Oakland Community College
Highland Lakes Library
7350 Cooley Lake Road
Waterford, MI 48327

5/10

DEMCO

TO SHAKE THEIR GUNS
IN THE TYRANT'S FACE

To Shake Their Guns
in the Tyrant's Face

LIBERTARIAN POLITICAL VIOLENCE AND
THE ORIGINS OF THE MILITIA MOVEMENT

Robert H. Churchill

THE UNIVERSITY OF MICHIGAN PRESS

ANN ARBOR

Copyright © by the University of Michigan 2009

All rights reserved

Published in the United States of America by

The University of Michigan Press

Manufactured in the United States of America

⊚ Printed on acid-free paper

2012   2011   2010   2009   4   3   2   1

A CIP catalog record for this book is available from the British Library.

Library of Congress Cataloging-in-Publication Data

Churchill, Robert H.

To shake their guns in the tyrant's face : libertarian political
violence and the origins of the militia movement / Robert H. Churchill.

p.   cm.

Includes bibliographical references and index.

ISBN-13: 978-0-472-11682-9 (cloth : alk. paper)

ISBN-10: 0-472-11682-7 (cloth : alk. paper)

1. Militia movements—United States—History.   2. Radicalism—
United States—History.   3. Government, Resistance to—United
States—History.   I. Title.

HN90.R3C485   2009

322.4'20973—dc22   2008048161

This book is dedicated to three men who
left without saying good-bye:

JAMES ALFRED JOHNSON 1931–1982

RODNEY GOVE DENNIS III 1930–2006

DONALD CHURCHILL 1928–1995

CONTENTS

ACKNOWLEDGMENTS

This book began at Rutgers University. It sprang from the training in early American history that I received at the hands of Thomas P. Slaughter, whose work continues to serve as an inspiration. The idea of writing a history that explores the early American roots of the contemporary militia movement emerged from a conversation with Paul G. E. Clemens in the spring of 1996. During my time at Rutgers I was a member of a remarkable learning community led by extraordinarily gifted teachers, including Michael Adas, Kathleen M. Brown, Dorothy Sue Cobble, Philip Greven, Allen Howard, Jan Ellen Lewis, and Joan W. Scott. David M. Oshinsky and Wilson Carey McWilliams served on my dissertation committee and offered me the benefit of their considerable insight into the modern Far Right. William Pencak, Owen S. Ireland, and Simon P. Newman read an early draft of the chapter on Fries' Rebellion, and the members of the Rutgers Center for Historical Analysis Seminar read an early summary of the argument of the book. I thank them all for their cogent criticism. Finally, I am particularly grateful for the friendship, advice, and encouragement offered by my colleagues Gregory T. Knouf, Peter C. Messer, Sara S. Gronim, Lucia McMahon, and Serena R. Zabin.

The path to becoming a historian and a teacher began long before Rutgers. The debts that I owe to the faculty of the Putney School, and especially to Hester and John Caldwell, David Calicchio, Felix and Marisa Lederer, Jim Johnson, Jeffrey Campbell, and Bob Mills can never be properly repaid. At Brown University, Robert H. Stanley sat me down one afternoon and told me that I thought like a historian even when I wasn't supposed to. Kurt A. Raaflaub, Philip Benedict, Gordon S. Wood, and Edward Beiser challenged me and encouraged me at key moments. Theodore R. Sizer offered an example of brilliant and compassionate teaching, and Paula M. Evans did more than anyone else to encourage me to take up education as my life's work. Elaine Temkin, Peter Santos, and Jacqueline Sutter did their best to make me a better teacher. My colleagues in the Law and Society program, the Brown Masters in Teaching program, and especially Beverly Schwartzberg and Shelley Warren, kept me sane along the way.

Since leaving Rutgers I have received advice and feedback on this project from a number of generous scholars, including Michael Barkun, Steven M. Chermak, Saul Cornell, Robert J. Cottrol, Jan E. Dizzard, Carolyn Gallaher, Glen Jeansonne, Gloria L. Main, Stuart McConnell, James M. McPherson, William Pencak, Christopher Waldrep, and David C. Williams. At the University of Hartford, my colleagues Michael F. Robinson and Leslie Lindenauer read the entire manuscript and offered detailed criticism that has made this a better book. Dean David Goldenberg and department chairs J. Holden Camp, Anthony T. Rauche, and Warren Goldstein have been enormously supportive of the process of revising the dissertation. I could not have asked for a better set of colleagues than the faculty of Hillyer College, whose cheerful dedication continues to inspire me.

Portions of the chapter on Fries' Rebellion draw upon Robert H. Churchill, "Popular Nullification, Fries' Rebellion, and the Waning of Radical Republicanism, 1798–1801," *Pennsylvania History* 67 (Winter 2000): 105–40, and appear here with the journal's permission.

This book involved research at a large number of manuscript repositories. I owe thanks to the staffs of the Historical Society of Pennsylvania, the Bucks County Historical Society, the Connecticut Historical Society, the Indiana Historical Society, the Indiana State Library, the Lilly

Library of Indiana University, the Lincoln National Life Foundation, the Illinois State Historical Society, the State Historical Society of Wisconsin, and the Walter P. Reuther Library of Wayne State University. I owe Steve Towne of the Indiana State Library Archives and Manuscripts Division a special debt for sharing his unparalleled knowledge of Indiana politics in the Civil War era. I wish to thank the Clerks of Greene County, Indiana, and Coles County, Illinois, for facilitating my research in local records.

I also received considerable assistance from the staffs of the National Archives in Washington, DC, and the regional branch archives in Philadelphia and Chicago. The Freedom of Information Act Request offices of the Michigan State Police and the Detroit Police Archives responded to my requests quickly and completely. Finally, I owe a debt to the staffs of the libraries of Rutgers University, Princeton University, Yale University, and the University of Hartford. The Interlibrary Loan Department of the Alexander Library at Rutgers and Christine Bird at the Mortensen Library at the University of Hartford have been particularly helpful in handling over a hundred ILL requests.

Doing primary research on the militia movement posed special challenges. Chip Berlet of Political Research Associates, Donald Cohen, director of the Detroit office of the Anti-Defamation League, and Mark Potok of the Southern Poverty Law Center opened their archives to me and gave me the benefit of their insights. They will probably disagree with the conclusions presented here. Any researcher on the Far Right owes a debt to Mark Pitcavage for the creation of his marvelous Web site, the Militia Watchdog. Mark also offered advice on relevant sources and secondary literature as I was just starting out on the project. He too will probably disagree with what I did with his advice. Rick Haynes of the Michigan Militia took an afternoon off of work so that I could cull through the Michigan Militia Multi-Information Archive stored in his home. He then refused payment for hundreds of photocopies. Michael Vanderboegh allowed me to carry away a crate of his personal papers so that I could survey them and copy what I needed. Finally, almost two dozen militia members have been willing to take the time to speak with me about the origins and aspirations of their movement and to share newsletters and other primary material. Without their cooperation and trust this study would not have been possible.

My work has been supported by generous grants of aid from the Department of History at Rutgers University, including four and a half years of graduate assistantship, a year of fellowship support, and a series of small but timely research grants. I have also received fellowship support from the Rutgers University Graduate School and the Rutgers Center for Historical Analysis. I received a Vincent Coffin Grant from the University of Hartford and two Gareau Faculty Development Grants from Hillyer College, which supported additional research for the book and gave me the time necessary to finish the manuscript.

The biggest debt of all I owe to my family. My late mother, Faith Churchill, provided me with a first-class education. Telling my mother that I had finished my Ph.D. was the proudest moment of my life. She and my sister Diana encouraged me at critical moments. Dave and Elaine Pardoe have been model in-laws and grandparents. They have taken up the slack to let me work on occasions too numerous to mention. John Hastie has been a staunch friend for many years. I think if he hadn't kept pestering me I might never have finished the book.

My father, Donald Churchill, died at the end of my second year of graduate school. I never discussed this book with him, but there is a great deal of him in these pages. He was a man who believed that great principles do not shift with the times, and these principles gave meaning to his life and his understanding of events around him. In knowing him, I learned to listen closely, even to those from whom others turn away. After my father's death, my uncle John Churchill, his son Derek, and my Churchill and Labovitz cousins adopted me as a wayward son, and this has done much to ease the burden of his passing.

My son Colin and my daughter Natalie have given up entirely too much of their childhood to this book. Yet they are still my most ardent cheerleaders, displaying a generosity of spirit that I find humbling. I must have done something very special in my life to deserve the two of them.

Rebecca Joanne Pardoe has been my best friend, an extraordinary partner, and my proofreader, editor, and sounding board for twenty-one years. She has held down the fort during long research trips and frantic months of revision. More than that, she has listened to me and helped me find my way through every challenge, professional and personal. This book is the fruit of our labor together. Let us now rest a while and enjoy each other's company.

INTRODUCTION

On April 29, 1994, twenty-eight men met in the woods of northern Michigan. Angered by the events at Ruby Ridge and Waco and alarmed by rumors of black helicopters and foreign soldiers hidden on American military bases, these men agreed to associate as the first brigade of the Northern Michigan Regional Militia. The militia was the brainchild of Norm Olson and Ray Southwell, the pastor and deacon of a small Baptist church near Alanson, Michigan. Those assembled elected Olson as their commander. He in turn laid down some basic principles under which they would proceed. First, the militia would operate publicly. If they believed that the government was a threat to their liberty, then it was their duty, as patriots and as men, to "shake their guns in the tyrant's face." Second, the militia would be open to men and women of principle regardless of race or faith. Olson believed that the government was utterly corrupt, but unlike other voices on the far right, he argued that the source of that corruption lay in the human heart and not in any Jewish conspiracy or in the loss of racial purity.

Finally, Olson portrayed the militia as an expression of popular sovereignty, a reincarnation of the Minutemen who had faced off against the king's troops at Lexington and Concord. The people's right to associate under arms to protect their liberty, Olson declared, was not subject to regulation by any government on earth. The purpose of that association was to create an armed force capable of deterring an increasingly abusive government. That April 29 meeting proved to be the genesis of the Michigan Militia.[1]

The Michigan Militia was one of hundreds of citizens' militias formed around the nation in 1994 and 1995. The Texas Constitutional Militia also held its first muster in April 1994. That same spring, J. J. and Helen Johnson began organizing E Pluribus Unum, a public discussion forum that would serve as a catalyst for militia activity in Ohio. Smaller organizations formed in Indiana, California, Alabama, Florida, and the states of the Northwest. Olson himself assisted in the organization of militias in Pennsylvania, Florida, and Wisconsin. His manual outlining the historical justification, organization, goals, and code of conduct of the Michigan Militia served as the basis for the manuals of militias in Missouri, Texas, and California.[2]

Some of these emerging militias followed Olson's model of holding public meetings and opening membership to all citizens. Others disagreed. The Militia of Montana, which began organizing in February 1994, offered a very different model. Founder John Trochman warned that America faced an apocalyptic invasion by the forces of the New World Order and consequently proposed an organizational structure based on closed, underground cells.[3] This more nativist and millenarian vision of the movement also spread to the Midwest. The Militia of Montana's manual was adopted by the early leadership of the Ohio Unorganized Militia. Mark Koernke, whose vision was similar to Trochman's, also began organizing local underground militias in southeast Michigan.

By the spring of 1995, hundreds of militias with as many as one hundred thousand members total had formed across the nation.[4] Most of the public became aware of the burgeoning militia movement only in the aftermath of the Oklahoma City bombing on April 19, 1995. Around the country, people reacted with shock, wondering what could possibly motivate citizens who claimed to be patriots to take up arms against their own democratically elected government. As journalists, self-appointed militia experts, and scholars rushed to offer answers, several explanations emerged. A loose coalition of civil rights organizations argued that the

movement was an outgrowth of a white supremacist paramilitary movement that had emerged in the 1980s, and constituted an attempt to
reestablish white supremacy by armed force. Other experts saw the movement as the product of millenarian impulses within the Christian Right.
Finally, some scholars and journalists compared the militia movement to
earlier populist vigilante movements, and argued that it was the product
of economic dislocation. All of these explanations portrayed the movement as an outgrowth of right-wing extremism in America.[5]

Like most Americans, I first learned of the militia movement in the
weeks after the Oklahoma City bombing. As I began to do research on
the movement, I became increasingly dissatisfied with these explanations. From the outset, I was struck by the lack of evidence behind the
charge that racism had played a significant role in the emergence of the
movement. It was also clear to me that economic concerns did not hold
a prominent place in the movement's analysis of the ills facing the nation. Finally, while some militias were clearly caught up in the sort of
elaborate conspiracy theories that characterized American millenarian
movements in the twentieth century, others went out of their way to debunk such theories.

Beyond this empirical unease, it seemed to me as a historian that the
concept of extremism begged a question: how do certain ideas, movements, and political impulses come to be considered extremist? As a citizen whose political identity was shaped by the late twentieth century, I
saw the militias' assertion of a right to use armed force to change government policy as new, threatening, and beyond the pale of legitimate
politics. But as a historian of early America I found achingly familiar
their assertion of a right to take up arms to prevent the exercise of unconstitutional power by the federal government. As a historian, then, I
was faced with a more specific question: how has the United States as a
political society come to view the assertion of that right as extremist?

Why did the militia movement emerge in 1994, and why do we view
that movement as extremist? On the surface they are simple questions,
and yet answering them involved reading the hundreds of newsletters
and Web pages in which militia men and women explained their movement to the public, to each other, and to themselves. It involved hours of

interviewing participants around the country, of sitting down and asking them what they were trying to do and listening carefully to the answers. Finally, it required tracing the history of the ideas that animated the movement, with a particular focus on the impact of those ideas on previous insurgent movements and on the relationship of these movements to the established political parties of their day.

As I listened to the disparate voices within the militia movement, the issue of political violence stood out above all others: the proximate cause of the movement lay in its members' perception that their government had turned increasingly violent. That perception may have been exaggerated, but it was firmly rooted in reality and fundamental to militia members' sense of their place in the world. The excesses committed by the federal government at Ruby Ridge, Idaho, and Waco, Texas, were the most important events driving this perception. But many joining the movement perceived a general trend at all levels of law enforcement toward the use of paramilitary tactics and military hardware, and several reported violent assaults and sieges reminiscent of Waco in their local communities. Finally, militia men and women feared that recently passed federal gun control legislation would be enforced with the same violence exhibited at Waco and Ruby Ridge. They feared that as gun owners they might become "next year's Davidians."

To defend themselves against what they perceived to be an imminent threat, a broad array of libertarians, gun owners, Christian millenarians, and survivalists seized upon the militia of association, an old political institution with a hallowed place within the collective memory of the founding period propagated by the gun rights movement. To explain the legitimacy of their new militia movement, members turned to ideas about political violence with similar eighteenth-century origins: they argued that popular political violence was a legitimate response to the denial of certain fundamental rights by agents of government; that insurgent violence against the state was a legitimate response to state-sponsored violence against its citizens; and that a state monopoly on violence, absent any popular deterrent against its abuse, yielded more violence rather than less.

In support of these assertions, the militia movement invoked one of the most radical intellectual legacies of the American Revolution. When Americans of the founding generation debated the limits of the right of revolution, two theories of legitimate political violence emerged. The first held that armed resistance to the oppressive acts of a representative government became legitimate only when that government infringed the constitutional means of opposition, such as access to the courts and the ballot box. But a second, more radical understanding of the meaning of the revolutionary conflict with Great Britain justified armed resistance to the acts of any government that repeatedly violated those rights, liberties, and privileges that the people believed they possessed as human beings and as citizens of a constitutional republic. Such transgressions of liberty were deemed illegitimate even if they had been enacted by a representative government following proper constitutional procedures. Under this theory, it was not only the right, but the duty, of all free men to embody themselves in a militia of the whole community and nullify the offending acts, by armed force if necessary. Many early Americans believed that those willing to undertake the duty of freemen to defend liberty and the constitutional order against the state exemplified the ideal of patriotic citizenship.

The eighteenth-century proponents of this ideal of patriotic insurgency based their claims for its legitimacy upon a particular interpretation of the meaning of the American Revolution. They described the Revolution not as a struggle for representation or to create an independent nation, but as a struggle to defend liberty against a corrupt and abusive state. I will refer to this interpretation as the *libertarian* understanding of the American Revolution. This interpretation was libertarian in the sense that it portrayed the Revolution as a struggle to protect liberty by enforcing inviolable constitutional restraints on the power of the state. Nevertheless, the early American proponents of this theory believed that liberty was best protected by a united community, and that an individual's freedom to act on behalf of either the people or the state was subject to the approval of the local community. They believed that the recourse to legitimate violence was neither public, in the sense of requiring state sanction, nor wholly private. This theory thus had little connection to the hyperindividualism of modern economic libertarianism.

In the 1790s, this libertarian understanding of the meaning of the American Revolution found its way into the ideas, rituals, and institutions of the Democratic-Republican Party. Over the next several decades, Democratic-Republican political culture and political rhetoric celebrated the Revolution as a legitimate exercise of popular violence against a despotic government. After the passing of the Revolutionary generation, the libertarian understanding of the Revolution retained a significant place within the collective memory of the Democratic Party. During the Civil War this libertarian memory of the Revolution fueled both political opposition and violent resistance to the war policies of the Lincoln administration.

In the last decades of the nineteenth century, however, the libertarian understanding of the American Revolution gave way in collective memory and public commemoration to a new ideal of patriotism and a new set of rituals emphasizing unquestioning loyalty and obedience to the nation-state. Within this new ideology of "one hundred percent Americanism," all forms of revolution took on the visage of an alien, subversive menace. So pervasive was this shift in patriotic ideology that in twentieth-century Independence Day festivities, celebrations of the justified recourse to popular violence against a lawful government bent on tyranny were entirely replaced by sanitized commemorations of the birth of the nation.

Deprived of its former place in public discussion and commemoration, the libertarian memory of the Revolution lived on at the extremes of the political spectrum. On the far right, the libertarian vision of righteous popular revolution blended with vigilante impulses rooted in white supremacy and the long history of American nativism. This fusion produced a series of paramilitary insurgencies, including the Depression-era Black Legion, and the Minutemen of the 1960s. On the far left, the libertarian justification of armed defense against state tyranny motivated radical civil rights activists such as Robert F. Williams to form local African American militias in the 1950s and 1960s. Within mainstream politics, however, the patriotic emphasis on countersubversion facilitated campaigns to suppress first communists, then fascists, and, after World War II, white supremacists and radical civil rights activists such as

Williams. Their willingness to resort to violence against the state marked all of these groups as extremist and un-American.

If the rise of American anticommunism played a key role in further driving the libertarian memory of the Revolution from the public sphere, the defeat of Communism opened the door to its return. In post–Cold War America, a wave of state-sponsored violence, real and imagined, encouraged some Americans to look at the American Revolution through new eyes. Some encountered the libertarian memory of the Revolution in a set of eighteenth-century texts that were widely disseminated by the gun rights movement. Others came across it as an idea articulated within far right discourse, where it was still entwined with white supremacist and nativist corollaries. From these encounters emerged distinct constitutional and millenarian wings of the militia movement, represented respectively by Norm Olson and John Trochman. Though operating on very different principles, these militias together rested on ideas about constitutionalism and political violence, on rituals of public armed deterrence, and on the eighteenth-century institution of the militia of association. Thus, in terms of ideology, organization, and cultural performance, the militias began in 1994 to do something that was both very old and very new.

Beyond the Narrative of 1995: Methodological Imperatives for Research on the Militia Movement

The militia movement has been the subject of at least a dozen books and hundreds of articles, yet it remains one of the most poorly understood political movements of the twentieth century. In the months after the bombing of the Oklahoma City federal building by Timothy McVeigh, civil rights organizations issued at least a dozen published reports on the militia movement, and civil rights activists offered "expert" commentary in hundreds of news stories. Within a year, books by leading figures associated with civil rights organizations, including Morris Dees, Kenneth Stern, and Richard Abanes, offered a coherent narrative of the origin of the movement.[6]

What America learned in these months was that the militia movement was an outgrowth of the racist Right. Civil rights activists portrayed the militias as the armed wing of a much larger "Christian Patriot" movement. They warned that Christian Patriots numbered in the millions and that Christian Patriotism called for the restoration of white, Christian, patriarchal domination. The Christian Patriot movement as a whole, and the militias in particular, were antidemocratic, paranoid, virulently anti-Semitic, genocidally racist, and brutally violent. Much of this literature suggested that Timothy McVeigh was the movement's highest expression. In this narrative, the militias and the Patriot movement took on the guise of the perfect, racist "other," and the threat they posed was best articulated by Morris Dees' apocalyptic vision of a "gathering storm."

This "narrative of 1995" produced by civil rights organizations, coupled with the horror of the Oklahoma City bombing, triggered what Steven Chermak has referred to as a moral panic. Through published reports, their influence over the news coverage of the movement, and testimony at prominent public hearings, leading militia "experts" injected their portrait of the movement into public consciousness and popular culture. In news coverage, popular novels, episodes of *Law and Order,* and movies such as *Arlington Road,* the public became well acquainted with the archetypal militiaman, usually portrayed as warped by racial hatred, obsessed with bizarre conspiracy theories, and hungry for violent retribution.[7]

The moral panic over the "militia menace" strongly resembled previous moral panics over the "communist menace" that had swept the nation in the aftermath of World War I and again in the early 1950s. Less well known than these two Red scares is America's "Brown Scare." In the late 1930s, political activists on the left warned that an array of far right opponents of President Roosevelt and the New Deal, including the Silver Shirts, the Black Legion, the German American Bund, and the Christian Front, constituted a fifth column composed of fascist brownshirts allied with Nazism and dedicated to the overthrow of democratic government in America. According to Leo P. Ribuffo, a leading scholar of the Depression-era Far Right, the ensuing moral panic facilitated a campaign of repression waged by the U.S. government against the Far Right during

World War II.[8] In 1995–96, the moral panic over the militia movement blossomed into a second American Brown Scare.

The literature produced by the second Brown Scare has had a significant impact on academic analysis of the movement, and this poses a problem for continuing scholarship. The civil rights organizations that produced the narrative of 1995 conceived of themselves as political opponents of the militia movement, and these organizations made the legal suppression of the movement one of their central political objectives.[9] That political objective has systematically shaped their reporting on the movement. Their analyses might serve as a primary source base for an interesting analysis of how the activist Left perceived the Far Right at the turn of the millennium. To use this literature as a primary source base in an analysis of the character of the militia movement itself is to allow the movement's opponents to define it.

Unfortunately, much of the scholarship on the militia movement produced in the last ten years has not broken free from the influence of the narrative of 1995. Too many scholars have relied on the reports and books generated by the Brown Scare as primary evidence of the character of the movement. Others who have avoided this first error have nevertheless allowed the narrative of 1995 to unduly influence their research agendas. Finally, even the best scholarship on militias tends to inappropriately conflate the militia movement with other movements on the far right of American politics and to overstate the influence of millennial thought on militia ideology.

Two of the first scholarly accounts of the movement relied almost entirely on Brown Scare literature as sources. David Bennett, historian of the Far Right, added a chapter on the militia movement to the 1995 edition of *The Party of Fear* that was based almost entirely on civil rights reports and news accounts. While Bennett was one of the first scholars to place the militia movement in a historical context, his source base led him to significantly overestimate the influence of nativism within the movement. Catherine McNichol Stock wrote *Rural Radicals: Righteous Rage in the American Grain* without conducting any primary research on her subjects. Her understanding of the militia movement came largely from Morris Dees and Kenneth Stern. As a result she placed a movement that was neither rural nor particularly violent within a historical context that emphasized the legacy of agrarian rebellion and populist vigilantism. More recently, sociologists Barbara Perry and Manuel Castells have published analyses of the movement based largely on Brown Scare sources.[10]

Other scholars have allowed the narrative of 1995 to dictate their research agenda and design. This has particularly been true of younger scholars. John Keith Akins accepted Kenneth Stern's contention that racism and anti-Semitism were central to the movement, and chose the case studies of his dissertation accordingly.[11] The most important statistical studies on the correlates of militia activity, by Sean O'Brian and Donald Haider-Markel, by Joshua Freilich, and by Nella Van Dyke and Sarah Soule, have all relied on lists of militia groups compiled by the Southern Poverty Law Center and the Anti-Defamation League. The inaccuracy of these lists, and their tabulation of militia groups by state rather than locality, has significantly diminished the utility of the only statistical analyses of the movement.[12]

The final academic legacy of the Brown Scare is an emphasis on the allegedly close association of militia groups with other far right organizations, such as white supremacist groups, Christian Identity ministries, common-law courts, and tax protest societies. The narrative of 1995 lumped all of these disparate far right groups together in the "Christian Patriot movement," a misguided simplification that has led a number of senior scholars to blur the lines between different groups with quite different worldviews. For example, Michael Kimmel and Abby Ferber, in a recent analysis of militia concepts of masculinity, accept *in toto* the narrative of 1995, concluding that "far right-groups are intricately interconnected and share a basic anti-government, anti-semitic, racist, sexist/patriarchal ideology." They then subject this "militia ideology" to a gendered analysis. But the texts on which they base this analysis were all generated by the white supremacist Right. The authors thus published what purports to be a gendered analysis of the militia movement without examining a single militia-generated text.[13]

The conflation of militia-generated texts with texts produced by other "Christian Patriot" groups has also undermined promising work by other senior scholars. Lane Crothers offers a fine analysis of militia ideology's complicated relationship to mainstream culture. But the manner in which he juxtaposes militia and Christian Patriot statements on conspiracism and racism leads to fundamentally misleading conclusions about militia ideology. Michael Barkun and Martin Durham have explored the role of millennial expectation within militia thought. Their work offers important insights into militia thought, but their reliance on texts circulating within Christian Patriot circles rather than on texts generated by militia members leads them to overestimate both the depth and reach of millennial concerns within the movement.[14]

Since the turn of the millennium, three scholars have begun the task of freeing scholarship on the militia movement from the narrative of 1995. In 2002 Steven Chermak offered a systematic critique of the media construction of the militia movement and journalists' extensive reliance on civil rights activists to provide expert opinion. He juxtaposed media depictions of militia ideology with primary source material drawn from dozens of interviews with active members of the movement. The following year, David C. Williams offered a book-length study that combined a thoughtful discussion of the political philosophy of the founding generation with an analysis of contemporary militia ideology, based on a variety of primary and secondary texts. Finally, in 2004, D. J. Mulloy offered the first sustained examination of the place of history and collective memory in militia ideology. His book also offers a thoughtful examination of the similarities between militia beliefs and those of "mainstream America."[15]

As a historian, I hope to contribute to this field an insight gained in the study of other partisan political crises in American history: in evaluating the ideology of an insurgent movement, one must not allow the movement's partisan allies, much less its partisan enemies, to speak for it. My analysis of the militia movement is based on the methodological imperative that militia ideology can only be analyzed by evaluating the primary source texts in which the movement itself speaks. In choosing these texts I have closely considered how the militia movement interacted with other groups on the far right. Though often described as a unified movement with a coherent ideology, the phenomenon of Christian Patriotism is best understood as the cultural product of an alternative public sphere in which a variety of far right political movements, including the militia movement, interact, exchange ideas, and often engage in fervent debate.

The public sphere is a forum in which "private people come together as a public" to express their opinions on matters of collective concern. In America, a public sphere has existed since the advent of newspapers and political societies in the eighteenth century. Debating societies, political parties, and the rise of partisan newspapers ensured vigorous debate and thorough public deliberation on political issues. Yet this public sphere has privileged some voices and excluded others. In the eighteenth and nineteenth centuries, racial minorities were excluded from the public sphere, and with the rise of "mainstream" journalism in the early twentieth century, groups on the far right found themselves barred from communicating in public forums.[16] As a result, far right groups generally fell back on private and binary modes of communication such as private lectures, newsletters, and direct mail to promote their message.

The telecommunications revolution of the 1990s transformed this binary model of communication. Far right activists were among the early pioneers in the use of new telecommunications media to better spread their message. As fax networks, computer bulletin boards, email discussion lists, shortwave and AM radio programming, and Web sites proliferated, an alternative public sphere emerged on the far right that facilitated real public discussion, deliberation, and debate among an array of groups that had previously had little direct communication with each other.[17]

Though inhabiting the same public sphere, and thus exposed to each other's messages, these groups did not necessarily share the same conceptual universe. Close observation of a variety of media within this sphere reveals a diverse collection of communities that butt up against each other. Interactions between these communities are as often characterized by vigorous debate, name-calling, and shouting matches as they are by agreement. Consensus, even among different militia groups, is rare.[18] Though civil rights groups generally describe the inhabitants of the Christian Patriot public sphere as dupes, devoid of intellectual

agency, those venturing into this public sphere behave more like con-
sumers, some avid and others more skeptical.[19]

The recognition that Christian Patriotism is best understood as a
public sphere suggests that militia ideology can only be analyzed by evaluating militia-generated texts. For the purposes of this study, I have used
several criteria to determine whether an individual or a group should be
considered part of the militia movement. First, a militia is an organization that has a membership and that conducts paramilitary training.
Plenty of individuals have belonged to militias that never extended beyond the bounds of their own imaginations. Some of them even created
Web sites.[20] There were many groups within the Christian Patriot public
sphere that never engaged in armed organization. None of these should
be considered part of the movement. Second, the militia movement
emerged in the aftermath of the assaults on the Weaver homestead on
Ruby Ridge in August 1992 and on the Branch Davidian compound in
Waco, Texas, in April 1993. There may have been far right paramilitaries
in existence prior to these events, but the militia movement as a historical phenomenon clearly began in the aftermath of Waco. Third, militias
generally self-identify as part of the movement.

Finally, some white supremacist groups, hoping to ride the wave of
popularity of the new militia movement, reorganized their paramilitary
wings in the mid-1990s and called them militias. For example, David
Duke's National Association of White People and several branches of the
Ku Klux Klan formed militias in the mid-1990s. I consider such groups
to be part of a distinct white supremacist paramilitary movement that
has existed since the late 1960s and that operates on foundational principles very different from those of the militia movement. In many cases
militias used the Klan and other white supremacist groups as a negative
referent in crafting their own identity.[21]

Following these methodological imperatives, my analysis of the militia movement is based on evidence drawn from militia Web sites, newsletters, email discussions, internal documents, videotapes, and manuals. Between 1996 and 2000 I periodically visited every identifiable militia Web
site and downloaded all substantive documents. I also visited the archives

of Political Research Associates, the Detroit office of the ADL, the Wilcox Collection on the American Far Right housed at the University of Kansas, and the Southern Poverty Law Center. In each of these visits I made paper or electronic copies of every militia-generated document to which I was given access. I supplemented this material with oral history interviews with prominent members of the militia movement conducted in the Midwest in 1998–99 and in other regions of the country in 2005–6. During these visits I received a great deal of additional written material to which I would never have had access, including material held in the Michigan Militia Multi-Information Archive and in the papers of Mike Vanderboegh. These documents included manuals, newsletters, and copies of internal communications otherwise unavailable.[22]

This source base does have some limitations. I conducted interviews only with members of the movement whose membership was public. Thus my findings may not adequately represent that portion of the movement which is "underground."[23] My source base also lacks geographic balance. My interviews and my document base are particularly strong for militias in the Midwest. I have incorporated additional material from groups in New England, Texas, Alabama, and the Pacific Northwest. I have not, however, collected significant material from California, the Southeast, or the Great Plains. The analysis offered here may thus underestimate regional variation.

An analysis based on oral history must assess the candor of the interviewee and the biases inherent in the interview process. In some of the interviews I conducted, the subjects offered accounts of the movement that were clearly self-serving. All of the subjects were probably motivated to give good account of themselves and their movement. In my approach to subjects I made it clear that I was interested in creating an oral history archive of the movement. Thus participants were aware that their words were being recorded for posterity.

With these issues in mind, I have attempted wherever possible to fact-check the content of the interviews against past public statements by the subjects, email communication between groups, and, where possible, internal communications. For example, much of the information contained in interviews with members of the Michigan Militia is corroborated by documents in the Michigan Militia Multi-Information Archive. Documents in Mike Vanderboegh's papers support his interview assertions at key points. Some statements simply cannot be checked, and here I must rely on my own impressions of the character and candor of those with whom I spoke.

There are many on the left and even within the academy whose perception of the Far Right is dominated by the figure of the "stealth Nazi," a dissembler who masks his genocidal intent behind a moderate and earnest public visage. Some would argue that only by posing as a militiaman could I encounter "the real militia mind" and would regard public statements by militia members as no more than public posturing. In my experience, however, most denizens of the Far Right, white supremacists included, wear their hearts on their sleeves. Many of my interviews developed into free-ranging and uninhibited conversations. Although all interviewees were given the opportunity to edit the interview transcript in any way that they saw fit, only one edited a transcript to change the substance of what was said, and the issue involved was trivial.

As for "infiltrating" the movement, the core ethical stricture governing research involving living human subjects can be summed up as "First, do no harm." I was initially leery of some standard oral history procedures, including the taping of interviews and allowing subjects to edit transcripts. I have come to realize, however, that these requirements simply represent good ethical practice. In any case it is unlikely that a research protocol based on deception would have received the approval of the Institutional Review Boards of Rutgers University and the University of Hartford.[24] Readers are of course invited to bring their own healthy skepticism to their encounter with the men and women of the militia movement. It is only those biases born of the Brown Scare that I would urge them to leave behind.

Exploring the Sources of Militia Identity: Race, Class, and Gender

Scholars of social movements, particularly those on the far right, have most often focused on the racial and class anxieties of their subjects.

From the post–World War II liberal pluralist studies that focused on status anxiety as the root of fascism to more recent examinations of the role of whiteness within Christian Patriotism, the application of social theory to scholarship on the Far Right has yielded insights, but it has also lent itself to condescension and caricature. Used cautiously, theory can help to explain ethnographic evidence and also place that evidence in a larger context. Theory can also overwhelm that evidence and allow political animus to masquerade as scholarship.

The insurgents described in this book occupied a broad range of class positions, from rural yeomen to middle-class professionals to corporate managers. Though the militia movement has often been described as rural and working class in character, analysts of the militia movement lack the kind of membership data that allowed earlier scholars to probe the class and occupational composition of, for example, the second Ku Klux Klan. An analysis of militia discourse may yield some insights, but here too the available data does not support firm conclusions. For example, some militiamen describe the threats they perceive in language laden with economic anxiety and class resentment, but others emphasize issues of sovereignty, political agency, and the potential for state violence. Given these limitations in the sources, a focus on class is unlikely to yield significant insight into the militia movement.[25]

Almost all of the insurgents discussed in this book were white. Race is a part of their story. Some militia members speak of the New World Order in language evocative of racial fear and animus, and some of the earlier insurgents discussed in this book were clearly motivated in part by white supremacy. But to sum up either the militia movement or earlier insurgencies as expressions of racial anxiety and identity runs the risk of effacing the complex influences of religion, rural culture, localism, and libertarianism. It would also bury the voices of many militia members who have denounced the doctrines of white supremacy as un-Christian, unpatriotic, and un-American. Race is a part of the story, sometimes a powerful part. It is not the whole story.

In recent years sociologist Eduardo Bonilla-Silva has offered an analytical perspective that is useful when evaluating the complex influence of race on the militia movement. Bonilla-Silva notes that racial ideology has shifted significantly in the aftermath of the civil rights movement. He argues that white Americans continue to enjoy systemic social and economic advantages due to their race, and to view race relations in terms that perpetuate these advantages. Bonilla-Silva's model of "color-blind racism" permits a nuanced evaluation of militia racial discourse and also suggests that this discourse mirrors the mainstream racial ideology of white America.[26]

Scholars of the Far Right and of earlier insurgent movements have until recently paid relatively little attention to the workings of gender. Yet conceptions of manliness have played a powerful role in shaping both early and modern American insurgent movements. Democratic-Republicans vowed to resist the Alien and Sedition Acts with "manly firmness," while leaders of the Civil War–era Democratic Party warned that violent resistance to conscription was "unmanly." Each of the movements under consideration here acted out of a sense of masculine duty, though their understandings of that duty were markedly different.[27]

Several observers have described the militia movement as an outgrowth of masculine anxiety, and cite James Gibson's *Warrior Dreams* to explain the contours of militia manliness.[28] Gibson's pathbreaking analysis of post-Vietnam masculine anxiety described attempts to shore up the cultural identity of white men whose social and political authority had been undermined by feminism, the civil rights movement, and defeat in the Vietnam War. Within a new subculture of books, movies, magazines, and games, authors created a "new war fantasy" in which archetypal warriors, freed from the restraining influences of family and society, would "retake and reorder the world" through the use of genocidal violence.[29]

Gibson's book was a tour de force, but the casual equation of the new war fantasy and the gender ideals of the militia movement is deeply problematic. An anecdote told by Steven Chermak illustrates a much more domestic and civic orientation within militia manhood. Chermak traveled to Knob Creek, Tennessee, to observe a militia meeting held at the annual Knob Creek machine gun shoot. As militia members left the meeting, two cars collided at a nearby intersection. After calling for emergency assistance, militia men ran to the scene, administered first aid, and began to direct traffic. When Chermak asked a journalist who had also witnessed this display of civic engagement whether he would describe the militia members' response in his story on the movement, the latter replied that "he was not in Kentucky to cover car crashes, but was sent to evaluate the militia movement." The journalist then returned to the machine gun shoot "to find his story."[30] In search of warrior dreams, the journalist proved blind to a live demonstration of militia manliness.

Gender theorist R. W. Connell's discussion of "complicit masculinity" provides a better theoretical foundation for a discussion of militia manliness than Gibson's warrior dream. Connell describes complicit masculinities as those that derive the benefits of patriarchy while remaining engaged in "marriage, fatherhood, and community life." Such engagement involves "extensive compromises with women rather than naked domination or an uncontested display of authority."[31] This theoretical lens helps to illustrate the contrast between militia masculinity and the new war fantasy. Many militiamen developed strong partnerships in their marriages. Concern for family and community animated all aspects of militia activity. To be sure, members of the militia movement brandished weapons and played at war, but within militia literature, imagined violence was deeply embedded in political principle and civic obligation, and there was rarely anything joyous about it. Theirs was a different warrior dream, one that, like all facets of militia identity, requires careful, sustained, and comparative analysis.

The Dynamics of Collective Memory and the Challenge of Writing a History of the Present

In addition to a close analysis of the militia movement, this volume discusses the history of the ideas that animated the movement and the currents of historical memory that have carried them across time. The theory of collective memory and my choice of events on which to focus this historical analysis therefore require a last bit of explanation.

The theory of collective memory offers insight into the process by which some political ideas are celebrated across time and others are marginalized, by which the past often acts to shape the present. Scholarship on collective historical memory is founded on Maurice Halbwach's insight that historical memory is a collective construction grounded in present social need. Political actors thus invoke particular historical memories to rally support for desired outcomes.[32] The transmission of ideas across time is embedded in the process of historical memory. Political actors have the creative capacity to reshape ideas and memories, and to combine them with new ones. Nevertheless, the dynamics of historical memory place limits on that creativity.

One limitation stems from the fact that the public commemoration of the past is often contested. John Bodnar, in tracing the evolution of public commemoration after the Civil War, argues that the contest over public memory involves a struggle between elite-sponsored "official memory" and "vernacular memories" held by "ordinary people." According to Bodnar, social and political elites compete with each other and with popular groups to reshape the history commemorated within the public sphere.[33]

Insurgent movements in American history have almost always sought to justify their acts by invoking the memory of the past. Creativity in the construction of that historical memory holds the potential to enhance these movements' freedom of action. But in an environment in which memory is contested, creativity can also alienate the audience whose political support a group seeks. The insurgents discussed here have been remarkably (and sometimes horrifically) creative in reshaping the memory of the American Revolution, but the most creative groups were the least successful in making a public case for their aims. The past thus shapes and limits the present, even as it is pressed into its service.

Once they have invoked a specific memory of the past, political actors may also find themselves captive to it. During the Civil War, northern Peace Democrats invoked the memory of the Virginia and Kentucky Resolutions of 1798, which articulated the right of the people to nullify unconstitutional legislation. When one of their number, Harrison Dodd, decided that the principles of 1798 justified a plot to overthrow the governments of four midwestern states, party leaders discovered that these principles represented a devastating political liability.[34] Ideas from the

past, incorporated into historical memory, bring with them consequences that cannot be easily escaped.

A final observation is crucial to the story of the militia movement: a
fundamental shift in the dynamics of public commemoration took place
in the post–Civil War era. Prior to the Civil War, public memory
emerged from an open competition of political parties, popular movements, and ethnic groups within the public sphere. Because the state
lacked the power to project a single unified memory, multiple competing
constructions of the past emerged from public debate and ritual. After
the Civil War, the capacity of the state and of national and local elites to
project an "official" memory into the public sphere and to mute the impact of popular, vernacular memories transformed public commemoration. John Bodnar argues that after the war, elite interest groups gained
the power to shape public discourse and to prevent the "meaningful"
public expression of competing constructions.[35] His model helps explain
the post–Civil War suppression of the libertarian memory of the American Revolution and the exclusion of the Far Right from the mainstream
public sphere after World War II. In the 1990s the communications revolution partially reversed this trend, allowing the vernacular memories
within the Christian Patriot public sphere to reach a much broader audience. As a result, the libertarian memory of the American Revolution,
long marginalized, found a renewed place in public discussion.

Tracing the intellectual roots of the militia movement and the manner in which collective memory has transmitted these ideas over time
poses a challenge. American history is crowded with agrarian rebels, insurgent slaves, working-class syndicalists, and vigilantes of all stripes.
Even confining the examination to those groups that have invoked the
American Revolution to justify the use of violence would still run the
risk of overwhelming an analysis of the militia movement with accounts
of its predecessors.

My solution to this problem is to confine the historical discussion as
much as possible to key turning points in the evolution of the collective
memory of the American Revolution: the political crises of 1798, 1863–64,
and 1936. In each of these crises, unprecedented assertions of federal authority triggered the emergence of an insurrectionary movement: Fries'

Rebellion in Pennsylvania, 1798–99, the Sons of Liberty conspiracy in Indiana and Illinois, 1863–64, and the Black Legion in Michigan and Ohio, 1932–36. In each case, insurgents threatened or enacted violent resistance to the authority of the federal government. Each of these groups invoked the libertarian understanding of the American Revolution and used that collective memory to justify political violence. Finally, each insurgency existed in complicated tension with a broader movement of political opposition to the party in power, and thus these crises illustrate the process by which the libertarian memory of the American Revolution was transformed from a mainstream creed to a badge of extremism.

There are several other insurgent movements in American history that at least partially fit these criteria. The Whiskey Rebels staged an insurrection against federal authority in 1794, and certainly merit inclusion. I have chosen to discuss Fries' Rebellion instead because it better illustrates the Democratic-Republican Party's embrace of the libertarian memory of the Revolution. Thomas Dorr led a working-class rebellion against the government of Rhode Island in 1842. Dorr invoked the memory of the American Revolution, but we have very little evidence of the ideological motivations of the rank-and-file members of his movement. The Dorr War's significance for the Supreme Court's repudiation of a constitutional right of revolution will be discussed at the end of Part I. Finally, the first Ku Klux Klan organized armed resistance to the authority of the biracial Reconstruction governments of southern states after the Civil War. Though the Klan waged a paramilitary campaign of violence and intimidation in the defense of local autonomy and white supremacy, it rarely invoked the memory of the American Revolution. Furthermore, as I discuss in the second chapter in Part II ("Cleansing the Memory of the Revolution"), Klansmen sought to assume state power, not to limit it.

The book is divided into three parts, corresponding roughly to three chronological periods in the evolution of the historical memory of the Revolution. Part I covers the years between the Revolution and the Civil War, a period that encompasses the Revolution itself, a series of political crises in which the meaning of the Revolution was fervently debated by those who participated in it, and the passage of the Revolution into historical memory. In this first period, the libertarian memory of the Revolution and celebrations of popular political violence continued to play a fundamental role in American political culture. The two chapters in this section explore the American recourse to political violence to nullify the Coercive Acts in 1774–75, the theoretical discussions of legitimate insurgent violence that emerged from the debates over the ratification of the Constitution and the Second Amendment, and the Democratic-Republican celebration of these precedents during the Alien and Sedition Act crisis of 1798. Part I concludes with a brief discussion of the transmission of Democratic-Republican principles and rituals of legitimate resistance into antebellum political theory and into the public commemoration of the Revolution in the first half of the nineteenth century.

Part II covers the era of American countersubversion that lasted from the beginning of the Civil War to the end of the Cold War. This period witnessed the Civil War, the rise of industrial class conflict and American anticommunism, and the emergence of a new, countersubversive ideal of patriotism, one hundred percent Americanism. The first of two chapters in Part II examines the violent political battle between Democrats and Republicans in the North over Lincoln's assertion of unprecedented powers during the Civil War. Midwestern Democrats invoked the memory of the Revolution and the Virginia and Kentucky Resolutions of 1798 and publicly denounced Lincoln as a tyrant. In response, Republicans crafted a new patriotic identity based on loyalty, obedience, and a state monopoly on violence. The second chapter in this part traces the process by which a new conception of patriotism, styled one hundred percent Americanism, drove the libertarian memory of the American Revolution out of mainstream public discussion and public commemoration after the Civil War. During the 1930s, Democrats joined the Republican embrace of countersubversive patriotism and warned that paramilitary organization by far right opponents of the New Deal constituted a "terrorist" threat to the Republic. Part II concludes with a brief discussion of Cold War–era efforts to reinforce Americanism's repudiation of revolutionary political violence and to contain paramilitary activity on the far left and far right.

Part III explores the militia movement's challenge to the state's monopoly on violence. Its first chapter examines the causes that generated militia organizing. Chief among these are the paramilitarization of law enforcement that led to the tragedies at Waco and Ruby Ridge, the opening of the Christian Patriot public sphere, and the revival of the libertarian memory of the Revolution. In addition to analyzing the movement's racial discourse and gender identity, the chapter traces the emergence of militias along America's suburban-rural frontier. The next chapter lays out the movement's perception and critique of the government's increasingly violent enforcement of the law and its growing intrusion into personal lives. It explores the distinct Whig and millenarian diagnoses of state violence offered by different voices in the movement, its program for reform, and its struggle to articulate clear boundaries for legitimate insurgent political violence. Finally, it narrates the gradual divergence of the millenarian and constitutional wings of the militia movement.

One final observation is in order: the invocation of the past to justify present action is a perpetual theme in American politics. It need not, however, command our deference. If there is a point at which the practice of history departs from the practice of collective memory, it is in the recognition that no word or deed from ages past can in and of itself justify the recourse to violence in the present. This is the story of men and women who asserted that the libertarian memory of the American Revolution enjoined them to fight for liberty at the turn of the twenty-first century. But history does not bind any of us. For the legitimacy of our acts, we must all seek judgment in a different realm.

PART ONE

THE PRECEDENT OF 1774: THE ROLE OF INSURGENT VIOLENCE IN THE POLITICAL THEORY OF THE FOUNDING

On September 6, 1774, representatives of the towns of Suffolk County, Massachusetts, recommended that the inhabitants of the county "use their utmost diligence to acquaint themselves with the art of war as soon as possible, and do for that purpose, appear under arms at least once a week." The purpose of this military training was to

> resist that unparalleled usurpation of unconstitutional power, whereby our capital is robbed of the means of life; whereby the streets of Boston are thronged with military executioners; whereby our coasts are lined and our harbors crowded with ships of war; whereby the Charter of the Colony, that sacred barrier against encroachments of tyranny, is mutilated, and, in effect, annihilated.

The people of Suffolk County responded to these resolutions by organizing militia companies, practicing military drill, and providing themselves with arms. They did so largely without recourse to organized government beyond the institutions of their local towns. Inspired by the Suffolk County Resolves, the people of New England took up arms in the fall of 1774 to nullify the Coercive Acts, legislation that they regarded as an all-out assault on their liberty.[1]

The Suffolk County Resolves ushered in the most radical phase of the American Revolution, a ten-month period in which Americans took up arms and overthrew their lawful governments. Even after the Revolution, the radicalism of this period would hover over American politics into the 1780s, to the dismay of many nationalists who feared the localism and violence of the Revolutionary impulse and its reenactment in Shays' Rebellion. Two legacies from this period would pass into American political culture and resonate with later insurgent movements. The first was a set of ideas that legitimated resistance to the tyrannical acts of a lawful government, even a government chosen by the people. The second was the emergence of a popular institution by which that resistance could be organized, a militia created by popular association at the local level.

The Precedent of 1774: Two Ideologies of Resistance

When the inhabitants of Boston threw a cargo of British East India Company tea into the harbor, they provoked a harsh response from the British Parliament. In the spring of 1774 Parliament retaliated by enacting a package of legislation, the Coercive Acts, designed to force Massachusetts to submit to Parliament's supreme authority. First, the Boston Port Act effectively closed the port until the town of Boston made restitution for the destroyed tea. The Massachusetts Government Act transformed the previously elected upper house of the colonial legislature into a Crown-appointed body. It also stipulated that judges and sheriffs would henceforth be appointed by the Crown, and would have the power to manipulate local jury selection. Finally, the act restricted the traditional institution of local self-government, the town meeting, to a single annual session unless the governor approved additional meetings. The Administration of Justice Act permitted royal officers accused of murdering colonists in the exercise of their duty to remove their trial to England. A new Quartering Act permitted the governor to requisition privately owned buildings (but not occupied residences) to house British troops. Finally, the colonists learned that the military commander of North America, General Thomas Gage, was to serve as their new royal governor.[2]

The Coercive Acts and the American response were the culmination of the imperial crisis between Britain and its North American colonies. In popular culture and public memory, that crisis is often portrayed as a conflict focused on taxation and representation. In fact, American opposition to the Coercive Acts developed along two tracks during the summer of 1774. The first mode of organized opposition, the nonimportation movement, did focus on taxation and representation. The second mode of opposition, armed organization, did not.

Upon hearing of the passage of the Boston Port Act, Americans immediately began to organize an economic boycott against Great Britain. This nonimportation movement drew upon ideas and tactics first worked out in the 1760s in the colonial protests against the Sugar and Stamp acts. These protests were rooted in a particular strain of English opposition thought dating to the late seventeenth century. Most often referred to as Country or Whig ideology, this set of ideas included demands for actual representation, a stress on the distinction between internal and external taxation, and a marked tendency to see the workings of corrupt conspirators behind adverse policy decisions. For example, Richard Bland responded to the 1764 Sugar Act by declaring that

> if Parliament should impose laws upon us merely relative to our INTERNAL government, it deprives us, as far as those laws extend, of the most valuable part of our birthright as Englishmen, of being governed by laws made with our own consent. . . . any tax respecting our INTERNAL polity which may hereafter be imposed on us by act of Parliament is arbitrary, as depriving us of our rights, and may be opposed.

Bland's argument was the foundation of American protests against the 1765 Stamp Act, and it was extended and elaborated upon throughout the 1760s and early 1770s in newspaper essays, pamphlets, and public resolutions.[3]

After the passage of the Coercive Acts, these Whig principles were the basis for the 1774 nonimportation movement. In dozens of counties across the southern and Middle Atlantic states, public meetings denounced parliamentary taxation and the Boston Port Act. For example, the freeholders of Middlesex County, Virginia, declared that "representation and taxation are inseparably connected by the essential principles of the British constitution." The inhabitants of Sussex County, Delaware, agreed, arguing that "it is the inherent right of British Subjects to be taxed by their own consent, or by Representatives chosen by themselves only; and that every Act of the British Parliament respecting the internal police of North America is unconstitutional, and an invasion of our just rights and privileges."[4]

In the face of Parliament's challenge to the right of actual representation, the nonimportation movement adopted the time-tested but passive strategy of an economic boycott. The freeholders of Sussex County, New Jersey, argued that "firmness and unanimity in the Colonies, and an agreement not to use any articles imported from Great Britain or the East Indies . . . may be the most effectual means of averting the dangers that are justly apprehended and securing the invaded rights and privileges of America." The inhabitants of Huntington, New York, similarly asserted that the cessation of all commercial intercourse with Britain and the West Indies would be "the most effectual means for obtaining a speedy repeal." This solution was offered in the published resolutions of dozens of local meetings during the course of the summer. Though advocates of nonimportation in a number of counties declared that the colonies should not submit to parliamentary taxation, they neither advocated active resistance nor undertook to organize such resistance. Instead, they urged the selection of delegates to a Continental Congress intended to coordinate economic retaliation against the Coercive Acts.[5]

By the end of the summer, however, not all Americans were centrally concerned with representation or satisfied with nonimportation as a remedy. Nonimportation may have seemed an adequate response to Whigs in the Middle Atlantic and Chesapeake regions because the Coercive Acts did not affect them directly or require active compliance on their part. In Massachusetts, however, the acts required active compliance at every turn. By reorganizing the government of the province and enhancing royal control over local courts, they forced the inhabitants to choose from three courses of action: submission, resistance, or withdrawal from public life.

In choosing to resist, the people of Massachusetts, and of New England generally, drew upon an ideology of dissent emphasizing the defense of liberty and the public good over the concerns with representation and internal taxation that preoccupied advocates of nonimportation. This more libertarian strain of English Whiggery originated in the writings of the same seventeenth- and early-eighteenth-century political theorists cited by the nonimportation movement, including John Locke, Algernon Sydney, Benjamin Hoadley, Francis Hutcheson, and John Trenchard and Thomas Gordon. It rested on a theory of English constitutionalism that conceived of parliamentary authority as subject to traditional restraints embodied in common law. The colonists saw in the Coercive Acts an assertion of parliamentary supremacy that threatened to sweep aside these constitutional restraints, deprive them of their liberty, and reduce them to "abject slavery."[6]

The first American expression of this more libertarian strain of English constitutionalism was Jonathan Mayhew's *Discourse Concerning Unlimited Submission and Non-Resistance to the Higher Powers*. Mayhew's *Discourse* advanced three ideas that would play a central role in 1774. The first was that obedience was due only to those rulers whose rule was substantively just, regardless of the form of government under which they ruled. A republic, he argued, was no more legitimate than a monarchy, except in that it was more likely to produce good government.[7]

Mayhew also asserted that resistance became legitimate when the people determined that their rulers had become oppressive. He ridiculed the notion that this responsibility could be vested anywhere else. "To say that subjects in general are not proper judges of when their governors oppress them and play the tyrant, and when they defend their rights, administer justice impartially, and promote the public welfare, is as great a treason as ever man uttered. . . . The people know for what end they set up and maintain their governors." Mayhew predicted that as mankind was disposed to obedience, popular resistance by the mass of the people would be confined to those situations in which it was wholly appropriate.[8]

Finally, Mayhew declared that rulers who demanded that their subjects transgress the will of God must be resisted, and he described their pronouncements as nullities: "All commands running counter to the declared will of the supreme ruler of heaven and earth are null and void, and therefore disobedience to them is a duty, and not a crime." Like Bland, Mayhew asserted that some acts of government were void and might be resisted without penalty. But he argued that the criteria for judging such acts was based on their degradation of liberty, justice, and the public welfare, rather than representation or jurisdiction.[9]

In 1774 two Virginians also voiced this more libertarian analysis of the Coercive Acts. Thomson Mason, George Mason's brother, denounced the Boston Port Act as "such a despotick invasion of property, that may be legally resisted, and ought not to be submitted to." He urged the colonists to send relief ships to Boston, prosecute any British officer who undertook to seize the ships, and raise an army if the British attempted to use force to interfere with these prosecutions. In July 1774, Thomas Jefferson devoted the first half of *A Summary View of the Rights of British America* to a substantive analysis of British legislation and reserved his fiercest condemnation for the Coercive Acts, complaining particularly of provisions that would allow Americans accused of murder and riot to be tried in England. He suggested that no American would "suffer a countryman to be torn from the bowels of their society in order to be thus offered as a sacrifice to Parliamentary tyranny."[10]

It was in Massachusetts, however, that the libertarian analysis of the Coercive Acts resonated most broadly. In a series of county conventions, the people of Massachusetts denounced the acts on the grounds that they asserted powers denied to Parliament under the English constitution, powers that the colonists believed transgressed the liberties of freemen. Within this libertarian analysis, articulated most forcefully in the Suffolk Resolves, the issues of representation and jurisdiction so central to the nonimportation movement were largely beside the point. The Resolves declared that the Coercive Acts were "gross infractions of those rights to which we are justly entitled by the laws of nature, the British constitution, and the Charter of the Province" and that "no obedience is due from this province to either or any part of the Acts above mentioned." Delegates from towns of Middlesex County complained that the acts deprived them of the rights of self-government, trial by jury, and assembly for the redress of grievances. They declared that "these late Acts, if quietly submitted to, will annihilate the last vestiges of liberty in this Province, and therefore we must be justified by God and the world in never submitting to them." The people of Bristol County denounced the Coercive Acts as "contrary to reason and the spirit of the English constitution, and, if complied with, will reduce us to the most abject state of servitude."[11]

The people of Massachusetts also asserted a right to be free from arbitrary state violence. In the Suffolk Resolves, the inhabitants of the county complained of a state of affairs "whereby the streets of Boston are thronged with military executioners; whereby our coasts are lined and our harbors crowded with ships of war." The specter of state violence hung over the warning by the people of Cumberland County that "the Ministry have borne their tyranny to such a length as to endeavor to enforce their wicked designs by military force." The people of Essex County complained of the "uncommon zeal, arbitrary exertions, and military violence" demonstrated in the British seizure of provincial gunpowder in Salem.[12] It was the threat of violent enforcement, as well as the unconstitutionality of the Coercive Acts, that prompted the people of Massachusetts to resist in 1774.[13]

In response, town representatives from Suffolk, Middlesex, Worcester, Cumberland, Essex, Hampshire, Plymouth, and Bristol counties organized a political campaign of public disobedience designed to nullify the Coercive Acts, calling for all officers appointed under the acts to resign and for the people to disobey those who refused to do so.[14] Across Massachusetts, the populace joined this campaign to render the acts null and void. In Middlesex County, a militia company forced the lieutenant governor and two members of the Governor's Council to resign and made the sheriff promise he would not enforce the acts in the county. In Worcester, a crowd of over five thousand, including at least one thousand armed militiamen, formed two lines and forced the judges and officers of the court to "pass and repass them, cap in hand, in the most ignominious manner, and read their disavowal of holding courts under the new acts of Parliament, no less than thirty times."[15] In Boston, the operations of the County Court were suspended by the refusal of the full venire of grand and petit jurymen to take their oaths. The jurymen's explanation illustrated the resonance of the libertarian analysis: they declared that the Coercive Acts appeared to us to be utterly repugnant to every idea of justice and common humanity and are justly complained of throughout America as highly oppressive to the good people of this province and manifestly destructive of their natural, as well as Constitutional rights. We believe in our consciences that acting in concert with a court so constituted, and under such circumstances, would be so far betraying the just and sacred rights of our native lands.[16]

The people of Massachusetts did not confine themselves to noncooperation and crowd intimidation. In the Suffolk Resolves, for the first time, they agreed to arm themselves, organize themselves into militia companies under officers of their own choosing, and train regularly under arms. Inspired by the example of the Suffolk Resolves, and the libertarian analysis on which it rested, communities across New England quickly followed suit. The people of Cumberland County, Massachusetts, declaring a "manly opposition to those cruel acts, and every measure which despotism can invent to 'abridge our English liberties,'" urged "every town and individual" in the county to arm and become "perfect in the military art." The delegates of the towns of New London and Windham counties, Connecticut, warned that the people of America were "threatened with the loss of our liberties and constitutional rights," and urged the officers and men of the militia to arm themselves and pay "due Attention to the cultivation of military skill and the art of war.[17]

As the resort to armed organization spread from New England to other regions, those taking up arms increasingly cited this libertarian critique of the Coercive Acts. The closer one gets to the time and place at which colonists decided to actually take up arms, the more their reasoning looks like that of Jonathan Mayhew, and the less it looks like that of Richard Bland. When the New Jersey Provincial Congress took steps to raise the militia in the summer of 1775, it denounced the Coercive Acts as "cruel and arbitrary measures adopted and pursued by the British Parliament and the present Ministry for the purpose of subjugating the American Colonies to the most abject servitude." When the Fairfax County, Virginia, Committee recommended that the freemen of the county associate in militia companies, the articles of association drawn up by George Mason declared that the threat of "the destruction of our ancient Laws and Liberty, and the loss of all that is dear to British subjects and freemen" impelled them to act.[18]

Between September 1774 and April 1775, thousands of Americans who had assembled at the local and provincial level determined that the Coercive Acts were "cruel and arbitrary measures" and "manifestly destructive of their natural, as well as Constitutional rights." Based on that analysis, they decided to render the acts null and void, by armed force if necessary.

Calls for a Continental Congress to coordinate the American response to the Coercive Acts originated in the nonimportation movement. When the first Continental Congress finally met in September 1774, it attempted to speak for both the nonimportation movement and the burgeoning insurrectionary movement in New England. In October 1774 Congress passed a series of resolutions that denounced the Coercive Acts as "impolitick, unjust, and cruel, as well as unconstitutional and most dangerous and destructive of American rights." Yet in outlining an "American Bill of Rights," Congress declared that these rights "cannot legally be taken away from them, altered, or abridged by any power whatever without their consent, by their Representatives in their several Provincial legislatures."[19]

In these resolutions Congress combined two distinct colonial ideologies of resistance in a manner that subordinated the defense of civil liberty to concerns over representation. But the people of New England were not associating in militia companies so that their own representatives could run roughshod over their liberties. In these resolutions Congress attempted to maintain the centrality of the principle of actual representation, despite the fact that it was no longer seen as central by those who were actually taking up arms against British authority.

Both ideologies were present in the Declaration of Independence as well. In the list of grievances with which Congress justified the recourse to revolution, the Declaration describes the Coercive Acts and other parliamentary laws as "pretended legislation," by a "jurisdiction foreign to our constitution and unacknowledged by our laws." Here the Declaration voiced the concerns over representation and jurisdiction that had animated the nonimportation movement. Nevertheless, in the Declaration this focus on representation is overshadowed by Jefferson's famous assertion that "when a long train of abuses and usurpations, pursuing invariably the same object, evinces a design to reduce them under absolute despotism, it is their right, it is their duty, to throw off such government, and to provide new guards for their future security."[20]

The libertarian ideology that animated the resort to armed organization and active resistance in 1774–75 was not the only strain of Whig thought at work in the American Revolution. But because it resonated most vibrantly at the local level, its influence on the Revolution and on American political theory has often been underestimated. Moreover, it offered a critique of oppressive government and state violence that would continue to apply to the acts of a fully representative republican polity.

The People Turn Their Arms against the State: The Militia as an Institution of Resistance

When the people of Suffolk County resolved to assemble in militia companies and engage in military drill, they seized control over a state institution regulated by law and transformed it into a popular institution operating extralegally. Under Massachusetts law, almost all men between sixteen and sixty were required by law to keep arms and turn out with those arms for military training four times a year. The laws of most colonies imposed similar obligations.[21] But when the people of Suffolk County reorganized that militia under popularly elected officers, they stripped the institution of its legal sanction under public authority. The sanction of town governments and county conventions gave these militias some legitimacy as public institutions, but the propriety of individuals banding together in militias of association was open to debate even within Whig political theory.

English Whig theorists were divided on the question of whether resistance to tyranny by private individuals was legitimate. Benjamin Hoadley, for example, argued that resistance was only legitimate when waged for the public good, and suggested that private individuals would usually have their private interests at heart. Francis Hutcheson argued that only the whole body of the people might legitimately make a revolution. But Algernon Sydney, John Locke, and John Trenchard and Thomas Gordon all argued that resistance by private individuals was legitimate so long as they resisted policies that injured the public good. For example, in the *Second Treatise on Government,* Locke asserted that resistance to the monarch was legitimate even where "the mischief and oppression has lighted only on some few, but in such cases, as the precedent, and the consequences seem to threaten all." To the charge that private resistance would lead to anarchy, Whigs answered that individuals would refrain from rising against the government unless their grievances were intolerable and widely enough felt to give resistance a broad public base, and thus some prospect for success. They argued that such occasions would rarely arise, and hence the social costs of private resistance would prove tolerable.[22]

The popular resort to quasi-private and extralegal militias of association thus pushed Whig political theory to its limits and set an important precedent. It also quickly spread beyond the environs of Boston. By late September 1774, Suffolk, Worcester, Cumberland, Hampshire, Plymouth, and Bristol counties had resolved to begin training militia companies outside of, and in opposition to, royal authority. At the end of the month General Gage reported that "the country people are exercising in arms in the Province, Connecticut, and Rhode Island, and getting magazines of arms and ammunition." It was not until October 26 that the Massachusetts Provincial Congress, the new representative body governing the commonwealth, would place this military activity back on a legal footing, the first province-wide representative body to do so.[23]

In New Hampshire, militia companies from three counties seized powder from a royal magazine in December 1774. In April 1775, after the Massachusetts militia fought British troops in the Revolution's first battle at Lexington and Concord, thousands of New Hampshire militiamen marched to join the siege of Boston. The New Hampshire Provincial Congress did not put this militia on a legal footing until June 1775.[24] In general, the militia that nullified the Coercive Acts in New England was locally constituted and self-armed. It was a popular political institution that was only later granted legal status under state control.[25]

In some regions of the South, the raising of the militia proceeded in a more orderly fashion. The county committees of Maryland deferred to the provincial convention, which in December 1774 became the first provincial body in the region to authorize the raising of militia companies. Similar deference prevailed in South Carolina, where the provincial congress followed suit on January 17, 1775.[26]

In Virginia, however, the process looked much more like that in New England. Local extralegal militias began forming in September 1774. George Washington and George Mason organized the first such militia, the Fairfax Independent Company of Volunteers, on September 21, 1774. This precedent was quickly imitated in other counties. James Madison noted in November that "in many counties independent companies are forming," and that many Virginians "publickly declare themselves ready to join the Bostonians as soon as violence is offered them or resistance is thought expedient." He expressed his hope that such extralegal militias would spread throughout the province. In December, Governor Dunmore complained to the Earl of Dartmouth that "every county, besides, is now arming a company of men, whom they call an independent company, for the avowed purpose of protecting their committees." On March 25, 1775, the Virginia Convention gave ex post facto legitimacy to this extralegal activity by adopting a plan to organize and arm the colony's militia.[27] Though some southern patriots proceeded conservatively, waiting for legal authorization to organize the militia, the case of Virginia suggests that the New England precedent of local, extralegal organization also resonated in the South.

It was in the Middle Atlantic states that militia organization was most spontaneous and carried the most radical implications. Most counties in New Jersey waited for the legal authorization of the Provincial Congress, which came on June 3, 1775. The inhabitants of Morris County and Upper Freehold Township in Monmouth County, however, organized themselves into companies in early May.[28] On the whole, the people of New Jersey were more hesitant than their neighbors in New

York and Pennsylvania. When word of Lexington and Concord reached New York on April 29, 1775, a public meeting of six to seven thousand inhabitants elected a Committee of Safety and vowed "to defend their liberty at all hazards." The crowd then seized the city magazine and distributed over four hundred stands of arms "among the multitude, formed themselves into companies, and trained in the streets." Two weeks later, six newly formed militia companies offered their services to the Committee of Safety.[29]

When the Continental Congress called for the arming of the New York Militia in late May 1775, the New York Provincial Congress responded by "recommending" that the colony's inhabitants "furnish themselves with arms" and "form themselves into companies." The provincial congress thus left the decision to take up arms against the king's authority to local communities rather than take the responsibility upon itself. Over the course of the summer, thousands of New Yorkers signed articles of association. In Newburgh, one group of associators declared that "we have no other alternative left but to repel force by force, or to submit to be slaves." In Suffolk and Dutchess counties, associators promised to "defend by arms these United colonies" against Parliament's attempt to enforce its "wicked and ridiculous claims." The Provincial Congress did not formally organize the militia until August 22, 1775. By that time, however, the willingness to associate in a militia company that lacked this explicit legal authorization was already understood as a test of membership in the body politic.[30]

In Pennsylvania and Delaware, the popular response to Lexington and Concord was equally swift and even more radical. There is evidence that companies had formed in York County and in New Castle County, Delaware, the previous winter.[31] Word of hostilities reached Philadelphia on April 25, 1775. The next day a meeting of eight thousand inhabitants of the city of Philadelphia unanimously agreed to associate under arms to defend against the enforcement of "the late cruel and unjust Acts of Parliament." The inhabitants of Reading began forming militia companies the same day. By the end of May, thousands of men had associated in militia companies in Berks, Bucks, Chester, Northampton, Lancaster,

Bedford, Cumberland, and Westmoreland counties, Pennsylvania, and in Kent County, Delaware, weeks before the Pennsylvania Assembly's June 30 act authorizing the establishment of a provincial militia.[32]

Even after this legal recognition, the Pennsylvania militia became an independent player in the radical movement that overthrew Pennsylvania's stubbornly loyalist government. In June 1776 the Continental Congress suggested that the people withdraw their allegiance from those colonial governments refusing to back independence. Militia companies in Philadelphia, Chester, and Lancaster counties responded by calling for a provincial convention to write a new state constitution, the first step in overthrowing the loyalist colonial assembly. When the assembly issued new regulations to the province's militia later that month, the Philadelphia Committee of Privates questioned the assembly's legitimacy and declared the militia independent of its control.[33]

The militias that associated across America in 1774 and 1775 were explicitly insurrectionary institutions, founded at the local level to enforce a popular determination to nullify the Coercive Acts. By the time the former colonies had established new written constitutions, the militia, even in Pennsylvania, had been brought back under statutory authorization and civil control. But the initial precedent of 1774 in which an irate populace took up arms and formed militia companies to resist the authority of an oppressive, albeit lawful, government would leave a lasting imprint on American political culture. Indeed, when the Federalists set out in 1787 to craft a government capable of commanding the obedience of the entire nation, control over the militia became a central issue in the ensuing debate.

The Militia and the Legitimacy of Resistance in the Ratification Debate of 1787–88

In the fall and winter of 1786–87, thousands of impoverished Massachusetts farmers closed the courts across the state in an attempt to block foreclosure on their farms. Led by Revolutionary War veteran Daniel Shays, the insurgents raised a large army and attempted to seize the federal arsenal at Springfield. They were eventually dispersed by an army raised by the state government. The state legislature denounced the in-surgents for waging an "open, unnatural, unprovoked, and wicked rebel-lion." Opponents of Shays' Rebellion declared that the rebels had misun-derstood the meaning of liberty in a republican polity. One Federalist essayist declared that within civil society, liberty consisted of "being sub-ject only to laws made in an equitable constitutional manner, and bind-ing alike on all the citizens of the state." Fear of the potential anarchy rep-resented by Shays motivated the Federalists gathered in Philadelphia to ensure that the new federal government would wield military powers sufficient to maintain its authority.[34]

The Constitution of 1787 provided these powers by giving the federal government the right to raise a military establishment in time of peace. The Federalists also ensured that the federal government would be able to put its own laws into force and coerce the obedience of individual cit-izens without requiring assistance from state institutions, which might withhold that assistance. In the militia clauses of the new Constitution, they gave the federal government the power to call forth the militia of the states to repel invasions, suppress insurrections, and execute the laws of the United States. These clauses also granted Congress the ongoing authority to ensure that the militia was adequately armed, trained, and disciplined to carry out this mandate. The militias remained under state control except when called up under federal authority, and the states re-tained the power to appoint officers.[35] All in all, these provisions granted the federal government a significant measure of coercive force.

When the work of the Philadelphia convention was published in the fall of 1787, opponents of the new Constitution argued that the delega-tion of these military powers would leave the people defenseless in the face of a federal government bent on tyranny. During the ratification debates Anti-Federalists gave full voice to their fears, rooted in Whig ide-ology, that the new federal government would grow as corrupt and tyrannical as had Parliament in 1774. They argued that the federal gov-ernment's power over the army and the militia would leave the people without an effective capacity to resist this tyranny. They particularly pre-dicted that the Constitution's militia clauses would pave the way to the destruction of the institution of the universal militia. The Federalists ridiculed these Whig fears, but they coupled this ridicule with a clear assurance that under the Constitution the people would retain the capacity to embody themselves in the militia and resist tyranny. The debates thus reveal that influential Federalists and Anti-Federalists continued to view the militia as a legitimate agent of resistance against a corrupt and violent state and that the Framers incorporated the libertarian strain of Whig ideology acted out in 1774 into the political theory of the founding.

Within eighteenth-century Whig ideology, the standing army had traditionally loomed as the greatest threat to popular liberty. Consequently, the clauses governing a federal military establishment were the initial focus of Anti-Federalist attacks on the Constitution's delegation of the power of military coercion to the federal government. In one of the most influential of Anti-Federalist essays, published on October 5, 1787, Centinel warned that the Constitution empowered Congress to levy internal taxes, and predicted that "their collection would be enforced by the standing army, however grievous or improper they may be." Other Anti-Federalist essayists soon joined in this attack. Brutus, for example, denounced the Constitution's provision of a standing army, declaring that "no government," regardless of how representative, "should be empowered to do that which if done, would tend to destroy public liberty." This, Brutus argued, was the foundational principle "of the late revolution."[36]

In essays published in early November, the Federal Farmer extended this analysis to the militia. He warned that Congress's power under the militia clauses would allow it to create a select militia, a militia composed entirely of unpropertied young men subject to continuous military training and thus dependent upon their pay for survival. Such an institution, he predicted, would support a "military execution of the laws" just as effectively as would a standing army. Indeed, the Federal Farmer saw in the select militia a far more subtle, and hence more dangerous, road to military despotism:

> Should one fifth or one eighth part of the men capable of bearing arms, be made a select militia, as has been proposed, and those the young and ardent

part of the community, possessed of little or no property, and all the others put on a plan that will render them of no importance, the former will answer all the purposes of an army, while the latter will be defenceless.[37]

When the dissenting minority of the Pennsylvania ratification convention summed up these fears of military coercion in December, they linked the army and militia clauses of the Constitution and charged that they marked a repudiation of the principles of the Revolution:

> The question will then be reduced to this short issue, viz. Whether satiated with the blessings of liberty; whether repenting of the folly of so recently asserting their unalienable rights, against foreign despots at the expence of so much blood and treasure, and such painful and arduous struggles, the people of America are now willing to resign every privilege of freemen, and submit to the dominion of an absolute government.[38]

In the apocalyptic tones of American Whiggery, the *Dissent of the Minority of the Pennsylvania Convention* warned that the representatives of this new government would abrogate the right of elections and levy internal taxes that "however oppressive, the people will have but this alternative, either to pay the tax, or let their property be taken, for resistance will be in vain. The standing army and select militia would enforce the collection." The minority predicted that the select militia, composed of young men, would be marched across the continent and used as "instruments of crushing the last efforts of expiring liberty, of riveting the chains of despotism on their fellow citizens."[39]

To balance this threat, most Anti-Federalists emphasized the importance of maintaining the universal militia, the traditional colonial American institution composed of almost all adult free white men. The people of New England had turned this institution against the British in 1774–75, and Anti-Federalists saw it as their best defense should the new central government begin to abuse its powers. There were several different strains of Anti-Federalist thought in 1787, but representatives of the different strains all articulated the belief that the militia should be composed of the body of the people.[40] Plebeian Anti-Federalists conceived of the militia as properly embodying the whole people and insisted the people retained a continuing right of resistance against abuses by their government. They acted out this belief when several members of an Anti-Federalist crowd in Carlisle, Pennsylvania, were placed under arrest. The inhabitants of the surrounding counties assembled in their militia companies, marched into Carlisle, and commanded the release of the prisoners.[41]

Middling Anti-Federalists were frightened by such displays of populist political violence, but they too argued that the Constitution must preserve the universal militia. The Federal Farmer, for example, criticized the militia clauses and argued that "the Constitution ought to secure a genuine and guard against a select militia, by providing that the militia shall always be kept armed, organized and disciplined, and include, according to past and general usage of the states, all men capable of bearing arms." This universal militia would, he argued, promote "free and mild government" as opposed to the "military execution of the laws" that he feared from a select militia.[42]

Even elite Anti-Federalists subscribed to the view that the militia might be called upon to protect the people from an abusive federal government. George Mason, a leader of elite Anti-Federalists, complained during the Virginia ratification convention that the Constitution threatened to undermine the universal militia. In proposing to amend the militia clauses, Mason explained that he feared "the natural propensity of rulers to oppress the people. I wish only to prevent them from doing evil. . . . if the clause stands as it is now, it will take from the state legislatures what divine providence has given to every individual—the means of self-defense."[43] Luther Martin, an elite Anti-Federalist who refused to sign the Constitution, authored one of the most bitter denunciations of the Framers, the *Genuine Information*, in which he accused the members of the Philadelphia convention of plotting the destruction of the states. He identified the militia and treason clauses of the Constitution as designed to deprive the states of the capacity to defend themselves and their citizens from the "arbitrary encroachments of the general government." That Martin considered such resistance proper he left no doubt.

"By the Principles of the American revolution," Martin declared, "*arbitrary power may* and *ought* to be resisted even by *arms* if necessary."[44]

Thus, leading spokesmen for all three strains of Anti-Federalism described the universal militia composed of the body of the people as normative and as a safeguard against military coercion. Few Anti-Federalists went as far as Luther Martin and the Anti-Federalists in Carlisle, Pennsylvania, in articulating a continuing right of resistance. There was substantial disagreement over how such resistance ought to be conducted. Nevertheless, most Anti-Federalists at least implicitly sanctioned armed resistance to domestic tyranny and saw the universal militia as the legitimate agent of such resistance. The precedent of 1774 was alive and well within Anti-Federalist thought in 1787–88.

Federalists replied to these Anti-Federalist fears with scorn. They argued that the representative government established by the Constitution could not possibly act despotically, and they consistently ridiculed Anti-Federalist warnings that federal representatives would betray their constituents. But ridicule alone was an insufficient response to the Anti-Federalist critique. In 1787, Federalists faced the argument that the power to raise an army and control the militia gave Congress the ability to coerce their constituents and thus marked a repudiation of the Revolution. From the enthusiastic reception of the *Dissent* of the Pennsylvania Minority and of Martin's *Genuine Information,* Federalists feared that this argument might resonate broadly enough to turn a majority against ratification.[45]

To meet this argument head on, Federalists consistently coupled their ridicule with discussions of legitimate resistance designed to demonstrate that the Constitution retained the people's capacity to wage such resistance. In a significant rhetorical concession, Federalists declared that were Congress to order the militia or the standing army to execute despotic measures, the militia, composed of the body of the people, would simply refuse, and would become the core of resistance. This Federalist response acknowledged the role of the militia as an agent of legitimate, albeit extralegal, resistance.

The first articulation of Federalist theories of resistance came in an essay published in Philadelphia on October 16, 1787. The author, styling himself "Impartial," conceded that the Constitution's provision of a standing army was a cause for alarm. Nevertheless, he declared that if Congress employed any illegal and unconstitutional mode of taxation, "they cannot subsist long where the rights of men are so well ascertained and so generally known. If remonstrances should not be sufficient to procure redress, the militia will always have it in their power to command it."[46]

Noah Webster picked up this argument in *A Citizen of America*, a response to Centinel that appeared the next day. Webster argued that the powers of raising an army and organizing the militia were necessary to any government and were retained in the hands of the people's representatives. He mocked Anti-Federalist warnings and described the powers of Congress as "little more than nominal." Nevertheless, he asserted that military coercion could never succeed in America because

> the whole body of the people are armed, and constitute a force superior to any band of regular troops that can be, on any pretence, raised in the United States. A military force, at the command of Congress, can execute no laws, but such as the people perceive to be just and constitutional; for they will possess the power, and jealousy will instantly inspire the inclination, to resist the execution of a law which appears to them unjust and oppressive.[47]

Two weeks after this, a New York Federalist, writing to the *Connecticut Journal*, struck the same chord. To warnings that the militia clauses contemplated a select militia, the Federalist author of a "Letter from New York" replied:

> But who are the militia? The militia comprehends all the male inhabitants from sixteen to sixty years of age; it includes the knowledge and strength of the nation. Against whom will they turn their swords? Against themselves!— to execute laws which are unconstitutional, unreasonable, and oppressive upon themselves! Absurdity itself could not have thought of raising an objection on that ground. . . . When the Congress resort to the militia, which is the body of the people, for the support of the laws of the Union, it is done in confidence that the laws are just and good, and worthy of the support of the

people, otherwise Congress can have no reason to expect support from that quarter.[48]

These Federalist contributions to the debate over the militia clauses described the universal militia as normative and attributed to the militia the power to "procure redress" and to "resist the execution" of unconstitutional and unjust laws. These statements did not contemplate the overthrow of the constituted government. Rather, they asserted that the militia, described as the body of the people, might legitimately serve as an insurrectionary check on government.[49] They suggest that the precedent of insurrectionary resistance set in 1774 influenced Federalist understandings of legitimate resistance.

In the winter of 1787–88, Alexander Hamilton and James Madison advanced some important variations on this argument. In *Federalist No. 28*, Hamilton suggested that insurrectionary resistance was never permissible but in cases of domestic tyranny, revolution was the proper recourse: "If the representatives of the people betray their constituents, there is then no resource left but in the exertion of that original right of self-defence which is paramount to all positive forms of government." Hamilton also argued that the federal system of contending national and state governments offered revolutionaries an advantage: should the federal government turn despotic, insurgents might use the state governments to coordinate their resistance. Without such organizational structures, Hamilton argued, "the citizens must rush tumultuously to arms, without concert, without resource; except in their courage and despair." With the federal system of rival governments, such organizational structures would always be available: "The people, by throwing themselves into either scale, will infallibly make it preponderate. If their rights are invaded by either, they can make use of the other as the instrument of redress."[50]

Two weeks later, in *Federalist No. 29*, Hamilton responded to the Anti-Federalist furor over the militia clauses by tying the militia into this discussion of revolution. In this essay he gave credence to Anti-Federalist fears by advocating the creation of a select militia. Though he likened these fears to the "inflammatory ravings of chagrinned incendiaries," he responded forthrightly to the "Address and Reasons for Dissent" of the Pennsylvania Minority by declaring that even a select militia could never be used to enslave the people:

> Whither would the militia, irritated by being called upon to undertake a distant and hopeless expedition for the purpose of riveting the chains of slavery upon a part of their countrymen direct their course, but to the seat of the tyrants, who had meditated so foolish as well as so wicked a project; to crush them in their imagined entrenchments of power and to make them an example of the just vengeance of an abused and incensed people?[51]

In contrast to earlier Federalist commentaries, Hamilton argued that the militia might legitimately enact revolutionary rather than insurrectionary resistance. He also offered a more nuanced interpretation of the relationship between state governments and the people. He described the militia as an independent agent, an embodiment of popular sovereignty. He emphasized the role of state governments as "instruments" that would organize and coordinate popular resistance to federal tyranny. He expressed doubt that insurgents could succeed without this coordination, but he refrained from identifying state action as a condition of legitimate popular resistance. Finally, Hamilton responded to Anti-Federalist suspicions of a select militia by arguing that such a militia would still perform the revolutionary role that Anti-Federalists assigned to the universal militia.

In *Federalist No. 46,* James Madison seconded Hamilton's contributions. Like Hamilton, Madison confined his discussion of legitimate resistance to revolutionary, as opposed to insurrectionary, solutions. He argued that "ambitious encroachments" by the federal government would trigger "the same appeal to a trial by force" as had the usurpations of Great Britain. Like so many other Federalists, he ridiculed Anti-Federalist fears of this outcome as the "incoherent dreams of a delirious jealousy." Nevertheless, he predicted that if the federal government should build a large standing army and marshal it against the states, it would be opposed by "a militia amounting to near half a million of citizens with arms in their hands, officered by men chosen from among themselves, fighting for their common liberties, and united and conducted by governments possessing their affections and confidence."[52]

This passage marks a change in agency within Madison's text. Up to this point Madison frames the discussion in terms of "encroachments of the federal government on the authority of the State governments." When turning to a discussion of resistance, however, Madison describes the "existence of subordinate governments" as "additional advantages," over and above the advantage of being armed, available to the people should they decide to resist a tyrannical federal government. Like Hamilton, Madison portrays the "free and gallant citizens of America," embodied in the militia, as legitimate agents of resistance. On one hand, he emphasizes the importance of the state governments; on the other, he relegates them to a supporting, instrumental role.[53]

Lesser Federalist authors continued the argument throughout the winter of 1788. In Connecticut, the "Republican" directly engaged the Anti-Federalist charge that the Constitution was "dangerous to liberty." He asserted that under the Constitution the "great barriers of liberty will still remain," among them "a militia of freemen." The people of America, he declared, "have arms in their hands; they are not destitute of military knowledge; every citizen is required by Law to be a soldier; we are marshaled into companies, regiments, and brigades for the defense of our country. This is a circumstance which . . . enables them to defend their rights and privileges against every invader." In Pennsylvania, Tench Coxe reiterated the argument that in cases of congressional usurpation, the people might "by virtue of those military powers, which are inseparable from their own persons, suspend every operation of Congress, which shall have thus ceased to be a lawful and constitutional power." Here Coxe reverted to the theme of insurrectionary resistance articulated by Noah Webster and others, and connected the right to keep and bear arms with the people's continuing capacity to wage such resistance: "Congress have no power to disarm the militia. Their swords, and every other terrible implement of the soldier, are *the birth-right of an American*. What clause in the state or foederal constitutions hath *given away* that important right."[54] These statements connected a general right to keep and bear arms within the universal militia with the people's capacity to resist their own government.

During ratification, Anti-Federalists argued that only a universal militia could preserve the capacity of the people and the states to resist domestic tyranny. In forcing Federalists to acknowledge an insurrectionary or revolutionary role for the militia, Anti-Federalists shifted the terms of the debate. Nor was this Federalist concession simply rhetorical. Anti-Federalists in Virginia and elsewhere incorporated their objections to the militia clauses in proposed amendments to the Constitution that recognized "that the People have a Right to keep and to bear Arms" and "that a well regulated Militia, composed of the Body of the People, trained to Arms, is the proper, natural, and safe Defense of a free state."[55] During the course of the framing of the Second Amendment, it would become clear that many moderate Federalists also approved of placing limitations on the military powers of the federal government.

A Note on the Second Amendment

A well regulated militia being necessary to the security of a free state, the right of the people to keep and bear arms, shall not be infringed.

Historians and legal scholars have debated the meaning of the Second Amendment with particular intensity over the last decade. The analysis that follows in no way does justice to the richness of the scholarship that has emerged. But when pressed to assign meaning to the Second Amendment, these historians have offered four possibilities for consideration. The first is that the amendment was intended to clarify that the power to arm the militia lay concurrently with the states and the federal government. The second is that the amendment recognized an individual right to own and use guns. The third is that the amendment was intended to give constitutional status to the institution of the universal militia. The fourth is that the amendment was intended to convey as little enforceable meaning as possible.[56]

The interpretation of the Amendment as a guarantee of the states' concurrent power to arm the militia is based upon an analysis of the debate over the militia clauses in the Virginia ratifying convention. During the course of debate, George Mason expressed his fear that the militia clauses gave Congress the power to "harass and abuse the militia" so as to "abolish them and raise a standing army in their stead." He also expressed the fear that Congress would use its exclusive authority to arm and train the militia in order to leave the institution disarmed and neglected.[57]

In response to Mason's objections, James Madison complained that there was no reason to expect that representatives in a republican polity would oppress their constituents. Still, he attempted to conciliate Mason with a concession. He declared that under the militia clauses, the power of arming the militia was held concurrently by the state and federal governments. He also noted that the militia would not be subject to martial law unless called into federal service. Neither Mason nor Patrick Henry, who joined the debate, were satisfied with this concession, however. Henry suggested that there was little to distinguish representatives from the rulers who had enslaved the people of other nations. Mason, for his part, repeated his assertion that the militia clauses gave Congress the power to undermine the universal militia.[58]

At the end of the convention, Virginia Anti-Federalists offered the following amendment as part of a proposed federal declaration of rights: "That the people have a right to keep and bear arms; that a well regulated militia composed of the body of the people trained to arms, is the proper, natural, and safe defense of a free state." This language was copied almost verbatim by the ratifying conventions of New York and North Carolina.[59] Alongside this provision concerning the right to keep and bear arms and the maintenance of a universal militia, the convention proposed a separate amendment on the issue of concurrency: "That each state shall have the power to provide for organizing, arming, and disciplining its own militia, whensoever the Congress shall omit or neglect to provide for the same." The same provision also recorded Madison's concession that the militia be subject to martial law only when called into national service.[60]

In contrast with the Virginia amendments' focus on the militia, ratifiers in Pennsylvania, Massachusetts, and New Hampshire offered language that explicitly recognized an individual right to keep arms. In Pennsylvania, Anti-Federalists proposed an amendment recognizing that "the people have a right to bear arms for the defence of themselves and their state, or the United States, or for the purpose of killing game; and no law shall be passed disarming the people or any of them, unless for crimes committed, or real danger of public injury from individuals." To enlist the support of Massachusetts Anti-Federalists, Samuel Adams proposed an amendment to the Massachusetts ratifying convention to make it clear that Congress had no power "to prevent the people of the United States who are peaceful citizens from keeping their own arms." Adams later withdrew his amendment. Finally, the New Hampshire ratifying convention proposed an amendment providing that "Congress shall never disarm any citizen, unless such as are or have been in actual rebellion."[61]

It is not clear whether the Pennsylvania or Massachusetts provisions came to Madison's attention before he drafted the Second Amendment. In any case, his original draft, "The right of the people to keep and bear arms shall not be infringed; a well armed, and well regulated militia being the best security of a free country," was clearly based upon Virginia's proposed declaration of rights provision. If Madison intended the amendment to recognize only a state's concurrent power to arm its militia, he ignored the language precisely tailored by George Mason to this narrow end in favor of the much broader language guaranteeing the right to keep and bear arms. He then placed this amendment alongside nine other provisions relating to the individual and collective rights of persons, as opposed to placing the amendment with the other provisions of his proposed new article 7 that addressed the separation of powers among the departments of government and between the states and the federal government.[62] There is nothing in the text of Madison's proposal, then, to suggest that it had anything to do with concurrency.

In interpreting the meaning of Madison's draft in a newspaper essay, Federalist Tench Coxe suggested that it offered recognition of an individual right to own guns:

As civil rulers, not having their duty to the people, duly before them, may attempt to tyrannize, and as the military forces which shall occasionally be raised to defend our country, might pervert their power to the injury of their fellow citizens, the people are confirmed by the next article in their right to keep and bear their private arms.[63]

While a contemporary commentary by a political ally would normally be considered important evidence of meaning, Coxe's interpretation stands at odds with the debate in the Virginia ratifying convention and also with the ensuing debate over the amendment in Congress. There was no discussion in those debates of the utility of an individual right to own guns. Though the language of the amendment may well have suggested to contemporaries that it protected an individual right to own guns, there is little evidence that this was the Framers' intent.[64]

The most significant alteration that Madison made in the Virginia text probably gives the clearest indication of what he believed was at stake. Madison deleted the phrase "composed of the body of the people" from his draft. In doing so he may have intended to water down Mason's call to maintain the universal militia and thus pave the way for the creation of the select militia advocated by Hamilton.[65]

The House of Representatives reversed the order of the two clauses in Madison's draft and restored the language that defined the militia as composed of the body of the people: "A well regulated militia, composed of the body of the people, being the best security of a free state, the right of the people to keep and bear arms shall not be infringed, but no person religiously scrupulous shall be compelled to bear arms."[66] The House's modifications suggest that the Federalists who controlled the chamber rejected Madison's language as too weak to accomplish Mason's goal of preserving the universal militia, a goal that many moderate Federalists shared.

The final draft of the Second Amendment was produced by the Senate, an institution that kept no records of its debates. The Senate once again deleted the language defining the militia as "composed of the body of the people."[67] Second Amendment scholars have offered two opposing explanations for this last alteration. The first is that the Senate, like Madison, intended to pave the way for the creation of a select militia system. The second is that the Senate was simply shortening the amendment for stylistic reasons. The first interpretation has this advantage: if the Senate agreed that the purpose of the amendment was to preserve the universal militia, it is unlikely to have deleted the language defining the militia as universal. On the other hand, the actions of the House tend to support the second interpretation. The House had already rejected the language that Madison had crafted to permit the creation of a select militia. Had the House understood the Senate language as having the same intent, it is unlikely to have conceded the matter without recorded objection. That the House accepted the Senate language without even sending it to the conference committee that considered disputed language in several other amendments suggests that it did not understand the Senate's alteration as being intended to have a substantive impact on the meaning of the amendment.

This interpretation is reinforced by the fact that the House remained steadfast in its opposition to the creation of a select militia for the rest of the first Congress. When Secretary of War Henry Knox sent Congress a plan to reform the militia along select lines, a coalition of moderate Federalists and Anti-Federalists purged the plan of all measures to intensify the training of a select corps of young men. During the debate Anti-Federalist congressman James Jackson of Georgia objected to the suggestion that only part of the militia be trained. Jackson declared it his opinion that "the people of the United States would never consent to be deprived of the privilege of carrying arms" and that "in a republic, every citizen ought to be a soldier, and prepared to resist tyranny and usurpation, as well as invasion."[68] Federalist Roger Sherman raised similar constitutional objections, declaring that "He conceived it to be the privilege of every citizen, and one of his most essential rights, to bear arms, and to resist every attack upon his liberty and property, by whomsoever made. The particular states, like private citizens, have a right to be armed, and to defend, by force of arms, their rights, when invaded."[69] Out of this debate came the Militia Act of 1792, which preserved the institution of the universal militia composed of the bulk of the nation's free white male citizens aged eighteen to forty-five.[70]

Of the four interpretations of the meaning of the Second Amendment, then, the first is the weakest. If Madison intended the Second

Amendment to recognize only the concurrent power of the state and federal governments to arm the militia, he chose the wrong language and sought to place it in the wrong part of the Constitution. The last interpretation, that the Senate stripped the amendment of its enforceable meaning, is plausible, but not compelling. One can read the amendment, deprived by the Senate of enforceable language, as "a mere statement of principle" that "generally endorsed the value of a well-regulated militia."[71] But any construction that deprives a provision of the Bill of Rights of enforceable meaning must meet a high burden of proof. Without direct evidence of the intent of the Senate, this interpretation cannot meet that test.

If its Framers invested the Second Amendment with enforceable meaning, then, they intended to protect either an individual right to own guns or the institution of the universal militia. Of these, the available evidence tends to point to the second. Though the debates of 1787–92 do include language evocative of an individual right, the overall discussion revolved around the institutional organization of political violence.[72] Nevertheless, under either of these interpretations, the purpose behind the amendment was the same: to vest in the Constitution the right of the people to retain the capacity to wage the natural right of resistance to tyranny.

The memory of the libertarian ideology of 1774 was carried by those who took up arms against their lawful government in the American Revolution. It was carried in the Declaration of Independence's celebration of the right and duty to throw off any government that subjects the people to a reign of "absolute despotism." Finally, the text of the Second Amendment served as an additional vessel that would carry this memory into the nineteenth and twentieth centuries.

THE REVOLUTION AS LIVING MEMORY: FRIES' REBELLION AND THE ALIEN AND SEDITION ACT CRISIS OF 1798–1800

On March 7, 1799, the inhabitants of several townships in Bucks and Northampton counties, Pennsylvania, forcefully resisted the execution of a federal law providing for a direct tax on houses, land, and slaves. Assembled in three militia companies, these insurgents marched on Bethlehem, Pennsylvania, and released prisoners in the custody of a federal marshal. Though the target of that resistance was the "house tax," the insurgents were motivated in large part by Democratic-Republican claims that the tax, an associated stamp excise, and the Alien and Sedition Acts were all part of the same Federalist conspiracy to enslave the people. In resolving to nullify the direct tax within their own communities, the insurgents articulated a memory of the American Revolution as a struggle to defend liberty. John Fries, who led a band of insurgents from Bucks County to Bethlehem and thereby gave his name to the rebellion, declared that "he had fought for liberty heretofore, and now the government was introducing again the same laws that he had fought against and he would not submit to them."[1] The campaign of resistance to the direct tax of 1798 is today considered the second insurrection against federal authority in United States history.

Fries' Rebellion marked the culmination of the Alien and Sedition Act crisis of 1798–99.[2] It would be easy to dismiss John Fries and his neighbors as misguided extremists, and many historians have done just that.[3] The rebellion was small, isolated, and easily suppressed. But Fries and his neighbors represented one voice in a larger national conversation. Appreciated in its full dimensions, the Alien and Sedition Act crisis demonstrates the continued resonance of the ideas that had led Americans to take up arms in 1774. Whig ideology, and particularly the libertarian commitment to armed resistance in the face of tyranny, retained an important place within political discussion, public commemoration, and the living memory of those who had fought the American Revolution. In 1798, Democratic-Republicans brought the moral imperatives of the American Revolution to bear upon the acts of a fully representative government of their own creation. Though some party leaders attempted to craft a more refined resistance of organized petitioning and state nullification, others continued to celebrate popular nullification and armed resistance. Together, they transmitted the ideas and rituals of colonial resistance into the politics of the new republic.

Love for the Honor of One's Country: The War Program of 1798 and the Reign of the Black Cockade

The Alien and Sedition Act crisis had its origins in a three-way diplomatic contest among the United States, Great Britain, and France that smoldered throughout the 1790s. French resentment over the favorable terms accorded Great Britain in a treaty signed by the United States in 1796 culminated in a state of "quasi-war" between France and the United States by the beginning of 1798. French naval commanders and privateers began a campaign of harassment against American shipping engaged in commerce with Britain. When President John Adams sent a delegation to Paris in 1797 to negotiate a new commercial treaty, agents of the French government, identified in diplomatic dispatches as "X, Y and Z," demanded a huge loan to the Directory, bribes for French officials, and the repudiation of President Adams's public complaints of French aggression. When the American delegates balked, the conduct of French officials became more threatening. They noted that France was poised to invade England and suggested that a similar fate might await America.

They warned that the "French party" in America, a veiled reference to the Democratic-Republican Party, would lay the blame for any conflict squarely at the feet of the Federalists.[4]

When dispatches describing these demands were made public in the United States in April 1798, war fever swept the nation. President Adams and the Federalist Party called upon all Americans to prepare to meet the threat of French aggression. Federalists warned of an imminent invasion. The tone of these warnings seems overwrought today, but the international situation in 1797–98 gave some substance to Federalist fears. As a result of a temporary ascendancy in its decades-long struggle with England, France did have the naval capacity to project military power across the Atlantic.[5]

At President Adams's suggestion, Congress took measures to guard against this menace. In 1797 it authorized an increase in the size of the navy and the construction of additional harbor fortifications and paid for these measures by levying a new federal stamp excise. After dispatches documenting the "XYZ Affair" were published in April 1798, Congress passed an additional increase in the size of the navy, quadrupled the size of the regular army to thirteen thousand, and began the organization necessary to raise a provisional army of fifty thousand troops. In addition, Congress abrogated the Franco-American treaties dating from the Revolutionary alliance. This program placed the country on a footing just short of declared war. To finance the new military establishment, Congress passed another internal tax, the direct tax on houses, land, and slaves. Congress also authorized the president to borrow unlimited sums at 8 percent interest in anticipation of tax revenues.[6]

Having taken measures to secure the country from invasion, the Federalists enacted a final set of laws in the summer of 1798 to guard the country against internal subversion. The Alien Acts authorized the president to restrain or deport any alien that he judged "dangerous to the peace and safety of the United States." The Sedition Act, on the other hand, was designed to guard against the subversive efforts of citizens. The first section made it a crime to enter into a combination or conspiracy to "oppose any measure" of the United States government. The balance of the act prohibited the "writing, printing, uttering or publishing" of any "false, scandalous, and malicious writing" tending to bring the government, Congress, or the president into "contempt or disrepute."[7]

In retrospect, these measures seem at odds with any rational calculation of the political interest of the Federalist Party. Many Republicans and even some Federalists perceived this program as a conscious assault on organized political opposition. Internal taxes were obviously prone to trigger public resentment, and standing armies had long been anathema within Anglo-American political culture. The Alien and Sedition Acts appeared to contravene several provisions of the Bill of Rights. The war program of 1798 set the Federalist Party on a collision course with public opinion.

When viewed through the lens of a shared masculine identity based on honor, however, Federalist behavior in this period becomes more comprehensible. Alarmed by the erosion of public deference in the increasingly democratic post-Revolutionary period, political elites in the 1790s crafted a code of honorable behavior to buttress their claims to leadership.[8] In 1798, Federalists described the war with France, the battle against the Republican press, and opposition to the democratization of American politics as matters of honor. They argued that the military establishment of 1798 was designed not only to defend against invasion, but also to vindicate the nation's honor. In an address to President Adams, the officers of the Delaware militia declared that the nation faced a choice between "disgraceful surrender" and "noble struggle." Adams agreed with their assessment of the situation, asking, "Where is the man of honor, virtue or public spirit, who can hesitate between dishonorable peace and necessary war?"[9]

When Republicans protested that further negotiation might bring a peaceful resolution of the conflict with France, Federalists expressed disgust at their passivity. A Federalist calling himself "Americanus" accused Republicans of a most "lamblike" patriotism: "How lukewarm must that love for the honour of one's country be, which, amidst insults heaping on insults, dares to do naught but hope for justice!" William Cobbett also denounced Republicans for preferring peace to war: "Thou man of mud! It is not the temporary preservation of thy land, nor of thy houses, nor thy dollars, nor thy scrip, that ought to be the first object with the government; it is the permanent good of the whole country, which is inseparable from its *honour*."[10]

Honor demanded not just a defense of the nation, but an aggressive defense of personal stature and reputation. Federalist justifications of the Sedition Act rested on the argument that reputation was an essential privilege owed protection by the Constitution and the rule of law. When Republicans launched a campaign of public criticism of measures taken by the government, Federalists complained that public opposition displayed a lack of trust that touched the honor of the officers of government, and suggested that such complaints breached the bounds of legitimate political expression. On a number of occasions, prominent Federalists even objected to public petitions that slighted the honor of members of the party. When the inhabitants of Prince Edward County, Virginia, sent Secretary of State Timothy Pickering an address to President Adams suggesting that the Alien and Sedition Acts reflected a design to strip the people of liberty, Pickering found it beneath his honor to forward the address to the president and returned it. If the freeholders of the county were "finally determined to insult the President and Congress, by persisting to offer the address," Pickering told them, "they may commit it to some person who is capable of debasing himself by presenting it."[11]

As war fever swept the nation in the summer of 1798, crowds of young men, soldiers, sailors, and militiamen demonstrated their support for the Federalist administration by wearing black cockades. These young Federalists' conception of honor lent itself to remarkably aggressive behavior that raised the specter of state-sponsored violence against political opponents. In September 1798, a troop of Federalist militia confronted Republican congressman Albert Gallatin in Harrisburg, bursting his effigy in front of him and warning him that such a fate awaited any man "who would quietly lie bye and suffer a foreign power to rob and insult us." Young men wearing the black cockade also harassed New York congressman Edward Livingston and Philadelphia news editor Benjamin Bache. The editor of the Norfolk *Epitome of the Times* was beaten by soldiers in 1798. Since the beginning of the 1790s, the Federalists had presented themselves to the public as the "Friends of Order," the party of stability and refinement. During the cockade fever of 1798–99, however, honor trumped order as the party's cardinal value.[12]

Within this culture of honor, however, aggression masked a deeper anxiety. Individual honor might be sapped by furtive campaigns of criticism, gossip, and slander. The preoccupation with such covert assaults made Federalist political ideology a fertile ground for themes of hidden subversion and conspiracy. Federalists warned of an "army of spies and incendiaries scattered through the continent," working in league with France. When Republican James Logan undertook a private diplomatic mission to France to try to prevent open warfare, William Cobbett suggested that he had gone to coordinate plans for an invasion. "Watch, Philadelphians, or the fire is in your houses and the *couteau at your throats.*" These fears reached their most apocalyptic form in the rapid dissemination of the grandest conspiracy theory of the age, John Robinson's description of the sinister Order of the Illuminati, an alleged international conspiracy of European origin dedicated to the overthrow of civil government and organized religion. In a May 1798 sermon, Federalist clergyman Jedediah Morse warned that the order had extended its tentacles across the Atlantic and aimed to overthrow the American government. He also suggested the order was recruiting from among the ranks of the Democratic-Republican Party.[13]

Federalists saw in the enslaved population of the South yet another hidden subversive force. In 1791 the onset of revolution in Haiti had sharpened the fears of slaveholding whites in America. During the 1790s newspapers across the nation published accounts of burning plantations and the slaughter of "innocent" whites. In 1798 Federalists warned that France might seek to export this revolution to the United States. Former secretary of war Henry Knox gave voice to such racially charged fears of subversion, warning President Adams of the possibility of an invasion from Haiti by "an army of ten thousand blacks and people of colour in vessels seized from our own citizens. They might land on the defenseless parts of South Carolina or Virginia. Under such circumstances, the slaves would instantly join them, and greatly encrease their force. I do not believe this picture too highly coloured." In defending the Alien Enemies

Act before the Virginia House of Delegates, George K. Taylor and General Henry Lee raised similar racial fears by warning that agents of France would "excite our slaves to insurrection." Should such a conspiracy come to fruition, Taylor warned, all in society would suffer equally: "The loudest in their wailings would be their wives and daughters torn from their arms, with naked bosoms, outstretched hands, and disheveled hair, to gratify the brutal passion of a ruthless negro, who would the next moment murder the object of his lust."[14] This arresting portrait depicted the sum of all Federalist fears, the ultimate annihilation of honor brought about by alien subversion of the racial order.

Firmness in Defense of Liberty: Republicans Debate the Boundaries of Legitimate Resistance

Republicans had pragmatic political reasons to resist the Federalist program of 1798. The party was unwilling to repudiate its attachment to the democratic principles of the French Revolution. The Alien Acts struck at French, Irish, and German immigrants, important constituencies within the party. More importantly, the Sedition Act held the potential to deprive the party of any means of communicating with its constituents. Political calculation thus played a role in the Republican response, but it cannot account for the party's open calls for resistance, which courted a devastating electoral backlash.

The key to Republican language and behavior in 1798 lies in their enthusiastic embrace of a traditional Whig analysis of the Federalist war program. A Republican writing under the pseudonym "Nestor" provides an excellent illustration of that embrace. In May 1798, Nestor accused President John Adams of renouncing the principles for which Americans had fought the Revolution. Seizing on Adams's comment that Americans had fought for independence only out of necessity, Nestor accused Adams of misinterpreting the meaning of the Revolution: "Did America resist because she wished only to be *independent?* No! Mr. Adams' assertion to the contrary, she contended for *freedom* as well as independence." Nestor insisted that in belittling America's struggle for freedom, Adams had revealed his hitherto veiled hostility to liberty. "The real enemy," Nestor warned his readers, "is assaulting the citadel of your dearest privileges—*Fleets, standing armies, debts and taxes* are preparing for you."[15]

Nestor clearly twisted Adams's words to the president's discredit. He suggested that Federalist policies represented the classical symptoms of corruption and despotism, "fleets, standing armies, debts, and taxes." In accusing Adams of standing for independence but not freedom, Nestor suggested that Adams had repudiated the struggle for liberty that had engaged Americans in 1774. He thus invoked the memory of the American Revolution and enjoined Americans to resist similar assaults on liberty by a government of their own creation.

In their denunciation of Federalist policies, Republicans laid heavy emphasis on the dangers of centralized power, the erosion of the separation of powers among the branches of government, and the violation of constitutional liberties, the same themes used by the Whig opponents of British imperial policy in the 1760s and 1770s. Confronted with what they saw as a classic example of a corrupt assault on liberty, the Republicans refused to grant any credence to Federalist protests that they were simply enacting temporary measures necessary for the protection of the nation. Like the Federalists, Republicans sought hidden explanations of Federalist behavior, and found them in a conspiracy to establish monarchical government in America.

Republicans portrayed the military buildup of 1798 and the taxes necessary to finance it as dangerous symptoms of corruption. Americans had regarded internal taxes with suspicion in 1765, and the fact that their own republican government had laid the stamp and direct taxes of 1797–98 did little to mollify Republican fears. Traditional Whig arguments against such taxes held that they were especially liable to promote corruption, because of the significant costs of collecting them. Whigs also believed that the enormous patronage powers associated with the appointment of thousands of tax collectors posed a threat to divided government, since legislators and members of their families could be rewarded with commissions as officers of the executive branch. Finally, Whigs had argued in 1765 that such inherently burdensome taxes should be enacted only at the most local level, by representatives intimately familiar with how best to levy them.[16]

In 1798, Republicans were quick to raise these objections against the stamp and house taxes, and to invoke the memory of British oppression. A correspondent to the *New London Bee* asked its readers if they would "Swallow every imp of Britain, stamp acts, gag laws, direct taxes, with double herds of collectors smelling into farm houses as well as grog shops?" In New Jersey, an "Essex Dutchman" warned that "if Congress, in their wisdom at their next session, should see fit to tax our day light, and our fire and candle light, it might also be necessary to appoint more such officers, and that would take more money."[17]

Republicans also denounced the creation of a standing army in peacetime, as the source of burdensome taxes and as dangerous in its own right. They saw in the army a locus of government power and patronage far greater than that represented by the direct tax. Thus, the Freeholders in Dinwiddie County, Virginia, warned that standing armies "have always been subservient to the views of the executive department, from which they derive their honors and emoluments." They also feared the army as a source of military coercion. The *Vermont Gazette* suggested that the army would free the government from popular control: "When the President has got his army well established, will he not be able to rain down stamp acts, salt tax, and any other tax, whether we will or not?"[18]

Finally, Republicans condemned the Alien and Sedition Acts as destructive of civil liberty and an attack on the whole constitutional order. Edward Livingston, a Republican congressman from New York and an early opponent of these measures, denounced the Alien Friends Act as a denial of the basic rights of due process under the Fifth and Sixth amendments. Livingston denied that these rights were restricted to citizens, and predicted that if the act was enforced against aliens, no argument could withstand its application to citizens: "What minute article in these several provisions of the constitution is there, that is not violated by this bill? All the bulwarks which it opposed to encroachments on personal liberty, fall before this engine of oppression."[19]

Republicans perceived the Sedition Act as an even greater threat, an attempt to shield the government from all criticism and to drive a wedge between Republican legislators and their constituents. Republicans argued that the freedom of speech and the liberty of the press were natural rights that had received explicit constitutional protection under the First Amendment. The citizens of Mifflin County, Pennsylvania, declared that the "free communication of thoughts and opinions is one of the most valuable rights of man, and cannot be abridged or restrained without an infraction of the liberties of the people and the law of nature." Republicans insisted that no government, no matter how representative, could invade the people's liberties in such a manner as the Adams administration had. This was the heart of Nestor's argument with John Adams over the meaning of the Revolution, and the citizens of Washington County, Pennsylvania, took it up in their petition against the Alien and Sedition Acts. "It matters but little to us," they declared, "whether our government be nominally democratical, monarchical, or despotic, if the powers of each be the same."[20]

Just as the Federalists searched for hidden Illuminati conclaves, the Republicans searched for the hidden causes of Federalist behavior. For those well versed in the Whig ideology of the Revolutionary period, a pattern of repeated assaults on liberty could have but one cause: conspiracy. As they viewed the Federalist program as a whole, Republicans insisted that it was the product of malicious human design. For example, Republicans in Amelia County, Virginia, and Orange County, New York, denounced the raising of a standing army as "dangerous to the rights and liberties of a free people, and calculated to introduce tyranny and oppression." Other Republicans saw a sinister connection between the standing army and the tax laws. The *Boston Independent Chronicle* called the tax laws "the first fruits of our late military institutions," reminding its readers that "impolitic laws are sometimes enacted that a standing army may be raised to execute them." For many Republicans, the Alien and Sedition Acts were the final pieces in the puzzle. In Orange County, Virginia, Republicans argued that the raising of internal taxes and a standing army under the pretext of danger from abroad was "sufficient to excite a suspicion of covert designs. But . . . attacking the principles of liberty at home has drawn aside the curtain."[21]

Comparing their situation to that faced by Whigs two decades before, Republicans concluded that they faced a Federalist attempt to establish the tyranny of absolute monarchy in America. To the Virginia House of Delegates, the explanation of events was clear: "Let history be consulted; let the man of experience reflect; nay, let the artificers of monarchy be asked, what further materials they can need, for building up their favorite system."[22] Though no less threatening, this Republican vision of a hidden conspiracy differed from the Federalist version in a number of notable respects. Republicans may have suspected some British involvement in Federalist monarchical ambitions, but the conspiracy they detected was largely if not exclusively domestic in scope. Furthermore, they suggested that any conspiracy was the product of the natural tendency of governments to become corrupt. The Federalist obsession with the infiltration of diabolically evil aliens was wholly absent in Republican discourse. Republican fears also lacked the explicit appeals to race and warnings of genocidal violence that characterized Federalist invocations of Haiti and slave rebellion.

Though Republicans of all stripes adhered to the Whig diagnosis of the political ills facing the nation in 1798 and 1799, they found themselves divided when searching for an appropriate cure. In the resolutions of dozens of public meetings and in newspapers across the nation, Republicans proposed solutions that fell along a spectrum of opinion concerning the legitimacy of resistance. Moderates within the party insisted that the legitimate redress of grievances must come through "Constitutional measures." Moderates defined constitutional opposition as encompassing petitioning and the use of the ballot to remove the authors of offending legislation. They insisted that the people must obey the laws until Congress repealed them. The *Newark Sentinel of Freedom* thus urged its readers to "pursue the constitutional mode of protesting . . . which is by convening together in township or county meetings, as convenience may dictate, and there request of your public agents, by way of remonstrance, to repeal the Alien and Sedition Laws." In a similar vein, Republican editor Thomas Cooper wrote of his hope that Federalist measures "will be steadily opposed, but opposed in the only justifiable way of opposition under a free government, by discussion in the first instance, and a change of persons by constitutional election if no other method will succeed."[23]

Moderate Republicans also warned against physical resistance. A Virginia Republican warned a colleague in Kentucky to "prevent the rash and inconsiderate part of your citizens from committing any outrages which may afford the government a pretext for punishing you."[24] Even when the petitioning campaign against the Alien and Sedition Acts failed to secure repeal, moderates refused to contemplate stronger measures. The citizens of Albemarle County, Virginia, suggested that prompt attention to their grievances would be a test of their faith in government and hoped that the repeal of the Alien and Sedition Acts would "yield grounds for the belief that the right of the people to remonstrate is not illusory." Yet when rumors began to circulate that Congress would reject repeal in March 1799, moderates neither voiced outrage nor proposed alternative measures.[25]

More radical elements within the Democratic-Republican Party were unwilling to abide by the judgments of a Congress and a judiciary dominated by Federalists. They argued that the threat to liberty represented by the Alien and Sedition Acts required active resistance. Radicals based their opposition on the premise, articulated within Whig thought, that any act that violated the Constitution was void. This idea of nullity was widely accepted: Alexander Hamilton had asserted in *Federalist No. 78* that "no legislative act . . . contrary to the Constitution, can be valid." But Hamilton went on to articulate a doctrine of judicial nullification in which the nullity of an act was a quality separate from the act itself, attached thereto by authoritative judicial pronouncement. Federalists and many moderate Republicans believed that nullity stemmed only from this sort of authoritative pronouncement.[26]

Radical Republicans understood nullity differently. They argued that the nullity of a law flowed from the law's substantive unconstitutionality, and thus nullity was an intrinsic quality of any unconstitutional law. Republicans in Essex County, Virginia, articulated this doctrine in 1798: "when laws are made contrary, both to the spirit and letter of the constitution, your memorialists are of the opinion, that such laws encroach upon the sovereignty of the people, and are in their nature void." This vision carried radical implications when linked to a second tenet of radical Republican faith: the belief that the people had the capacity to judge the constitutionality of laws for themselves. The *Albany Register* expressed this belief when it denounced the doctrine "that a decision as to the constitutionality of all legislative acts, lies solely with the judiciary department; it is removing the cornerstone on which our federal compact rests; it is taking from the people the ultimate sovereignty." Republicans in Richmond, Virginia agreed, denying that "the legislature is to be the judge, when the constitution is infringed. The *people* are the dread tribunal."[27]

The combination of these two strands of Republican ideology led to a logical conclusion: that the people, embodied in public meetings at the local level, had the right to nullify laws by recognizing their unconstitutionality, publicly declaring their nullity, and withholding their obedience. The citizens of Orange County, New York, acted on this right in the fall of 1798 by publishing a series of resolutions declaring that laws abridging the freedom of speaking and publishing were "unconstitutional and not obligatory." New York congressman Edward Livingston agreed, and went so far as to call for open resistance. In his speech to Congress on the Alien Friends Bill, Livingston delivered one of the earliest pronouncements of the doctrine of popular nullification. "Whenever our laws manifestly infringe the constitution under which they were made," he declared, "the people ought not to hesitate which they should obey: if we exceed our powers we become tyrants, and our acts have no effect." He warned his colleagues that the states and the people would resist the Alien and Sedition Acts: "If we are ready to violate the constitution we have sworn to defend—will the people submit to our unauthorized acts? Will the states sanction our usurped powers? Sir, they ought not to submit. They would deserve the chains which these measures are for them if they did not resist."[28]

Radical Republicans responded to Livingston's speech by calling public meetings across Kentucky, Virginia, and the Middle Atlantic states. At these meetings Republicans gathered and publicly pronounced the nullity of the Alien and Sedition Acts.[29] Some Republicans followed Livingston's lead and openly called for resistance. At a dinner for Con-

gressman John Clopton of Virginia, Republicans from the counties surrounding Richmond listened to an address that concluded that "acts that
violate our chartered rights have no binding force, and are not entitled to
the respect or obedience of the people."[30] Republicans in the neighboring county of Powhatten asserted an equally radical understanding of
popular sovereignty. Where the majesty of the people is abused by
"tyranny or usurpation," they declared,

> It is the right of the people (and what is their duty) to resume the delegated
> power, to call their trustees to an account, to resist the usurpation, extirpate
> the tyranny, to restore their sullied majesty, and prostituted authority, to
> suspend, alter, or abrogate those laws, to punish their unfaithful and corrupt
> servants. Nor is it the duty only of the united body, but every member of it,
> ought, according to his respective rank, power, and weight in the commu-
> nity, to concur in advancing and supporting those glorious designs.[31]

Other public statements that recognized the nullity of the Alien and
Sedition Acts stopped short of an overt call for resistance. For example,
the resolutions of a meeting in Fayette County were typical of the sentiments of radical Republicans in Kentucky:

> Resolved, that the privilege of speaking and publishing our sentiments on
> public questions, is inestimable; that it is unequivocally acknowledged and
> secured to us by the constitution of this state, as well as that of the United
> States; that all laws made to impair or destroy it are void; and that we will as-
> sert and exercise our just right to this privilege, in opposition to any law
> which has been, or may be passed, to deprive us of it.[32]

This statement avoided the mention of any specific law. Nevertheless, the
Republicans of Fayette County knew that a public declaration that they
would speak and publish their sentiments notwithstanding "any law that
has been, or may be passed" might be itself illegal under the Sedition Act.
Their public resolution to this effect was in itself a popular nullification
of the Sedition Act, an act of overt defiance designed to render the law
unenforceable.[33]

None of these public statements advocated the immediate recourse to armed organization that the Suffolk Resolves had recommended in 1774. Radical Republicans in Virginia and Kentucky placed great emphasis on petitioning their legislatures in an effort to secure the repeal of the Alien and Sedition Acts. Their resolutions made it clear, however, that petitioning was only the first resort, and several asserted the right of revolution in the last eventuality if their petitions went unheard. The citizens of Essex County, Virginia, for example, declared that "every expedient ought to be adopted before a recourse is had to revolutionary principles." The citizens of Bourbon County, Kentucky, offered a similar warning, declaring that "we are yet disposed to pursue constitutional means to effect a change of measures and a redress of grievances, and we deplore heaven that we may not be forced to reiterate our appeal by any other means."[34]

Ultimately, radical Republicans did not seek to overturn the established order or to dissolve the Constitution. They hoped that popular nullification would serve as a middle ground between obedience and revolution, a hope expressed in the assurances of the citizens of Bourbon County: "We disavow any intention to oppose the Constitutional laws of our country—that we will, and every good citizen ought, to render and assist to enforce a prompt obedience to all such laws."[35]

As they sought to check the exercise of unconstitutional power by the Federalist administration, Republicans turned to the institutions and rituals that had supported resistance to Great Britain in 1774. Though the Constitution gave the federal government the authority to call out the militia to "execute the laws of the union, suppress insurrections, and repel invasions," Republicans ascribed a fourth purpose to the militia: to defend liberty against domestic tyranny. The officers of the Philadelphia brigade of the Pennsylvania militia illustrated this belief when they offered the following toast: "the militia of the United States—May they ever be ready to resist tyranny either foreign or domestic."[36]

Republicans around the country looked to the militia to serve as the bulwark of resistance to the Alien and Sedition Acts. Militiamen in Amelia County, Virginia, declared that they would not lend any assistance in enforcing the acts, while a militia regiment in Madison County, Kentucky, resolved that "the Alien and Sedition Bills are infringements of the Constitution and of natural rights, and that we cannot approve or submit to them."[37] Republicans in Fayette and Bourbon counties urged the citizens, embodied in the militia, to prepare to take the defense of liberty into their own hands, resolving that "a well organized militia are the proper, and the only safe defenders of our country; that for that purpose the general and state governments ought to provide them with arms and ammunition; that as they have neglected to do this, every freeman ought to consider it his duty to provide both for himself."[38]

Just as honor was central to the masculine identity of Federalists in 1798, Republicans celebrated the masculine quality of "firmness" that would animate the defense of liberty. The officers of the Philadelphia brigade of the Pennsylvania militia, for example, toasted "The people— may they have the discernment to know their rights and the firmness to maintain them." The militia of Morris County, New Jersey, celebrated the same spirit when assuring President Adams that no one would muster against an invasion with more "firmness and alacrity" than they would. They then warned Adams that they "would as soon crush a domestic tyrant, or any man who would propose a hereditary President, as we would repel the French or any other foreign foe."[39]

In contrast to the aggressiveness of the Federalist culture of honor, Republicans argued that firmness required an unyielding, but defensive stance. For example, the militia of Morris County declared themselves ready to fight "when war is really necessary, and purely defensive, and the good of the community at large and the security of the common people are the only objects."[40] For Republicans, the aggressiveness of the black cockade fever raised serious doubts about the manhood of the young men involved. The New York Journal ridiculed the heroism and "love of order" of the young Federalists who raided Mendham, New Jersey, and cut down the liberty pole, noting that they had terrorized the women and children of the community while the men were busy in the fields. Republicans also described the young Federalists who joined the standing army in glaringly feminine terms. A correspondent to the Aurora attributed to these young men a fondness for "pageantry, a love to rule and hatred to be ruled, indolence and effeminacy."[41] The Republican discourse of manly firmness thus offered a gendered critique of Federalist celebrations of honor.

Throughout the summer and fall of 1798, at public meetings, militia musters, Independence Day celebrations, and liberty pole raisings, Republicans combined political messages, masculine performance, and gunfire. For example, July Fourth celebrants at Newburgh, New York, commemorated the heroism of those who took up arms against tyranny in the Revolution, and resolved that they would "reason with calmness, fight with courage, and bring down tyrants." This celebration culminated in a volley of musket fire. Republicans across the Middle Atlantic states also raised liberty poles as a token of defiance. In Slaughterdam, New Jersey, in March 1799, local Republicans raised one such pole with a flag inscribed, "We will defend our rights." To clarify the point and further demonstrate their resolve, they fired off a volley.[42]

In 1798, these local rituals combining words, masculine performance by the militia, and gunfire were captured in print descriptions of the festivities and injected into the national public sphere. The resulting political message carried more than a hint of the potential for political violence. For example, when the citizens of Orange, New Jersey, celebrated Independence Day in 1798, they toasted "the citizens of the United States—may their active spirit and undiminished zeal in support of the constitution, be proof against all attacks of foreign invaders and domestic usurpers." They punctuated this toast with a volley of musketry.[43] Everyone in Orange and everyone who read the published account of the celebration understood that this volley was aimed as squarely at John Adams as at any foreign nation.

In the summer and fall of 1798, the potential for popular resistance to the Federalist war program was widely discussed, and demonstrated, within the public sphere. In the context of this debate over the legitimacy of resistance, the Virginia and Kentucky Resolutions of 1798 represented a mix of radical and moderate ideas. The discussion of nullification in Madison's original draft of the Virginia Resolutions was quite veiled. Madison simply asserted that the states, as parties to the constitutional compact, had "the right, and are in duty bound, to interpose for arresting the progress of the evil, and for maintaining within their respective limits, the authorities, rights, and liberties appertaining to them." The resolutions were silent about what form that interposition might take, a silence that allowed Madison to argue two years later in the *Report of 1800* that the resolutions had never contemplated any remedy beyond petitioning for repeal.[44]

Jefferson's draft of the Kentucky Resolutions, on the other hand, explicitly articulated a doctrine of state nullification:

> In cases of an abuse of the delegated powers the members of the general government being chosen by the people, a change by the people would be the constitutional remedy; but where powers are assumed which have not been delegated, a nullification of the act is the rightful remedy: that every state has a natural right, in cases not within the compact . . . to nullify of their own authority all assumptions of power by others within their limits.[45]

Even this passage clearly described nullity as stemming from the authoritative act of a state government. It was thus closer to the moderate theory of judicial nullification than it was to the more radical doctrine of nullity. Nevertheless, Jefferson's draft included radical language as well. Jefferson's declaration that the Alien and Sedition Acts were "altogether void and of no force" evoked the definition of nullity as a quality inherent in the acts' unconstitutionality.[46]

John Breckinridge, who introduced the Kentucky Resolutions in the state legislature, tried to moderate Jefferson's original draft. Breckinridge dropped Jefferson's call for other states to declare they would not permit the exercise of unconstitutional laws within their borders. He substituted a more moderate call for congressional repeal in its place. He also deleted the passage previously quoted describing nullification as a legitimate exercise of state authority.[47] Ironically, in the context of the overall debate of 1798, that last deletion rendered the resolutions, as passed by the Kentucky legislature, more radical, rather than less. Without the language describing nullity as the product of an authoritative institutional procedure, what was left was the assertion that the Alien and Sedition Acts were substantively "void and of no force." This assertion evoked the language of popular nullification in a manner that, perhaps inadvertently, vindicated the stance of the most radical expressions of Republican opposition.

"We Will Have Liberty": Fries' Rebellion as the Culmination of Radical Republican Opposition

The outbreak of armed resistance to the Federalist program of 1798 did not come in either Virginia or Kentucky. It came in Northampton County, Pennsylvania, and in several adjoining townships in Berks, Bucks, and Montgomery counties. Resistance to the direct tax began building in these townships in October 1798 during the federal election campaign. When tax assessors held meetings in late November to explain the law and present their commissions to the local populace, they found their neighbors aroused against the law. Those assessors appointed to assess their own communities came under heavy pressure from neighbors to resign their commissions. At least six did so. Those who persisted began executing the law in early December, visiting every local homestead to measure houses for the purposes of assessment. Within days, their neighbors confronted them with threats of violence sufficiently credible that most of the assessors desisted from further attempts to execute the law. In several townships, women doused the assessors who approached their homes with hot water and the contents of chamber pots. In a dozen townships, male residents joined voluntary associations and committed themselves to resist the law and defend against any attempt to arrest those organizing the resistance.[48]

The emergence of the resistance movement in Northampton County was caused by a potent combination of ideology, political culture, and ethno-political conflict. Insurgent ideology contained many of the central elements of radical Republican criticism of the war program of 1798, including a distrust of internal taxation, a suspicion of a malicious conspiracy within the Federalist Party, and a commitment to the right of popular nullification. The movement was also influenced by the particular currents of ethnic politics in southeast Pennsylvania.

The region most affected by the house tax resistance was largely populated by Germans of the Reformed and Lutheran churches. These

"Kirchenlute," or church people, as opposed to German pacifist sects such as the Moravians and Mennonites, allied themselves increasingly with the Republican Party in the late 1790s. Federalists, on the other hand, drew the bulk of their support from local Quakers and Moravians. During the War of Independence, many of the Kirchenlute had served in the Continental Army and in the militia. The bulk of Pensylvania's pacifist community, however, refused to contribute to the struggle for independence or even to swear allegiance to the commonwealth, thus contributing to lasting tension between these communities.[49] In the 1790s Pennsylvania Republicans skillfully played on ethnic tensions and made very public efforts to help Kirchenlute candidates obtain their proper share of local offices. Consequently, Montgomery, Berks, and Northampton counties produced Republican majorities for the first time in the elections of 1798.[50]

When the Federalist administration appointed commissioners to carry out the house tax assessment, these appointments fell almost exclusively on the local Quakers and pacifists.[51] The notion that Quakers and pacifists who had refused service in the war should collect the house and stamp taxes struck the Kirchenlute as a repudiation of everything for which they had fought. Insurgents began to refer to local Federalists, Quakers, and other pacifists as "Tories" and "stamplers." John Fries complained, "All these people who were tories in the last war mean to be leaders—they mean to get us quite under—they mean to make us slaves." Insurgents in Macungie Township resolved that the assessment "should not be made by any man who had not done duty in the last war, or by any tory."[52] The insurgents also had doubts about how honestly their political opponents would administer the direct tax. There were widespread complaints in post-Revolutionary Pennsylvania that local tax officials were either collecting more tax than was owed and embezzling the balance or withholding the sums unaccounted for by the Treasury and using the money for speculative purposes.[53]

The resistance to the house tax, however, was about more than just ethnic competition and frustration over corrupt tax gathering. The broad outlines of Republican opposition thought are clearly present in the statements of the insurgents of Northampton and Bucks counties.

Insurgents echoed the Whig hostility to internal taxes by distinguishing between the federal direct tax and normal county property taxes. When John Butz, tax assessor for Macungie, came to take the county rates for insurgents Daniel Haverly and Adam Stephan, both made it clear that he was welcome to do so, but that they would not permit him to assess their property under the house tax. John Fogel Jr. noted that most people in that neighborhood had no objection to paying a tax if it were "laid as they were used to," *i.e.*, by the state government to pay for local services.[54] Insurgents also expressed their objections to internal taxation by describing the house tax and the stamp tax of 1797 as a repetition of the measures against which the Revolution had been fought. John Fries, a Revolutionary War veteran, declared "that he had fought for liberty before, and now the government was introducing again the same laws he had fought against, and he would not submit to them." Insurgents in Plainfield, Williams, Macungie, and Weissenberg townships in Northampton County used almost identical language to connect the house tax with their memory of the internal taxes of the Revolutionary period.[55]

During the election campaign of 1798, local Republican politicians suggested that a hidden, malicious design lay behind the house tax. In Heidelberg Township, Blair McClenachen, a Philadelphia congressman, warned that new internal taxes on milling grain and killing livestock were on the way, and that "if things were to go on the way they had begun, we should have a number of great lords and the people would be slaves, and also that the President would make himself to be a king of the country." In Plainfield, Abraham Horn, another state legislator, warned that "the President has sold the states and that the people should oppose the laws."[56] These warnings of a conspiracy to enslave the people clearly had an impact on the insurgents, though the ethnic tensions in the region contributed a particular gloss to insurgent fears of conspiracy. In several townships, insurgents expressed the desire to wait until other counties, such as the Quaker-dominated counties nearer Philadelphia, had paid the tax, just to be certain they were not being duped.[57]

The insurgents also accepted the Republican argument, reprinted in the columns of the *Aurora* and the *Readinger Adler*, that the war program of 1798 represented a conscious attempt to deprive them of liberty. James

Williamson, the assessor for Plainfield township, reported that the insurgents connected the house tax "with the stamp tax and the Alien and Sedition Acts, and said that they had fought against such laws once already, and were ready to do it again." Cephas Childs, the assessor for Lower Milford Township, reported that John Fries and his neighbors "damned the house tax and the Stamp Act, and called me a stampler repeatedly. They damned the alien law and sedition law, and finally . . . the government and all the laws the present Congress had made." When Childs asked them why they were determined to resist, they replied, "We are determined to oppose the laws, and we have met to do it; the government is laying one thing after another, and if we do not oppose it, they will bring us into bondage and slavery, or make slaves of us. We will have liberty."[58]

The insurgents were aware of radical Republican calls for popular nullification resonating in other parts of the nation. According to local Federalists, the *Aurora*, which reprinted almost all of the most radical Republican petitions and resolutions of 1798 and early 1799, circulated widely in the area. In addition the local German paper, the *Readinger Adler*, translated Edward Livingston's speech on the Alien Friends Act and the declaration of the militia of Morris County, New Jersey, into German.[59]

Furthermore, according to several insurgents, Republican officeholders in Pennsylvania had also explicitly advocated armed resistance. John Fogel Jr. claimed to have consulted with General Robert Brown, newly elected to Congress from the district, in February 1799. According to Fogel, Brown advised him of the petition campaign against the Alien and Sedition Acts, and told him that the Federalist program of 1798, including the house tax, would almost certainly be repealed by the new Congress meeting in March. Fogel told his neighbors that Brown advised them "to keep the assessors back so that the rates should not be taken before the new Congress met." Insurgent leader Henry Ohl also claimed that Philadelphia congressman Blair McClenachen had urged the residents of Heidelberg "that if the laws were put in force, the people should meet and arm themselves and make way with government officers."[60]

On the basis of these influences, the insurgents committed themselves to render the house tax void and of no force. In Chestnut Hill

Township, Reverend Jacob Eyerman declared that "Congress . . . had no right to make those laws, and that the people were under no obligation to obey the laws of Congress." Assessor Jacob Oswald reported that the people of Lynn Township "thought congress had no right to tax them." When he tried to explain to the insurgents that Congress did indeed have that power, they still insisted that he should stop assessing houses. Attempts to explain the law failed to persuade the insurgents of other towns as well. In Plainfield Township Valentine Metz expressed his neighbors' decision that "the law was too bad for many people to put up with." When tax commissioner Jacob Eyerly attempted to persuade the insurgents of Upper Milford to submit, the following exchange ensued:

> George Shaeffer jumped up before me, and said, "Mr. Eyerly, it is no law." I told them that if they did not believe me, they might enquire of squire Schymer whether it was or not. Mr. Schymer then told them it was a law; upon which Shaeffer replied, "admitting it is a law, we will not obey it."

When Eyerly offered to let the insurgents of Upper Milford and Hamilton townships choose their own assessors, they refused, saying, "if we do this, we at once acknowledge that we will submit to the laws, and that is what we won't do."[61]

The insurgents deviated from the national conversation about resistance only in two respects. Though most Republicans had made the Alien and Sedition Acts the target of their campaign of popular nullification, Fries and his neighbors took up arms to resist the execution of the house tax. The commissioners responsible for measuring houses under the direct tax law were charged with the task of visiting every homestead and business in the nation. By contrast, only six individuals were prosecuted under the Sedition Act prior to Fries' Rebellion, and all but one of these prosecutions took place in Federalist New England.[62] Given Republican arguments that the tax laws, the standing army, and the Alien and Sedition Acts were all part of a concerted program to deprive the people of liberty, it is not surprising that Fries and his neighbors chose to resist the part of this program that brought Federalist tax assessors to their doorsteps.[63]

The insurgents also stood out in the national debate for the grounds on which they nullified the house tax. The radical Republicans of 1798 were careful to couple declarations of the nullity of the Alien and Sedition Acts with a clear constitutional analysis. The house tax, however, clearly lay within the power of direct taxation granted to the federal government under the Constitution. John Fries did make a constitutional objection to the progressivity of the tax, arguing that this violated constitutional provisions for the equal apportionment of taxes. Jacob Eyerman also claimed the tax was unconstitutional, but his argument on this point consisted of waving a book that he claimed was the Constitution. Most insurgents, however, articulated a "higher constitutionalist" argument, avoiding discussions of the text of the Constitution and simply declaring that the house tax was a bad and substantively oppressive law that infringed their liberty. They traced the nullity of the house tax to its oppressiveness, rather than to its lack of conformity with the text of the Constitution. George Seider and Henry Jarrett, leaders of the insurgents in Upper Milford and Macungie townships, both argued that the house tax was a "bad law" that should not be executed. Reverend Eyerman, when not waving his constitution, told his neighbors that "they ought not to suffer the Direct Tax law to be put in execution, that it was too hard and if the people did suffer it to be done they would be as bad off as they were in Europe." Insurgents in Lower Milford Township described the tax somewhat generically as a threat to liberty and declared that therefore their resistance was legitimate.[64] Though one might hear in this higher constitutionalism a distant echo of Jonathan Mayhew's distinction between good law and oppression, it departed from most Republican constitutionalism in 1798.

The insurgent movement incorporated the style and rituals of Democratic-Republican political culture, but in a particularly radical and populist form. Some moderate party leaders in Northampton County attempted to calm the aroused populace and channel dissent into constitutional forms of protest by circulating a petition denouncing the Alien and Sedition Acts. Because the petition made no mention of the house tax, and thus ignored popular grievances, the effort failed.[65] For the most part, the movement was organized at raucous public meetings held in taverns and attended by all the male citizens of the neighborhood or township. When tax commissioners attended these meetings to explain the law, they often found that their legal expertise was dismissed by the assembled populace. James Chapman attempted to explain the law at a meeting in Lower Milford, but "the people would pay no attention to them, and huzzaed and shouted for liberty. . . . Conrad Marks said he knew the law as well as they did." Some of the insurgents had brought muskets to the meeting, and one told Chapman that "they had made a law of their own, that this [brandishing his gun] was their law."[66]

Like Democratic-Republicans across the country, the insurgents took great pains to demonstrate that the authority to resist the house tax flowed from the consensus of the people, expressed in meetings of the local community. The insurgents performed that consensus ritually. At an early meeting in Upper Milford, John Shimer called upon those who would stand against the house tax to follow him outside. When all but a few of the sixty or so townspeople present did so, he asked that "all those that are for liberty shall waive their hats and huzza for liberty, upon which they huzzaed." Shimer then led the party back inside and informed the local assessor that "the township are all agreed." The crowd at a town meeting in Plainfield told James Williamson to stop taking assessments. He later reported that "the whole body seemed to rise and give their assent to this." He interpreted this gesture as "declaring the sense of the township that I should not make the assessment."[67]

Once the insurgents established the "sense of the town," they expected all members of the community to abide by it. The insurgents did not hesitate to coerce individual dissenters, even their social betters. In the communities that resolved upon resistance, the insurgents met dissent with threats of violence credible enough to make many local Federalists and quite a few tax assessors fear for their lives. Penn Township assessor Peter Zeiner resigned after being threatened by a party of fifteen to twenty men. He declared that he could not proceed "for fear of injury to his person or property." In Upper Milford, assessor Christian Heckwelder's guide abandoned him, saying that he dared not accompany Heckwelder any further, "that his neighbors would not permit it, and that he would be a dead man if he did it."[68]

The insurgents also promised to support those willing to observe the community decision. Resurrecting the institutions of 1774, the insurgents of several townships bound themselves into associations for mutual support and coordination. Six hundred men from Williams, Lower Saucon, Upper Saucon, and Upper Milford townships signed an association binding themselves to resist the tax. Other associations formed in Weissenberg, Heidelberg, Albany, Lehigh, Macungie, and Lower Milford townships. Militia companies in Lower Milford, Upper Milford, Macungie, and Lower Saucon supported the resistance, and the insurgents attempted to enlist the commanders of several other companies in the area.[69] The offer of mutual support also extended to those of their neighbors who had taken commissions as tax assessors. Insurgents in Plainfield Township, Northampton County, and Albany Township, Berks County, promised local tax assessors that they would be "indemnified of all costs and fines" if they would cooperate by ceasing to take rates.[70]

This support included the promise to interfere with the arrest of any of their neighbors. The associators of Williams, Upper and Lower Saucon, and Upper Milford townships committed themselves to resist the law and to "break the gaol" if any of their number were arrested. At one meeting, George Shaeffer taunted Jacob Eyerly publicly, promising that if he was arrested, "you shall see how far you will bring me." Insurgents insisted that if any of their number were to be tried for acts of resistance, they should be tried "in their own courts, and by their own people."[71]

Organized in a masculine sphere of public meetings, associations, and militia musters, the resistance was animated by the same spirit of manly firmness that Republican leaders had been lauding all summer and fall. By forcing the tax assessors to cease measuring houses, the insurgents effectively nullified the house tax in Northampton County. When the Federalist authorities took a series of steps to enforce the law, the insurgents met each with the same stance of unyielding defiance. At every step in the escalating conflict, the insurgents calculated the minimum force necessary to prevent the execution of the law.

In January 1799, Jacob Eyerly attempted to convince the people of Upper Milford Township to appoint their own assessor. The residents physically abused him for his troubles. He then persuaded Northampton County justice William Henry to begin taking evidence against the insurgents. In response, militia captain Henry Jarrett mustered his company outside the tavern where Henry was sitting court. The presence of the company reminded potential witnesses that they would have to deal with their neighbors long after Henry left. Two of the militiamen, George Shaeffer and Henry Shankwyler, invited one of the witnesses whom they had threatened to relay their threats to Henry, and to tell him that the threats now extended to the judge himself.[72]

When federal marshal William Nichols arrived six weeks later to arrest Shaeffer and Shankwyler, a crowd gathered to prevent their arrest, and the two insurgents refused to submit. Shankwyler, along with many other young members of the crowd, invoked the memory of the valor that their fathers had demonstrated in the Revolution. Shankwyler told Marshal Nichols that he had fought against the stamp tax and would not submit to it now. When Nichols observed that Shankwyler appeared too young to have fought during the war, Shankwyler refused to back down. His father had fought against the British, he insisted, and he refused to surrender to the law.[73]

That night, word spread that those whom Nichols had managed to arrest would be transported from the Sun Tavern in Bethlehem to Philadelphia for trial. The insurgents controlling the standing militia companies of three nearby townships marched into Bethlehem on the morning of March 7 and paraded under arms in front of the tavern. John Fries, the leader of a company from Bucks County, forced Marshal Nichols to set the prisoners free.

During this confrontation, Fries used the minimum necessary force to achieve his purpose. When Fries demanded the release of the prisoners, Nichols insisted that he could not simply yield. "I cannot give them up willingly," Nichols told Fries, "but if you take them by force, I cannot help it." Fries, correctly thinking he heard a deal offered, collected his men. He told them they must force their way up the stairs of the tavern to the room where the prisoners were being held. He warned that they must not hurt anyone unless the marshal's men fired upon them. If the Federalists should fire, Fries told his men, they should shoot back until the smoke blinded them. As they forced their way upstairs, Fries told the marshal that he could not guarantee the safety of tax commissioners Stephen Balliett and Jacob Eyerly, and Judge William Henry, who were also at the tavern. The militia companies outside the tavern had pointed their guns every time these men appeared at the windows. This last threat gave the marshal a legitimate reason to let the prisoners go without the appearance of dishonorable capitulation.[74]

Resistance to the tax collapsed within weeks of the rescue of the prisoners. At a March 18 meeting, a committee of the inhabitants of the affected area advised the people to submit to the tax. The quick collapse of resistance allowed Republicans to claim later that the insurgents had never intended to rise in arms against their government. Their decision to submit, however, was based not on a surrender of principle, but on another calculation. For months prior, the insurgents had been contemplating the possibility that they would have to take up arms against a military force sent to enforce the house tax. They knew that they could not hold out against such a force for long, but they believed that they were part of a larger resistance movement, one that included the radical Republicans of Virginia and Kentucky. Insurgents from Upper Milford and Macungie discussed rumors that an army "would come from the backcountry to support them." In Lower Milford, a mysterious letter had encouraged the insurgents by informing them that George Washington would march to their aid with an army of ten thousand Virginians.[75]

After the rescue, Henry Jarrett and other leaders continued to urge resistance. In the week after the rescue, however, rumors of assistance evaporated and word arrived that President Adams had issued a proclamation that declared their communities in a state of insurrection and branded them as traitors. Faced with a choice between permitting the assessment and facing a national army on their own, the insurgents agreed to submit to the tax. Manly firmness was one thing. Collective martyrdom on the scaffold was another matter.[76]

The Preservation of Order and Tranquility:
The Suppression of Fries' Rebellion

When word of the rescue in Bethlehem reached Philadelphia, the *Gazette of the United States* immediately declared that the insurrection was connected with the French threat.[77] Federalists worked themselves into a renewed countersubversive fever, declaring that the French plot about which they had been warning for a year was coming to a head. Within weeks, the *Gazette* was pushing the argument to the hilt:

> We are driven from outrage to outrage, from insurrection to insurrection. . . . It is effecting but a partial purpose to put down the insurrection of a few counties, whilst a band of French mercenaries dispersed over the commonwealth are preparing an insurrection of the whole state, under the auspices of a thorough going French Revolution, who would soon league poor Pennsylvania with the land of slaves in her holy work of dismembering the union, and soon deliver us, bound hand and foot, to the dominion of the Directory.[78]

In New England, Jedediah Morse renewed his warnings that the Illuminati were spreading their influence throughout the nation. William Cobbett agreed that the unrest in Northampton was part of a larger scheme, and warned darkly that the entire spirit of opposition confronting the Federalists must cease: "Merely to quell such an insurrection as this will answer but little purpose. It is a weed that has poisoned the soil; to crop off the stalk will only enable it to spring up again and send out a hundred shoots instead of one. It must be torn up by the root; the *principles of insurrection must be eradicated,* or anarchy must ensue."[79]

On April 4, over two weeks after the insurgents had agreed to submit to the tax, an army of two thousand men began its ponderous march through Bucks, Northampton, and Berks counties. Many of the insurgents had already surrendered themselves and posted bail for their appearance in the U.S. district court in Philadelphia. Nevertheless, over the course of two and a half weeks, the troops succeeded in capturing John Fries and dozens of other insurgents. The Federalists, however, intended to use the army to restore the honor of the government, as well as its authority. That second purpose lent an aggressiveness to the army's behavior. Detachments of soldiers searching for fugitives turned the countryside upside-down and searched dozens of homes in the middle of the night. Furthermore, the soldiers took it upon themselves to find and destroy every liberty pole in the affected area. When Jacob Schneider, printer of the Republican *Readinger Adler,* published a satire on the "Herculean adventures" of the Lancaster County troop of light horse, who had cut down several liberty poles, members of the troop abducted him from his printing office. On orders of their captain, soldiers whipped Schneider in the market square of Reading. William Duane published an account of this assault in the *Aurora* on May 13. Two days later, he too received a public beating from members of several troops of the light horse that had taken part in the march.[80]

The trials of the insurgents in April and May also provided the Federalists with an opportunity to elaborate on the connection between Fries and a broader conspiracy. John Fries was indicted for treason, and Federalist prosecutors Samuel Sitgreaves (a recently defeated Federalist congressman from Northampton County) and William Rawle played up spurious evidence of a French connection. Depositions taken immediately after the release of the prisoners in Bethlehem describe three or four different bands of insurgents arriving in Bethlehem at different times. According to early testimony, some of the younger members of one of these companies were in the habit of wearing red, white, and blue cockades in their hats as a symbol of opposition to the Federalist Party (whose adherents wore black cockades). When the same witnesses testified six weeks later, their testimony was sufficiently altered that William Rawle was able to describe a parade into Bethlehem by a unified military force, adorned with "French" tricolor cockades and under the unified command of John Fries. Fries did indeed play a central role in Lower Milford Township and in the release of the prisoners at Bethlehem. However, this may have had less to do with his selection by the authorities as the leader of the insurrection than a passing comment he had made to one of the assessors. Fries often warned of the threat of the house tax in the following terms: "If we let them go on, things would be as in France—we would be as poor as snakes." At the trial this expression was twisted into the declaration, "It shall be as it is in France!" Federalists began referring to the insurrection in Northampton and Bucks counties as Fries' Rebellion because Fries could be most easily portrayed as the pro-French subversive so central in the Federalist imagination.[81]

The trial also served as a forum in which another aspect of the Federalist ideology could play before a national audience. For a year Federalists had complained that the campaign of public opposition and criticism launched by Republicans in 1798 was an illegitimate usage of political speech. They argued that the only proper activity of the people between elections was quiet obedience to the laws. At Fries's trial, Federalist justice James Iredell attempted to write these tenets of Federalist political culture into law by arguing that treason began with public criticism. Treason in a republic, he argued, would never involve a direct assault on the Constitution. Rather, those bent on treason

> go about their design by more insidious means; art will be used, and pains taken to promote a dislike to a certain law, this evil prejudice is encouraged until it becomes general among the people, and they become ripe for insurrection as in the present case. Nor would the evil cease with the destruction of one law: they may declare they mean to stop at one act, but having destroyed it, and finding their power above that of the government, is it not to be apprehended that they would destroy another, and another, and so on to any number they disapprove of.[82]

Iredell used this domino theory of opposition to argue that opposition to a single law, the house tax, was treason even in the absence of any intent to overthrow the federal government. Yet his charge described a slippery slope beginning with criticism and implied that even the constitutional opposition of Republican moderates was a species of treason.

Juries convicted John Fries and two others of treason, and Federalist judges sentenced them to hang. Dozens of other insurgents were convicted of sedition. In a display of the magnanimity of the federal government, President Adams granted full pardons to Fries and the others in May 1800.

The ease with which Federalists portrayed John Fries as a pro-French subversive allied with the Republican Party proved embarrassing for Republicans in Pennsylvania and the nation. Federalists had accused the Democratic Republican Societies of 1794 of inciting the Whiskey Rebellion, simply on the basis of their criticism of the Whiskey excise. The societies had collapsed in the subsequent backlash. In 1798, Republicans had gone much farther in invoking the memory of the Revolution and calling for popular nullification. Recognizing John Fries as the unanticipated product of this campaign, they made a strategic decision to back away from the radicalism of 1798. Thomas Jefferson was one of the first Republicans to advise a retreat. In a letter to Edmund Pendleton in mid-February, Jefferson took note of the trouble brewing in Northampton County:

> In this state we fear the ill-designing may produce insurrection. Nothing could be so fatal. Anything like force would check the progress of public opinion and rally them around the government. This is not the kind of opposition the American people will permit. But keep away from all show of force, and they will bear down the evil propensities of the government, by the constitutional means of election and petition.[83]

In calling for moderate, "constitutional" opposition, Jefferson stepped back from his assertion the previous November that nullification was the "rightful remedy" to the Federalist assault on liberty.

Republicans were also quick to distance themselves from Fries at his trial. Republican attorney Alexander James Dallas volunteered to serve as Fries's defense attorney. But Dallas did not argue for Fries's innocence: he argued that Fries should be prosecuted under the Sedition Act rather than under the law of treason. That Fries should be punished Dallas left no doubt. He described the march on Bethlehem as "a great unjustifiable riot—seditious in its origins, daring in its progress, and iniquitous in its effects." Though this defense was designed to save Fries's life, it flew in the face of earlier Republican protests that the Sedition Act was unconstitutional. Furthermore, Republican attorneys refused to serve as counsel for the vast majority of the insurgents charged under the act, forcing the defendants to throw themselves on the mercy of Federalist judges. When Federalists accelerated prosecutions under the Sedition Act in the spring of 1799, Republicans made no attempt to interfere. Despite the previous autumn's call for nullification and interposition, the Republican authorities of Virginia permitted the prosecution of newspaper editor James Callender under the Sedition Act. [84]

Jefferson's letter and the Republican repudiation of John Fries marked the beginning of a general retreat from the radical Republican discourse of 1798. Republicans sent no further petitions to Congress or to the state legislatures. They raised no more liberty poles. When Congress refused to repeal the Alien and Sedition Acts, Republicans made no formal or coordinated response. While falling silent on the issue of nullification, Republicans clearly repudiated the insurgents of Northampton and Bucks counties, extolling instead the virtues of electoral opposition. William Duane had initially attempted to dismiss the entire episode as nothing more than a "hot water war" waged by the women of Northampton County. Once it became clear that ridicule would not suffice, Duane denounced the insurgents, arguing that "no Republican can justify the conduct of those people who resisted the Marshal. . . . It was highly reprehensible and ought to be punished." The editors of the *Newark Sentinel of Freedom* likewise exhorted their readers "in the name of all that can be estimable to freemen, never to suffer the hideous monster insurrection to rear its baneful head amongst you." The *New York Argus* noted that citizens had the right "not to resist the executive—but to complain, and to use every constitutional measure for redress."[85]

At a more popular level, Republicans continued to celebrate the anniversary of independence by toasting the militia as a bulwark against despotism and the abuses of a standing army, but these toasts sounded a new note. In Philadelphia, members of the city's militia legion drank to their company: "The Militia Legion of Philadelphia, may it be conspicuous for discipline and respect for the laws." The militia of Queen Anne's County, Maryland, drank to "Wholesome, Constitutional Laws, and strict obedience to them." In Newark, Republicans celebrated the disbanding of the standing army in June 1800 by toasting "the Freedom of speech and liberty of the press, devoid of licentiousness."[86]

There were a few lingering traces of radicalism in the Republican discourse of 1799. The *Albany Register* continued in a radical vein through the spring, publishing a Republican "creed" that asserted that a constitution "openly outraged" by the government was "no longer binding" on the people. The *Aurora* printed an "Address to the Germans of Cumberland County" that asserted that "If Congress should pass an unconstitutional law, the people are not bound to attend it at all, for in truth it is no law." Nevertheless, a new moderation is evident in Republican discourse. Republicans replaced denunciations of the Alien and Sedition Acts and other Federalist usurpations with complaints about the disorderliness and abuses committed by the standing army. The *Baltimore American,* the *Richmond Examiner,* the *New London Bee,* the *Kentucky Gazette,* and the *Albany Register* joined Duane's *Aurora* in describing a series of depredations committed by members of the standing army and the naval forces throughout the summer of 1799. A witness describing himself as "A Real Lover of Order" described acts of thuggery committed by crewmen of the naval vessels anchored in New York Harbor. The *Albany Register* complained of the "spirit of despotism" displayed by marine recruits who incited a brawl with the city's cartmen.[87]

Republicans also began to write an alternative narrative of the unrest in Northampton County that described the insurrection as another example of Federalist disorderliness. In the spring of 1799 William Duane of the *Aurora* denied that the unrest had anything to do with nullifying any laws and declared that the insurgents were, in any case, all Federalists. Duane's narrative was reprinted in Republicans papers around the country.[88] In the same vein, the Republican establishment of Pennsylvania opened the 1799 gubernatorial campaign with repeated accusations that Federalist candidate James Ross had helped to foment the Whiskey Rebellion. William Duane printed this accusation in the *Aurora* five times in the final weeks of the campaign. The language employed in this effort was striking for its wholesale adoption of the Federalist countersubversive rhetoric of 1798: "Does any man love *peace?* Let him not vote then for a promoter of bloodshed. Does any man love *good government?* Let him not then vote for a promoter of opposition to the laws." On election day, Duane's summary of the campaign themes extolled McKean as an "Asserter of the Laws" while damning Ross as "A Fomenter of Western Insurrection."[89]

In the summer of 1799, then, Republicans represented themselves as "asserters of the laws" and aspired to the mantle of the "Friends of Order" hitherto worn by their Federalist opponents. A second set of Kentucky Resolutions in 1799 and Madison's *Report of 1800* were part of this overall trend toward moderation. The *Report of 1800* offered a moderate interpretation of the state compact theory and the doctrine of interposition. Madison suggested that the states were sovereign parties to the Constitution only as an expression of the "highest sovereign capacity" of their citizens. As for interposition, Madison suggested that the state legislatures might petition Congress directly or through their representatives in the Senate, and that they might ask either for a repeal of the objectionable acts or for new amendments to the Constitution. All of these remedies, Madison insisted, fell "strictly within the limits of the Constitution."[90]

The Kentucky Resolutions of 1799 also represented a partial repudiation of the resolutions of 1798. The legislature continued to declare that the Alien and Sedition Acts were "palpable violations" of the Constitution and that "a nullification by those sovereignties [the states that ratified the Constitution] of all unauthorized acts done under color of that instrument, is the rightful remedy." Nevertheless, the legislators conciliated their countrymen: they promised that "this commonwealth . . . will bow to the laws of the Union" and that Kentucky would oppose all violations of the Constitution "in the constitutional manner." Kentucky thus abandoned even the appearance of resistance to the Alien and Sedition Acts.[91]

The political contest between Federalists and Republicans came to a head in February 1801. The Republican victory in the presidential election had been thrown into doubt by a deadlock between Jefferson and his running mate Aaron Burr in the Electoral College. Therefore, the election was thrown into the House of Representatives, where Federalists would hold a majority until December 1801. With President Adams due to leave office in March, Republicans feared that Federalists would invoke a 1792 statute to swear the president pro tempore of the Senate into office as president during the interval. They warned the Federalists not to suspend constitutional government in order to keep the executive branch in their own hands. Members of both parties began warning darkly that they would mobilize the state militias and decide the contest by force of arms.[92]

In the midst of this constitutional crisis, leading Republicans decided that they would in fact use force to ensure the election of a Republican president, and they took steps to prepare for that eventuality. In a letter drafted during the crisis, but sent only after it had passed, Thomas McKean, former "Asserter of the Laws," advised Thomas Jefferson that he had prepared to use the state militia, a force of twenty thousand fully armed men, to arrest all Federalist members of Congress in Pennsylvania. James Monroe, governor of Virginia, made preparations to use that state's militia to seize a federal arsenal in New London, Virginia. In a letter to Monroe, Jefferson himself indicated that leading Republicans in the new capital city of Washington had communicated to the Federalists in Congress their resolve to resist any attempt to place a Federalist in office: "We thought it best to declare openly and firmly, one & all, that the day such an act passed, the middle states would arm, and that no such usurpation, even for a single day, should be submitted to."[93]

In the end, Federalists in the House relented and permitted Jefferson to take office peacefully. Jefferson allowed the Sedition Act to lapse into oblivion, and Republicans in Congress repealed the internal taxes of the 1790s, including the direct tax of 1798. Jefferson's decision to repudiate the radicalism of 1798 and pursue electoral victory proved to be based on an accurate assessment of the public mood. As to the question of whether the people might resist the acts of a government of their own creation, the stand taken by Republicans in March 1801, together with their response to Fries' Rebellion, constituted a very different answer than that offered by the party in the fall of 1798. In the end, Republicans concluded that the people might resist only when their right to create that government through lawful elections had been abridged. Should lawfully elected officials exercise undelegated power, the people might defend their liberties and vindicate their sovereignty only by petitioning for redress and turning out the offenders in the next election.

Republicans may have successfully captured a moderate middle ground, but they could not erase 1798 from memory. The Virginia and Kentucky Resolutions of 1798, the primary texts transmitting the memory of 1798 to later generations, bequeathed legacies not anticipated by their authors. The resolutions carried into memory not only the state compact theory that would animate Southern secessionists, but also the language of popular nullification and the mentality of Whig ideology. Thus, over two generations of partisan political competition, even northern Democrats would continue to find meaning in Jefferson's warning "that it would be a dangerous delusion, were a confidence in the men of our choice, to silence our fears for the safety of our rights: that confidence is everywhere the parent of despotism; free government is founded in jealousy, and not in confidence."[94] In the first half of the nineteenth century these Whig sentiments would be incorporated into constitutional discussions of the right to keep and bear arms, and they would continue to be ritually performed at political meetings and militia musters. Despite the Democratic-Republican retreat in 1799, over the next two generations the libertarian understanding of the American Revolution would continue to hold an important place in public memory.

THE LIBERTARIAN MEMORY OF THE
REVOLUTION IN THE ANTEBELLUM ERA

In January 1830 Senators Daniel Webster of Massachusetts and Robert Hayne of South Carolina engaged in a passionate debate over the nature of the Constitution and of the union. The debate was a key moment in the articulation of the competing antebellum constitutional doctrines of states rights and national supremacy. It also illustrates the continuing hold of the Revolution and the Alien and Sedition Act crisis upon the collective memory and the political theory of the nation even after the passing of the Revolutionary generation.

In the debate Hayne defended South Carolina's nullification of the tariff of 1828 and offered James Madison's Virginia Resolutions of 1798 as

---

Fig. 1. *(facing page)* Tompkins Harrison Matteson (American, 1813–84), *The Spirit that Won the War*, 1855. Chrysler Museum of Art, Norfolk, VA.

In this painting, Matteson captures the memory of the events of 1775. The scene depicts a household's preparations for the march of the militia. As the militiamen of the neighborhood gather, a family works together to prepare weapons, equipment, and provisions. Even the children are engaged in casting bullets. The militiaman's wife adjusts his pack while his mother warns him to pay heed to the will of the Creator. The wooden leg of his father symbolizes the sacrifices of prior generations.

an authoritative statement of the legitimacy of state nullification.[1] In his response, Webster repudiated the doctrine and argued that a state had no constitutional authority to resist a federal law. Such resistance, he argued, was treason, even when authorized by a state government: "If John Fries had produced an act of Pennsylvania annulling the law of Congress, would it have helped his case? Talk about it as we will, these doctrines go the length of revolution. They are incompatible with any peaceable administration of government." Webster's famous concluding celebration of "liberty and union, now and forever, one and inseparable," was an early and passionate articulation of the nationalist sentiment that would carry the nation through the Civil War.[2]

Nevertheless, Webster did not deny the right of revolution against a "tyrannical government." He embraced both the natural right of revolution and the right of the people "to resist unconstitutional laws, without overturning the government." But he argued that such resistance was lawful only if the federal judiciary had exercised its exclusive authority to declare the law unconstitutional. Any state magistrate or individual citizen who resisted the law in the absence of such a ruling engaged in revolution and courted the penalties of treason thereby: "I cannot conceive that there can be a middle course, between submission to the laws, when regularly pronounced constitutional, on the one hand, and open resistance, which is revolution, or rebellion, on the other."[3]

In response to Webster's charge that South Carolina's nullifiers were inciting revolution, Hayne appealed to the memory of Anglo-American struggles for liberty:

Sir, I will put the case home to the gentleman. Is there any violation of the constitutional rights of the states, and the liberties of the citizen, (Sanctioned by Congress and the Supreme Court,) which he would believe it to be the right and duty of a state to resist? Does he contend for the doctrine "of passive obedience and non-resistance?" Would he justify an open resistance to an act of Congress sanctioned by the Courts, which should abolish the trial by jury, or destroy the freedom of religion, or the freedom of the press? Yes Sir, he would advocate resistance in such cases, and so would I, and so would all of us. But such resistance would, according to his doctrine, be *rev-*

olution; it would be *rebellion.* According to my opinion, it would be just, legal, and *constitutional resistance.*[4]

Considered together, the positions outlined by Webster and Hayne demonstrate that the terms of the debate over the right of revolution and the legitimacy of insurrectionary resistance had changed little between 1798 and 1830. Both men recognized a natural right of revolution. Both men also sought to carve out an authoritative procedure by which unconstitutional acts could be nullified without recourse to political violence, much as Madison and Jefferson had in 1798. Finally, both men acknowledged that resistance to unconstitutional laws short of revolution was legitimate in some circumstances. For Webster, constitutional resistance was legitimate only when the executive ignored a judicial decree. Hayne offered a broader view. Articulating Democratic-Republican principles from the 1790s, he asserted a duty to resist, and suggested that that duty fell upon individuals as well as states.

The continued resonance of the right of resistance in the antebellum era can be traced in part to its incorporation within Democratic-Republican political ritual. On July 4, 1826, for example, the inhabitants of Petersburg, Virginia, gathered to celebrate the Jubilee of American independence. In addition to the reading of the Declaration of Independence and the public exercise of the militia, the citizens gathered for the stock ritual of American political festivity, a dinner punctuated by toasts. After toasting the fiftieth anniversary of Independence, the celebrants drank to the following sentiment: "The People—the only source of Legitimate Power; they know it, and will speak in thunder to those who forget it." This toast was accompanied by six rounds of gunfire, six cheers, and the singing of Yankee Doodle.[5] The toast was a protest against the corrupt bargain of 1824, in which John Quincy Adams had been chosen by the electoral college despite losing the popular vote to Andrew Jackson. It demonstrates that celebrations of popular resistance remained a routine part of Democratic political ritual and of the commemoration of the Revolution.[6]

Such celebrations were not confined to popular political culture. When Americans discussed the right to keep and bear arms and the institution of the militia in the first half of the nineteenth century, the constitutional importance of maintaining the capacity of an armed people to resist domestic usurpation and reenact the drama of 1774 was a standard feature of the discussion. In 1807, for example, Congress debated a bill to provide arms for the militia. During the debate, Eziekiel Bacon of Massachusetts rose to explain the purposes for which the institution of the militia had been maintained:

> They were not only that the great mass of the people should be prepared on any sudden emergency to oppose the sudden invasion of a foreign external foe, and to suppress internal commotions, but that they should at all times be both ready and able to defend themselves against those arbitrary exactions and unconstitutional oppressions, with which they might in process of time be loaded, even by the machinations of their own rulers; for this purpose it was essential that the arms that they might be called upon to wield should be exclusively their own, subject to their entire control, and which no power on earth had a right lawfully to wrest from their hands.[7]

In 1833, Joseph Story, associate justice of the United States Supreme Court, offered a similar explanation of the importance of maintaining an armed militia:

> The militia is the natural defense of a free country against sudden invasions, domestic insurrections, and domestic usurpations of power by rulers. . . . the right of citizens to keep and bear arms has justly been considered, as a palladium of the liberties of a republic; since it offers a strong moral check against usurpation and arbitrary power of rulers; and will generally, even if these are successful in the first instance, enable the people to resist, and triumph over them.[8]

In 1840 the Tennessee Supreme Court grounded an influential decision interpreting the right to keep and bear arms on the same memory of legitimate political violence: "every free white man may keep and bear arms. But to keep and bear arms for what? . . . The free white men may keep arms to protect the public liberty, to keep in awe those who are in power, and to maintain the supremacy of the laws and the constitution."[9]

Each of these statements fell back upon the memory of Anglo-American struggles for liberty and anticipated a return to legitimate political violence in response to domestic tyranny.

If the memory of 1774 and 1798 lived on in political culture and constitutional theory, the Jacksonian Era also witnessed some important countertrends. In his analysis of the evolution of judicial supremacy, Larry D. Kramer argues that the popular constitutionalism of 1798 had given way by 1830 to an increasing emphasis on judicial nullification as the authoritative mode of settling constitutional disputes.[10] The development of Edward Livingston's constitutional thought supports Kramer's analysis in part. Livingston, the New York congressman who was one of the first radical Republicans to suggest popular resistance to the Alien and Sedition Acts, moved to Louisiana and returned to Congress to represent his new home in 1823. In 1831, Livingston became Andrew Jackson's secretary of state, and as such authored the proclamation of December 1832 with which Jackson threatened force against South Carolina.

In March 1830, Senator Livingston joined in the congressional debate initiated by Webster and Hayne. Hoping to rein in the South Carolina nullifiers while vindicating the Democratic-Republican opposition of 1798, Livingston attempted to craft a middle ground between Senator Hayne's assertion of a broad right of state nullification and the consolidated nationalism of Senator Webster.

Livingston dwelled at length upon the events of 1798, and offered an answer to Senator Hayne's question concerning the legitimacy of resistance to an unconstitutional law that had been sanctioned by the federal courts. He began by declaring that the states had given up "every constitutional right of impeding or resisting the execution of any decree or judgment of the Supreme Court . . . even if such decree or judgment should, in the opinion of the States, be unconstitutional." In such a case, he declared, the states might protect their citizens:

> by remonstrating against it to congress; by an address to the people, in their elective functions, to change or instruct their representatives; by a similar address to the other states, in which they have a right to declare that they

consider the act as unconstitutional, and therefore void; by proposing amendments to the constitution, in the manner pointed out by that instrument; and finally, if the act be intolerably oppressive, and they find the general government persevere in enforcing it, by a resort to the natural right which every people have to resist extreme oppression.[11]

In these passages Livingston embraced the centrality of judicial review to the settlement of constitutional disputes and a minimalist interpretation of the Virginia Resolutions of 1798. Further, he made it clear that any resistance that came in defiance of a Supreme Court decision would be revolutionary in nature and would court the "risk of all penalties attached to an unsuccessful resistance to established authority."[12] Clearly by 1830 Livingston had backed away from the popular constitutionalism that he had done so much to stimulate in 1798.

Nevertheless, Livingston's discussion displays a lingering discomfort with the stark choice between obedience to institutional authority and revolution. He argued that political opposition might continue even in the face of Supreme Court validation of a law, and invoked Madison's prediction in *Federalist No. 46* that federal usurpation would be met with "the disquietude of the people, their repugnance, and, perhaps, refusal to cooperate with the officers of the union, the frowns of the executive magistracy of the state, the embarrassments created by legislative devices which would often be created on such occasions." He went on to note Madison's discussion of the militia's continuing capacity for revolutionary resistance. Finally, he suggested that the states' capacity for both active political harassment and forceful resistance would allow them to face the federal government down in cases of obvious usurpation regardless of court rulings: "An organized body, ready to resist either legislative or executive encroachment, round which the people, whenever oppressed, might rally, will always keep oppression in awe."[13] In the Jacksonian era, then, even nationalists were willing to acknowledge the legitimacy of an active constitutional resistance so long as it stopped short of outright violence.

In practice, the growth of the party competition over the next two decades brought stability to American politics, and with it, a growing preference and expectation that political conflict would yield to institutional remedies. In the 1840s, as the second party system fostered new rituals and symbols of popular sovereignty, the militia gradually lost its central role in popular political culture. Militia musters, public meetings, and volleys of musketry gave way to partisan speeches, parades, banners, and torches. The integration of local, state, and national parties and the mobilization of partisans in electoral campaigns at all levels of government sent a powerful message that the people had a continuing capacity to correct adverse policy decisions and even infringements of liberty by participating in the next election.[14]

The 1840s also witnessed the collapse of the universal militia system, as many states repealed the legislation mandating militia training for free white men under forty-five. The universal militia gave way in the 1840s to volunteer companies largely composed of bourgeois citizens. As antebellum political commenters called for a politics of rational deliberation and denounced violent protest as an expression of passion unsuitable to a democratic society, magistrates and political leaders became increasingly willing to use these volunteer militias to suppress rioting and social disorder.[15]

This increasing emphasis on order and stability shaped the national response to Rhode Island's Dorr War. In 1841 Providence attorney Thomas Dorr led a movement to hold a popularly elected convention to replace Rhode Island's colonial-era charter and establish a more democratic government for the state. After the resulting People's Charter was ratified by a majority of the adult male residents of the state, Dorr was elected governor under its provisions. When the legislature authorized under the old charter refused to yield power, Dorr and his followers attempted to seize the state arsenal. Dorr fled the state after the attempt on the arsenal failed, but was arrested two years later and convicted of treason against the state.[16]

Nationalists reacted to Dorr's assertion of a people's sovereign right to alter their form of government with outrage. Joseph Story argued that without the institutional approval of the constituted government, the people had no authority to act: "What is a Republican government worth if an unauthorized body may thus make, promulgate, and compel obedience to a Constitution at its own mere will and pleasure?" Story later joined the federal circuit court decision that rejected Dorr's assertion of the peaceable right of revolution.[17] In *Luther v. Borden,* the Supreme Court of the United States upheld Story's opinion. The court refused to consider Dorr's appeal to the Anglo-American Whig tradition and to the memory of the Revolution as justification for his acts, ruling that the legitimacy of the People's Charter was a political question over which the court had no jurisdiction.[18]

Even as nationalists and conservatives grew less comfortable with constitutional resistance, peaceable revolution, and politics out of doors, abolitionists found use for the memory of the Revolution as a struggle to preserve liberty. In 1854, Massachusetts abolitionist Richard Hildreth, whose critique of southern society proved influential among early leaders of the Republican Party, invoked the memory of the Revolution as he rejected the argument that opponents of slavery must obey a national government bent on upholding the institution:

> Law, so far as it has any binding moral force, is and must be conformable to natural principles of right; indeed, that in this conformity alone its moral binding force consists, and that so far as this conformity is wanting, what is called law is mere violence and tyranny, to which a man may submit for sake of peace, but which he has a moral right to resist passively at all times, and forcibly when he has any fair prospect of success. Such indeed was the principle upon which the American Revolution was justified.[19]

Hildreth's argument represented a reworking of the most radical principles of 1798. He combined abolitionist "higher law" doctrine with the ideology of popular nullification. In Hildreth's view the validity or nullity of a law depended upon its conformity with "natural principles of right," a variation on the "letter and spirit of the constitution" by which Democratic-Republicans had measured the Alien and Sedition Acts. Hildreth also referred to resistance as a moral rather than a constitutional right, but he clearly saw such resistance as legitimate.

For the people of Massachusetts, the libertarian memory of the Revolution retained its power to move, both emotionally and violently. In 1854 that memory was at the center of the popular outrage over the return of Anthony Burns to slavery. Burns, a fugitive from Virginia living in Boston, was arrested under the Fugitive Slave Act of 1850. When all efforts to secure Burns's release failed, the city turned out in mourning to witness his transportation back to slavery. The posse that escorted Burns to the harbor required an escort of half a dozen military companies. As church bells pealed in mourning, the marines and militiamen marched through streets dressed in black crepe, and passed beneath a yoke composed of a large black casket, signifying the death of liberty, suspended across the street by rope. Several observers noted that the procession passed close by the site of the Boston Massacre and beneath the spire of the Bunker Hill monument, and expressed outrage that the militia that had fought tyranny in 1775 had mustered to enforce slavery in 1854. Repeatedly protesters broke into the line of march and members of the militia companies restraining the crowds found themselves publicly cursed by name. The following year Massachusetts passed a personal liberty law designed to render the Fugitive Slave Act unenforceable.[20]

Here then were the popular repugnance and the official embarrassments that Madison had spoken of in *Federalist No. 46*. Furthermore, some observers expressed frustration that embarrassment was all that had occurred. The Reverend George B. Cheever, writing in the *New York Independent,* denounced the governor of Massachusetts for employing the militia to enforce the decision to return Burns to slavery rather than in a "just and legal armed resistance to unjust law." Drawing upon Justice Story's commentary on the Second Amendment, Cheever argued that the people of Boston, backed by the militia, would have prevented Burns's enslavement, and thus placed "an irresistible moral check against usurpation."[21]

Webster's 1830 appeal to "liberty and union" was prescient: his vision of nationalism represented America's future. Yet the embers of the Age of Revolution still glowed, and they would burst forth in flame one last time in 1860. Only in the aftermath of its most devastating war would America begin a generations-long process of turning its back on the memory of 1774. The Republican Party would lead that process and fashion a new patriotic identity based on loyalty to the nation. Democrats would exhibit a greater reluctance to part with the memory that had played such an important role in the creation of the party, but in time they, too, would leave behind the memory of eighteenth-century struggles for liberty.

PART TWO

THE ROOTS OF MODERN PATRIOTISM: CONSCRIPTION, RESISTANCE, AND THE SONS OF LIBERTY CONSPIRACY OF 1864

In February 1863, Ohio congressman Clement Vallandigham rose in the House of Representatives to speak against the extraordinary exercise of emergency war powers by President Abraham Lincoln. Vallandigham's speech addressed the particulars of the conscription bill then before the house, but his sentiments applied with equal measure to Lincoln's suspension of habeas corpus, to a wave of military arrests across the nation, and to the Emancipation Proclamation, which had taken effect seven weeks previously. Vallandigham denounced this program as an attempt "to abrogate the constitution, to repeal all existing laws, to destroy all rights, to strike down the judiciary, and erect upon the ruins of civil and political liberty a stupendous superstructure of despotism." He warned darkly that the people of America would no longer submit. "Sir, it is this which makes revolutions. . . . and if, indeed, we are about to pass through the usual stages of revolution, it will not be the leaders of the Democratic party . . . but some man among the people, now unknown and unnoted, who will hurl your tea into the harbor."[1]

Republicans protested that the policies of the administration were necessary to the preservation of the Union, and were thus constitutional by definition. They denounced Vallandigham's criticism as disloyal, and suggested that patriotism demanded unquestioning loyalty in a time of crisis. Democrats were unwilling to accept this redefinition of patriotism. The party's response to Lincoln's war policies was steeped in the historical memory of the Revolution, and some midwestern Democrats publicly revived the radical language of 1798 and declared that the Conscription Act was "not entitled to the obedience of a free people." In the spring of 1863 rural Democrats in Indiana and across the Midwest began to reenact that memory: they formed extralegal militias and took up arms against their government. That resistance culminated in a plot by leaders of a Democratic secret society, the Sons of Liberty, to overthrow the governments of four midwestern states and withdraw them from the Union. The partisan conflict of 1862–64 thus illustrates both the continued resonance of the libertarian memory of the Revolution and the rise of a new conception of patriotism based on loyalty and obedience to the state.

Traitors in their Midst: Republicans Confront Domestic Opposition

Lincoln is regarded today as one of the nation's greatest presidents for two distinct reasons. He is celebrated in public memory as the great liberator, who freed the slaves and set the nation on a course toward racial equality. He is also a symbol of national survival and perseverance in the face of total war. But many of Lincoln's actions during the war rested on the premise that any measure necessary to secure the safety of the nation was by definition legitimate. Within the Republican Party this doctrine of necessity led to a corollary: that anyone opposing such necessary measures countenanced the destruction of the nation and was guilty of disloyalty. For most Republicans this equation of dissent and disloyalty brought with it the fearful expectation that the disloyal would congregate and conspire to bring about the downfall of the nation. Republican ideology and political culture during the Civil War thus rested on three themes: necessity, loyalty, and conspiracy.

The period from September 22, 1862, when Lincoln issued the preliminary Emancipation Proclamation, to his reelection in November 1864 was one of intense political and ideological struggle in Indiana and across the Midwest. Since the beginning of the rebellion, Lincoln and Republican majorities in Congress had enacted a series of measures they believed necessary to the defense of the Union. These measures included a new tax on incomes, the creation of a national banking system, and the wholesale confiscation of "rebel property," including property in slaves and the proceeds of illegal smuggling. Lincoln intensified this program in the fall of 1862. In September he suspended the writ of habeas corpus and began a campaign of military arrests to suppress smuggling and desertion. He also issued the Emancipation Proclamation, due to take effect at year's end. Finally, in March 1863, Congress passed the Conscription Act, which established the first federal military draft and created a federal military police force within every congressional district in the nation with the power to appoint subordinate officers in every township.[2]

Lincoln and most Republicans justified the suspension of habeas corpus, the Emancipation Proclamation, and conscription as necessary to the preservation of the union. Explaining his actions in a letter in 1864, Lincoln asserted that "measures, otherwise unconstitutional, might become lawful, by becoming indispensable to the preservation of the constitution, through the preservation of the nation." Republicans around the nation embraced this expansion of executive war powers. Republicans in Bartholomew County, Indiana, for example, declared that in the exercise of necessary war powers the president was bound only by "a reasonable discretion."[3]

Local Republican officials and subordinate military officers proved quite willing to push this doctrine of necessity to its limits. In Indiana and Illinois, Democrats won control of the state legislatures in the elections of 1862. In Indiana Democrats attempted to force Republican governor Oliver P. Morton to share military authority with a council of subordinate state officers dominated by Democrats. In response, the Republican minority of the state senate bolted from the chamber, depriving the legislature of a quorum. As a result, the legislative session ended on March 8, 1863, without the passage of annual appropriations bills. For the next two years, Governor Morton suspended constitutional government and administered the state without a legislature. He funded state operations with loans from Republican officials and financial assistance from the Lincoln administration. Governor Richard Yates resorted to similar expedients in Illinois.[4]

Issued on April 19, 1863, General Ambrose Burnside's General Order No. 38, which prohibited "sympathy for the enemy" and "treason, expressed or implied," was another expansive application of the doctrine of necessity. In effect, Burnside promulgated a new Sedition Act based on his own military authority as commander of the Department of the Ohio. When Clement Vallandigham repeated the sentiments of his remarks to Congress in a speech in Mt. Vernon, Ohio, openly defying Burnside's order, the general ordered Vallandigham's arrest. A military commission tried Vallandigham for "declaring disloyal sentiments and opinions with the object and purpose of weakening the power of the government" and convicted him. President Lincoln subsequently exiled Vallandigham to the Confederacy.[5] Another military commission tried Indiana state senator Alexander J. Douglas for publicly advocating armed resistance to military arrests. Only the Lincoln administration's reversal of Burnside's order brought about Douglas's release: the military commission found him guilty of the specified act but dismissed the charge against him.[6] General Milo Hascall, implementing Burnside's order in Indiana, issued General Order No. 9, ordering the suppression of any newspaper or speaker endeavoring to bring "the war policy of the government into disrepute." Hascall subsequently sent notices ordering several Democratic newspapers to "publish a loyal paper hereafter" or cease publication. He suppressed the *Columbia City News* under this order in May 1863.[7]

Hascall's demand that Democratic editors "publish a loyal paper" reflected a growing Republican conviction that Democratic opposition to "necessary" war measures was grounded in disloyalty. Republicans demanded that all citizens pledge obedience to the constituted authorities of the Union and abstain from criticism that might undermine the war effort. The Union League of New York captured this new Republican patriotism in its constitution, which stated that "the condition of membership shall be absolute and unqualified loyalty to the government of the United States." The new Republican understanding of patriotism as unquestioning loyalty to the nation-state was propagated through religious sermons, the pamphlets of the Loyal Publication Society, and the activities of the Union League, a new social and political organization that quickly spread throughout the North.[8]

Midwestern Republicans accepted this doctrine without qualification and used it to partisan advantage. The Republicans of Johnson County, Indiana, declared that "in the present calamities of our government, we recognize no party line but that drawn between loyalty and disloyalty—between those who sustain the government and those who oppose it." When Democrats protested that they remained loyal to the Union even though they were unwilling to support the policies of the administration, Republicans refused to relent. Republicans in Franklin, Indiana, for example, declared that the "newly invented doctrine, making a distinction in time of war between the Administration and the Government, is treasonable and tends to the destruction of all government, and we regard no man as truly loyal who is not as patriots in by gone days 'for their country right or wrong.'" Midwestern Republicans used this jingoistic standard of loyalty to justify every administration attempt to curb dissent.[9]

Republican political discourse and political culture took on an increasingly militarized tone as the war progressed. During the winter of 1862–63, Republican editors in Indiana and Illinois approvingly printed dozens of resolutions from Union regiments threatening to return home to "crush" treasonous Democrats. The *Indianapolis Daily Journal*, for example, published resolutions from two Indiana regiments who warned the Democratic members of the state legislature to "beware the retribution that is falling upon your coadjutors at the South, and as your crime is tenfold blacker, will swiftly smite you with tenfold more horror should you persist in your damnable deeds of treason."[10]

In this atmosphere of intense loyalism, militarism, and partisan suspicion, violence came easily and often into the lives of Indiana Democrats. In August 1863, a military force was sent to Columbia City to arrest a man for resisting a provost marshal. As the soldiers were about to depart the town with their prisoner, a crowd of Democrats sent up three cheers for Vallandigham. The soldiers rushed the crowd with revolvers drawn, shot one prominent Democrat, arrested another, and assaulted all those who protested their conduct. Furloughed soldiers assaulted Judge Charles Constable, a prominent Illinois peace Democrat, in the winter of 1864 and forced him to take an oath of allegiance.[11] Members of returning regiments also displayed a predilection for destroying Democratic newspaper offices and printing presses. In Indiana alone the offices of at least five Democratic papers were destroyed during the war, and attacks on several others were narrowly averted.[12] Heated words and contested symbols also sparked brawls among civilians. An argument over a butternut pin (a badge denoting the Southern heritage of many Democrats in the southern part of the state) in Danville, Indiana, resulted in a pitched gun battle in April 1863. In Sullivan County, Republican members of a local religious congregation assaulted a female member during church services, held her down, and forcibly stripped her of a butternut pin. Such incidents were common during the war.[13]

The ideological connection between Democratic dissent and disloyalty also led Republicans to search for evidence of subversive conspiracies. In the summer of 1862, Republicans in localities across Indiana charged that their Democratic neighbors were plotting treason. State officials were flooded with letters describing clandestine military drills by rural "copperheads," a pejorative label that compared Democrats to poisonous snakes hidden in the grass, ready to strike. In their public statements and even their private correspondence, Indiana Republicans began to use the terms *Democrat, butternut, copperhead,* and *KGC* interchangeably. The last term referred to the Knights of the Golden Circle, a prewar Southern secret society that had organized private "filibustering" expeditions intended to establish proslavery governments in South America.[14]

Republicans built the grandest conspiracy theory of the 1860s around rumors that the KGC had taken root in the north. In a series of investigations and exposés, Republicans alleged that thousands of Democrats had organized KGC temples across the Midwest and sworn allegiance to Jefferson Davis.[15] As the war progressed, this conspiracy theory grew in scope. An Indianapolis grand jury reported in August 1862 that the KGC had fifteen thousand members in Indiana, and that these members had been trained to recognize members in the Confederate army and had sworn not to fire upon them. In January 1863, Republicans announced that the purposes of the order had expanded to encompass the encouragement of desertion and the secession of the northwestern states. Republicans in Indianapolis warned darkly that they would meet the "traitor sympathizers of the North" with "powder and ball" should they "dare to trample the old flag under their feet."[16]

As Republican conspiracy discourse expanded in scope, it increasingly emphasized nativist and apocalyptic themes. Republicans portrayed the subversive conspiracy as alien in origin, having emerged in the Confederacy. They thus suggested that Democrats had bound themselves to foreign (Confederate) masters just as Federalists had suggested that Democratic-Republicans had bound themselves to French Illuminati in 1798. Republicans also began to portray the conspirators in diabolical terms. The editor of the Indiana *Daily Journal* described them as a "living, restless brood of poisonous serpents impatiently awaiting the hour to strike the government." He denounced the leadership of the Democratic Party for harboring the conspirators: "The leaders of that party associated with these reptiles not only understand their movements, but direct them, urge them forward in their devilish work."[17] As the war continued, Republican fears grew more exaggerated. In July 1864 Republicans charged that a new secret society, the Sons of Liberty, was conspiring with Confederate agents to set the city of Chicago on fire.[18] This image of the region's largest city set ablaze offered as compelling a vision of the apocalypse for northern Republicans as the image of servile insurrection had offered for southern Federalists in 1798.

Though they repackaged earlier conservative fantasies of alien conspirators, Republicans offered an understanding of patriotism that was distinctly modern. In the place of the Federalist obsession with personal honor, Republicans embraced a vigorous national state as the object of their devotion. They sought the widest possible latitude for state action, denounced almost all criticism as disloyal, and justified the violent repression of dissent. Many Democrats believed that this new patriotic order posed as profound a threat to constitutional liberty as southern secession.

"To Battle Manfully for Their Rights": Democratic Opposition and the Response to General Order No. 38

Given the enthusiasm with which Democrats had rallied to the Union at the outset of the war, the bitterness of Democratic opposition to Lincoln's war policies by late 1862 is remarkable. The cause of this change in sentiment lay in the policies adopted by Lincoln in the fall of 1862. The doctrine of necessity flew in the face of sixty years of Democratic belief in limited government and strict construction of the Constitution. The Emancipation Proclamation put the national government on a collision course with a long-standing Democratic commitment to white supremacy. Conscription threatened to coerce Democrats into military service alongside black soldiers and to force them to fight for the abolition of slavery, a cause that most abhorred. Military arrests and violent attacks by crowds of Republicans and soldiers threatened to deprive Democrats of their civil liberties and their political voice.

Democratic opposition rested in part on a fundamental rejection of the Republican doctrine of necessity. Democrats argued that the Constitution established inviolable limits on the powers of the national government and of the president in particular, and that those limits must be enforced in times of war as well as peace. Democrats in Brown County, Indiana, for example, declared that "the plea of military necessity is the tyrant's plea, and if suffered to overthrow the Constitution in war will bring it into contempt in peace."[19]

Democrats also rejected Republican assertions that patriotism demanded loyalty to the nation and to its constituted authorities. American patriotism, Democrats insisted, rested on loyalty to the Constitution. The Democrats of two congressional districts in northeast Indiana repudiated "as slavish, and having no foundation in the principles of our free democracy, the doctrine that loyalty to the government of the United States consists in unconditional adherence to the measures or policy of any administration." They insisted that it was the "inalienable right of the people" to judge such measures by "the infallible test of the Constitution, fidelity to which is the criterion of loyalty."[20]

In rejecting the doctrines of necessity and loyalty, Democrats invoked the memory of Anglo-American struggles for liberty. Democratic politicians were no longer as intimately familiar with the writings of Locke, Sydney, and Trenchard and Gordon as the Revolutionary generation had been. Nonetheless, Democratic speeches and convention resolutions celebrated the Anglo-American revolutions of the seventeenth and eighteenth centuries. They portrayed these revolutions as struggles for constitutional liberty and insisted that fidelity to the sacrifice of their revolutionary forebears obligated Americans to defend the Constitution from the Republican assault.

The most articulate narrator of this historical memory was Indiana congressman Daniel Voorhees. In "The Liberty of the Citizen," a February 1863 speech delivered before the House of Representatives, Voorhees surveyed the constitutional struggles that had produced the Magna Carta, the Petition of Right, and the English Bill of Rights. He contended that these episodes illustrated the continuing necessity to defend liberty against the corrupt human desire to wield unlimited power:

> The usurper seizes the moment when the constitution of his country is weakened by some deadly peril to assist in breaking it down. He watches the opportunity when the laws are unsettled to trample them under his feet and substitute his own imperious and unhallowed will in the place of their well-defined and peaceful operations.[21]

Voorhees employed this historical memory to portray Lincoln as a tyrant and his war policies as symptoms of the corruption so central to Whig thought. Lincoln's suspension of the writ of habeas corpus had, Voorhees declared, "usurped the powers of the judicial and legislative departments of the Constitution to an extent which is totally subversive of republican institutions." Under Lincoln, the multiplication of offices and the expansion of government expenditures had led to a new age of "the courtier and the parasite. At every new aggression, at every new outrage, new advocates rise up to defend that source of patronage, wealth, and fame." If the people submitted to the Lincoln administration's violations of their liberty, Voorhees declared, "our own martyred host, robed in glory, who fell for freedom in the battlefields of the Revolution, will have tasted the bitterness of death in vain."[22]

In 1863 and 1864, Democrats across the Midwest appealed to the memories of the Revolution and of the Alien and Sedition Act crisis and argued that Lincoln's policies and his adherence to the doctrine of necessity marked a return of the measures and constitutional doctrines that Americans had rejected in 1774 and 1798. In a Fourth of July oration, Indiana Supreme Court justice Samuel E. Perkins declared that the Revolution was fought for "the liberty of the people—freedom from arbitrary power in government." He charged that arbitrary power manifested itself "in arbitrary arrests of the citizens, in depriving them of free conscience, speech, press, and suffrage," all powers that the Lincoln administration had recently asserted. To live up to the heritage of their "patriot ancestors," Perkins concluded, the people "must compel the administration to confine itself strictly within constitutional and legal limits." Samuel Winter, editor of the *Huntington Gazette,* accused the Republicans of repeating the "forced constructions" of the Constitution employed by Federalists in 1798. He then quoted the Kentucky Resolutions in support of the proposition that "whenever the general government assumes undelegated powers, its acts are unauthoritative, void, and of no force."[23]

Democratic opposition in 1863 combined this libertarian memory of the Anglo-American revolutionary heritage with a powerful commitment to white supremacy. Democrats across the Midwest greeted the Emancipation Proclamation with especially bitter condemnation. The *Chicago Times* called it "the deed which converts the war from a constitutional contest for the integrity of the union to an unconstitutional crusade for the liberation of three millions of negro barbarians and their enfranchisement as citizens." J. J. Bingham, editor of the *Indiana State Sentinel,* denounced the proclamation in similar terms: "It is the act of an usurper; it is the exercise of despotic power. It is infamous. It means servile war—the butchery of white men not in arms, of helpless white women and children, by a race of semi-barbarians."[24]

The Emancipation Proclamation, conscription, and the enlistment of African Americans in the army struck at Democrats' sense of racial and gender identity as well as their understanding of liberty and citizenship. Democrats believed that citizenship was a privilege of whiteness. Conscription alongside black soldiers to fight to abolish slavery would inevitably undermine that racial privilege. Democrats in Bartholomew County, Indiana, gave voice to their dismay at this prospect, resolving that "this government was made on the white basis, by white men for the benefit of white men, and their posterity forever, and that the scheme now before Congress for making soldiers of the negroes is a step toward negro equality that Democrats cannot approve."[25]

Given their embrace of the Whig memory of Anglo-American struggles for liberty, Democrats were quick to attribute Republican policies to malicious intent. The Democrats of the Tenth and Eleventh congressional districts condemned the administration "because many of the official acts of the Administration have been acts of usurpation and tyranny, and have evinced a despotic temper, that they find their parallel in the worst acts and spirit of the Stuart dynasty of England." A correspondent to the *State Sentinel* charged that Republicans "would not consent to be interfered with in their attempt to establish military despotism." The Democracy of Brown County complained that Lincoln had pledged to observe the Constitution in return for Democratic support, "but when the 'men and money' are obtained, the disguise is thrown off."[26]

There were two facets of this Democratic conspiracy discourse. Democrats portrayed the suspension of habeas corpus, the Conscription Act, the secret arming of the Union League, and the interference in elections in Maryland and Kentucky as part of a coordinated plan to undermine the electoral process and establish Lincoln as a military dictator. In a column reprinted in the *Indiana State Sentinel,* the *Chicago Times* asked, "What is the purpose of this? Can any man doubt it for a moment? Look at Maryland and Kentucky. Let your readers contemplate in those states the despotism to which all the states are hastening." In contrast with the millennial tone of Republican warnings of the alien and diabolical Knights of the Golden Circle, Democratic conspiracy discourse rested on the traditional Whig vision of a domestic threat posed by ambitious and corrupt officials grasping for power.[27]

Some Democrats, however, saw abolition and black citizenship as the first steps of an even more sinister design. The *Chicago Times* warned that miscegenation and social equality would be the next steps in the Republican program. The *Indiana State Sentinel* was apocalyptic in its warning that "the two races cannot live upon terms of equality. The attempt will result in the extermination of one of them. The administration has deliberately chosen to invite such a contest, and aid the negroes in the destruction of the white race."[28]

At the outset of 1863, a broad range of Democratic voices in the Midwest asserted that the memory of the Revolution and the defense of white manhood alike enjoined them to resist Lincoln's war program. J. J. Bingham, editor of the *Indiana State Sentinel*, greeted the Emancipation Proclamation with a January editorial declaring that "if this act of usurpation passes unrebuked, then we may bid farewell to constitutional liberty." He then asserted that "the President had no more right to issue such a decree than had any other citizen, and it should be of no more effect."[29]

Though the Emancipation Proclamation posed the gravest threat to Democrats' racial identity, there was little that free-state Democrats could do to resist it directly. Military arrests, however, brought Lincoln's suspension of habeas corpus directly to bear upon many predominantly Democratic communities. The Democratic Party in some of those communities called for resistance. In February 1863, Democrats in Greene County declared the suspension of habeas corpus "should be resisted by the strong arm of a free people." In April, the Democracy of Brown County resolved that "illegal and arbitrary arrests, without law and warrant thereof, will not be submitted to, if in our power to prevent." As late as June 1864, the Democrats of Kosiusko County pledged to defend "peaceably, if we can, forcibly, if we must" against "all arbitrary and military arrests."[30]

In addition to these calls for popular nullification, other Democrats called for state interposition. The Democracy of Orange County argued in February 1863 that "the suspension of the writ of *habeas corpus* by the President of the United States, is unconstitutional—an act of Executive usurpation, and absolutely void and should be disregarded by those who are entrusted with the execution of and the administration of the laws." Party meetings in Lawrence and Shelby counties joined this call for interposition against military arrests.[31]

Democrats also called for resistance to the Conscription Act. In January, as Congress debated the act, the Democracy of Rush County embraced the following resolution:

> That in the name of justice, right and humanity we enter here our solemn protest, and register here our unrelenting opposition to the passage by congress of any conscript or drafting act, whereby men of our country shall be taken from their quiet homes and the peaceful pursuits of life, to fight in an abolition war for the freedom of the negro. …. Such a law, so manifestly unjust, unconstitutional and oppressive, would be null and void and not entitled to the obedience of a free people.[32]

A few days later, the Democratic festival in Shelby County held in honor of U.S. senator Thomas A. Hendricks passed the same resolution. Samuel Winter, editor of the *Huntington Democrat,* made a similar assertion at the end of February. He predicted that conscription could not be enforced and argued that resistance would be legitimate: "going upon the principle that this government was made for man, and man not for the government, which is the true theory, the people have the authority vested in them to resist conscription." In April the Democracy of Warren County resolved that since the Conscription Act was "unconstitutional in its provisions and dangerous to the liberties of the people, the authority of each of the states should sternly resist the operation of a scheme so fatal to the relations which should always exist between Federal and State governments."[33]

General Order No. 38, issued on April 15, 1863, and the ensuing campaign to suppress public criticism of the administration, forced Democrats to reconsider their public calls for resistance to conscription and military arrests. Over the next two months, party leaders and newspaper editors amended these early calls for resistance, reminding their readers that obedience to the laws was a basic duty of citizenship. The duty of obedience had been a theme of Democratic discourse earlier in the year as well. The *New Albany Ledger*, a leading organ of the party's "war faction," had sternly warned as early as March that citizens must not resist the law.[34] The appearance of such statements in the pages of the Democratic newspapers alongside the calls for nullification and interposition spoke of the confusion among Democrats over how to meet the challenge of the Republican war program.

In May, the state Democratic Party attempted to resolve that confusion by articulating a new set of constitutional red lines. At the state Democratic Mass Meeting in Indianapolis on May 20, attended by seventy-five thousand Democrats from all over the state, party leaders Joseph McDonald and Senator Thomas Hendricks both urged their listeners to obey the law so long as freedom of speech, freedom of the press, and free elections were maintained. The resolutions of this meeting reflected this new constitutional stance:

> Whilst constitutional guarantees—among others the right of free discussion; of appeal to the courts, as against unconstitutional laws and illegal acts; of resort to the legislative power to abrogate bad laws; of removal of obnoxious officials through an untrammeled, uncorrupted ballot box, remain inviolate, it is the duty of the citizen to aid those who are rightfully in authority in all lawful proceedings; but, if these rights are set at naught by their official servants, the people may assert their inherent sovereignty, and resume the powers thus being abused.[35]

In articulating this new stance, the party did not repudiate the right of resistance. At the May 20 meeting Joseph McDonald declared that "if the time ever comes when peaceful remedies will no longer avail us . . . it shall become our duty to vindicate our rights by means of an armed resistance." Rather, the party revised the grounds on which it would advocate resistance to the administration. Party leaders determined that the rights of freedom of speech and the press, violated under General Order No. 38, would be defended by force. The party also announced that any attempt by the military to interfere with elections in Indiana, Illinois, and Ohio would trigger civil war in the North.[36]

In the spring of 1863, Democratic leaders made a tactical decision to back away from an imminent confrontation over conscription and military arrests. The leadership recognized that the party was unprepared for the large-scale political violence that such a confrontation would likely trigger, and, as men of property and standing, party leaders feared disorder. They warned, in language that conveyed a profound fear of revolution, that resistance to conscription would bring devastating consequences. Senator Hendricks, speaking in Rush County, warned that resistance would degenerate into "guerilla strife, against which the organized military force of the government would be brought, striking and destroying separate bands, and leaving the localities of the struggle reeking with blood and smoking ruins." Prominent Democrats also shrank from the prospect of sharing Clement Vallandigham's fate. The freedom of speech and suffrage on which their public lives depended was an interest worth defending, even at the risk of arrest and detention. Freedom from a draft that was unlikely to affect them directly was not.[37]

Bourgeois concepts of masculine identity also lay behind the retreat from resistance to conscription. Party leaders inhabited a bourgeois culture that saw writing, public speaking, and the other intellectual rituals of party politics as the highest exercise of manhood.[38] This connection between manliness and participation in the activities of party politics led bourgeois Democrats to two conclusions. The first was that the preservation of the liberties upon which party politics depended—speech, press, and suffrage—was a masculine duty. The second was that it was unmanly to engage in violent resistance in lieu of politics. Senator Hendricks thus urged Democrats to "vindicate their rights and their manhood at the ballot box" and denounced the use of force as illegitimate. The editor of the *Bloomfield Southern Indianan* denounced the destruction of another Democratic printing press, declaring that "the abolitionists have not the manliness nor the courage to meet an honest, outspoken enemy face to face, and battle with argument against argument." The *State Sentinel* reprinted a *New York News* editorial criticizing the conduct of the New York draft rioters: "If they have determined to resist the conscription act, let the resistance be that of men. . . . Remember, fellow citizens, that it is our duty to prove that we are superior, in the attributes of manhood, to those in power."[39]

Thus class interests and a class-based understanding of manliness led party leaders to reshape the contours of calls for resistance. In the winter of 1864, three Democratic congressional district conventions resolved that "there is a point at which forbearance merges a man into a slave and resistance becomes a duty. Whether that time in the history of times has arrived, may be debated. But we will resist by force any attempt to abridge the elective franchise."[40] Despite denunciations of "unmanly" violence, the party retained its assertion that resistance would be a legitimate response to the denial of the rights of speech, press, and suffrage. As events unfolded, however, it became clear that the party's rural rank and file had a different understanding of the duty of freemen.

"The People Say They Will Not Stand It": Rural Democratic Resistance to Conscription

Confronted with the local enforcement of federal power, an increase in local political violence, and significant restrictions on the liberties of their persons, thousands of Democrats in rural Indiana took up arms to defend themselves and their communities. In the spring of 1863 rural yeomen and laborers organized local mutual protection associations in townships and neighborhoods across Indiana. These associations performed the same functions that local militia companies had celebrated in the 1790s: the protection of local communities from coercion by distant central authority and the defense of liberty in the face of government usurpation.

In 1863, Democrats could no longer depend on the state's organized militia to protect them. When reorganizing the Indiana Legion, the state's legally sanctioned militia, at the outset of the war, Republican authorities took pains to ensure its "loyalty." Local Republicans urged Governor Morton and Indiana adjutant general Laz Noble to deny recognition and arms to "disloyal" companies composed largely of Democrats.[41] As a consequence of the politicization of militia service, rural Democrats organized mutual protection associations to serve as a Democratic shadow militia.

These associations were active in at least twenty counties in Indiana,

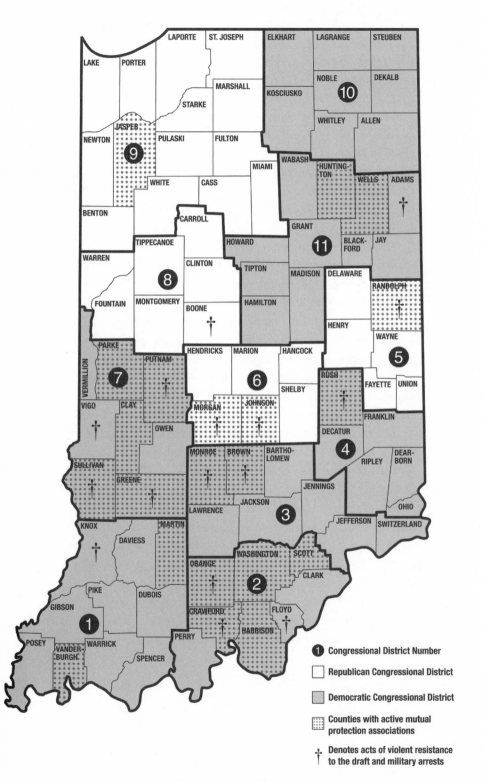

Democratic Resistance in Indiana, 1863–64

and similar organizations spread across Illinois. In some counties, these groups remained secretive. In Indiana's Second and Third congressional districts Democratic leaders consistently denounced armed partisan organizations. Consequently, mutual protection associations in Martin, Orange, Scott, Brown, and Monroe counties met secretly, usually at night in barns and abandoned schoolhouses. Sometimes these bands met in secluded pastures for military drill. In the Seventh Congressional District, local party leaders openly advocated armed organization for local defense. Here mutual protection associations drilled openly, often in conjunction with Democratic political meetings.[42]

Local Republicans frequently charged that these associations were local branches of the pro-Confederate Knights of the Golden Circle. Democrats responded that the associations were a defensive response to the formation of local Union Leagues in early 1863.[43] In fact, these societies were neither pro-Confederate nor purely defensive: they were popular insurrectionary institutions similar to the militias of association that had formed in 1774. A series of incidents in the first half of 1863 amply demonstrated the determination of these societies to resist the arrest of deserters, the implementation of the Conscription Act, and the military arrest of civilians, particularly of Democratic political leaders.

In February 1863, armed men drove off a small detachment of soldiers sent to arrest a band of deserters hiding in Morgan County. The authorities responded by sending a troop of twenty-five cavalry to secure the deserters. Warned of the impending arrest, a local mutual protection association rumored to number more than five hundred men resolved to ambush the cavalry troop and rescue the prisoners. The insurgents' plan failed, however, when the cavalry followed an alternative route. Incidents of organized resistance to the arrest of deserters also took place in Rush and Brown counties in the ensuing months.[44]

In Sullivan County in June, a detachment of forty soldiers sent to arrest deserters beat a hasty retreat before a crowd variously estimated at between five hundred and two thousand Democrats. The populace believed that the soldiers had orders to arrest Andrew Humphreys, a prominent local Democrat, for his role in organizing mutual protection associations in three local townships. Humphreys subsequently offered to travel to Indianapolis to submit to civil arrest in order to calm his neighbors' anger over the use of the military to arrest civilians.[45]

The implementation of conscription brought more serious violence. The Conscription Act called for the enrollment of every eligible draftee before the commencement of the draft lottery. In order to complete the rolls, enrollment officers visited every community, neighborhood, homestead, and workplace in the nation to collect names and other essential information. As June progressed, resistance to the enrollment broke out across Indiana and Illinois, beginning with the assassination of two enrollment officers in Rush County on June 9.[46] Over the next two weeks, mutual protection associations conducted a concerted campaign of resistance across southern Indiana.

In the second week of June, forty armed members of a mutual protection association on the border between Morgan and Johnson counties resisted the arrest of George Burgess, who had earlier threatened an enrollment officer with a gun. A troop of cavalry escorting the U.S. marshal who came to arrest Burgess scattered the insurgents and captured seventeen.[47] Over the course of the next week, one or more mutual protection associations in Putnam County staged coordinated acts of resistance in five townships. Separate armed bands, each numbering at least fifty, stormed the houses of enrollment officers James Sill and Herman Craig on the same night, demanding they surrender the enrollment papers. Committees of local residents visited the enrollment officers in two other townships and warned them that their lives were in danger if they proceeded. A fifth officer had his papers seized by force of arms.[48]

By the third week in June, Republican authorities were discussing the possibility that martial law might be necessary to complete the enrollment in Indiana's Seventh District. On June 18, members of the local mutual protection association assassinated Fletcher Freeman, the enrollment officer of Cass and Jefferson townships, Sullivan County. Freeman had received a letter warning him to stop enrolling the townships. When he ignored the warning, assailants concealed by a foliage blind shot him dead on the road near his home. Robert Garvin, another enrollment officer in the same county, reported that he too had been shot at while riding in the woods, but his assailant's gun had misfired.[49]

The day after Freeman was shot, eighty armed members of a mutual protection society that had been drilling in Monroe County forced the enrollment officer of Indian Creek Township to surrender his lists. The authorities decided that the time for decisive action had come. A regiment of infantry marched into Monroe County to recover the lists and enforce the enrollment. When it appeared that these troops might march into Greene and Sullivan counties, a force of at least five hundred members of the mutual protection societies of Greene County assembled on the border to meet them.[50]

At the end of June, Democratic Party leaders, including Seventh District congressman Daniel Voorhees, succeeded in calming Democratic tempers, and local provost marshals completed the enrollment. Resistance continued for several weeks in the neighboring counties of Illinois's Eleventh Congressional District, however, and there was a serious outbreak of violence in Holmes County, Ohio, as well.[51] The breadth and seriousness of the resistance raised questions about whether the authorities could enforce an actual draft call in the affected districts. Many in the Midwest feared that in the event of a draft, resistance would boil over into the open insurrection that had been so narrowly avoided.

The insurgents of 1863 left far less evidence of their thoughts and motivations than did John Fries and his neighbors.[52] Nevertheless, one can discern in the available evidence strong indications that the insurgents of rural Indiana, Illinois, and Ohio accepted the Democratic Party's constitutional critique of Lincoln's war policies. Several insurgents expressed the belief that it was their right to resist this law because it was unconstitutional. For example, Franklin Newkirk, a member of the mutual protection association in Sullivan County, explained that members of the society "decided that the conscript law was unconstitutional and would not obey it." It was this belief, according to Newkirk, that led them to target Fletcher Freeman for assassination. A Republican in Moultrie County, Illinois, similarly warned that his Democratic neighbors swore that "they wont stand the draft for it is contrary to the constitution." A member of a mutual protection association in Washington County reported that the assembled members resolved to preserve the "constitution and union as it was," a Democratic slogan that summed up the party's commemoration of traditional strict construction and rejection of the doctrine of necessity.[53]

In opposing the policies of the administration, Democratic leaders repeatedly warned that they would soon be faced with a choice between resistance and submission. From May 1863 onward, party leaders argued that interference with elections would mark the moment at which that choice would become unavoidable, and they declared that their identity as freemen would enjoin them to resist. Many rural Democrats, however, perceived the draft enrollment as the intolerable moment of submission. Franklin Newkirk explained that the mutual protection societies of Sullivan County had resolved that "they would resist the draft, by force of arms, if necessary, because they were not willing to submit to the government." When an enrollment officer in Johnson County named Taylor came to the home of John A. Burgess, an old friend, Burgess met him in the dooryard with a rifle in his hand and a revolver in his belt. Burgess made it clear that he would not submit to enrollment or the draft. When Taylor asked him his age, Burgess replied, "There is danger here, for I do not want my friends to force me into this matter. I do not want you to put my name on that roll." For Burgess, compliance with the ritualized surrender of one's personal identity, even to a friend and neighbor, was incompatible with his sense of liberty.[54]

Submission to conscription was particularly threatening to insurgent identity because it undermined their status as free white men.[55] This racial anxiety is illustrated in the frequency with which insurgents referred to conscription as the product of abolitionism. When Brink Marratt confronted the group of truculent laborers in Boone County, their first objection to the enrollment was that "this was a damned abolition war, and they were not going to be enrolled." An enrollment officer in Carroll County received a similar response when he asked for the names of a group of farm laborers. One of the laborers replied, "That is for you to find out—I will not give my name to any damned abolitionist." When the officer protested that he was no abolitionist, the laborer stalked off; the officer was shot at in the woods shortly after this confrontation. The insurgents who assassinated Knox County enrollment officer Eli Mc-Carty did so because "if he was killed, they would not then be drafted into the abolition army."[56]

Faced with the threat of conscription and military arrests, party leaders offered manly resistance in the form of political speech. Rural insurgents offered a different ritual performance of manly resistance: they drilled under arms before a community audience. In June 1863, for example, over one hundred Democrats gathered at the farm of William Frazier on the open prairie of Coles County, Illinois. Half these men drilled with arms, and then those assembled gathered in a circle to listen to Bryant Thornhill speak. Thornhill declared that Jefferson Davis and the men of the South were fighting for their rights and that he himself would resist the draft until death. He then asked the crowd gathered around him, "Gentlemen, what have we met here for?" According to one witness, those assembled responded by declaring as one body that they were ready to resist. A similar exercise took place in Indiana that same month, when the insurgent Democrats of Greene and Sullivan counties gathered to celebrate "Vallandigham and the Constitution" by organizing military companies and conducting drill.[57]

The threat that conscription posed to yeoman identity was intertwined with the threat that it posed to community autonomy. For the most part, resistance to the draft was concentrated in regions of the state that were isolated from transportation links and other physical connections to translocal markets.[58] In such regions household subsistence depended on exchanged tools, traded foodstuffs, and the loan of dependent laborers at harvest time. The withdrawal of the labor of even a few adult men in these tightly knit communities could have catastrophic consequences. The editor of the *Sullivan Democrat* recognized the economic burden conscription placed on rural households and advised enrollment officers to be cautious and courteous, as their visits were "more odious than that of a sheriff with an execution for the last cow."[59] As the economic impact of conscription fell heavily on women left to run agricultural households without the labor of adult men, resistance often became a family affair. Women assaulted draft enrollment officers in Knox, Vigo, Randolph, and Boone counties.[60]

Given the role of the community in reinforcing masculine identity and economic subsistence, insurgents viewed the autonomy of their neighborhoods, townships, and counties from outside interference as essential to the preservation of liberty. Insurgents viewed conscription and military arrests, which involved the physical intrusion of agents of the federal government into local neighborhoods, as especially threatening. William Clayton, a member of a mutual protection association in Warren County, Illinois, expressed this threat in terms of the physical proximity of the government to the local community. Asked by the judge advocate at the treason trial of Harrison H. Dodd why he and his neighbors had gathered for military drill, Clayton answered:

A: The government was using such tyrannical efforts that probably there would be a time come when we should have to stand in defense of our rights.

Q: Did you feel the tyranny of the government yourself?

A: We were afraid that the government would crowd us.

Q: Did the government crowd you any?

A: No, but there had been talk about conscripting.

Other insurgents expressed a similar sense of physical intrusion. A leader of the insurgent Democrats in Washington County later testified that they had taken up arms to "defend themselves from oppression and wrong, and to fight anything that came to fight them."[61]

The preservation of local autonomy was also the primary motivation for resistance to military arrests. The insurgents of Sullivan and Greene counties committed themselves to preventing the arrest of Andrew Humphreys, saying that they would instead take him to be tried by "the civil authority" in their own county court. Insurgents in Holmes County, Ohio, released four men in the custody of a provost marshal and forced him to swear never to return to the county. They explained that they "were tired of permitting people to be carried off by arbitrary arrests without due process of law" and that they had resolved to "resist the marshal in any attempt he may make to carry away one of the citizens beyond the limits of the county to be tried by a military tribunal."[62]

Local Democrats stood by those who defended the community against conscription and brought their wrath to bear on those who co-operated with authorities. The fines levied on the Morgan County insurgents were paid by community subscription. The identities of the assassins of Fletcher Freeman in Sullivan County and Frank Stevens in Rush County were widely known. The fact that no one was ever brought to trial for these crimes suggests a communal resolution to protect the guilty. On the other hand, those who did inform on their neighbors often received anonymous warnings to leave the community. Joseph Morris was warned to leave Rush County for informing on deserters, and William Bennett received a warning in Sullivan County that he had been "tried in a secret political association . . . for the crime of reporting."[63]

Resistance to federal authority in the rural Midwest thus sprang from a particular convergence of ideology and political culture that justified violence in the defense of liberty, community autonomy, and white manhood. Thousands of Indiana yeomen resorted to overt acts of resistance during the course of the Civil War. Indiana furnished enough volunteers to the war effort to avoid the repeated draft calls of 1863 and early 1864, but with President Lincoln's call for five hundred thousand men in the summer of 1864, Indiana's number was up. Every Democrat in the state faced the prospect of actual conscription in the draft of September 5, 1864. In the summer of 1864, Indiana was ripe for insurrection. The leadership for that insurrection would come from within the bourgeois establishment of the Democratic Party.

"The People Are Prepared for Revolution": Harrison Dodd and the Indianapolis Sons of Liberty Conspiracy of 1864

In 1799, the leadership of the Democratic-Republican Party repudiated the forceful resistance of John Fries and confined itself to electoral opposition to the Federalist administration. Though Democratic Party leaders appeared to choose the same strategy in 1863, their repudiation of force was far more equivocal. Few in the party dared to publicly advocate resistance after May 1863. Nevertheless, a significant portion of the party leadership in the Midwest continued to adhere to the principles that sanctioned resistance. One private refuge in which leading Democrats continued to give these principles voice was a new secret society, the Order of American Knights.

The Order of American Knights first emerged in Illinois, and by the spring of 1864, it had spread into Indiana, Missouri, and Kentucky. Phineas C. Wright, an itinerant lawyer, organized the first Indiana "temple," or lodge, in August 1863 in Terre Haute. Over the course of the next year bourgeois Democrats organized additional temples across the state. At a meeting of the Indiana Grand Council in June 1864, the order's secretary reported temples in fifty-one counties in the state. The order organized temples in Indianapolis, Evansville, Fort Wayne, New Albany, Sullivan, Linton, Salem, Peru, Logansport, Plymouth, Laporte, Huntington, and Bluffton. In Illinois, it established temples in Quincy, Peoria, and Springfield, and was strongest in the Wabash and Illinois river valleys. The most reliable estimates put the strength of the order at ten to twenty thousand in each state. In Indiana that membership included the two highest-ranking Democratic officeholders, a former congressman, and several dozen newspaper editors, state legislators, and county officials.[64]

The order's ritual rested on an odd blend of elaborate fraternal ceremony, historical memory, and radical Democratic ideology. J. J. Bingham, editor of the *Indiana State Sentinel* and one of the first members of the Indianapolis temple, testified that the order was designed to "educate the people in the old fashioned republican doctrines, the same as those entertained by Jefferson and Madison." Samuel Winter, editor of the *Huntington Democrat,* testified that he understood that the order was intended to spread the principles of the Kentucky Resolutions.[65] According to the ritual, all first-degree initiates were required to give their assent to the following statement:

Whenever the officials to whom the people have intrusted the powers of the government shall refuse to administer it in strict accordance with the constitution, and shall assume and exercise power or authority not delegated, it is the inherent right, and imperative duty of the people, to resist such officials, and, if need be, expel them by force of arms. Such resistance is not revolution, but is solely the assertion of right.[66]

The order thus invoked the doctrine of popular nullification that had motivated radical Democratic Republicans in 1798–99. The Indiana Democratic Party had publicly abandoned this stance in May 1863, yet prominent members of the party testified that they continued to believe in the right of resistance in principle. Stephen G. Burton, a prominent Sullivan County Democrat, testified that he understood the ritual to mean that "when one political party assumes power, and begins to trample on the rights of other citizens, these can take up rights in their own hands, and defend them by force of arms." Wilson B. Lockridge, editor of the *Miami County Sentinel,* testified that he expected that the order would "protect us if any of our personal rights were invaded," by force if necessary. He added that each member of the order was free to judge the extent of the rights to be protected.[67]

The leading figure in the order in Indiana was Harrison H. Dodd. Dodd had ambitions that far outstripped his station in Indiana political society in 1863. He bought a printing establishment in Indianapolis and invested heavily in a modern steam printer, but he never secured the necessary backing to start up a second Democratic newspaper in the state capital. Dodd also made himself available as a political speaker at Democratic political meetings across the state but never gained a place among the party's preeminent orators. Dodd shared the resentment of many Indiana Democrats at the abuse they so often received from Republicans. On March 30, 1863, a crowd of young, armed men interrupted Dodd's speech at a Democratic meeting in Danville and demanded that he "talk to suit them or receive a volley." In responding, Dodd cut a figure of bourgeois manliness. He declared that he would "finish his speech in his own way" and asked them "to take good aim and give him notice that he might stand still." When Dodd returned to the rail depot at Cartersburg, a crowd of armed men cursed and threatened him. Dodd later claimed that the crowd never laid a hand on him, but it seems likely that he was "manhandled" during these proceedings.[68]

Dodd continued to travel about Indiana on speaking engagements, and in September another confrontation took place, this time with a very different outcome. On September 5 local authorities arrested Dodd after a speech in Rensselaer because local Republicans complained that he had uttered "treasonable language." At dawn the next day eight hundred armed men assembled a mile outside town. These insurgents, probably members of a local mutual protection association, demanded Dodd's release and, according to some reports, threatened to burn the town. The authorities released Dodd and allowed him to proceed to Indianapolis unimpeded.[69]

This demonstration of the utility of collective force in the defense of liberty had a profound impact on Dodd. When Phineas Wright traveled to Indiana to peddle his hybrid vision of politics and fraternalism, Dodd leapt at the chance to organize the order in Indiana. He convened the Indiana Grand Council of the order on September 10. At that meeting Dodd proposed that the order should build its own military organization. The Grand Council subsequently divided the state into four districts and appointed major generals for each.[70]

At the beginning of 1864, Dodd and several other leaders revised the ritual and renamed the organization the Order of Sons of Liberty. They traveled to Canada, where Clement Vallandigham had taken residence after his exile to the Confederacy, to ask him to join in their endeavor and offer him the honorary rank of supreme commander of the order. Vallandigham agreed, but he urged Dodd to pare back the elaborate fraternal ritual and to emphasize appeals to the memory of the founding generation. Dodd responded by writing the key passages of the Virginia and Kentucky Resolutions into the ritual of the order, and he portrayed the order as the reincarnation of the Revolutionary Sons of Liberty at the February 1864 meeting of the Indiana Grand Council, noting that "this great brotherhood is entitled now to the respect of mankind for the part it enacted in the period anterior to the Revolution of 1776." The Grand Council responded to his speech with a resolution that began by paraphrasing the Declaration of Independence: "the right to alter or abolish their government, whenever it fails to secure the blessings of liberty, is one of the inalienable rights of the people." "Therefore," the resolution continued, "we declare that patriotism and manhood alike enjoin upon us resistance to usurpation as the highest and holiest duty of freemen."[71]

At this meeting the council also reappointed military commanders for each of the state's four districts, but the purpose of the order's military organization remained ambiguous. Clement Vallandigham later testified that the order would have taken up arms in response to "the destruction of the right of election."[72] S. Corning Judd, grand commander of the order in Illinois, had a more expansive vision. He explained in a letter to President Lincoln that the order was prepared

> to defend free speech and free press; and to defend against what we regarded as arbitrary arrests—arrests in our state outside military lines, without offense charged, and without due process of law—if no remedy could be secured through the authorities or the ballot box; and to defend against the indiscriminate disarming of Democrats, which we understood was threatened by the Union Leagues.[73]

For his part, Harrison Dodd began to conceive of a fully revolutionary purpose for the order. Dodd concluded the November 1863 council meeting by saying that the time had come "to kick down the walls of decency and talk treason for a while," acknowledging that military organization and revolutionary activity went beyond the bounds of bourgeois decency. He argued that if the order successfully recruited the rural insurgents of Indiana, it would be strong enough to take control of the state.[74]

The order embarked on a recruiting campaign that winter and achieved some success. Dr. William A. Bowles, the order's military commander for southeast Indiana, began to reorganize the rural mutual protection associations of Orange, Martin, Washington, and Harrison counties and incorporate them into the Sons of Liberty. The mutual protection associations of Sullivan and Greene counties already looked to Andrew Humphreys, appointed major general for southwest Indiana, and to Stephen G. Burton, William G. Moss, and Benjamin Cisson, all members of the order, for leadership. In northeast Indiana, Lambdin Milligan and other members controlled mutual protection associations in Huntington and Wells counties.[75]

In the spring of 1864 Dodd and a small group within the leadership began to conspire to overthrow of the governments of Indiana and Illinois. The conspirators believed that the time for revolution had come and that they could not afford to wait for elections.[76] They crafted an

Fig. 2. The Sons of Liberty conspirators, from the frontispiece of Benn Pitman, *The Trials for Treason at Indianapolis* (1865).

The five defendants are, clockwise from the top, William Bowles, Andrew Humphreys, Stephen Horsey, Horace Heffren, and Lambdin Milligan. Missing is Harrison Dodd, who had escaped from prison during his trial.

elaborate scheme for the simultaneous release of Confederate prisoners at Camp Morton in Indianapolis, Camp Douglas in Chicago, and Rock Island in Illinois on August 16. The released prisoners and the armed forces of the Sons of Liberty would capture the arsenals in Chicago, Springfield, and Indianapolis, and then rendezvous with Confederate forces in Kentucky and Missouri to capture Louisville and St. Louis. The conspirators hoped that withdrawal of Indiana, Illinois, Missouri, and Kentucky from the Union would end the Civil War. In an ironic instance of life imitating art, Dodd and his fellow conspirators breathed substance into years of apocalyptic Republican warnings of a subversive conspiracy within the Democratic Party.[77]

On June 14, Dodd sent up a trial balloon at a meeting of the Indiana Grand Council to see if the order as a whole would back his plan for an uprising. According to one participant the council discussed the subject of military organization "for the purpose of resisting the government," but the council refused to act because "the majority of the members did not want any military action, but preferred to wait for a change through the election." Another participant remembered a decision that each temple should procure arms.[78] To further this purpose, Dodd, John C. Walker, and James Barrett and Joshua Bullitt, leaders of the order in Illinois and Kentucky, each accepted large sums of money from Confederate agents in Canada for the purchase of arms. In the middle of August, Dodd and Walker arranged a shipment of pistols and ammunition from New York City. The first lot of 290 pistols and over one hundred thousand rounds of ammunition arrived in Indianapolis on August 15.[79]

A second, multistate meeting to finalize preparations for the uprising took place in Chicago on July 20. This meeting also broke into discord, with some conspirators proposing that the plot be launched on August 16 and some demanding a delay until the promised Confederate forces made an appearance. When those demanding a postponement carried the day, Dodd and Bullitt decided to proceed with a rising on the sixteenth anyway. At the end of July, Bullitt returned to Louisville with money for the purchase of arms, and asked Felix Stidger to send for his chief lieutenants so that he could inform them of the plan. Stidger, a government detective who had gotten himself appointed as the grand secretary of the order in Kentucky, arranged for Bullitt's arrest before the latter could put the plan in motion.[80]

Unaware of Bullitt's arrest, Dodd had his grand secretary, William Harrison, send word to Bowles and Lambdin Milligan, the major general for northeast Indiana, to come to Indianapolis for a council of war. Milligan refused to go to Indianapolis.[81] Bowles, on the other hand, agreed to proceed, and warned the insurgent Democrats of Washington, Orange, Harrison, and Floyd counties to stand ready. Local congressman Michael C. Kerr reported that his district was on the verge of panic, and state authorities received several reports that large numbers of men had gathered in the vicinity of Bowles's residence at French Lick Springs in Orange County. The Sons of Liberty had incorporated mutual protection associations in Kerr's district with as many as three thousand members.[82]

In order to assemble the members of the Sons of Liberty in Indianapolis, Dodd needed the cover of a large political meeting. On August 3 he went to J. J. Bingham, who was chairman of the Democratic State Central Committee, to ask him to call a mass meeting for August 16. When Dodd related the details of the plot, an appalled Bingham refused to give any assistance. Bingham then called a meeting of prominent Democrats, most of them members of the order, on August 5. At this meeting, Dodd and John C. Walker made one last attempt to persuade the leaders of the party that the time for revolution had come. They insisted that "the people were prepared for revolution; that they would not submit to the draft; and that it was better to direct the revolution than to have revolution direct us." In their last attempt to realize their revolutionary dreams, Dodd and Walker revealed that they had adopted the understandings of liberty, masculinity, and the duty to resist held by the insurgent yeomen whom they hoped would serve as the Sons of Liberty's foot soldiers. The assembled party leaders, including gubernatorial candidate Joseph McDonald, angrily repudiated Dodd's revolutionary impulse, and warned him that they would inform the authorities if he did not shut the plot down.[83]

In fact, the Morton administration and the state's military authorities were well versed in the details of Dodd's plot. When a second shipment of pistols purchased by Dodd and Walker arrived in Indianapolis on August 20, authorities seized it, and began making arrests. Dodd was arrested when he returned to the city from the Democratic national convention on September 3.[84]

Dodd may have been naive in believing that party leaders would back his plans. He was not naive, however, in believing that Indiana was ripe for an uprising. In August 1864, the state was home to thousands of desperate men facing the draft lottery of September 5. In mutual protection associations across Indiana there were serious discussions during August and September about whether to submit or resist. Members of mutual protection associations debated the feasibility of coordinated resistance in Wells, Huntington, Sullivan, and Greene counties. From Rush County, William S. Hall, reputed leader of the local mutual protection association, wrote to Charles Lasalle, a prominent member of the Sons of Liberty from Cass County. Hall took care to veil any discussion of resisting the draft. He reported that the Democrats of his region were convinced that the draft call for September 5 would trigger political violence and martial law. "Believing that 'resistance to tyrants is obedience to God,'" he continued, "they have resolved, by the aid of the Democracy, that they will have their constitutional rights at all hazards." Hall went on to ask, "what can be relied on from your part of the state?" He noted that he had sent similar inquiries throughout Indiana.[85]

Though these last-ditch attempts at statewide coordination failed, there were significant acts of resistance to the draft of September 1864. Insurgents assassinated enrollment officers in Knox and Adams counties. Another two officers were shot to death in Illinois. Other draftees simply "skedaddled." One-quarter of the drafted men in the Second Congressional District failed to report, and in Sullivan County the evasion rate was 32 percent, double the rate in the state as a whole.[86] Large bands of draft evaders gathered in Clay and Greene counties in October. Soldiers broke up the camps after the insurgents fired on an officer bearing draft notices.[87] In the Second Congressional District, where the preparations for Dodd's plot had gone farthest, Democrats and members of mutual protection societies began looting the homes of local Republicans after their attempts to coordinate resistance to the draft came to nothing. The Indiana Legion easily dispersed them.[88]

Given the intensity of the uncoordinated resistance in Indiana and Illinois in the fall of 1864, a call to arms from Harrison Dodd and the leadership of the Sons of Liberty, issued in August before the draft lottery had divided Democrats into the saved and the damned, might well have been heeded by thousands of midwestern Democrats. Indiana weathered the draft of September 1864 in large part because the leaders willing to coordinate statewide resistance had been taken off the stage. At the crucial moment, Harrison Dodd and William Bowles were in jail on charges of treason.

The Democratic Party continued to work diligently to prevent serious resistance to the draft of September 1864. J. J. Bingham, on behalf of the party establishment, sent a subtle message to Democrats around the state when in the *State Sentinel* he juxtaposed the list of draft men for Marion County with the proceedings of the first day of Dodd's treason trial.[89] To those contemplating resistance, this illustration of the consequences must have been clear. Local party organizations also helped defuse the conflict by organizing the procurement of substitutes. In regions where insurrectionary sentiment was the strongest, communities raised large sums of money to pay bounties with which drafted men could buy substitutes and thus avoid submitting their persons to the government. In Sullivan County, the voters approved a levy on county funds for this purpose, and similar collective relief was provided in parts of Putnam and Allen counties where antidraft sentiment was strong.[90]

But even as party leaders reminded their rank and file that conscription was the law of the land, they announced their own program of revolutionary organization. On August 12 the Democratic State Central Committee met to ensure that Dodd had closed his plot down. At the same meeting the committee wrote an "Address to the People of Indiana." Though the address denounced "any attempt at resistance of the laws before constitutional remedies are exhausted," it reiterated the party's commitment "to maintain by force, if need be and at all hazards, the right of the people to free and fair elections." It then noted the "well founded apprehensions" that the authorities would interfere with the fall elections. To prepare for this eventuality, the committee declared that "the constitutional right of the people to keep and bear arms as a necessary means of defense to a free State, should not be violated nor abandoned; and it is the right and duty of all good citizens to co-operate in open lawful organizations for the protection of the freedom of elections and for the preservation of the peace and constitutional order and the rights of the people within the state." The committee concluded by recommending the formation of such organizations at the county and township level.[91]

With this address the Democratic Party in Indiana sealed its political fate in the elections of 1864. Party leaders had just discovered that an organization to which many of them belonged was plotting treason. In shutting the plot down they themselves had conspired to conceal it from the authorities. To discuss armed organization at this moment clearly opened the party to politically disastrous charges of complicity with treason. Given a choice between electoral success and fidelity to constitutional principle and historical memory, the party chose the latter.

When the Republican press published the details of Dodd's plot and exposed the membership of many of the state's most prominent Democrats in the Order of Sons of Liberty, the party's attempt to distinguish between secret plots to resist the draft and open armed organization to resist interference with elections lost luster with voters. In September, one Republican observer of the political scene commented that "the exposure of the Sons of Liberty is tearing the ranks of the Democracy all to flinders. McClellan stock is not quoted at all. McDonald stock is fast going down."[92] In the fall elections, Republican Oliver Morton decisively defeated Democratic gubernatorial candidate Joseph McDonald. Joseph Ristine and Dr. James Athon, the two highest-ranking Democratic officeholders in the state, were also defeated. The Democrats held on to four of Indiana's eleven seats in Congress, but the state gave its electoral votes to Abraham Lincoln in November 1864, an outcome that few in the state expected even six months before.[93]

Memory, Law, and Justice: The Sons of Liberty Trials and *ex parte Milligan*

In September 1864, a military commission convened at Indianapolis to conduct the trial of the Sons of Liberty conspirators. Of the conspirators, John C. Walker avoided arrest by fleeing to Canada, and William Harrison, Horace Heffren, and James B. Wilson turned state's evidence. Harrison Dodd was the sole defendant in the commission's first trial. As the trial came to a close and conviction seemed certain, Dodd escaped from his cell and fled to Canada. Subsequently, the commission placed four other members of the Sons of Liberty, William Bowles, Lambdin Milligan, Andrew Humphreys, and Stephen Horsey, on trial. In November the authorities described a second plot to release Confederate prisoners of war held at Camp Douglas in Illinois. Additional members of the order were tried by a military commission that convened in Cincinnati in January 1865.[94]

These trials proved to be yet another arena for partisan combat. The prosecution and the defense offered starkly different visions of the applicable law, of constitutional principle, and of historical memory. Given that the commission featured a jury composed largely of Republican military officers, the prosecution's appeal to the broadest applications of martial law, to the doctrine of necessity, and to a nationalist memory of the Founding era, all found a willing audience. The Indianapolis proceedings were thus stacked against the defendants from the outset. When the defense asked the judge advocate to produce a witness in military custody who promised to provide exculpatory evidence on Dodd's behalf, the commission pronounced the very request as "an insult to the court, and intended as such." Republican members of the commission condemned the defendants in public speeches while the proceedings were still under way. At several critical points the court refused to hear testimony that Andrew Humphreys had resigned from the order before the advent of the conspiracy. Benn Pitman, the official trial recorder, published a heavily edited transcript of the proceedings that concealed these irregularities and exaggerated some key testimony.[95]

The trials did nonetheless establish beyond a reasonable doubt that Dodd and Bowles had conspired to levy war against the United States, and both men were convicted and sentenced to hang. The evidence implicating Humphreys, Milligan, and Horsey was much more ambiguous. The judge advocate failed to present any evidence that any of them knew of the planned rising of August 16.[96] Both Humphreys and Milligan had been appointed major generals in the order, but both denied accepting the appointment. The commission seemed unduly swayed by evidence that the two had been vocal critics of the war policies of the Lincoln administration. Horsey had stockpiled weapons for a mutual protection association in Martin County but was otherwise a minor figure. The commission nevertheless found the three defendants guilty of all charges and specifications. They sentenced Milligan and Horsey to hang alongside Bowles. Because Humpheys' lawyer demonstrated, over vigorous objections, that his client had dropped all association with the Sons of Liberty and repudiated his appointment as major general, the commission sentenced him to home confinement for the duration of the war.

The military commission proceedings also offered a forum for competing articulations of patriotism and collective memory. During closing arguments before the Indianapolis commission, J. R. Coffroth, Milligan's counsel, concluded by beseeching the commission to defend the right to trial by jury by repudiating its jurisdiction: "It was in defense of it that Hamden fell, that Sydney bled, that Washington fought, and for which the battlefields of our holy Revolution were incarnadined with the best blood of our patriot fathers." Coffroth declared that if the nation could be saved "only by the sacrifice of constitutional liberty, and the inalienable rights of our race, I say let it die."[97]

H. L. Burnett, the judge advocate who presided over the commission that tried the conspirators, responded to Coffroth by arguing for a higher loyalty. "A strict observance of the written laws, is doubtless *one* of the highest duties of a good citizen, but it is not *the highest*. The laws of necessity, of self-preservation, of saving our country when in danger, are of higher obligation." In an emotional conclusion crafted to appeal to military officers, Burnett urged the commissioners to remember the sacrifices of their comrades under arms: "Remember that while the Revolution gave your nation birth, that from that bloody struggle was achieved national existence, through this second bloody struggle, through this second baptism of fire and sword, she is to achieve immortality."[98]

Dodd's escape left Lambdin Milligan to challenge the jurisdiction of the military commission before the United States Supreme Court. In the landmark decision *ex parte Milligan*, the court ruled that even in mo-

THE ROOTS OF MODERN PATRIOTISM

ments of grave national emergency, military courts had no jurisdiction over civilians in regions where the civil courts were open and functioning.[99] Justice Davis's majority opinion gave voice to the same Whig memory articulated by Coffroth and other leading Democrats during the war. The opinion repudiated the doctrine of necessity as inconsistent with the preservation of civil liberty and celebrated the memory of the founding generation:

> The lessons of history informed them that a trial by an established court, assisted by an impartial jury, was the only sure way of protecting the citizens against oppression and wrong. . . . But it is insisted that the safety of the country in time of war demands that this broad claim of martial law shall be sustained. If this were true, it could be well said that a country, preserved at the sacrifice of all the cardinal principles of liberty, is not worth the cost of preservation.[100]

Milligan may have secured the Supreme Court's vindication of Democratic constitutionalism and libertarian historical memory, but the tide of memory was running against him. For Burnett and many Republicans, the struggle for "national birth" displaced the struggle for liberty as the central meaning of the American Revolution. Further, he offered his fellow military officers a vision of a future collective memory in which their own shared struggle would eclipse that of the founding generation. Burnett's vision would prove prophetic. The precedent set in *ex parte Milligan* and the historical memory on which it was based would fall into disuse.[101] Over the next two generations, the principles of necessity, loyalty, and national preservation would displace the libertarian ideals of the American Revolution, and the nationalist commemoration of the Civil War would become the foundation of modern patriotism.

CLEANSING THE MEMORY OF THE REVOLUTION: AMERICANISM, THE BLACK LEGION, AND THE FIRST BROWN SCARE

At the end of the Civil War, the dispute over the nature of American patriotism persisted. Republicans during the war had embraced loyalty to a strong national state and that state's monopoly on legitimate violence as the essence of patriotism. In contrast, even at the war's end, Democrats continued to insist that fidelity to the Constitution and to eighteenth-century understandings of liberty and limited government defined a patriotic citizen. They argued that patriotism sometimes demanded the use of revolutionary violence against the state.

Beginning in the 1870s, however, a variety of bourgeois voluntary associations undertook the task of easing the war's divisions by remaking the nation's collective memory of the Founding era, and out of this effort emerged a new patriotic ideal, "one hundred percent Americanism." By the early decades of the twentieth century, the memory of the American Revolution had been recast to emphasize the birth of a national state to which all Americans owed unquestioning obedience. In a similar vein, twentieth-century commemorations of the Civil War emphasized sectional unity, virtuous self-sacrifice, and the noble struggle between the white brethren of the North and South. The libertarian political philosophy that had animated Americans to take up arms against their lawful governments in 1776 and 1863 passed out of mainstream public discussion. From this refashioning of the past emerged an ideal of American-ism that combined the emphasis on loyalty and on the state's monopoly on violence within wartime Republicanism with the assertion of white supremacy so embedded in the culture of rural Democrats during the war.

Yet the memory of the Revolution as a libertarian struggle against the state continued to resonate on the far right of American politics. The Black Legion, the largest right-wing paramilitary organization in the United States during the Great Depression, combined a far right under-standing of liberty as the preservation of white Protestant supremacy and patriarchal control of the home with a memory of the American Revolution that justified the use of revolutionary violence to defend these liberties. The legion accordingly hatched a plot to overthrow the Roosevelt administration in September 1936.

This plot met with widespread condemnation, especially among Democrats and others on the political left. Its disclosure triggered Amer-ica's first Brown Scare, a campaign by the Left designed to demonize op-ponents on the right and far right by portraying them as a "fascist fifth column." In the process of this campaign, Democrats and others on the left embraced the state's monopoly on violence and denounced their po-litical enemies as un-American. They thus crafted their own vision of Americanism and abandoned the libertarian memory of the Revolution that had defined the party's response to the crises of 1798 and 1863.

The Transformation of American Patriotism: Memory, State Power, and the Rise of One Hundred Percent Americanism

In the aftermath of the Civil War the refashioning of collective memory was integral to a generation-long process of crafting a new ideology of American patriotism. The human and psychic losses generated by the Civil War stimulated popular interest in the preservation and celebra-tion of the past. The rise of private organizations such as the Grand Army of the Republic, the Sons and Daughters of the American Revolu-tion, and a host of genealogical societies reflected this desire to honor personal ancestors and national values. These organizations lent themselves to the process of healing the divisions of the war and fashioning a new patriotism based on shared symbols and values. They also brought together members of both political parties and thus ameliorated the partisan strife that had dominated political and social life before and during the war.[1]

As Woden Sorrow Teachout observes in her dissertation on the Sons and Daughters of the American Revolution, Americans in the Gilded Age came to regard the Founding era as central to their search for timeless American values. During the centennial of the Declaration of Independence, these societies collected and preserved artifacts and manuscripts from the Founding era and celebrated the founders as exemplars of true Americanism. These celebrations advanced the cause of national reconciliation by offering the era of the Revolution as a symbol of national unity and self sacrifice, and as a victorious war that all Americans could celebrate without bitterness. Americans thus remembered the Revolution as part of a larger process of forgetting the Civil War. But the remembrance of the Revolution in this period was itself oddly apolitical. The Sons and Daughters lavished loving attention on Revolutionary War uniforms and colonial spinning wheels, objects that illustrated sacrifice but carried no larger political meaning. The libertarian political philosophy and pervasive political violence of the Revolutionary era were wholly absent from these celebrations. In some sense, then, the need to forget so much of the lived experience of the Civil War demanded that political struggles of the Revolution be forgotten as well, even as the Revolution's commemoration became a subject of national attention.[2]

The organizations most responsible for the new culture of patriotic commemoration based membership on proof of lineage dating to the founding or colonial eras. Their memberships were dominated by a bourgeois elite that conceived of the community of "True Americans" in class-specific terms. Thus, in 1876, when the nation confronted a wave of labor radicalism and violent nationwide strikes, these bourgeois organizations all embraced a state monopoly on force in response to the threat of working-class violence. Cecelia O'Leary notes the impact of the railway strike of 1877 on the Grand Army of the Republic, which denounced the strikers as lawless and declared that its members were "willing to take up arms in the cause of law and order," just as they had "crushed treason and rebellion in the past." Teachout argues that the Pullman strike had a similar effect on the Sons and Daughters of the American Revolution. The New York SAR warned that labor unrest posed a greater threat "to our nation and our civilization than did the British Redcoats in '76 or Lee's armies in '61."[3]

This bourgeois embrace of a state monopoly on violence is also reflected in the creation of a new national select militia, the National Guard. Efforts to rebuild the state militia system in the aftermath of the Civil War received new impetus after the railway strike of 1877, particularly in the industrial heartland encompassing New York, Pennsylvania, and the Midwest. These efforts produced voluntary militia organizations that received state recognition and state and federal funding. The officer corps of the Guard was drawn exclusively from the bourgeois elite, and the rank and file was highly transient, guaranteeing that a bourgeois vision of law and order would predominate within these organizations. Industrial magnates frequently provided the Guard with additional funds over and above state and federal appropriations, and just as frequently called upon the Guard to crush strikes. Thus, in the late 1870s, state legislatures and industrial magnates created a new national militia shorn of the insurrectionary legacy of the eighteenth-century militia system. When Illinois workers organized their own militia in 1879 to protect them against the depredations of National Guardsmen and the private police force employed by local industrialists, the Supreme Court ruled in *Presser v. Illinois* that their militia constituted an illegal, private paramilitary.[4]

This embrace of a state monopoly on violence had profound implications for the memory of the Revolution and for the political content of the new Americanism that the various patriotic societies promoted. According to Teachout, the celebration of the Revolution in the 1890s turned increasingly into a celebration of the foundation of the state. Liberty remained a prominent concept within patriotic ideology, but liberty was now more often defined as the opposite of license and anarchy than as the opposite of tyranny. The SAR and DAR began to highlight the contributions of those founders of a Federalist orientation, and in their celebrations the Constitution took pride of place from the Declaration of Independence. These organizations also began to compare the American Revolution to the contemporary struggle against subversion by immigrants, socialists, and anarchists, an outright inversion of the earlier libertarian memory of the struggle. Thus, one patriotic society portrayed its members as "rebels against the socialism and populism of the times," likening their struggle to that of the founders who had rebelled against King George.[5]

In adopting the American flag as a preeminent symbol of patriotism, the patriotic societies practiced a similar inversion. They took the liberty pole, a potent symbol within the libertarian memory of the Revolution, and turned it into the preferred location for the display of the preeminent icon of the national state. In the ritual culture that surrounded the display of the flag in the 1890s, the flag came to stand above all for the sacrifice of the individual to the nation. Presenting a flag to an orphanage in 1894, Major Edward Hunter told the assembled orphans to pray that God would help them to "daily increase in that spirit of Americanism symbolized in today's gift of the sons of the American Revolution, until my flag becomes to me more precious than my blood and as sacred as my religion."[6]

A public commemoration of the Civil War on Memorial Day, 1902, illustrates that manner in which these themes led to the wholesale refashioning of collective memory. On that day, the people of Indiana celebrated the dedication of the Soldiers and Sailors Monument, erected in Indianapolis's Governor's Circle. The festivities began with a march of veterans of the Civil War carrying their regimental banners from the State House to the monument. The marchers entered Governor's Circle and formed ranks before a cheering crowd estimated at 250,000. The monument featured a central pedestal topped with a statue representing Victory. At each corner of the pedestal's base stood a statue of a military leader who had led the state in a time of war. To symbolize the struggle and sacrifice of the Civil War era, a statue of Governor Oliver P. Morton was placed at the monument's southeast corner. Morton's widow featured prominently in the dedication ceremony. The speeches of dedication and the proceedings of meetings of the Grand Army of the Republic and of regimental associations over the course of the weekend emphasized the qualities of loyalty and self-sacrifice with which the people of Indiana had met the crisis of the Union.[7]

In crafting this collective memory of the Civil War as a time of loyal sacrifice under the leadership of Governor Morton, the marchers and spectators expunged the memory of Democratic opposition to the war, even though many of them had been Democrats during the war and some had probably actively participated in that opposition. After the ceremony the veterans marched down Market Street to the State House to lay down their regimental banners for the final time. On this return march they passed the east portico of the State House, where almost forty years before, on May 20, 1863, Democratic congressman Daniel Vorhees had denounced Abraham Lincoln and Governor Morton as co-conspirators in a plot to enslave the people of Indiana. On this spot, five years later, the city would dedicate a second statue of Governor Morton.[8]

Only at one moment during the memorial weekend did the discord of the past rear its head. The day before the dedication, the Indiana branch of the Grand Army of the Republic lashed out at the growing public criticism of the conduct of the United States Army in suppressing the Philippine insurrection. Angered by reports criticizing the army for employing the "water cure" during interrogations of captured insurgents, the meeting passed resolutions denouncing the criticism: "The veterans of the war for the union abhor and despise all citizens of the Unites States who refuse to support our government during the war and cannot see wherein the copperheads of 1898 to 1902 are less venomous than their ancestors." In a resolution cut from the final draft of the statement, but dutifully reported by all of the city's newspapers, the GAR called upon the president to "arrest all such persons, and send them outside our lines."[9] In remaking the memory of the war in a manner that transcended their wartime partisan identities, the assembled GAR delegates banished the name of Clement Vallandigham to a realm of unutterable shame.

By the turn of the century, the themes on exhibit in Indianapolis, loyalty to the state, self-sacrifice, and the intolerance of dissent, had begun to coalesce into a new ideology of patriotic citizenship, one hundred percent Americanism. As this ideology continued to evolve, proponents crafted a limited vision of membership in the newly redefined body politic and excluded those belonging to "unworthy" races and ethnicities. As David W. Blight has noted, the process of national reconciliation demanded the North's acceptance of the South's violent reimposition of white supremacy. As a consequence, African American veterans were effectively erased from the memory of the Civil War, and indeed none of Indiana's black veterans took part in the celebrations of 1902. Furthermore, spokesmen for Americanism proposed denying suffrage to the new wave of immigrants from southern and eastern Europe. They argued that these aliens displayed a racial propensity for subversive and revolutionary activity that demonstrated their unfitness for membership in the body politic.[10]

The 1915 film *The Birth of a Nation* further illustrates this racialization of patriotism. At the end of the film, northern and southern whites regenerate the nation by joining together in the Ku Klux Klan to protect Aryan liberty and white womanhood against the depredations of barbarous blacks, thereby redeeming the battlefield sacrifices of thousands of white men during the war. In its most stirring—or for us, most shocking—moments, the film portrays the castration and lynching of a would-be black rapist, the double marriage of the descendants of a radical Republican congressman and a Southern slaveholder, and the military discipline and prowess of the Klan. The film gave the first Ku Klux Klan a hallowed place in the pantheon of the patriotic defenders of liberty and American institutions.[11]

At first glance, the first Klan seems an unlikely candidate to model the qualities of Americanism. The Klan had begun its career during Reconstruction as an insurgent organization and had offered violence to the officers and policies of the national state.[12] However, according to René Hayden, the Klan did not seek to curb state power so much as seek to restore the relationship between state power and the private enforcement of racial and patriarchal subordination.[13] In his analysis of Reconstruction-era North Carolina, Hayden contrasts the Klan with African American militias that sought to defend the black community against white supremacist violence. Of the two groups, it was the African American militias that behaved in a manner reminiscent of earlier libertarian insurgencies. Organizing military drill before a community audience, displaying arms and military regalia as symbols of popular sovereignty, and acting in daylight to establish their presence within the public sphere, these militias shared the rituals and purposes of the mutual protection associations of the Civil War North. For example, in October 1868 an African American militia in Wayne County, North Carolina, mustered under arms to face down a white posse that had been conducting warrantless searches of the homes of freedmen.[14]

In contrast, the Klan operated for the most part nocturnally. The Klan donned ghostly disguise, thus invoking the supernatural rather than the symbols of popular sovereignty. Klansmen reveled in the brutalization of their victims and used this brutality to terrify both African Americans and whites who transgressed community understandings of gender order. The Klan engaged not only in assassinations, but in rapes and highly sexualized floggings. While the Klan may occasionally have made a pretense of standing against arbitrary power, it in fact sought to reestablish a pre–Civil War order in which the state sanctioned the private and community recourse to arbitrary power to enforce racial and gendered subordination.[15] The Klan was willing to embrace the strong state envisioned by the proponents of Americanism, so long as that state left "patriotic citizens" free to police the hierarchies of race and gender.

As America entered World War I, the tenets of this new ideology of patriotism hardened. Indianapolis celebrated Memorial Day in 1918 with a smaller parade than in 1902, but with a much broader appeal to loyalty, unity, and obedience. Governor James Goodrich declared to the Republican state convention that "there can be no middle course in this war. There are just two kinds of people in America—patriots and traitors. . . . It is the imperative duty of all true Americans to yield cheerful and unquestioned obedience to the government." The rhetoric of the day was also laden with appeals to violence. Indiana senator Harry New declared, "It is a time that demands the most unwavering loyalty from every party and of every man and woman in the country. Who falters should be scourged and who fails us should face the firing squad."[16]

Keynote speaker Albert Beveridge summed up the transformations of collective memory and patriotic identity when he promised the assembled veterans that the soldiers of the Great War would form a new Grand Army of the Republic, "a solid and unmixed host of pure and unadulterated Americanism. Unspoiled by alien dyes, the old flag that you and your fathers carried to victory will wave above them, once more triumphant, the unfading symbol of an undying nation. The members of this new Grand Army will keep your camp fires burning; and their clear voices and strong arms will uphold your principles of loyalty to the republic and devotion to liberty."[17]

Beginning in the summer of 1919, that new Grand Army would take the field. Soldiers returning home from World War I would ally themselves with the American Legion, the Ku Klux Klan, and the attorney general of the United States. Together they would unleash a wave of political and racial violence from the streets of Washington, DC, to the union halls of the Northwest, to the African American neighborhoods of Tulsa, Oklahoma.[18] In the 1920s, many of those returning soldiers would join the second Ku Klux Klan. A decade later some of them would join the Black Legion.

The Black Legion and the Far Right Appropriation of the American Revolution

The origins of the Black Legion lay in the political, economic, and ethnic tensions that had been building in the industrial Midwest for several decades. The industrial cities of the region had absorbed hundreds of thousands of migrants since the turn of the century. Native-born white Protestants who had migrated from the rural areas, African American migrants from the South, and Catholic and Jewish immigrants from Europe competed for jobs and neighborhoods. Industrialists exacerbated tensions by playing on ethnic divisions and importing large numbers of African American workers as strikebreakers. In the 1920s, the second Ku Klux Klan grew rapidly across the entire region, numbering twenty-four thousand members in 1924 in the Detroit region alone.[19]

The Great Depression hit Michigan particularly hard, and the competition for the rapidly shrinking number of industrial jobs further intensified racial and ethnic tensions. In 1933, the national banking panic peaked in Michigan. Automobile and steel plants in Ohio and Michigan laid off hundreds of thousands of workers. In Detroit alone a quarter of a million people were on relief rolls. Communist-organized unemployment councils set up soup kitchens, interfered with evictions, and organized full employment rallies. When Dearborn police fired on a council-organized march to the Ford auto plant in March 1932, sixty thousand Detroit residents turned out for the victims' funeral and marched down Woodward Avenue singing the Internationale.[20]

The coming of the New Deal in 1932 politicized these tensions. Democrats represented groups whose political participation Americanism had disdained, including industrial workers, Catholics, Jews, and African Americans. Furthermore, the New Deal represented the repudiation of the constitutional orthodoxies of the Gilded Age. The New Deal rested on sweeping delegations of legislative power to the executive branch, novel interpretations of the federal government's taxing power, and the creation of dozens of government agencies at the state and federal level. For example, the National Recovery Administration's attempt to regulate the marketplace broadly interfered with the rights of property and contract as they had been interpreted since the Civil War.[21] In Michigan and Ohio, the refusal of the state and federal governments to use force against striking workers transformed the balance of power between workers and employers. The United Auto Workers responded by launching sit-down strikes to organize the automobile industry. The UAW campaign began a wave of sit-down strikes that brought Detroit business to a standstill in February and March 1937.[22]

The New Deal soon came under political attack from conservatives of all stripes. Conservative Democrats led by Al Smith and John W. Davis organized the American Liberty League and charged that the New Deal had destroyed the constitutional balance among the branches of the federal government and had usurped powers reserved to the states. The league argued that this centralization of power within the executive branch was but the first step of a secret plan to establish Roosevelt as the nation's dictator. In the words of Raoul E. Desvernine, the chairman of the league's National Lawyers Committee, New Deal measures represented "an attempt to substitute Americanism with Totalitarianism—

Constitutional Democracy with Autocracy." The league also suggested that open disobedience of federal law might be a legitimate mode of opposition.[23]

The language used by far right critics of the New Deal was more violent, and contained a strong dose of conspiratorial anti-Semitism. For example, William Dudley Pelley, founder of the Silver Shirt Legion and one of the most prominent figures on the American far right in the 1930s, charged that a "Judeo-Bolshevik" cabal based in Europe was in firm control of Roosevelt's administration. In 1936, he predicted that this cabal would overthrow Roosevelt and establish a dictatorship, at which point the Silver Shirts would take up arms to defend the nation from the conspirators.[24] Father Charles Coughlin, a Detroit-area priest who broadcast a nationally syndicated radio show, came out in opposition to Roosevelt and the New Deal in the middle of Roosevelt's first term. In 1936, Coughlin repeatedly charged that Roosevelt was in league with Communists and "Jewish international bankers." In a speech in Cincinnati, Coughlin warned menacingly that "when any upstart dictator," a reference to Roosevelt, "succeeds in making of this nation a one party form of government, and the ballot becomes useless, I shall have the courage to stand up and advocate the use of bullets."[25]

At the local level, anti-Communist organizations, some organized by the region's automobile manufacturers, threatened vigilante violence against the Left. The leader of one Michigan organization declared that "when American workingmen had to pay dues to a union in order to hold a job the time had come to fight." In 1936, a Pontiac judge suspended the sentences of vigilantes who had publicly flogged members of the city's unemployment council, noting that Communist agitation had aroused the defendants' "zeal for the American flag."[26]

It was in this climate that the Black Legion made its debut on the national stage. Dr. William Shepard, a Bellaire, Ohio, Klansman, founded the legion in 1925 in an attempt to reinvigorate the second Klan by returning to the drama and ceremony of the Klan's first, Reconstruction-era incarnation. Whereas the second Ku Klux Klan in the North had enjoyed its greatest popularity as a social and political organization that operated in the light of day, Shepard returned to nocturnal meetings as a recruiting device and wrote an elaborate initiation ritual designed to enhance the "mystery" of the Klan. Legion initiations took place in darkened basements, re-creating the atmosphere of the underground caves in which the first Klan had initiated members. Shepard also reinstituted the rituals of coerced initiation practiced during Reconstruction, when Klansmen had taken the oath with a noose around their neck. In Shepard's ceremony, initiates were handed a pistol cartridge, and warned that if they ever attempted to leave the legion, they would get the other half (i.e., a bullet). Whereas Midwest leaders of the second Klan had focused on amassing political power at the polls and frowned on violence as a blot on the Klan's reputation, Shepard disdained public parades and open political organization. He created the legion "to maintain southern chivalry and the ideals of the South before the Civil War," and under his leadership, the legion engaged in vigilante "night riding" to enforce prohibition and punish moral transgression.[27]

Shepard envisioned the legion as an elite organization within the Klan, and he dressed his followers in black robes to set them off against the white robes of the Klan rank and file. His methods put him at odds with Midwest Klan chief James Colescott, however, and Colescott expelled Shepard and his followers from the invisible order. Nevertheless, the Black Legion established units of at least several hundred members each in the prominent towns in the Ohio River valley surrounding Bellaire, as well as in the industrial cities of Cleveland and Youngstown.[28]

In 1932, Virgil Effinger, a Lima, Ohio, electrician, paid Shepard a visit and proposed to establish legion units in western Ohio and southern Michigan. Shepard agreed to let Effinger use his ritual and retained the figurehead title of national commander.[29] In Effinger's hands, the legion turned into a larger, more violent, and potentially revolutionary organization. Effinger organized it along explicitly paramilitary lines, departing from Shepard's emphasis on fraternalism. The basic unit of legion affiliation was a company of one hundred members, divided into five-man squads. Larger units included regiments with a nominal strength of sixteen hundred men, commanded by a colonel. In Oakland County, Michigan, companies met for military drill in a secluded field outside Pontiac. The legion also conducted firearms training at general musters of Michigan regiments in Saline and at training sessions for Ohio regiments in Bowling Green. Legion gatherings of up to five thousand members took place in Oxford, Michigan, and at a farm outside of Toledo, Ohio.[30]

The legion spread quickly across the industrial heartland of southeastern Michigan, northern Ohio, and the lake shore cities of Indiana. Isaac "Peg Leg" White, a retired Detroit policeman, and Arthur Lupp, a Detroit milk inspector and lay preacher, founded the Michigan organization in 1932. The Detroit metropolitan area had six active regiments by 1936 with a total strength of eight thousand. The legion organized additional units in Oakland, Genesee, Monroe, and Jackson counties and in Saginaw, Battle Creek, and Grand Rapids.[31] In Ohio, units in Toledo and Lima enrolled over three thousand members each, and smaller units were organized in Wayne County, Bucyrus, Akron, and Sandusky. In Indiana, legion units with a total membership of less than one thousand organized in Fort Wayne, Gary, and South Bend.[32] The best estimate of total legion membership is fifteen thousand in Michigan and ten thousand in Ohio and Indiana combined.[33]

The legion recruited the bulk of its membership from two occupational categories, semiskilled workers in the industrial plants surrounding Detroit and Pontiac and public employees. The legion also included a smattering of professionals, businessmen, and aspiring politicians in its ranks. Significantly, however, the Detroit legion segregated businessmen into a separate regiment, indicating that the legion's leaders feared that the organization's working-class culture would grate on middle-class members.[34] Two other common denominators among legion members were southern origin and previous Klan affiliation. Of the defendants tried in the murder of Charles Poole, two-thirds were from states where slavery had been legal before the Civil War. Five top-ranking legion officers in Michigan tried for breaking up a political meeting in Detroit were all born in the upper South. Finally, almost all of the legion defendants and many of those who testified during grand jury investigations in Michigan reported previous membership in the Klan. According to several witnesses, legion recruiters targeted former Klansmen and sometimes told initiates that the legion was a "higher degree" of Klan affiliation.[35]

The ideology of the legion was best illustrated on a spring night in 1934, when fifteen hundred residents of the Detroit suburbs gathered in a field outside of Romeo, to witness the initiation of recruits. After the initiates had been sworn in, the colonel of the legion's Eighth Regiment stepped forward to explain the origin and purposes of the organization. The legion, he explained, was descended from the Boston Sons of Liberty, and the Minutemen who fought the Revolution had been members. More recently, the guerillas who fought under abolitionist John Brown and Confederate William Quantrill had carried on the tradition. The legion, he claimed, had organized the original Ku Klux Klan under Nathan Bedford Forrest. As members of the legion, he declared, "We regard as enemies to ourselves and our country all aliens, Negroes, Jews and cults and creeds believing in racial equality or owing allegiance to any foreign potentate. These we will fight without fear or favor as long as one foe of American liberty is left alive."[36]

This juxtaposition of the appeal to the founding of the nation and the fight against Jews, Catholics, and Communists was central to legion ideology. The Black Legion of Genesee County similarly declared that it was ready to take up arms to fight "political Romanism, Judaism, and Communism and all other isms which our forefathers came to this country to avoid."[37] Legionnaires saw themselves as fighting for the liberty that was their birthright as descendants of the founding generation. In their minds, liberty, as Communism's antithesis, stood for economic independence, decentralized government, the end of elite control, and, most importantly, the right to actively enforce white Protestant supremacy and patriarchal morality. The legion saw the defense of these facets of liberty as a patriotic duty, and as a masculine prerogative.

Arthur Lupp, the Michigan commander of the legion, summed up the organization's objective as taking "the Jew out of business and the Catholic out of Politics." Another legion member from Genesee County noted that "the Republican Party was controlled by the Jewish bankers of Wall Street, and the Democrats were controlled by the Pope of Rome."[38] The vision of a conspiracy of elite Jewish bankers was an anti-Semitic reworking of traditional themes within nativist conspiracy discourse dating back to the Illuminati scare of the 1790s. It illustrated the class anxieties and economic insecurity generated by the Depression. Jews in this vision came to stand for both the industrial elite and immigrant workers. Both groups threatened the class position of native workers and small businessmen, and the legion perceived both as an alien, international menace. As the legion's ritual put it, "the native born white people of America are menaced on every hand from above and below. If America is in the melting pot, the white people of America are neither the aristocratic scum on top nor the dregs of society on the bottom."[39]

References to the pope revealed the legion's sectarian hostility toward Catholicism. Members swore at their initiation to oppose "by force of arms if necessary" the use of public funds to support the institutions of the Catholic Church, a common source of sectarian tension in this period. The legion distributed literature warning that the Catholic clergy posed a profound threat to the sanctity of the family and to patriarchal authority. For example, in Highland Park members handed out the *Rail Splitter,* an anti-Catholic newspaper published by Illinois KKK figure William Lloyd Clark. But references to the pope also signified resentment of distant and hierarchical control. As Dayton Dean, the legion gunman who killed Charles Poole, explained it, the legion directed its animus not toward Catholics as individuals but toward "those who ran the church, because . . . the Catholic people were compelled to take their orders from the Pope in Rome." The growing federal regulation of the economy during the Depression, the advent of the union shop, and the experience of regimentation in the relief programs of the New Deal brought new experiences of distant authority to the lives of many in the industrial Midwest. Legionnaires proved viscerally hostile to these trends.[40]

If the legion's preoccupation with Judaism and Catholicism thus represented economic insecurity coupled with a dose of sectarian bigotry, its preoccupation with Communism stemmed from more profound issues of identity. Legionnaires saw Communism as a threat to Christianity as a whole, to patriarchy, and to whiteness.

Arthur Lupp and regimental commander Wilbur Robinson saw Communist atheism as a threat to all religious life. They feared that a central objective of Communists in America was to undermine Christianity in America much as they had in Russia. A leaflet written by the legion purporting to be a campaign manifesto of Detroit labor lawyer Maurice Sugar portrayed Sugar as a Communist whose motto was "close the churches and make the buildings into shelters for the homeless men and women. Down with the religion that is the opium which the ruling class feeds to you to keep you satisfied with the miserable existence which you lead. There is no God."[41]

But members of the legion were even more concerned with Communism's celebration of racial and gender equality. When officers explained the history of the legion to new recruits, they described the maintenance of white supremacy as part of the organization's patriotic heritage: "After the Civil War, the northern politicians attempted to regard the South as conquered territory to force racial equality on the people. It was then that the Rider Organization under the great General Nathan Bedford Forrest organized the Ku Klux Klan." Virgil Effinger also articulated the legion's desire to uphold the racial order of white supremacy, explaining that the organization aimed to "encourage the colored man to have enough pride in himself to accept his place in the scheme of things. He is better off if he remains the way he is, a race apart." For the legion, the preservation of white liberty meant the absence of contact between the races. One member testified that he had been initiated at a meeting called to protest a black family's purchase of a house in a white neighborhood. A Detroit policeman testified that he joined the legion because it was "organized to keep negro children out of schools attended by white children."[42]

The legion proved quite willing to use violence against African Americans who stepped out of their "place in the scheme of things." During legion initiations, recruiters asked potential members their attitude toward lynch law and offered the specific example of the rape of a white woman by a black man to encourage a positive response.[43] Alongside stereotypes of black criminality, the legion played on fears of black self-assertion. The leaflet written by the legion to discredit Maurice Sugar also purported to address Detroit's black community (and thus targeted the fears of neighboring whites) as follows: "This man will fight for your right to marry white women. This man will fight for your right to live in any white neighborhood that you choose."[44] In 1936, members of the legion plotted to murder Clarence Oliver, a black man who had dared to participate in the political process by working for the campaign of Ecorse mayor William Voisine.[45]

The legion used violence to police the hierarchies of gender as well as race. One high-ranking legion officer, convinced that Communism would overthrow moral order in favor of "free love," participated in burning down a Communist organized labor camp in Farmington, Michigan, because he believed it was the site of sexual orgies. The legion also flogged husbands for failing to enforce patriarchal control of households, and most legion violence involved the control of sexuality. The Michigan legion flogged two men in Jackson County as a warning "not to bother other men's wives." In Oakland County, the legion whipped at least one man accused of molesting a young girl. In Ohio, William Shepard's organization targeted women as well as men, tarring one woman and threatening two others with hanging for sexual transgressions.[46]

The masculine anxiety behind this sexualized violence also pervaded the legion's public performances. In large open-field musters, legionnaires came together to engage in performances of virility and armed self-assertion. During the day members practiced shooting with "every type of gun that you can imagine." At night regiments gathered shoulder to shoulder around bonfires to witness the initiation of new recruits at gunpoint. Here, under the midnight sky, these men may have found a masculine agency that few men experienced during the Depression. Yet the legion's performance of masculinity quickly degenerated into caricature. The chaplain's address given to all new legion recruits just before they took their oaths evoked an exaggerated hypermasculinity: "You have already signified a desire to cast your fortunes with us. By doing so, remember that our purpose is to tear down, lay waste, despoil, and kill our enemies. Mercy belongs to sycophants and emasculated soldiers. It has no place in a fighter's outfit."[47]

As performed by members of the Black Legion, however, the manly violence of "southern chivalry" proved uncontrollable and ultimately senseless. In May 1936, Black Legionnaires in Detroit murdered Charles Poole, a Catholic WPA worker. Poole's sister-in-law had heard that Poole was beating his wife, who was eight months pregnant. When legion

Fig. 3. Police officers posing with Black Legion robes and weapons, 1936. *Detroit News.*

The robes and weapons shown here were intended to terrify the enemies of the legion, but with the exposure of the murder of Charles Poole, they quickly became symbols of legion criminality.

colonel Harvey Davis got wind of a Catholic man beating his Protestant wife, he presented the matter to a legion meeting and offered those assembled the opportunity to demonstrate their virility. They responded by calling for Poole's punishment: some yelled, "whip him," others, "hang him," and at least one called out, "shoot him." Later that night members lured Poole to a deserted road on the outskirts of the city. Davis stepped up to Poole and told him, "you've beaten your wife for the last time." Poole protested that his wife was in the hospital having a baby, whereupon Dayton Dean, who would later become the state's central witness against the legion, shot Poole eight times.[48]

Davis later testified that he had only intended to scare Poole and hadn't expected Dean to shoot him. This testimony may have been self-serving, but it is also possible that Dean was so stirred by the frenzy that erupted at the meeting and so intent on proving himself worthy of serving in a "fighter's outfit" that he missed the point of the exercise. Other legion assaults showed a similar volatility. When the legion targeted Clarence Oliver for assassination, they could not locate him. Rather than let the matter go, Harvey Davis picked a black man, James Armour, at random, as Armour was walking home. Davis walked up to Armour and shot him. Armour survived only because his metal lunch pail deflected the bullet.[49]

The murder of Silas Coleman, an African American laborer, displayed legion masculinity at its bleakest. In May 1935, a year before the Poole murder, Harvey Davis had told Dean that he "wanted to know what it was like to kill a Negro." He told Dean to bring a likely candidate out to his vacation place on Rush Lake for some "entertainment." Dean went to a friend, Charles Rouse, who suggested that they take Coleman, with whom he had worked on a building site. They lured Coleman by telling him that they were taking him to find a contractor that owed them all money. When they arrived at Davis's house, Davis told his guests, all legionnaires, that it was time to "have some fun." He said that Coleman had beaten up a white man and they were taking Coleman on a "one-way ride." They took Coleman to the lake, got him out of the car, and opened fire. Coleman escaped into a patch of swamp but died of his wounds before morning.[50]

Taken to its farthest extreme, the legion's definition of liberty asserted the right to kill, at random, for the sheer thrill of it. The *Toledo News-Bee* captured that impulse when it published a cartoon of armed legionnaires parading under an American flag emblazoned with the slogan "The Right to Murder."[51] But in a nation that witnessed an average of twenty lynchings a year as late as 1935, the thrill killing of an African American laborer was not entirely beyond the bounds of Americanism.

It was a plot to overthrow the government of the United States that put the legion beyond the pale of one hundred percent Americanism. During the winter and spring of 1936, the organization's leaders called upon members to prepare themselves to overthrow the Roosevelt administration on September 16, 1936. Some legionnaires interpreted the planned rising, which they referred to under the code name "Lixto," as a legitimate use of force to counter un-American subversion. For example, Carl Moore, a legion colonel in Genesee County, explained that if the code word was issued, "it meant that the enemy was ready to invade the country. Members were to converge upon Washington or Chicago, or wherever the seat of trouble was, to defend the flag, and use forceful means, guns or clubs." Wilbur Robinson, commander of a legion regiment in Detroit, described the legion's readiness to "strike against the reds whenever they attempt a revolution. We'd be ready for them. We were going to volunteer our services to the government. Maybe the army and navy couldn't do the job alone." This emphasis on countersubversive violence to stave off a Communist coup resonated broadly on the far right, and was entirely consistent with the prevailing definition of patriotic Americanism. Thus Wilbur Robinson declared: "If the Legion isn't within the law, I'll quit. I'm 100 per cent American."[52]

There was, however, a second interpretation of the Black Legion's plan for September 16 that suggests that legion ideology transcended the ideological boundaries that had constrained the conservative establishment and most other far right voices in the 1930s. According to multiple witnesses, leaders of the legion broke with every other native-born conservative group and called for an armed rising against the Roosevelt administration on the basis of its policies alone.[53] Charles Harris, an Ohio FBI informant, explained that the legion claimed that "certain laws have been passed, and lots coming up that they object to and will try to beat them by ballot and if they can't they will issue a call for all members to take up arms and fight." A Genesee County informant told the Michigan State Police that the object was to defeat Roosevelt "by vote if possible, by arms if necessary." Dayton Dean testified that Effinger, Lupp, and Isaac White had used similar language, saying, "we'd have to fight them and get the government. If it couldn't be done by ballots, it would have to be done by bullets."[54]

According to these witnesses, the leadership of the legion was actively organizing an insurrection. Dean testified that Effinger had spoken at several meetings in Michigan in which he warned that the legion would "take over the government" on September 16. Dean also charged that a select group of three hundred "Night Riders" had been chosen for the task of "taking over all government buildings and arsenals, power plants and public buildings." George Scheid, a former legion colonel in Allen County, Ohio, told the FBI that he, too, had heard Effinger talk about taking over government buildings. He later told his son that "they were talking about raiding government arsenals and taking away arms and ammunition and starting a revolution against the government." He claimed he had dropped out because of such "revolutionary tactics." Charles Dexter, a legion captain in Detroit, testified that he was told to be prepared for action on September 16, 1936, and that another officer had explained that "we have got to beat the other side to it in the killings."[55]

In 1936, even the most bitter opponents of Roosevelt, including the Liberty League, Charles Coughlin, and William Dudley Pelley, largely refrained from advocating violence against the state. The key to the legion's capacity to transcend Americanism's prohibition on revolutionary violence appears to lie in the role of the American Revolution in the legion's collective memory. For all that legion ideology and ritual owed to Nathan Bedford Forrest, the Ku Klux Klan, and one hundred percent Americanism, the organization's celebration of the memory of the Revolution seems to have allowed members to justify a broader range of violent activity, including the overthrow of a government they deemed a threat to "American liberty."[56]

In a typescript describing the history of the legion, the organization is portrayed as a working-class version of the Order of Cincinnatus. According to this history, the order was founded "by a man by the name of Samuel Adams, and its first escapade was the Boston Tea Party. The Minutemen who fought the Revolution were members, and it was organized in all of the thirteen colonies." The typescript continues to trace a genealogy through "Jim Lane of the Jayhawkers and John Brown" described as "two of the most famous northern riders."[57]

What Samuel Adams, the Minutemen, and John Brown shared was the impulse toward extralegal violence against the state. In celebrating this patriotic lineage, the legion crafted a collective memory that justified insurrectionary violence. Andrew Martin, a legion officer from

Detroit, declared that legion initiates pledged to fight "a guerilla war in defense of the United States Constitution" and cited the Boston Tea Party as an example of American patriots "taking things into their own hands." The memory of the Revolution as a struggle against a despotic state was also articulated in the Genessee County legion manifesto, which declared:

> we believe that the first 10 amendments of the Constitution of the United States . . . mean exactly what they say and if there is no other honorable way to maintain respect for the Constitution and amendments, we of the Black Legion will fight for the preservation and obedience of same by all who want to be citizens of this great republic, as did our forefathers against the tyrannical rule of King George III of England.[58]

In searching for a text on which to ground the libertarian memory of the American Revolution, legionaries settled on the Second Amendment rather than the Declaration of Independence. When interviewed by the FBI in April 1936, Virgil Effinger quoted the Second Amendment in support of the proposition that "it is sometimes right and necessary, in his opinion, for the patriotic citizens of this country to take the law into their own hands." Choosing the Second Amendment as the vessel of this memory allowed Effinger to avoid the Declaration of Independence's avowal of human equality. The Second Amendment thus allowed legionnaires to celebrate the memory of armed resistance in the past alongside their quest for racial and patriarchal domination in the present. Arthur Lupp illustrated the potency of combining these themes when he urged listeners to defend the right to bear arms "if you have any of the spirit of the forefathers who fought and died to preserve this nation, if you have any love for your family, if you have any desire to protect the lives of little children against the attacks of criminals, if you have any desire to maintain the semblance of your constitutional rights, if you have any spark of that thing that is called manhood in your makeup."[59]

The legion thus fused the exclusionary vision of the body politic on which one hundred percent Americanism rested with an older vision of Americanism that celebrated the capacity of the people to take up arms and throw off a "traitorous" government. The legion resurrected the libertarian memory of patriotic revolution suppressed after the Civil War and sought to use it to advance the Far Right's agenda of ridding the nation of Roosevelt and his supposed cabal of Communists, Catholics, and Jews.[60] In 1936, however, the legion's vision of a popular uprising lacked any connection to political and organizational reality: the militia structure employed by Civil War–era Democrats was long gone, and gone with it were the homogenous communities that had given the mutual protection associations their political force. In the event that they were called to arms under the code word Lixto, legionnaires were told to grab their guns and start walking down the road to Washington, DC. Someone, they were assured, would give them a lift. Presumably that someone would also know where to go and what to do.

The plan for September 16, 1936, was far-fetched, and long before then, the legion had collapsed under the pressure of multiple criminal indictments and mutual recrimination. Nonetheless, critics on the left regarded the plot as all too real, and they charged that the legion represented the cutting edge of a new species of alien subversion, the coalescence of a fascist fifth column in America.

The Suppression of the Black Legion, the Brown Scare, and the Democratic Negation of the American Revolution

The news of the legion's responsibility for the murder of Charles Poole broke on May 22, 1936, ten days after his death. In June, investigators announced that they had uncovered evidence of the plot for September 16. Over the course of the summer, as state authorities in Michigan and Ohio systematically dismantled the Black Legion, evidence of other legion crimes, including the shootings of James Armour and Silas Coleman, came to light. State authorities secured indictments against much of the organization's leadership for the murders of Poole and Coleman, as well as several attempted murders, kidnappings, and arsons. Local governments in Michigan began a systematic purge of legion members from public payrolls. Michigan authorities soon reported that Black Legionnaires were burning their robes. Finally, at the end of August a

Michigan grand jury indicted legion chief Virgil Effinger and twenty-two others for violating Michigan's criminal syndicalism statute, a 1919 law criminalizing the advocacy of violence as a means of political change.[61]

The defendants were convicted and punished for their crimes, but they were condemned for their thoughts. Moreover, the public condemnation of the legion created a climate that led to the prosecution of other members of the Far Right on the basis of their political philosophies and public statements alone. News editorials and political figures were quick to denounce the legion. Condemnation was bipartisan, but the content of the liberal response to the legion was particularly striking, for in denouncing the vicissitudes of the Far Right, New Deal Democrats and their political allies in the far left Popular Front embraced the rhetoric of Americanism. The legion, they argued, represented a degraded class of un-American terrorists and the cutting edge of an alien conspiracy against American freedom.

The depiction of Black Legionnaires as a particularly degraded class of humanity began within days of the news of Charles Poole's murder. The *Detroit News* denounced the membership of the legion as vigilantes of "abysmal ignorance, of despicable intolerance, and a predisposition to violence of a craven sort." Michigan governor Frank Fitzgerald warned that the legion was evidence that America harbored "a fanatical and ignorant element eager to bring about the destruction of our democracy." Governor George Earle of Pennsylvania, speaking in Detroit in early June, went further, charging that the legion was "an example of the new fascism preying on ignorance and petty human vanity, spawned in the diseased minds of fanatics and bigots."[62]

As for the principles for which the legion stood, Democrats did not hesitate to brand them as un-American. Governor Fitzgerald ridiculed the legion's embrace of Americanism: "In actuality they are a group of one hundred percent anti-Americans. And as such they should be regarded by all patriotic citizens." A group of thirty prominent liberals wrote a public letter to Roosevelt in support of a congressional resolution calling for an investigation of the Black Legion and other organizations "spreading similar un-American propaganda of religious, racial, or subversive political prejudices." The *Washington Times* declared, "Intolerance has no place in the American scheme of things, and homicidal fanatics of the Black Legion type have no place in America."[63]

If intolerance marked the legion as un-American, so too did its advocacy of violence against the state. Democrats were quick to join Republicans in declaring that the legion's embrace of insurgent political violence marked them as un-American. The Republican *Indianapolis News* blasted the legion in an editorial, declaring that "in a free country the duty of every citizen disaffected with the policies of government is to work for improvement by use of the ballot. No other plan can be tolerated. Terrorism in any form is a menace to free government, and to peace and good order, and its authors are enemies of society." Governor Fitzgerald argued that the legion's "reign of terrorism" was all the more despicable for its attempt to "hide its crimes behind the Constitution." He promised that "every ounce of power and authority vested in the state" would be brought to bear on "this organized outlawry." The *New York Post* also called for a vindication of the state's monopoly on violence, declaring that "America doesn't want and should not tolerate secret armed terrorist bands."[64]

Progressives were quick to charge that the legion was part of a larger fascist conspiracy that had taken root in America, a theme that originated on the far left but quickly spread into mainstream discussion. In June, a headline in the *Daily Worker* announced that a "united front with Hitler" was the objective of the legion and its allies on the far right. The *Detroit News* and *New York Times* published stories suggesting that the Black Legion's exposure had interrupted its plans to amalgamate with William Dudley Pelley's Silver Shirts. Both papers also quoted Detroit prosecutor Duncan McRae's suggestion that the legion represented the tip of a national organization that was preparing a fascist coup similar to an alleged plot that Major General Smedley Butler had warned of in 1934. Governor Earle of Pennsylvania drew the circle wider still: "I say to you that the money changers and the great industrialists behind the Liberty League and the present Republican party leadership cannot escape responsibility for this creature of their malicious, shameless propaganda against the Government of the United States. The Black Legion is the first fruit of their campaign for Fascism, and the blood of Charles Poole is on their hands."[65]

Progressives called for the legion's suppression with language that mirrored the violence of calls for the suppression of dissent during World War I. The *Detroit Free Press* responded to the legion with an editorial titled simply "Stamp It Out." The *Detroit News* applauded Detroit police commissioner Heinrich Pickert's order that "the gang murderers who styled themselves the Black Legion" should be "exterminated." The *Asbury Park Press* and the *Washington News* also called for the "extermination" of the legion. An editorial cartoon in the *Hartford Times* depicted the legion as a collection of masked snakes under the headline "Wipe Out the Whole Brood!" A cartoon in the *Washington Times* depicted the legion as a snake whose head had been crushed by a rock labeled "Americanism."[66]

In these statements lie the seeds of a liberal embrace of important aspects of one hundred percent Americanism. New Deal liberals rejected the nativism and white supremacy of legion ideology as un-American. They thereby accepted Americanism's exclusionary vision of a body politic to which some Americans must be denied entry. In the 1930s progressives placed the racist, nativist "other" into the civic exile previously reserved by proponents of Americanism for racial and ethnic minorities. Moreover, secure for the first time in their control of the violent apparatus of the state, progressives also embraced the principle of a state monopoly on violence. In 1936, progressives sought to rhetorically and legally "stamp out" revolutionaries of the Right, to cast them out of the body politic just as Communists and socialists had been suppressed in the heyday of one hundred percent Americanism.

Though New Deal liberals did not call down vigilante violence upon far right groups, they did launch a systematic campaign of public condemnation and state repression that Leo P. Ribuffo has dubbed the "Brown Scare." Sustained attention to the allegedly fascist tendencies of the American Far Right had begun in 1934 in the pages of the *Nation*, the *New Republic*, and *American Mercury*, and in the hearings of Congressman Samuel Dickstein's Special Committee on Un-American Activities. Hollywood also turned its attention to the problem, using documentary newsreels, particularly *The March of Time*, to alert the public to the dangers of "the lunatic fringe."[67]

The Brown Scare intensified after the exposure and suppression of the Black Legion. Friends for Democracy and the Institute for Propaganda Analysis, both founded in 1937, provided an institutional foundation for the analysis of the American Far Right and the publicizing of its dangers. The institute sponsored educational outreach programs to train high school and college students in propaganda recognition. Perhaps more importantly, Friends of Democracy initiated the collection of dossiers on leading figures of the Far Right, relying in part on material collected by confidential informants. Both organizations publicized the danger that the American Far Right posed to the nation as a potential source of support for a fascist coup. Their activities contributed to the publication of a wave of books and reports over the next five years, including Harold Lavine's *Fifth Column in America* and Avedis Derounian's *Under Cover*.[68]

As the United States entered World War II, the rhetorical assault on the Far Right that had intensified with the breakup of the Black Legion was enhanced by a systematic campaign of state repression. In late 1936, President Roosevelt ordered FBI director J. Edgar Hoover to investigate "subversive activities in the United States, particularly Fascism and Communism." In the ensuing years, Hoover built files on far right subversives and began a "custodial detention index." Government investigations spread from far right agitators like William Dudley Pelley to more mainstream opponents of American entry into World War II. FBI investigations often involved covert surveillance, interviews with neighbors and employers, the opening of mail, and leaks of grand jury testimony to the press.[69]

Government efforts to suppress the Far Right reached their culmination during the war in a series of political show trials. Though the Black Legion had engaged in armed organization and criminal activity, most of those prosecuted during the Brown Scare had not gone beyond the realm of political speech. In 1942, the administration prosecuted William Dudley Pelley in federal district court for conspiring to disseminate information designed to impair the operations of the armed forces. To remove Pelley from the political scene during the war, Roosevelt used precisely the same tool that Woodrow Wilson had used against socialist leader Eugene Debs a quarter century before: the Espionage Act of 1917. The government then launched the sedition prosecution of thirty leaders of the Far Right, including Pelley, Gerald Winrod, Elizabeth Dilling, Lawrence Dennis, James True, Robert Edmonson, and Gerhard Wilhelm Kunze. Finally, the city of Chicago prosecuted Gerald L. K. Smith and Arthur Terminiello for breach of the peace, a charge stemming from a 1945 lecture in Chicago at which protesters turned riotous and the city authorities blamed the two speakers for inflaming the crowd.[70]

Though the government played up spurious evidence linking the defendants to Nazi Germany, at their core these cases involved the suppression of far right political philosophy and the denial of the right of free speech. In each trial the prosecution bolstered its claim that the defendants were part of an international subversive conspiracy by denouncing their ideas as un-American and beyond the pale of legitimate politics. According to Leo Ribuffo, the roots of these Brown Scare prosecutions lay in a liberal embrace of "liberty for our side only," and in the denigration of far right speech as "propaganda" tending to "poison" the minds of "innocent dupes."[71]

For the American Left generally, the adoption of the countersubversive tenets of Americanism came at a cost. The institutions and rhetorical tactics of the Brown Scare would come back to haunt the Left after World War II, as a resurgent Republican Party launched a second Red Scare under the leadership of Joseph McCarthy and Richard Nixon.

For the Democratic Party in particular, the cost was higher still: in branding the Black Legion's vision of revolution as fascist terrorism, the party suggested that any assertion of the right of revolution was itself un-American. The party thus surrendered a fundamental tenet of its collective memory and a linkage to its eighteenth-century roots. That ideological sacrifice is perhaps best symbolized by the central New Deal contribution to the commemoration of the American Revolution: the Jefferson Memorial. The memorial, inaugurated in 1943, featured a towering bronze statue of the cofounder of the Democratic Party, surrounded by four marble panels with inscriptions from Jefferson's writings. As Pauline Maier has observed, when the Jefferson Memorial Commission crafted the inscription to commemorate Jefferson's authorship of the Declaration of Independence, they decided to cut from the final text Jefferson's articulation of the right of revolution: "That whenever any Form of Government becomes destructive of these ends, it is the Right of the People to alter or to abolish it, and to institute new Government, laying its foundation on such principles and organizing its powers in such form, as to them shall seem most likely to effect their Safety and Happiness." With this simple bureaucratic decision, New Deal Democrats effaced the meaning of the American Revolution as Jefferson and much of the founding generation of the Democratic Party had understood it.[72]

By the onset of the Cold War, both parties had accepted a state monopoly on legitimate political violence and denied that revolutionary violence had any place within American political theory. Though the patriotic celebration of a continuing right of revolution lived on at either end of the American political spectrum, political leaders sought to brand this idea as extremist and deny its adherents access to the public sphere. This impulse to silence consumed the words of Thomas Jefferson just as it had earlier consumed those of Clement Vallandigham.

THE MAKING OF THE SECOND BROWN SCARE:
LIBERAL PLURALISM AND THE EVOLUTION OF
THE WHITE SUPREMACIST RIGHT

The Republican embrace of a new ideal of patriotism during the Civil War marked the beginning of a new era in American history. Over the next century, first Republicans and later Democrats repudiated the insurgent violence that had characterized the onset of the American Revolution. They also abandoned the libertarian memory of the American Revolution that had played a fundamental role in early American politics. In the nineteenth century, American conservatives fashioned a nationalist memory of the Revolution as a tool in their campaign against working-class "subversives." A generation later, with the onset of the New Deal, it was American liberals who argued that fantasies of revolutionary violence marked the Far Right as "un-American."

After World War II, attempts to exclude the Far Left and Far Right from access to the public sphere received reinforcement from social scientists concerned by the rise of Senator Joseph McCarthy. Employing modern psychology and social theory, Theodore Adorno, Richard Hofstadter, Daniel Bell, Seymour Martin Lipset, and Alan Westin offered an evaluation of right-wing movements in the postwar world that defined a boundary between "mainstream" liberal pluralist politics and a realm of "extremism" characterized by paranoia, Manichaean political thought, and intolerance. In drawing this line, liberal pluralist scholars generally agreed that groups engaging in "hate mongering" and the "advocacy of violence" belonged within the realm of "extremism."[1]

The liberal pluralist theory of extremism perpetuated the exclusionary vision of Americanism that the Left had embraced during the Brown Scare. In 1955 Richard Hofstadter famously denounced the "pseudo-conservatives" of the extremist Right as enemies of Americanism. Quoting at length from Adorno's *Authoritarian Personality*, Hofstadter declared that "the pseudo-conservative is a man who, in the name of upholding traditional American values and institutions and defending them against more or less fictitious dangers, consciously or unconsciously aims at their abolition." The two qualities that marked this false patriot, Adorno and Hofstadter argued, were fearfulness and violence: "'conventionality and authoritarian submissiveness' in his conscious thinking and 'violence, anarchic impulses and chaotic destructiveness in the unconscious sphere.'"[2]

In crafting the mainstream/extremist paradigm, liberal pluralists maintained that their task was the accurate characterization of the observable political and psychological behaviors that they dubbed the "Paranoid Style." But liberal pluralism was from its inception a prescriptive political program. When confronted with the question of what was to be done with American extremists, pluralists suggested that the answer lay in a concerted program of intellectual and cultural containment consistent with the mainstream norm of tolerance. Alan Westin, for example, suggested that the solution lay in "policing the boundaries" of "respectable" conservatism: "the containment of the radical right is at hand. But it will always be containment, rather than extinction."[3]

In practice, combining "containment" and "tolerance" proved problematic. The containment of the Far Left and Far Right during the Cold War proceeded well beyond "resistance to their destructive proposals through public debate and the defense of policies."[4] It involved the systematic policing of the public sphere to prevent the transmission of "extremist" content. After World War II opponents of "extremism" utilized a combination of cultural authority, exclusionary rhetoric, and influence within mass media institutions to contain the ideas, personalities, and organizations of the Far Left and Far Right and wall them off from the public sphere.

The task of maintaining this containment fell largely to private civil rights organizations. Some of these organizations had played a significant role in promoting the scholarship of liberal pluralism. The American Jewish Committee, for example, supported Theodore Adorno's research and published the first edition of *The Authoritarian Personality*. The Anti-Defamation League played the same role in the publication of Seymour Martin Lipset's *Politics of Unreason*. These two groups would have a central part in the containment of the Far Right. When Gerald L. K. Smith, a leading figure on the Far Right, began prop-agating conspiratorial anti-Semitism after World War II, Rabbi S. A. Fineberg of the American Jewish Committee coordinated the efforts of the AJC and other organizations to block Smith's access to the media. These efforts involved securing the cooperation of major media outlets and persuading them to ignore Smith's public events. Civil rights orga-nizations also persuaded Smith's opponents to let Smith speak without protest, thereby depriving him of the public incident that would force the press to cover his activities. Perfected against Smith, this strategy of "dynamic silence" was again utilized against George Lincoln Rockwell, the leader of the American Nazi Party (ANP), in the early 1960s.[5]

The Anti-Defamation League tended to take a more activist ap-proach to containing the Far Right. The ADL began to collect dossiers and conduct covert surveillance of far right activists shortly before World War II. The organization publicly denounced Gerald L. K. Smith's anti-Semitism before the U.S. Senate in 1950. It also employed the court system, filing an amicus brief in favor of the prosecution of Smith and Arthur Terminiello for breach of the peace and suing to prevent the ANP from holding private rallies in 1960. Finally, the ADL lobbied local gov-ernments to prevent road construction that would provide improved ac-cess to a biblical theme park built by Gerald L. K. Smith in Eureka Springs, Arkansas.[6]

Within the borders of this proscribed realm of "extremism," the ideo-logical justification of revolutionary violence took new forms. Some groups on the far left and far right continued to celebrate the American Revolution. Others modeled themselves on twentieth-century totalitar-ian movements. A few creative intellectuals crafted entirely new collective memories with which to justify violence. Some groups cooperated and shared ideas, while others shared nothing but their common exile and the frequent experience of political, legal, and cultural repression.

On the far left, Robert F. Williams, leader of the NAACP in Monroe, North Carolina, organized an African American militia in 1957 to defend Monroe's black community against white supremacist attacks. Williams's militia had roots in a tradition of African American collective self-defense dating from Reconstruction, but he also drew upon the memory of the American Revolution to justify his recourse to armed organization. "Tom Paine, Washington, Jefferson, and Patrick Henry were honorable men," he wrote in 1960, "who are supposed to represent the true spirit of America. These noble men advocated violence as a vehicle of liberation." For his advocacy of violence, Williams was banished from the NAACP, reported to the FBI as a Communist infiltrator by Thurgood Marshall, and eventually forced to flee the country.[7]

On the far right three ideological developments reinforced earlier connections between white supremacy and revolutionary violence. The first was the emergence of Christian Identity, an elaborate racist theology crafted from British-Israelism, conspiratorial anti-Semitism, and Christian premillennialism. British-Israelism held that the Anglo-Saxons were the true descendants of the lost tribes of Israel. Identity built upon earlier versions of British-Israelism by its elaboration of several variants of "two-seedline doctrine," which maintained that Jews and other nonwhite races were the racial product of a separate creation from whites. Within Christian Identity theology, Jews were described as the seed of the union of Eve and Satan, the literal "spawn of Satan." Christian Identity thus racialized Christianity in a manner that dehumanized both Jews and nonwhites.[8]

Christian Identity had a significant influence on William Potter Gale, one of the authors of the second significant evolution in far right thought, a new strain of constitutionalism that would serve as the basis of the Posse Comitatus movement. Rejecting the strong Cold War state and its dedication to pluralism, Gale justified the radical decentralization of state power by crafting a memory of the Founding era that left the Constitution of 1787 entirely forgotten. In 1971, Gale argued that "in the formation of this constitutional republic, the county has always been and remains to this day, the true seat of the government for the citizens of who are inhabitants thereof." He argued that the ancient Anglo-Saxon institution of the posse comitatus, composed of all male citizens eighteen to forty-five, remained the sovereign lawmaking body. The members of the posse could sit as a "citizen jury" to try violations of the posse's edicts, and could embody themselves in an "unorganized militia" to support the sheriff in enforcing the posse's mandate.[9]

Gale suggested that this new radical localism was somehow rooted in the "constitutional republicanism" of the Founding era, but in 1971 his historical justification lacked detail. A decade later, Gale crafted a more elaborate historical memory to justify the seizure of state power by the white supremacist Right. He argued in 1984 that the 1781 Articles of Confederation were still the supreme law of the land. He dismissed the subsequent Constitution of 1787 by asserting that the Articles were an expression of biblical law that could not be superseded. He then declared, correctly, that Congress had assumed powers to tax and regulate that were not authorized under the Articles. Finally, Gale noted that the Articles provided that during a congressional recess its powers would be wielded by a "Committee of the States." In July 1984 Gale and forty-two others signed a declaration dissolving Congress and appointing themselves the Committee of the States and the "Lords and Masters of this self-governing Republic known as the United States of America."[10]

In the 1980s several Christian Identity ministers, including Richard Butler and James Wickstrom, began to organize institutions and local sovereignties along the lines suggested by Gale. They infused Posse ideology with conspiratorial anti-Semitism and organized separatist Posse townships designed to allow sovereign white citizens to separate themselves from the authority of the "Zionist Occupation Government" (ZOG). When the farm crisis hit the Great Plains in the early 1980s, hundreds of farmers saw in Posse ideology an explanation of their troubles, and some began to organize "common law courts" in an effort to halt debt collection and farm foreclosure proceedings.[11]

In response to illegal tax protests, crowd interference with farm auctions, and paramilitary training among farmers and Posse activists, federal and local officials began to prosecute Posse Comitatus activities more aggressively. An attempt to organize a Posse township in Medina, North Dakota, in 1983 ended when federal and local law enforcement officers tried to arrest Posse activist Gordon Kahl. Kahl shot three officers in the incident, one of them fatally. Several months later Kahl and a local sheriff died in a raid on the house where Kahl was hiding. The FBI, unaware that Kahl had been killed in an exchange of gunfire with Sheriff Gene Mathews, poured diesel fuel into the house and set it on fire.[12]

If Gale significantly recast the memory of the Founding period, another far right revolutionary dismissed the Founding as irrelevant. The third development on the far right in the 1970s and 1980s was the propagation of an American strain of Nazism by William Pierce, one of George Lincoln Rockwell's protégés. Pierce founded the National Alliance in 1974, and laid out his program for Aryan rebirth in his 1978 novel *The Turner Diaries*. The novel depicts a white America under siege from the multiple threats of integration, gun control, and cannibalistic violence perpetrated by blacks and Jews. Through the systematic application of guerilla violence, protagonist Earl Turner and his fellow Aryan warriors gain control of California. They then exterminate the forces of evil, composed of minorities, Jews, "mongrels," and race traitors, in the "Day of the Rope." Once the Aryan warriors of the "Order" gain control over the United States, they reenact this genocidal rebirth upon the entire globe. They stage pogroms in Europe to eliminate "the offspring of generations of dysgenic breeding" and "sterilize" the rest of the globe with chemical, biological, and nuclear weapons.[13]

If Pierce's outright advocacy of genocide was extreme even for the American white supremacist Right, it was the book's political philosophy that set it apart from earlier white supremacist discourse. In *The Turner Diaries*, Pierce dismissed the entire tradition of constitutional republicanism that Gale had attempted to reforge. In the novel, Earl Turner derides a conservative general who has set up an independent republic in northern California as insufficiently authoritarian: "he has been issuing idiotic proclamations about 'restoring the Constitution,' stamping out 'communism and pornography,' and holding out new elections to 're-establish the republican form of government intended by the Founding Fathers,' what ever that means."[14] Historically, most American white supremacists had embraced the principles of white equality and limited government embedded in the "herrenvolk democracy" of the Jacksonian period. Even Gale's revision of the memory of the Founding ultimately stems from this tradition. Pierce's explicit celebration of a totalitarian state controlled by a revolutionary elite took American white supremacy in a radically new direction.

In the mid-1980s Richard Butler attempted to bridge the gap among these disparate strains of white supremacist thought. Butler founded Aryan Nations and began to hold annual sessions of the "World Aryan Congress" to bring skinheads, Klansmen, Identity adherents, and neo-Nazis together as one cohesive movement. Butler's emphasis on networking and Pierce's fantasy of authoritarian revolution together inspired the creation of the Order, a violently racist group devoted to overthrowing the United States government and establishing an Aryan republic. The activities of the Order included bank robberies and the murder of Denver talk show host Alan Berg. Federal authorities eventually arrested most of the group's members and cornered group founder Robert Matthews in a rented house on Whidbey Island in Washington. After Matthews repeatedly fired on FBI agents laying siege to the house, the authorities set fire to the house with a flare. Matthews perished in the flames.[15]

The rise in right-wing violence in the 1980s prompted civil rights organizations to abandon the policy of quiet containment. The Southern Poverty Law Center was founded in 1971 as a law firm specializing in civil rights violations. In 1979 the center organized the Klanwatch project, devoted to monitoring white supremacist groups. Klanwatch began to publish the *Intelligence Report* in 1981. The Center for Democratic Renewal, based in Atlanta and dedicated to combating hate groups, was founded in 1979. Throughout the 1980s the SPLC, the ADL, and the Center for Democratic Renewal published exposés of far right activity with such titles as *Hate Violence and White Supremacy* and *Aryan Nations: Far Right Underground*. These organizations also significantly influenced book-length studies of the Far Right by James Ridgeway and James

Coates. This literature described the Nazification of the third Ku Klux Klan, the development of a pan-Aryan ethos based on Christian Identity theology, and a growing menace posed by paramilitary training and revolutionary organization on the far right. Though these developments were real, this literature also fostered an exaggerated perception of a united Far Right dedicated to a genocidal Aryan revolution along the lines described in the *Turner Diaries*.[16]

By the end of the 1980s, then, the necessary ingredients of a second Brown Scare were all in place. The fusion of white supremacist and revolutionary ideologies stimulated a wave of paramilitary activity on the far right. The ideologies of Aryan Republicanism and the Posse Comitatus flouted the repudiation of revolutionary violence that had been a defining characteristic of mainstream politics since the advent of one hundred percent Americanism. Civil rights organizations responded with warnings of a secret subversive alliance among the disparate groups of the racist Right. These warnings marked a return to the rhetorical tactics that had characterized the first Brown Scare. When civil rights groups began to hear of militia groups forming in the early 1990s, they charged that the militias represented a new wave of extremists, a "gathering storm" of racial hatred and "terrorist" violence. Civil rights activists were wrong in their association of the emerging militia movement with the white supremacist paramilitaries of the 1970s and 1980s. But they were right in their assertion that the militias celebrated violence against the state as a legitimate act of patriotism.

PART THREE

THE ORIGINS OF THE MILITIA MOVEMENT:
VIOLENCE AND MEMORY ON THE
SUBURBAN-RURAL FRONTIER

Sometimes change is sudden, and so dramatic that we can hardly believe our eyes. On November 9, 1989, I came home from teaching high school and turned on the television. I had followed the events in Eastern Europe closely that fall, but it still took me twenty minutes to fathom the live images of young people dancing atop a concrete wall. I simply could not grasp what I was seeing. The newscasters reporting the fall of the Berlin Wall were themselves speechless.

Sometimes change is imperceptible, until one day we are forced to confront a new state of affairs and realize that it has been twenty years in the making. I grew up in a variety of communities, urban, suburban, and rural. In one of those rural communities I once attended a Fourth of July celebration in a parking lot in the middle of town. It was a tailgate party attended by most of the town's high school students, who stood in a small crowd drinking beer, in wholesale violation of the town's open container laws and the state's minimum age regulations. At the entrance to the parking lot, about fifty yards from the crowd, the town's chief of police sat in his cruiser. As every underage celebrant left the party, they stopped by the cruiser and chatted for a while with the chief, before heading up the road. The chief seemed to know each of them by name: he'd grown up in the community, and he'd probably stopped in to watch his share of Little League games and soccer matches while on his appointed rounds. I'm quite sure he was the happiest law enforcement officer in the county that night. The law lay prostrate, but he had all his ducks in one pond.

Several years later I took my first teaching job at a suburban public high school in the same state. After school I usually did some paperwork and then headed across the street to watch my students play soccer on the adjacent field. Often their mothers came to watch them play, and usually their fathers would take half an hour off from work to come watch as well, parking their cars along the edge of the field. One day that first fall one of the town police officers arrived at the game in his cruiser. Though he knew a few of the school's "bad apples," he didn't actually live in the community, and he didn't appear to know any of the parents. He did, however, know his job, and so he was perfectly professional and correct as he began to ticket the illegally parked cars belonging to the parents who had come to watch their children play. And one by one the fathers ran to their cars and drove back to work.

Most Americans live in suburban and urban communities. They may see what happened in that first community as an abdication of responsibility and what happened in that second community as one of life's typical frustrations. But as someone who had never before lived in a suburb, I was shocked and disoriented by the spectacle of a community that had surrendered control of its policing. My sense of having entered a new world was as strong that day as it would be when I watched the Berlin Wall fall just a few weeks later. But I had entered that new world voluntarily: I had moved to take a job in this community and accepted the change in social norms that came with it. Many Americans in the 1980s and 1990s found themselves in that new world through no action of their own. It simply grew up around them. Born in the first town, they woke up one day in the second, and were left to wonder how it had happened, how they had lost control of their world. Between the end of Communism, the transformation of rural communities undergoing suburbanization, and the increasing pace of economic globalization, millions of Americans experienced this disquieting loss of control in the early 1990s.[1]

For some, the sense of shock and loss, and even of rage, was aggravated in the early 1990s by a wave of state-sponsored political violence stemming from the arrival of paramilitary policing in the heartland. The paramilitarization of law enforcement was nothing new in America. SWAT teams originated in Los Angeles in the late 1960s, but in the late 1980s, paramilitary tactics and weapons were adopted by the enforcement arms of a variety of federal agencies and also by a number of suburban police and sheriff's departments. Paramilitary policing thus came into the lives of rural and suburban communities that had never experienced it before. The federal law enforcement assaults at Ruby Ridge, Idaho and Waco, Texas were the most visible product of this broader trend toward paramilitary policing. But many concerned citizens, especially gun owners, saw Ruby Ridge and Waco as the tip of a much bigger iceberg, and observed that federal and local agencies were employing the same weapons and tactics in communities closer to home.

The sense of threat and alienation that many felt after witnessing Ruby Ridge and Waco reverberated within a new alternative public sphere that emerged as a result of the communications revolution of the 1990s. Using talk radio, fax networks, Internet discussion lists and chat rooms, and the World Wide Web, gun owners, tax protesters, white supremacists, and common-law activists all came together to discuss what they perceived as a growing threat from their own government. Concerned individuals also banded together in local civic organizations, such as patriot discussion groups and gun clubs.

Finally, and crucially, these years also witnessed the revival of the libertarian memory of the American Revolution within the gun rights movement. As gun rights activists entered into this new public sphere, they brought with them an insurrectionary understanding of the Second Amendment, a familiarity with eighteenth-century Whig ideology and the Whig diagnosis of government abuse, and a more civic understanding of the institution of the militia. These ideas offered an alternative to the millenarian, white supremacist, and anarcho-libertarian ideas that had been circulating on the far right for half a century.

The first groups of what would become the militia movement began to operate in the winter and spring of 1994. From the outset two competing models, linked to differing perceptions of the threat, governed militia organization. Constitutionalists began to organize militias on the basis of public meetings and open membership. They saw the growing threat of state-sponsored violence as a symptom of a corrupt and abusive government, and argued that the militia, if public, could act as a deterrent against further government abuse. Millenarians began to organize on the basis of a closed cell structure hidden from public view. Their vision was millennial and apocalyptic: they saw militia organization as the only way to survive an imminent invasion by the forces of the New World Order. Over time, these divergent worldviews would produce the distinct constitutionalist and millennial wings of the militia movement.

Sometimes change is sudden and startling. Sometimes it is gradual and imperceptible. The militia movement represented the anxious response of a group of white suburban Americans to change. In the 1990s, militia men and women perceived a fundamental alteration in their relationship to their government, and in that government's capacity for violence. The movement was born out of its members' perception that government, both local and federal, posed an increasing threat to their liberty and their lives, a threat that was political, violent, and intolerable.

The Road to Ruby Ridge and Waco: The Growth of Paramilitary Policing and the Declaration of a War on Guns

During the 1980s, law enforcement agencies across America embraced the use of paramilitary weapons and tactics. The number of police paramilitary units in urban and suburban communities grew rapidly in the post-Vietnam era. In a 1995 survey of police departments serving communities with populations of over twenty-five thousand, criminologist Peter Kraska found that over 75 percent of departments had organized a paramilitary unit, the vast majority within the previous ten years. More importantly, such units took on a significantly expanded role after 1985. According to Kraska, the number of annual callouts for police paramilitary units (PPU's) increased an average of 538 percent between 1980 and 1995 in the 193 departments serving cities of over fifty thousand that deployed units for the full period. Furthermore, these units shifted their focus from reactive responses to hostage situations and "barricaded persons"—their original purpose—to such proactive tasks as investigatory drug raids and "warrant work." The expansion in PPU activity occurred in departments serving smaller communities as well: the median number of callouts tripled in departments serving a population of twenty-five thousand to fifty thousand. Much of this proactive work involved no-knock entry into private residences, with very high risks to all concerned. Kraska refers to the expansion of paramilitary policing into progressively smaller communities as the "militarization of Mayberry."[2]

The 1980s and early 1990s also witnessed a significant increase in cooperation and joint operations among local, state, and federal law enforcement agencies. Kraska has noted that the federal government began to take an active role in training and equipping local police paramilitary units in this period. At the end of the Cold War, the federal government began to donate helicopters, armored vehicles, and other equipment to local law enforcement agencies as part of its effort to dispose of surplus military equipment. The war on drugs also produced new interagency programs called Multi-Jurisdictional Task Forces (MJTF), in which local, state, and federal officials combined their policing resources to combat drug trafficking. Some of these operations involved the cordoning off and systematic searches of multiple city blocks. One such operation took place in Shreveport, Louisiana, in September 1994.[3]

Finally, the early 1990s brought a renewed interest in urban warfare. After battles in Panama City and Mogadishu showed up deficiencies in the U.S. military's capacity to conduct operations in urban settings, the army and marines began to hold military exercises in cities and suburban areas around the country. For example, 125 soldiers from various military units along with several helicopters conducted an exercise in the Chicago suburb of Lamont in June 1995, complete with simulated gunfire and the use of explosive charges. Similar exercises took place around the country in the mid-1990s. At least some of these exercises carried the suggestion that the MJTF model might be expanded to involve actual military forces in domestic law enforcement. An exercise planned for Detroit in July 1994 featured cooperation between U.S. Army Special Forces and the Detroit police SWAT team. In 1996, Pittsburgh

SWAT teams participated in an urban warfare exercise alongside troops from Fort Bragg, North Carolina.[4]

Though the trend of paramilitarization had its roots in America's prohibition on illegal drugs, paramilitary tactics were eminently applicable to the prohibition on guns that was an ascendant priority in the 1990s. In 1989 the Bush administration banned the importation of some types of semiautomatic weapons. After 1992, the Clinton administration made the tighter regulation of guns a legislative priority. The 1993 Brady bill required that purchasers of handguns undergo criminal background checks before completing the purchase. The 1994 assault weapons ban prohibited the sale of certain types of semiautomatic weapons. On February 28, 1994, the day that the Brady bill went into effect, much broader follow-on legislation was introduced into the Senate that would have required the registration of all handguns, the safe storage of all weapons, and special licenses for owners of more than twenty guns. The bill, widely dubbed Brady II, included an expanded version of what would become the assault weapons ban, and a 50 percent sales tax on ammunition.[5]

More than anything else, it was the application of paramilitary tactics to an emerging war on guns that produced Ruby Ridge and Waco. Randy and Vicki Weaver moved from Iowa to Bonners Ferry, Idaho, in 1983. Millenarians obsessed with the impending end of time, they built a cabin on Ruby Ridge and adopted a survivalist lifestyle. Randy attended several events at Richard Butler's Aryan Nations compound in nearby Hayden Lake. The Weavers' religious views gravitated increasingly toward Christian Identity belief. Though they were clearly comfortable socializing with white supremacists, the Weavers were at most only peripherally involved in the white supremacist paramilitary activity taking place in the region in the mid-1980s.[6]

The Weavers were, however, acquainted with the family of John Trochman, who would later found the Militia of Montana. In 1989, the Bureau of Alcohol, Tobacco, and Firearms suspected that David Trochman, John Trochman's brother, was trafficking in illegal firearms. BATF informant Kenneth Fadely was instructed to see if Weaver might introduce him to the Trochmans. Fadely asked Weaver to supply him with sawed-off shotguns. Once Weaver supplied two such weapons, illegal without a government permit and a registration fee of two hundred dollars, he had committed a crime. In June 1990, BATF agents gave Weaver a choice: he could either go to jail or inform on the Trochmans. Weaver told the agents to "go to hell." For years the Weavers had believed that during the tribulations of the end times, agents of the Zionist Occupation Government would come to destroy them. In 1990, the federal government chased Randy Weaver up his mountain and made his fears real. For the next two years, a standoff ensued, with Randy Weaver refusing to surrender to the authorities.[7]

On August 21, 1992, federal marshals conducted a dawn surveillance sweep of the Weavers' property. As the marshals were preparing to leave, the family's dog, Striker, detected them. Randy Weaver, his fourteen-year-old son Sam, and family friend Kevin Harris followed Striker into the woods in hopes that he had found some game to add to the family's meager food supply. All were armed. The agents retreated, but Striker pursued them. Randy tried to circle around the prey that Stiker was stalking, and caught sight of the agents. He ran back to the cabin and called out for Kevin and Sam to return as well, but they did not hear him, and continued to follow Striker. Finally, one agent shot Striker, only to be confronted by Sam Weaver, who cursed him and opened fire. In the ensuing exchange of gunfire, Agent William Degan was killed, probably by Kevin Harris, and Sam Weaver was shot in the back while running home. Randy Weaver took no part in this exchange.[8]

The Federal Bureau of Investigation took over the case that night, and FBI snipers moved into position around the Weavers' cabin. In the midst of considerable confusion over what exactly had happened that morning, the FBI fixed its attention on several details: the bureau determined that Randy was an Aryan Nations member and that the Weavers' home was a "fortified white supremacist compound." With this information in mind, the Justice Department issued special rules of engagement for use in the Weaver case. The new rules provided that "deadly force can and should be used to neutralize" any armed adult male on the property. Given that prior surveillance had revealed that all members of the

Weaver family habitually carried arms outside the cabin, these rules were a virtual death sentence against Randy Weaver and Kevin Harris. FBI sniper Lon Horiuchi agreed with his team leaders that if Randy Weaver and Kevin Harris left the cabin armed, the snipers would kill them. Weaver and Harris left the cabin later that morning to visit Sam's body in an outbuilding. As they approached the shed where Sam's body was stored, Horiuchi opened fire, wounding Weaver. As Weaver and Harris ran for the safety of the cabin, Horiuchi drew a bead on Harris, and fired a second shot as he passed through the cabin door. Vicki Weaver was behind the door (which opened outward) holding it open. On its way to its intended target, Horiuchi's second shot blew Vicki Weaver's head off.[9]

Randy Weaver and Kevin Harris surrendered eleven days later. The white supremacist community of the Northwest was enraged by the deaths of Vicki and Sam and considered them martyrs for the cause. But outrage at the events at Ruby Ridge extended well beyond the racist Right. As the truth of what had happened emerged in the ensuing trial of Randy Weaver and Kevin Harris, many Americans began to question whether the failure to purchase a two-hundred-dollar permit justified the massive show of force on Ruby Ridge and the order to shoot Randy Weaver on sight.

During the trial of Weaver and Harris, on April 19, 1993, the government's assault on the Branch Davidian compound in Waco, Texas, resulted in more deaths and more questions. The Branch Davidians, a small isolated religious sect led by charismatic preacher David Koresh, were suspected of illegal weapons trading. The initial BATF assault on the Waco compound on February 28 was ostensibly intended to serve a search warrant, but extensive preparations to film the raid suggested that it was also planned in part as an exhibition of the agency's martial prowess with an eye on the upcoming federal budget cycle. The assault plan featured paramilitary "dynamic entry tactics" and involved the use of helicopters and flash-bang grenades. The raiders' first task was the "neutralization" of the compound's dogs.[10]

The plan depended on the element of surprise, but agents realized the morning of the raid that the Davidians had been tipped off. Thus when agents rushed the compound, they found the Davidians armed and determined to defend their community. Once again, the best evidence indicates that BATF agents fired the first shots at the compound's dogs. The ensuing gun battle left four agents dead and fifteen wounded. At least three Branch Davidians died that day, and David Koresh was wounded, but the total number of Davidian casualties on the twenty-eighth is unknown.[11]

After the failure of the initial assault, the FBI's elite paramilitary squad, the Hostage Rescue Team, took over from the BATF. For the next fifty days agents laid siege to the compound. In round after round of fitful negotiations, they persuaded Koresh to send out a few of the residents' children, and a few adults left voluntarily. By the end of two weeks, however, the HRT was losing patience with Koresh and began to employ more aggressive psychological tactics, including cutting off electricity to the compound and using music and sound recordings to create sleep deprivation and irritability among the Davidians. Finally, on April 19, the FBI used armored vehicles to inject CS gas into the compound. Several hours later fire swept through the structure. Nine Davidians escaped the flames. Seventy-five others died in the fire. Thirty-three, including all of the remaining children, took refuge in a concrete room at the center of the compound. The children huddled together with their mothers under wet blankets and slowly asphyxiated as the fire raged over their heads. After the fires died out federal agents raised the BATF flag over the ashes.[12]

There were striking similarities between Waco and Ruby Ridge. In both cases armed confrontation degenerated into a mêlée when the authorities fired the first shot at a dog. In both cases, critics later questioned whether the use of force was proportional to the original offense. In both cases, the offense in question revolved around the purchase and possession of firearms. American gun owners, in particular, looked at Ruby Ridge and Waco and wondered who was next.[13]

Gun rights organizations took pains to publicize other incidents which they believed illustrated a broader pattern of abusive law enforcement tactics directed at gun owners. For example, the Second Amendment Foundation circulated a report on eleven botched paramilitary raids conducted by the BATF and other federal agencies around the country between 1991 and 1995, several of which resulted in serious injuries to civilians. National Rifle Association president Tom Washington published a letter to former president George H. W. Bush in which he described several cases in which entirely innocent civilians had been shot in botched raids.[14]

One final tragedy, this time initiated by local law enforcement, illustrated the perils of the paramilitarization of suburban policing. John Lekan lived in Brunswick, Ohio, a suburb of Cleveland, with his wife Beverly and nine-year-old son John Jr. Lekan suffered from mental illness, and neighbors had reported instances of odd behavior. Home health aides frequently visted the Lekan home to care for Beverly, who was bedridden with multiple sclerosis. In March 1995 the aides complained to supervisors that Lekan had displayed firearms while they were in the home. A request from the nursing agency that Lekan sign an agreement to refrain from such behavior in the future seemed to agitate him. Meanwhile, word of Lekan's behavior reached the Brunswick Police Department. On the afternoon of Friday, March 31, 1995, two officers were dispatched in plain clothes to check on the situation. Lekan refused to let the officers into his home, and they later reported that he lapsed into incoherence when talking to them through an open window about his constitutional rights. The officers decided that Lekan represented a danger to his family, and kicked in the door to the house, though they had no warrant to enter the home. Lekan responded by shooting officer Sam Puzella in the chest. Five hours later Lekan shot two more officers when a five-man SWAT team attempted to rush the house.[15]

Thereafter some 250 police officers, including four SWAT teams, laid siege to the house. Police snipers had orders to shoot Lekan on sight. They fired tear gas into the house at 6:00 a.m. Saturday morning, and attempted to further intimidate Lekan at 11:00 a.m. by using a thirteen-ton armored assault vehicle named "Mother" to ram holes in the house. We will never know exactly how Lekan perceived Mother as it smashed through the walls of his home, but the coroner's report indicates that he responded by shooting his son in the head and then killing himself. Beverly Lekan believed that her husband may have been trying in his own way to protect their son from the hostile forces arrayed against him. She buried John Jr. in his father's arms.[16]

Some Americans looked upon the events at Ruby Ridge and Waco and placed the blame squarely on the shoulders of Randy Weaver and David Koresh. Some looked upon these events as tragedies without clear villains or victims. But for some, the experience of bearing witness to these events transformed their perception of their place in the world and their relationship to their government. Jim McKinzey, cofounder of the Missouri 51st Militia, described this paradigm shift in terms of his understanding of patriotism:

> Ruby Ridge was a wake-up call for a lot of people in the country, including myself. Until Ruby Ridge came down the pike, I could care less about politics. . . . "This is the greatest country in the world, love it or leave it" type attitudes. . . . And then, they're starting to shoot children, and shooting unarmed women in the head. "Wait a minute now, I need to pay attention to what's going on here." Then, what, less than a year later, these same people are now down in Texas, taking on women and children, and that is really what did it.[17]

The perception among those who would join the militia movement that paramilitary policing had brought a wave of state violence into suburban communities may have been exaggerated. Few police departments kept statistics on the proportion of raids that yielded injuries and significant property damage or that were conducted on innocent parties. As a result, the size of the problem cannot be fully calculated. Anecdotal research by Radley Balko of the Cato Institute indicates that botched raids were not isolated incidents. Balko has documented sixty-nine cases between 1985 and 1994 in which police actions led to deaths or in which the police raided the premises of an innocent party. His sample is composed only of cases that generated news coverage and does not include nonlethal raids that generated injuries or significant property damage. His research does, however, demonstrate that for those caught up in it, the consequences of the state's resort to paramilitary violence were often devastating.[18]

Tragedy Finds a New Forum:
The Rise of the Christian Patriot Public Sphere

The events at Waco played out before a national television audience. Ruby Ridge, by contrast, received only brief coverage in national news media, and most of the other events discussed here did not make it into the national news at all. But these events reverberated within a new public sphere that had emerged in the early years of the 1990s. This public sphere offered adherents of a variety of far right ideologies a forum for the discussion of political grievances, looming threats of state violence, and new modes of political organization. The individuals that communicated in this forum, though sometimes lumped together as "Christian Patriots," did not represent a unified political movement. It was access to a new, alternative public sphere, which I will refer to as the Christian Patriot public sphere, that bound them together. Advances in communications technology offered diverse voices on the far right new ways to spread ideas long considered unpublishable within the mainstream public sphere and fostered communal discussion and deliberation across space and time in a manner that had never been possible before.

Some of the technology in use within this new public sphere was actually quite old. Politicians across the political spectrum had used radio broadcasts to reach a broad audience since the 1930s. In the late 1980s, however, conservatives were the first to see the potential of the new format of talk radio for fostering discussion and debate of key ideas and for community building. The 1987 repeal of the fairness doctrine requiring broadcasters to present controversial public issues in a balanced manner facilitated the emergence of a new style of partisan and inflammatory political discussion on broadcast radio, particularly on the right. Leading conservative radio hosts included Rush Limbaugh and G. Gordon Liddy. On the shortwave bands, World Wide Christian Radio offered a forum to more radical voices from the far right, including conspiracy theorists Chuck Harder and Bill Cooper, Christian Identity minister Pete Peters, and militia proponent Mark Koernke. All of these programs offered listeners the opportunity to call in and join the on-air discussion.[19]

Two new technologies supplemented the web of connections offered by talk radio. The advent of cheap plain paper fax machines at the end of the 1980s offered activists a means of rapidly transmitting documents to large numbers of recipients. The American Patriot Fax Network (APFN) was founded during the trial of Randy Weaver to distribute daily reports to those concerned by Ruby Ridge. It then began to send reports on the Waco siege that began one week later. When Linda Thompson, an Indianapolis attorney, called for a militia to muster in Waco and pressure authorities to lift the siege, APFN distributed the call to arms.[20]

Personal computers and modems brought an additional set of communications technologies into the hands of conservative and far right political activists. Electronic bulletin board systems allowed individuals with computers to dial into a server and upload and download messages. Fidonet, founded in 1984, grew into a worldwide BBS (Bulletin Board System) network connecting hundreds of thousands of users. In April 1994 Linda Thompson posted her infamous call for a militia march on Washington, DC, to her own node of this network, AEN News Service, and sent it out over Fidonet.[21]

A more sophisticated level of communication was facilitated by Internet news and discussion groups that allowed users to post comments and respond to other users in an ongoing discussion. The Usenet system hosted hundreds of such groups, all open to any computer user connected to the Internet. Discussions of militia organization appeared on alt.politics.guns and alt.politics.usa.constitution as early as 1992, and in April 1994 Jon Roland and Norm Olson used Usenet discussion groups to announce the formation of the Texas Constitutional Militia (TCM) and the Michigan Militia Corps (MMC). Because of the high level of militia-related traffic on these lists, Usenet started a new list dedicated to issues related to militias, misc.activism.militia, on April 14, 1995. Local Internet service providers and private individuals hosted additional discussion groups. Other important militia-related discussion groups included patriots@kaiwan.com and the Patriots Information Mailing List, piml@mars.galstar.[22]

Email alert systems also allowed institutions and individuals to send emails with news and commentary to thousands of subscribers. The National Rifle Association and Gun Owners of America organized email

systems to keep their memberships informed about legislative developments and law enforcement abuses of gun owners' rights. The Militia of
Montana (MOM) organized a similar list to publicize "intelligence" concerning the impending New World Order invasion.[23]

Finally, the World Wide Web allowed political activists of a wide variety of stripes to create Web pages and online newsletters and to link
them together in a dense web of connections. White supremacists were
among the first to capitalize on the Web and to use the new medium to
publicize their views and attract recruits. In the mid-1990s more generic
Christian Patriot sites offered links to hundreds of Web pages hosted by
tax protest groups, gun rights organizations, survivalist catalogs, Christian Identity churches, and militia groups. By early 1995 over two dozen
militia groups had created Web sites of varying sophistication. These
sites featured news, essays on preparedness, and political commentary.
The Michigan Militia Web site published Norm Olson's *Michigan Militia
Corps Manual,* and several militias published newsletters online.[24]

Perhaps the most important of the early militia-related sites was Jon
Roland's Constitution Society Web page. Roland's site included links to
militia Web sites around the country, a link to the subscription page for
the Patriots Information Mailing List, and a directory of county contacts
for the Texas Constitutional Militia. Roland also used the site to publish
essays, known collectively as the *Texas Militia Papers,* that discussed
eighteenth-century political philosophy and its application to his project
of reviving the universal militia. Finally, Roland created an electronic library containing classic texts of Anglo-American political philosophy in
html format. This collection has grown over time, and his site is now one
of the leading online repositories of Anglo-American political theory
from the early modern period.[25]

Alongside these marvels of the technological revolution of the 1990s,
the Christian Patriot public sphere also depended on more traditional
modes of political organization and discussion. Participants often
brought the news, opinions, and information generated in online discussion networks into local political discussion groups that met periodically to ponder political developments and national events. Some of
these groups coalesced around an interest in gun rights, but others cov-

ered a broader array of concerns, including taxation, home schooling, and religion. Face to face conversations in these discussion groups often served as the catalyst for the formation of local militias. For example, in Columbus, Ohio, the Central Ohio Unorganized Militia sprang from the patriot discussion group E Pluribus Unum. A discussion group called the Indiana Patriots gave birth to the Indiana Citizens Volunteer Militia. In Kansas City, the Western Missouri Shooters Alliance played a similar role in the founding of the Missouri 51st Militia.[26]

Preparedness expos, which began to tour the country in the early 1990s, served as additional nodes in the Christian Patriot public sphere. Essentially a combination of traveling bazaar and political road show, expos offered far right activists the opportunity to sell literature, videotapes, and survival gear and offered national spokesmen for various causes the opportunity to spread their messages across the country. The appearance of militia figures such as John Trochman, Mark Koernke, Jack McLamb, and J. J. Johnson tended to reinforce local efforts to organize militias.[27]

The Christian Patriot public sphere thus facilitated a combination of nationwide communication and local face-to-face discussion that fostered the rapid growth of the militia movement. The tragedies of Waco and Ruby Ridge were constant topics of discussion on early patriot Internet discussion groups. The National Rifle Association and Gun Owners of America used email to keep their memberships well informed of continuing BATF abuses. Talk radio kept up a steady beat of criticism of the "jackbooted thugs" responsible for Waco, and G. Gordon Liddy famously advised listeners that if the BATF should come to disarm them, they should "kill the sons of bitches." Calls for militia organization by Linda Thomson, Norm Olson, and Jon Roland went out over popular Usenet lists and reached hundreds of local political discussion groups all over the country. Within those groups, small numbers of individuals came together to discuss the idea of forming a militia, held initial meetings, contacted existing militias like the MOM or the MMC for assistance, and then began to recruit members.

The militia movement, like most insurgent movements in American history, was sparked by the perception of an urgent threat, a perception that grew and matured through a process of public discussion and deliberation. What set that discussion apart was that it took place within a new alternative public sphere made possible by the communications revolution of the early 1990s. As a consequence, these deliberations, though public and national in scope, took place outside the notice of most Americans. They touched on topics, like revolutionary violence, long banned from the mainstream public sphere. Finally, the entire process of discussion and political organization occurred at an accelerated pace. As a result, to many Americans, the militia movement seemed to come out of nowhere.

The Racial Ideology of the Militia Movement: Color-Blind Patriotism as an Expression of Mainstream Racial Discourse

Throughout the 1990s civil rights activists argued that the militia movement was an outgrowth of the racist Right. In 1996 Morris Dees and Kenneth Stern argued that the movement was conceived at a 1992 meeting of leading white supremacists at Estes Park, Colorado. Other activists charged that the movement had adopted major tenets of white supremacist ideology, including the theology of Christian Identity, the doctrine of Fourteenth Amendment citizenship, and the concept of "leaderless resistance." Activists were careful to emphasize that not all militia members were racist, but the Southern Poverty Law Center asserted that 45 of the 224 militias that it had identified in 1995 had "ties" to white supremacist groups. According to this "narrative of 1995," racism was a central animating cause of the militia movement.[28]

Many militia members were indignant at this portrait. Denying that racial animus played any role in their motivation, they argued that their racial views had been misrepresented. They pointed out that principled statements of antidiscrimination and antiracism had been a part of militia discourse from the first days of the movement. Nevertheless, most scholarship on the movement has either accepted the civil right charge or taken an equivocal stance.[29]

Recent work in sociology offers a more fruitful approach to evaluating the racial ideology of the militia movement and the role of racism in its emergence. Sociologist Eduardo Bonilla-Silva observed in 2001 that the racial order of the United States had been transformed during the civil rights era, but that structured racial inequality had nevertheless persisted. According to Bonilla-Silva, structured racial inequality gave members of the dominant race a stake in its perpetuation: "actors in superordinate positions (dominant race) develop a set of social practices . . . and an ideology to maintain the advantages they receive based on their racial classification." He argued that in the post–civil rights era the racial ideology of white Americans can best be characterized as "color-blind racism."[30]

In Bonilla-Silva's view, color-blind racism rested on ideological beliefs, or "sincere fictions," with which white Americans justified the persistence of racial inequality. The first of these ideological frames was "abstract liberalism," which combined a faith in the market economy's capacity to produce racially equitable outcomes and a laissez-faire rejection of state regulation as a tool of social reform. A second frame described racial outcomes such as de facto segregation as the natural product of free choice. In a third frame, whites substituted ethnocentric cultural disdain for older racial stereotypes. They asserted that cultural deprivation, rather than racial inferiority, prevented minority groups from taking advantage of the equal opportunities open to them. A final frame denied the importance of racial discrimination as a lasting influence on inequality. Bonilla-Silva noted that this dismissal of the continuing impact of discrimination rested on taking the incorporation of minorities to signify the nonracial character of social institutions and also on the marginalization of "old style" biological racists.[31]

Bonilla-Silva's observations offer an interpretive model for evaluating the racial discourse of the militia movement. As libertarians and critics of overreaching government, militia members placed a decided emphasis on abstract liberalism as a frame in racial discourse. This often took the form of criticizing the intrusion of the state into what they considered to be essentially private decisions: whom to hire, whom to do business with, and where to send their children to school. Many emphasized that they did not discriminate when making such choices, yet they resented what they considered to be state coercion. For example, Charlie

Morrison, a member of the Central Ohio Unorganized Militia (COUM), complained:

> The government tells me that I have to hire, I can't discriminate when I hire, and personally I think I should be able to discriminate when I hire. I discriminate in every other field. I say you don't know enough about electronics, so I'm not hiring you—I'm discriminating against him. But when it comes to sexuality, race, creed, color, whatever, I'm not allowed to be prejudiced. Now I'm going to back up what I said there by stating that I do have a lesbian who works for me, she's worked here for ten years, best employee this company has ever had, ever will. I have a black man working for me. I have—well that's about all of the minorities I can claim, except obviously the lesbian is a woman. So I wouldn't want to discriminate, but I think that it is my right to handle my company the best way that it is for me.[32]

Samuel Sherwood, founder of the United States Militia Association, also argued that freedom demanded a broad latitude for private discrimination, even while criticizing those who would use it: "Why shouldn't you be free to sell your home to whom you want to? Why shouldn't you be free to hire whom you want to? Now, if you want to be a jerk and discriminate against somebody on the basis of their color because you don't want to work with them because they're Latino, well, okay, then don't hire them, okay?"[33]

Bonilla-Silva found in his own research that whites were relatively reluctant to apply the second frame by describing racial outcomes like segregation as natural.[34] Such sentiments were equally rare among militiamen, but they did occur. For example, the manual of the Militia of Montana contained the following warning: "Beware of someone whose intellect, education, and background appear different from those with whom he attempts to associate. Most people inter-relate with others of similar interests and background."[35]

More common among militia members were examples of Bonilla-Silva's third frame, expressions of cultural disdain that served to explain racial inequality. These varied from racially charged humor to fears of urban unrest to outright expressions of the cultural inferiority of minority communities. The newsletter of the Gadsden Minutemen, for example, reprinted a parody of a "Los Angeles City School Test" that offered crude stereotypes of inner-city minority youth as promiscuous, drug-addled criminals. Jim McKinzey, cofounder of a racially integrated militia in Kansas City, expressed cultural disdain when describing his fear of urban unrest: "The welfare class is a major threat to this country. . . . Y2K comes around and all these government checks, they stop. They've never had to rely on themselves for nothing. . . . Well, these people, their checks aren't coming in and their food stamps aren't coming in, do you think they're going to go out and get a job or you think they're going to come over and try to steal what I have?" McKinzey denied that the culture he was describing was racially distinct: "I just see angry scared people that are more willing to hurt me than to go out and try do what's right and take care of their own families." For his part, Joe Pilchak, commander of one faction of the Michigan militia, asserted that most technological innovations have "basically come from the white race." But he insisted that this was the product of cultural environment, not inherent racial superiority: "The environment that people lived in has made some people superior in their ability to do things."[36]

Bonilla-Silva's fourth frame, the denial of structural discrimination, offers an explanation of militia antiracism that renders it consistent with these other aspects of militia racial discourse. This interpretive model suggests that militia antiracism served the ideological function of allowing members to believe that discrimination was marginal in their movement and in society as a whole. This interpretation of militia antiracism is acceptable only if offered in conjunction with a full accounting of its power and persistence. This antiracism consisted of efforts to welcome minorities into the movement, albeit often at a token level, as well as efforts to resist the attempt of white supremacists to infiltrate the movement. Militia men and women also publicly repudiated some of the racist doctrines circulating within the Christian Patriot public sphere, including Christian Identity and Fourteenth Amendment citizenship, and in some cases actively harassed white supremacist groups. Finally, the movement embraced the principles of equal protection and due process of law for all Americans.

Almost all militias, including those in the millennial wing, disclaimed any intent to discriminate in terms of membership. Within the constitutional wing, many militias took pains to advise potential recruits that minorities were welcome to join, but racists might not feel comfortable. For example, the Regiment of Dragoons, a constitutional militia in New Hampshire, declared that "the Regiment is anti-racist, anti-sexist, and multi-ethnic. . . . We are all the children of immigrants, regardless of when we arrived." The Wayne County Brigade of the Michigan Militia explained, "The very concept of racism is hateful to the true freedom loving patriot." They further advised potential recruits that racists "are not welcome. We aim to make anyone who would oppress, by word or deed, as uncomfortable as possible. Officially, we will 'suffer the fool.' Say what you will, but don't be surprised to be ridiculed, shouted down, or confronted by our members."[37]

Several members of constitutional militias described this stance as important to their own comfort with joining the group. Chuck Wittig described his desire in joining the Missouri 51st Militia to ensure that he was "not becoming involved with a group of white supremacists or ZOG conspiracy proponents." John Hakes, a brigade commander in the Indiana Citizens Volunteer Militia, described watching the crowd at one ICVM organizational meeting to discern their reaction to minority members of the audience: "I spent a lot of time watching people. And I did key in on that because I wanted to see what the makeup of this bunch was. And it heartened me to see that nobody, very few people in that room, took any exception to these two men."[38]

The result was that in the constitutional wing of the movement, many militias had at least a token minority membership. In some militias, there were substantial numbers of minority members. One member of the Cuyahoga County chapter of the OUM reported that approximately one-third of the group's members were African American. There was a significant Hispanic presence in some of the militias in the Southwest. At the same time, members of the ICVM, the MMC, and the COUM reported turning away members who were Christian Identity adherents or casual bigots. Tom Plummer and Charlie Morrison described discouraging two Aryan Nations members simply by advising them, "Our unit leader is black. Would that bother you?"[39]

Constitutionalists within the militia movement also publicly denounced the ideological doctrines of the racist Right. In 1996, Mike Vanderboegh, an Alabama militiaman and prominent spokesman for the constitutional wing of the movement, placed the blame for the Oklahoma City bombing on "neo-Nazis and self-described 'Christian Identity' racists and anti-Semites from Elohim City, Oklahoma, who hope to ignite a civil war that will destroy the American Republic thus giving way to a Nazi American Reich." In a 1997 email exchange, Oral Deckard, an Indiana militiaman, ridiculed the doctrine of Fourteenth Amendment citizenship for its suggestions that blacks had no rights that the government need respect: "The contention that states have the authority to deny people the right to vote based on their race is not only racist, but unpatriotic, in that it violates the very foundation upon which this country was based, that is, government by the consent of the governed. Denying them the right to vote was government without the consent of the governed, the very definition of tyranny. Any patriots for that?"[40]

Some militia members grounded their antiracism in libertarian principle. During this email discussion of Fourteenth Amendment citizenship, Deckard observed, "Well I, for one am for States Rights. I am also for individual rights. And individual rights come from God, and are not subservient to states rights. In a republic, individuals have rights that no government, federal or state, has any authority to violate." The antiracism of other militia members was grounded in Christianity. Joe Adams, an Ohio militiaman, attributed his own antiracism to "being a student (albeit a very imperfect one) of the One who came to earth as an olive-skinned Jewish carpenter." Norm Olson similarly declared, "I have absolutely no use for Christian Identity. I think it mocks this true nature of mankind. It mocks the spiritual nature of mankind. It mocks the very purpose and the reason why Jesus Christ came to redeem all men."[41]

Militia antiracism manifested itself in deeds as well as in words. Members of the Missouri 51st Militia picketed a Klan gathering in Lone Jack, Missouri, in 1996 and also protested against racial profiling in Kansas City's Swope Park. Members of the Tri-States Militia publicly harassed several white supremacists linked by Mike Vanderboegh to the Oklahoma City bombing. According to Vanderboegh, Tri-States members also conducted a quieter campaign dubbed "Operation White Rose" that involved breaking into the homes of white supremacists suspected of collaborating with Timothy McVeigh and leaving mechanical rats that when disturbed would thrash about as though in their death throes. Vanderboegh explained that the campaign was intended to warn these individuals that any further terrorist attacks would bring retribution from the militia movement.[42]

As they imagined themselves as a community of patriots, militia members argued that race was irrelevant to membership and indeed suggested that membership transcended racial identity. At the Tri-States meeting, Vanderboegh asked the assembled constitutional militia members, "Do you suppose that any of our ancestors who were at the Boston Massacre cared that the first guy who died was Crispus Attucks? Do you think that they cared that his skin was black? Did it matter? Did it matter that the sniper who killed Pitcairn at Bunker Hill was named Peter Salem? Did it matter that he was black? Did it matter that he was a slave? No, it didn't matter. He killed Pitcairn, didn't he? He's an American, by God, in my eyes." J. J. Johnson, the most influential African American in the militia movement, also argued that the movement transcended race. In his 1998 novel *Cracking the Liberty Bell,* J. J. Johnson ruminated on the nature of patriotic identity. He portrayed a confrontation between an African American FBI agent captured during an assault on a separatist religious community and an elderly African American member of this community of patriots who had been his Sunday school teacher. The agent is astonished to find her among the congregation, and says, "I didn't know you were in here. I didn't know any black people were in here." She replies by pointing to the bodies of congregants killed in the assault: "Look at these folks covered up here. Both black and white. These folks is our folks. They ain't got color no more."[43]

Militia expressions of this "color-blind patriotism" distinguished them from the "old-style" racists of the white supremacist Right. Nevertheless, the militia movement inhabited the racialized social system of late twentieth-century America, and its white members were complicit in the social practices and "sincere fictions" with which white Americans defended their privileged position in that system. Bonilla-Silva's structural explanation of the contours of racial ideology in the post–civil rights' era thus captures the central themes of militia racial discourse, though it does not predict the passion and activism of militia antiracism. This interpretation places militia racial discourse squarely within the mainstream racial ideology of white America at the end of the twentieth century. With regard to race, militiamen and militiawomen were not ideologically distinct from those colleagues and neighbors who never contemplated joining the movement. A full evaluation of "color-blind patriotism" thus undermines the assertion that racism was an animating cause of the militia movement.

From Warriors to Citizens: The Emergence of Civic Masculinity in Post–Cold War America

A number of sociologists studying far right paramilitary activity have argued that the phenomenon was rooted in a crisis in masculine identity. In particular, James Gibson, Michael Kimmel, and Abby Ferber have interpreted far right paramilitary organization as a hypermasculine response to the decline in status and authority faced by rural and working-class men in the post-Vietnam era. These scholars have identified downward mobility, resentment of female self-assertion, and anger at economic and political competition from minorities as the central features of an embattled paramilitary masculinity. According to Gibson, the warrior dream behind paramilitary organization was to reforge patriarchal domination and to retaliate against those who had undermined it. Gibson described a "new war fantasy" at the root of paramilitary culture in which men enjoyed freedom from ethical constraints, civic obligations, and domestic ties. Gibson, Kimmel, and Ferber have argued that this new war fantasy lay at the center of militia masculinity.[44]

Developments in masculine identity at the turn of the twenty-first century were indeed important to the emergence of the militia movement and to the identity of its members. But most militia members viewed the practices associated with Gibson's warrior dream as the antithesis of true manhood. Militiamen fashioned a masculine identity in which the paramilitary warriors of both the white supremacist Right and the BATF served as negative referents. Though martial in character, militia manhood was not so much an extension of the warrior dream as a reaction to it.

In 1995 sociologist R. W. Connell referred to those gender practices tending to reproduce a patriarchal domination based on violence, aggression, and competition as hegemonic masculinity. Connell argued, however, that within the gender order of contemporary Western society, hegemonic masculinity existed in tension with other, distinct, masculine identities: complicit, subordinate, and marginalized. In particular, he described complicit masculinity as that practiced by men who "wield the patriarchal dividend" but also respect the women in their lives, provide for their families, and refrain from domestic violence. He argued that such men were embedded in "marriage, fatherhood, and community life" and that these relationships were based on negotiation rather than "naked domination or an uncontested display of authority." Connell suggested that challenges to hegemonic masculinity might emerge out of this complicit identity, and offered Robert Bly's Men's Movement as one example.[45]

On close observation, the identity of many militiamen offered a similar challenge to the hegemonic masculinity of the warrior dream. Most militiamen grounded their identity in a sense of personal accomplishment and civic contribution and described their participation in the movement as the fulfillment of a civic obligation to serve as active citizens. Their understanding of civic duty encompassed active political participation, disaster preparedness, and the martial defense of liberty. Women participated in most militia groups, and militiamen saw their female colleagues as full partners in the civic duties of political action and emergency preparedness. Though many militiamen saw the martial aspects of citizenship as essentially male, even this most masculine facet of militia identity remained rooted in domestic attachment.

Militiamen often expressed an identity that was firmly grounded in personal and professional accomplishment. Chuck Wittig of the Missouri 51st Militia described his colleagues as follows: "We are the doers and the thinkers of the world. We are the people who make things work. We bring power to the light meters and dial tones to the phone system.

We are the mechanics who keep the automobiles running. We are the network managers and programmers that maintain the computer nets." Mike Vanderboegh similarly described the members of the groups he had associated with as successful in their professional and domestic lives: "Most of these guys . . . are successful within their own chosen field. I mean, for a time my executive officer was, not then, but is now, the vice president of a bank here in town. Most of these guys make good money. They've got wives and kids, as well adjusted as—certainly better than me, I suppose." These observations were borne out by two small surveys, both of which found that militia members were significantly more likely than the general population to hold a bachelor's degree.[46]

The identity of most militia members revolved around their sense of obligation as citizens to strengthen the larger community, rather than a sense of alienation. In 1999 Mike Vanderboegh gave a speech to the Birmingham Libertarian Club in which he described citizenship as the fulfillment of this masculine duty: "along with the rights and privileges as citizens, comes the duty to fight against the tyrannies of our day. . . . We're stuck with the duty. It comes right along with the title 'citizen.'" Tom Plummer agreed that the defense of liberty and the Constitution was an obligation for men (though optional for women): "That's why I'm doing this. I feel I have an obligation as a citizen." Vanderboegh dubbed those willing to undertake that duty as "sheepdogs," a designation that described them as neither sheep nor wolves, neither victims nor victimizers. And he explained that the fulfillment of this duty reinforced the identity of those involved: "You come to understand that being a sheepdog is a pain in the butt, but it also is self-affirming. It is like I said, the big things don't love you back, but you can take joy in your small successes and you can make a difference."[47]

This ideal of citizenship encompassed political and civic, as well as martial activity. In elaborating on his understanding of masculine duty, Vanderboegh discussed the political responsibilities of citizenship:

First, to inform myself on the issues of the day, so that I may make cogent arguments of my beliefs to other citizens and so that I will cast my ballot based upon facts not propaganda and party line. . . .

Second, a citizen must stand ready to serve in the jury box. . . .

Third, to vote at every election. It is our duty to exercise our franchise at the ballot box at every opportunity. . . .

Fourth, and this really is no laughing matter, it is our duty to fight the corruption of the political process wherever it occurs and in every way we can. We must hold the leaders we elect accountable to the law and even, as shocking as it may seem, to their campaign promises.[48]

J. J. Johnson offered a similar vision of active citizenship that emphasized political rather than martial activity: "If we grab onto the first amendment and use it every day, then we won't need to use the second. Those of you who own twenty guns, go out and sell a couple and buy a computer. Set up a home page on the internet and teach people about the first amendment. Start a shortwave radio program. Get the message out."[49]

Militia members also placed considerable emphasis on a citizen's civic duty to contribute to the larger community in a crisis. In 1994, Norm Olson urged militia members to prepare to offer safe haven to refugees in the event of the collapse of the federal government. Jim McKinzey expressed his sense of civic obligation in a program of survivalist preparation. He stored arms, food, clothing, medical supplies, and other essentials far in excess of the needs of his family in order to be able to provide refuge for others: "You come over to my house right now and I can arm fifteen people, totally arm them, and put them in the field and, in my basement, I have well over a year's supply of reserve groceries." Mike Vanderboegh argued that citizens had an obligation to serve others in moments of crisis: he defined citizens as "the people who had the smarts and the determination, and more importantly the ethos, the social philosophy that they needed to take care of the wider community as well."[50]

Women participated in almost all militia groups from the earliest days of the movement, and most militiamen acknowledged the desirability of female participation in the political and civic responsibilities of citizenship. John Hakes noted that at the second meeting of his local unit of what would become the ICVM, the wives of those assembled came into the garage where their husbands were meeting, and said, "Hey, we've been in here talking, and we think we should be part of this too." Hakes described the roles filled by these women as "medical, food, a lot of things like communications." In discussing the role of women in the movement, Charlie Morrison described women as full partners in E Pluribus Unum, a political discussion group associated with the Ohio Unorganized Miltia: "You'll find at least half of them are women and they've got the same goals, as far as the Constitution. They write their congressman, senators, make their phone calls, we pass out flyers, have a newsletter going on, that kind of thing."[51]

Nonetheless, many militiamen expressed ambivalence toward female participation in the martial aspects of citizenship. Tom Plummer and Mike Vanderboegh both celebrated individual female members of their militias who had mastered the military arts. But both expressed an anxiety that female participation in combat transgressed natural gender roles. Vanderboegh noted that when women were wounded in combat, their male colleagues abandoned the fight to tend to them, and this disrupted unit cohesion at a critical moment. Plummer suggested that men might not be able to withstand the psychic trauma of watching women killed in combat: "If we ever would happen to get into hard-core combat, it might not be as easy for a woman, and when you're into seeing people's guts all over the place, it's unpleasant. It would be less, really unpleasant if it were a woman."[52]

Other militiamen simply insisted that women had no place in combat. Oral Deckard, for example, argued that female self-sacrifice in combat was unnatural: "Instinctively, I think, most men will go into mortal combat, sacrificing their own life, to defend their wife and children. I'm not going to advocate that women take on the same attitude. If they do that heroic, well, then, I'll commend them, but it's not in their best interests of their children that they sacrifice themselves. That's the job of the man."[53]

Although most militiamen saw the martial aspects of citizenship as essentially male, they also conceived of that role as rooted in their attachment to family and community. A description of weekend field exercises conducted by the Missouri 51st Militia demonstrated a close connection between martial citizenship and domestic life: "rifle and pistol practice included first time shooters and youngsters. . . . It was apparent that the militiamen were proficient in the use of their arms. . . . Though the training was enthusiastic and done in earnest, this was a family affair. Husbands, wives, and kids were very much a part of the group." Norm Olson described his motivation for participating in the militia movement as driven primarily by his relationship with his children and his descendants, a relationship characterized by obligation and affection: "The only thing we can leave to our children is a legacy of who we were and what we could do. And one day when they come out to your grave site, they're going to either stand over your grave with hallowed respect and whispering soft words and cherished words of admiration and thanksgiving because you did everything you could do, or else your grave will be covered with brambles and they'll come out and they'll curse the day that you lived because you did nothing when you had the chance."[54]

The militia movement was indeed influenced by the tensions in masculine identity at the turn of the century. But the civic ideal of citizen-as-guardian espoused by militiamen bore little resemblance to the Gibson's warrior dream. To the contrary, it represented a new conception of civic masculinity that directly challenged the hegemonic masculinity of the warrior dream.

The Last Necessary Ingredient: The Recovery of the Libertarian Memory of the American Revolution

The idea of reviving the militia as a revolutionary institution gained currency on the far right as early as the 1980s and it took several different forms. In 1984 William Potter Gale envisioned the "unorganized militia" as a county-based military force that would enforce the mandates of the Committee of the States. In 1992, white supremacist Louis Beam wrote an essay entitled "Leaderless Resistance," in which he argued that "those who love our race" should form leaderless cells for the purpose of resisting a government whose corruption he measured by its enforcement of civil rights and equal protection for minorities. He suggested that such cells would strike proactively at the government in a manner impossible to predict: "Those idealists truly committed to the cause of freedom will act when they feel the time is ripe, or will take their cue from others who precede them." When white supremacists gathered in Estes Park in 1992 to formulate their response to Ruby Ridge, Beam offered his essay as the organizational model for a new militia movement.[55]

These far right conceptions of a revived militia would not, however, serve as the intellectual inspiration for the bulk of the movement. The final necessary factor in the emergence of the militia movement was the recovery of the libertarian memory of the American Revolution by the gun rights movement. In the mid-1970s, the National Rifle Association adopted a much more militant stance in its political lobbying, arguing that all forms of gun control violated basic constitutional principles. To make its case more persuasive, the NRA promoted legal scholarship to support the thesis that private gun ownership was constitutionally protected under the Second Amendment. This individual rights interpretation of the Second Amendment, though common in the nineteenth century, had fallen out of favor with judges and most legal scholars in the twentieth century.[56]

One of the most important early reevaluations of the Second Amendment was a 1976 article in the *Fordham Urban Law Journal* by David I. Caplan, a lawyer and gun rights activist. In "Restoring the Balance: The Second Amendment Revisited," Caplan offered the first modern articulation of what has become known as the insurrectionary interpretation of the Second Amendment. Caplan argued that the Second Amendment recognized a right of private gun ownership because the Framers believed that private arms had a role to play in the constitutional balance between the people and their governors:

> The founding fathers were, after all, revolutionaries who had seen that the success of the American Revolution was in no small part attributable to militia action, some of it in the nature of guerilla-type warfare. In striving to protect the "security of a free state" from tyranny, the second amendment draftsmen apparently believed that the private keeping of arms played a significant role in deterring any Presidential attempts at usurpation.[57]

Several other lawyers connected with the gun rights movement, including David T. Hardy and Stephen P. Halbrook, elaborated on this insurrectionary interpretation of the Second Amendment. In a series of law review essays, and also shorter articles in gun rights publications such as *The Rifleman,* they explored eighteenth-century understandings of the militia, and discussed statements by prominent founders, including Noah Webster, the Federal Farmer, Tench Coxe, Alexander Hamilton, and James Madison, supportive of the right of revolution and the right to keep and bear arms. Halbrook summed up his work in a monograph, *That Every Man Be Armed,* in 1986, and Hardy published a short sourcebook on the Second Amendment the same year.

Beginning in 1989, scholars unconnected with the gun rights movement began to take this interpretation seriously. Sanford Levinson, professor of law at the University of Texas, argued in 1989 that the insurrectionary interpretation was worthy of serious academic scrutiny. Other scholars at leading law schools, including Akhil Reed Amar, David Williams, Robert Cottrol, Glenn Reynolds, and Randy Barnett, followed Levinson's lead.[58]

The result of this scholarship was the recovery of the libertarian understanding of the American Revolution within the collective memory celebrated by the gun rights movement. As the highlights of this new scholarship began to filter down to rank-and-file gun rights activists, some began to read the *Federalist Papers,* prominent Anti-Federalist tracts, and various other texts from the era of ratification for themselves. Others turned amateur historian and began to comb through more obscure eighteenth-century texts and compile quotes supportive of the insurrectionary interpretation. The most comprehensive of these collections, *The Origin of the Second Amendment,* published by David E. Young in 1991, contained hundreds of excerpts from early American texts mentioning the militia and the right to keep and bear arms.[59]

What gun rights activists found within these texts was a set of eighteenth-century ideas about the nature of government, the right of revolution, and the role of the militia as an armed deterrent against government abuse. In the Anti-Federalist discourse of the ratification period they encountered the Whig fear that all governments, regardless of their structure, inevitably tend toward centralization, the exercise of undelegated power, and the military enforcement of the laws. In the Federalist responses to these texts they found repeated assurances that an armed militia would deter such abuse, and would in the last extremity intervene to protect the people from their governors. In these texts, the modern gun rights movement encountered the most radical legacy of the American Revolution, the idea that the people have a right and duty to take up arms, even against an elected government, should that government exercise unconstitutional power.

Together these ideas became a fundamental part of the collective memory of the gun rights movement, and gun rights activists carried this memory into the Christian Patriot public sphere and into the militia movement. The work of David Hardy, Stephen Halbrook, and Robert Cottrol and Sanford Levison was posted to Usenet groups between 1989 and 1992. Clayton Cramer, a gun rights activist and a prolific researcher and author on the topic of the right to keep and bear arms, posted an early draft of his monograph *For the Defense of Themselves and the State* to the Usenet discussion group ca.politics in 1991.[60]

With these texts available online, and with the distribution of Halbrook's monograph and Hardy's and Young's sourcebooks by gun rights organizations, references to and brief quotes from ratification-era texts entered into the public discussion of the Second Amendment. An impression of this process can be gleaned through an examination of the Google Usenet archive, a searchable database of every Usenet post from 1981 to the present. According to this database, the first reference to Tench Coxe, the Federalist author of several commentaries on the right to keep and bear arms, appeared in a 1991 post to ca.politics by Clayton Cramer. In 1994, Coxe was mentioned in ninety messages posted to newsgroups. While the number of postings was not large in absolute terms, the audience for these discussions was growing exponentially. The Second Amendment was mentioned in 194 messages posted to Usenet prior to 1991. Over the next four years, almost twenty thousand posts to Usenet mentioned the amendment.[61]

A 1994 essay by Mike Vanderboegh offered another glimpse of this process. Vanderboegh observed that during the American Revolution the subject of political liberty was no longer monopolized by a "civil and priestly hierarchy," but became the "object of universal attention and study." A similar phenomenon, Vanderboegh suggested, had overtaken America in the 1990s:

> A good friend listened not long ago to a two-hour discussion of the Federalist and Anti-Federalist papers on a radio call in show in Columbus, Ohio. The callers argued about the substance of the founding father's writings and also shared information on where the Federalist Papers books could be purchased and engaged in a fascinating discussion of why the books were not available at most local bookstores. Two truck drivers were recently overheard discussing the same subject on CB radio, when in the middle of making a point, one said, "Wait a minute, I got to pull over and find out what George Mason said about that." The conversation resumed after he found the citation. When we no longer rely upon the "civil and priestly hierarchy" of the news media and political parties to tell us what to think, we have come full circle to the pre-revolutionary times of our forefathers.[62]

The impact of the libertarian memory of the American Revolution on the militia movement is clear. Jon Roland's 1994 essay "Reviving the Ready Militia" was one of the most widely read and reproduced texts within the militia movement. Roland did not cite fellow Texan Louis Beam, but he did cite Halbrook's *That Every Man Be Armed*. Samuel Sherwood, one of the movement's first organizers, was influenced by a broader range of intellectual currents percolating in the Northwest, especially by Mormon constitutionalism. Nevertheless, Sherwood's 1992 volumes, *The Little Republics* and *Guarantee of the Second Amendment*, owe much to eighteenth-century republicanism and draw heavily on eighteenth-century texts. John Trochman, founder of the Militia of Montana, would base his *Information and Networking Manual* on Sherwood's work. Mike Vanderboegh and Michael Johnson, an early militia spokesman in Florida, grounded some of their early writing on the eighteenth-century texts cited by the 1980s gun rights literature.[63] Without this collective memory of the eighteenth century, there might still have been a right-wing paramilitary response to the rise in state-sponsored violence in the 1990s, but it would have been a very different movement.

A Force upon the Subdivision:
The Militia Movement Takes the Field

The first component militias of the movement began organizing in early 1994. Though there was no one point of origin for the movement as a whole, there were several currents of intellectual influence by which we can trace its spread. The first of these begins with Idaho organizer Samuel Sherwood. Sherwood began to publish his ideas for a militia movement in 1992, as part of a larger vision of constitutional restoration. Sherwood's vision, outlined in *The Little Republics,* called for a return to original constitutional principles through the creation of new democratic republican governments at the county level. He argued that the growth of the welfare state had brought corruption, socialism, and control of the individual in its wake. In describing his solution he invoked the romantic language of a return to the glorious freedom of the Anglo-Saxon shire prior to the arrival of the Norman yoke. Medieval romanticism aside, his blueprint called for the creation of new county governments based on eighteenth-century principles of limited government, popular participation and representation, the separation of powers, and the preservation of inalienable rights. In some sense, Sherwood offered an alternative to William Potter Gale's vision of local sovereignty as a path to national regeneration. Whereas Gale had envisioned empowering the posse comitatus as a fully sovereign body, Sherwood sought to retain the national government established by the "original constitution" of 1787; he simply sought to strip the national and state governments of the powers they had accumulated over the centuries and return them to the people to exercise at the local level. Whereas Gale sought to empower a revolutionary elite in the Committee of the States, Sherwood insisted on open public government and strict democratic accountability for all officeholders. His call for civic regeneration was also free of the white supremacist taint of the Posse Comitatus movement.[64]

Like Gale, Sherwood called for the reinstitution of the militia as part of his framework for county government. In a companion volume, *The Guarantee of the Second Amendment,* Sherwood laid out his vision for the militia. Sherwood is a Latter-day Saint, and his vision was significantly influenced by biblical texts, but he also quoted extensively from the eighteenth-century texts resurrected by the gun rights movement, including *Federalist Nos. 29* and *46* and the essays of Tench Coxe. He used these passages to assert that the people had an inherent right to reconstitute the universal militia and to reclaim "the right to keep and bear arms, have a militia, and maintain a civilian counter balance to the terror of the force of government." He called for concerned citizens to organize militias in their communities and outlined the policies of the United States Militia Association as an umbrella group. In training materials, published in 1994, Sherwood made it clear that the militia would be a public institution. He instructed organizers to publicly announce meetings and invite local magistrates and law enforcement. He urged them to seek charters from state or local officials. He also made it clear that while the USMA was a private organization, membership was open to all who would uphold the Constitution and abide by the laws of the state and nation. He explicitly suggested members of the white supremacist groups operating in the Northwest, who generally rejected the authority of the federal government, would not be permitted to join.[65]

Sherwood had previously operated a home-schooling resource center called Nauvoo Academy. Access to this national network of home schoolers led to the rapid dissemination of Sherwood's call for militia organization. His vision began to bear fruit in the summer of 1994, as units of the United States Militia Association began springing up around the country. The organization first took root in a belt of counties running from Pocatello to Tetonia, Idaho. It also spread into the suburbs of Boise; Portland, Oregon; Philadelphia; and Las Vegas. Additional units emerged in more rural areas of New Mexico and northern Utah.[66]

Sherwood's work had some degree of influence on John Trochman, who joined with his brother David and his nephew Randy to found the Militia of Montana. Trochman had been angered by the federal assault on the home of Randy Weaver, with whom he was friends. He also appeared to move comfortably within the social and intellectual circles of the white supremacist Right in the Pacific Northwest. Trochman participated in programs held at Richard Butler's Aryan Nations compound on at least two occasions, and he is rumored to have been a Christian Identity adherent. When Trochman first began discussing the creation of a militia in Montana, he consulted Sherwood. As a result, the first half of the Militia of Montana *Information and Networking Manual* consisted of a significantly condensed paraphrasing of Sherwood's *Guarantee of the Second Amendment*. But Trochman used Sherwood's words to take the militia movement in a very different direction. Whereas Sherwood envisioned the militia as operating in cooperation with state and federal government, Trochman's vision was much more local. Two deletions from Sherwood's text may also reflect white supremacist influences on Trochman's thought. Sherwood's articles of association stated that "the militia shall at all times be interested in fairness, equality, and justice." Trochman deleted "equality" from this sentence. Sherwood also insisted that the militia "shall always be under the authority of, and be subject to, the penalties of the civil law of the land." Trochman altered this to read "the penalties of the Constitutional laws of the land," a formulation that suggested that militiamen might pick and choose which laws to abide by. Trochman's manual also stated that any citizen might call out the militia to oppose "any armed force" not authorized under state law, a provision that suggested that the militia might turn out to oppose any armed federal officer.[67]

In addition to modifying Sherwood's model for the militia, Trochman's manual offered two additional models of paramilitary organization. MOM's manual included a second section on organizing "militia support groups," public organizations that would fulfill the same role as the militia in states with antiparamilitary activity statutes. These support groups were pyramidal organizations designed to organize a statewide structure of "neighborhood guards." When Trochman later testified that MOM was nothing more than a big neighborhood watch, it is probably this model to which he was referring.[68]

The final model offered in the manual would become the best known and most controversial. Inspired by Louis Beam's essay, "Leaderless Resistance," Trochman included advice on how to form seven-man underground cells. This last section of the manual also suggested that white supremacists might be welcomed into the militia: Trochman warned his potential recruits, "Do not react to the buzzwords: White Supremacists; Tax Protesters; Cultists; Bigots; Nazis; and other words which the masses

Fig. 4. John Trochman at a Preparedness Expo in Spokane, Washington, February 1997. Associated Press.

Trochman, cofounder of the Militia of Montana, is seen here selling militia material and videotapes. Trochman was one of the leading voices in the millenarian wing of the movement.

Fig. 5. Norm Olson in his gun shop, Alanson, MI, 1995. Paul Paiewonsky.

Olson, cofounder of the Michigan Militia, was a licensed gun dealer in one of the northernmost counties of Michigan's Lower Peninsula. He was one of the leading spokesmen for the constitutional wing of the movement until May 1995.

Fig. 6. J. J. Johnson addressing a meeting of the Virginia Citizens Militia, Richmond, VA, July 1996. Associated Press.

Johnson was the cofounder of E Pluribus Unum, a patriot discussion group in Columbus, OH. He was also an early leader of the Ohio Unorganized Militia.

Fig. 7. The Gadsden Minutemen on the firing line. Copyright, *The Birmingham News*, 2008. All rights reserved. Reprinted with permission.

Target practice and military training were a fundamental part of militia activity in the 1990s. Here the Gadsden Minutemen practice marksmanship with a variety of semiautomatic weapons.

are conditioned to hate. After the media has demonized the target, as in Weaver and Waco, the government is free to murder as it chooses."[69]

The Militia of Montana began holding public recruiting meetings in February 1994. As an actual paramilitary organization, the MOM was largely restricted to the state's northwest corner. Nevertheless, Trochman had a broader intellectual influence. He opened a mail-order "information clearing house" of militia and preparedness information and videotapes and toured the country, speaking at gun shows, preparedness expos, and even at Yale University.[70]

Trochman's intellectual influence outside of the Northwest is most evident in Ohio. In early 1994, the Ohio Unorganized Militia (OUM) was organized by an uneasy alliance of libertarians and white supremacist sovereign citizens. The manual of the OUM was a revision of Trochman's MOM manual. Here again, Trochman's product was put to new uses, and the OUM made significant alterations to his manual. The OUM styled itself as an association of "Nationals of the Ohio Republic." The OUM manual further defined "nationals" as follows: "Term used in reference to people, recognizing their sovereignty, as opposed to the word citizen, which indicates 'the property of.'"[71] The term was a reference to the theory of sovereign citizenship that grew out of the Posse Comitatus movement of the 1980s. The theory of sovereign citizenship argues that after the Civil War, Americans had been duped into accepting the complete control of the state and federal governments and had thereby given up the rights and privileges of free men. To regain these freedoms and return to the original status of individual sovereignty, individuals must rescind all contracts acknowledging the sovereignty of government. Such contracts include birth certificates, drivers' licenses, and social security numbers. An explicitly racist variant of this theory, dubbed the theory of Fourteenth Amendment citizenship, argues that African Americans may only aspire to a lesser category of citizenship devoid of inalienable rights, and that sovereign citizenship is only available to Caucasians.[72]

The incorporation of this theory into the original OUM manual had serious implications. Whereas Sherwood and Trochman had stipulated that the militia might never use violence against unarmed citizens, the

OUM manual stated that this protection applied only to unarmed nationals, suggesting that the militia need respect only the rights of sovereign citizens. The manual also stipulated that the militia could be called out against the police or state government by its commander. Sherwood had insisted that only the "representative authorities within their jurisdiction," such as the governor, state senate, or assembled county commissioners, could issue such a call.[73] In sum, the manual suggested that the OUM might have been conceived as a tool of the white supremacist movement in Ohio.

If there is an identifiable line of influence from Samuel Sherwood to John Trochman to the early OUM, a second line of influence emerged almost simultaneously in Texas and Michigan, one much closer to Sherwood's original vision. In Texas, Jon Roland and Bill Utterback organized the first muster of the Texas Constitutional Militia on the first anniversary of the final assault on Waco, April 19, 1994. In response to Roland's public call, several dozen individuals assembled at daybreak on the outskirts of San Antonio. Only two dozen individuals came to the first muster, but subsequent meetings served as the genesis of the first county units of the TCM.[74] Roland outlined his vision for the militia in his essay, "Reviving the Ready Militia." He began with George Mason's question to the Virginia ratifying convention, "Who are the militia? They consist now of the whole people, except for a few public officers." Roland explained that his intent was to revive the eighteenth-century institution of the universal militia. He argued that the Dick Act of 1902, which scrapped the universal militia system mandated by the Militia Act of 1792 and institutionalized the National Guard in its place, had violated the Constitution's intent to ensure that the states would continue to organize and train the whole militia. "If the state fails to do so," Roland declared, "people have not only the right but the duty to organize and train themselves locally, using their own arms." Roland recognized that the militias he was organizing would be composed of "volunteers, who may not constitute a cross section of the general population. In this situation," he observed, "the militia members must make a special effort to avoid having the militia unit take on the attributes of a private association, such as by always calling up the militia using public notices, and allowing any responsible citizen to participate. It must also avoid any suggestion of partisan or sectarian bias, and limit itself to constitutional actions." Roland urged militia members to reach out to local and state officials, and to involve themselves in community affairs. By the spring of 1995, the TCM had organized militias in thirty-eight counties, concentrated in the San Antonio, Houston, and Dallas metropolitan areas.[75]

On April 29, 1994, ten days after the TCM's initial muster, Norm Olson and Ray Southwell organized the First Brigade of the Michigan Militia in Emmett County. Like Roland and Utterback, Olson and Southwell argued that the militia must operate publicly and be open to all: "Call the assembly meeting. Make them public. Stay focused. Stay constitutional and cling to the rule of law, due process, and the Bill of Rights. Open your militia to all races, creeds, religions. This is what America is really all about." Olson also appealed to the memory of the American Revolution. He quoted at length Patrick Henry's call upon the Virginia Provincial Convention to embody the militia as a precedent, and he argued that "it was clear to the early patriots that the militia was independent of the organized government, and made up of the people who stood ready to repel a tyrannical government from denying the rights of liberty under the Constitution." Over the next year, Olson and Southwell organized brigades of the Michigan Militia Corps in almost all of Michigan's eighty-three counties.[76]

Together, Samuel Sherwood, Jon Roland, and Norm Olson offered a more constitutionalist, civic, and racially inclusive vision of the militia than that propagated by John Trochman. Their vision had a broad appeal. In Ohio, libertarians and gun rights activists were by the end of 1994 becoming increasingly disenchanted with the white supremacist overtones of the early OUM. In February 1995, J. J. Johnson, the African American cofounder of E Pluribus Unum, issued a new manual offering a much more constitutionalist vision for the OUM. In that manual, Johnson reprinted Roland's "Reviving the Ready Militia" and Olson's essay "Is the Citizen Militia Lawful?" Thereafter, in the fall of 1996, Ohio militias of a constitutionalist orientation organized the Ohio Unorganized Militia Advisory and Assistance Command as a new umbrella group. In 1998 it claimed to have organized units in as many as fifty counties.[77]

As was true of Sherwood, Roland's and Olson's outreach stimulated militia organization in many states. By 1996, Olson's manual for the Michigan Militia served as the basis for the manuals of militias in Texas, Florida, Pennsylvania, Missouri, and California, and Roland's essay had been republished in militia newsletters in Alabama and Ohio.[78]

One further source of inspiration proved especially important in the Midwest. In early 1994 Mark Koernke began broadcasting a radio program called the *Intelligence Report* over the stations of World Wide Christian Radio. Koernke's program, and a videotaped presentation entitled *America in Peril*, warned of an imminent invasion by the forces of the New World Order. Koernke urged patriots to form underground cells along the lines suggested by John Trochman. He claimed to have formed his own Michigan Militia at Large, and had some significant influence over some of the brigades of the Michigan Militia forming in southeast Michigan. Koernke also joined the preparedness expo circuit and helped stimulate militia organization in Ohio and Pennsylvania.[79]

From these multiple influences, hundreds of militia groups began to organize in the fall and winter of 1994–95. The movement had relatively little presence in the Northeast, but emerged in various degrees of organization in most other regions of the country. The Indiana Citizens Volunteer Militia, the South Carolina Citizens Militia, the Oregon Militia, and the New Mexico Citizens Regulated Militia adopted the model of statewide organization pioneered in Texas, Michigan, and Ohio.[80] In other states, multicounty organizations emerged. For example, the Northern Illinois Minutemen organized in the suburban counties surrounding Chicago, and the Florida State Militia spread through the counties of Florida's Treasure Coast.[81] In other states, organization was ad hoc, with independent groups springing up at random. In Alabama, militias emerged independently in the suburbs of Gadsden, Birmingham, and Montgomery. In California a dozen independent groups organized in different parts of the state, from the suburbs of San Diego and Sacramento to the foothills of the Sierras.[82]

Several journalists and scholars observing the movement have described it as rural in character, and many participants would agree with this characterization.[83] An examination of a sample of over two hundred militia counties lends itself to a very different conclusion. In the twenty-two states in which I have been able to assemble significant information on the militia movement, stable militias organized in 246 counties. Of these counties 139 (57 percent) fell within metropolitan areas as the federal government defined them in 1993, the vast majority of them in metropolitan areas with a population of greater than 250,000. In other words, the bulk of the movement emerged in counties that had experienced significant urban and suburban development. Another 52 (21 percent) counties sat adjacent to the metropolitan boundaries that marked the suburban-rural frontier, and of these 15 would be "captured" in the next decade. Only 55 (22 percent) of the 232 counties lay entirely unconnected to the suburban-rural frontier. Of these, 5 would be captured by 2003 and the metropolitan frontier would move adjacent to another 10.[84]

Looked at overall, the bulk of the militia movement emerged in suburban and suburbanizing communities. In Texas the movement expanded through the suburbs of San Antonio, Houston, and Dallas. In New Mexico, the movement grew out of the emerging suburbs of Albuquerque and Santa Fe. The strength of the United States Militia Association lay in the suburbs of Boise, Portland, and Philadelphia. In Ohio, the movement grew up rapidly in the suburbs of Cleveland, Columbus, and Cincinnati, and around smaller cities like Dayton, Findlay, and Akron. In Indiana and Illinois, the movement gravitated around the suburbs of Indianapolis and the Chicago–South Bend metropolitan area. In Florida, Alabama, and South Carolina, the movement emerged similarly in the suburbs of major cities like Birmingham and Palm Beach and subsidiary cities like Greenville-Spartanburg and Gadsden.

When militias emerged outside of metropolitan boundaries, they often took root in counties where a combination of rapid population growth and the proximity to more urbanized communities raised the prospect of incorporation into metropolitan America. Large units of the Indian Citizens Volunteer Militia emerged in Brown, Owen, and Greene counties, all incorporated during the 1990s. The same phenomenon of exurban growth probably played a role in militia formation in Torrance County, New Mexico, and in Bibb County, Alabama.[85]

Even where the movement took root in fully rural communities, it tended to emerge in communities that were growing rapidly. Twenty-one of the fifty-five rural militia counties experienced population growth in excess of 20 percent over the course of the 1990s. Of the most rural militia counties, those scoring a nine on the USDA's nine point rural-urban continuum, all but one were growing faster than the national average.[86] Two examples illustrate the importance of this growth. The Militia of Montana's greatest recruiting success lay in Flathead County, centered on the Kalispell, a popular vacation destination. Flathead County's population grew 26 percent during the 1990s, a figure that does not capture the boom in second-home construction. When county officials refused to appropriate funds to update the county's master plan to provide new zoning to regulate land use, a private association of recently arrived homeowners hired a planner and crafted a revision of the master plan. When they submitted a revised plan to the county government, local landowners complained bitterly that the planning process and zoning regulations were being imposed by "outsiders." MOM's warning of the threat posed by the shadowy cabal behind the New World Order found a fertile environment in a community riven by the process of rapid growth.[87] Emmet County, Michigan, birthplace of the Michigan Militia, experienced a similar growth rate and for a similar reason—Michigan's northern and western lakeshore counties were booming in the 1990s as they became desirable vacation and retirement destinations.[88]

In sum, even to the degree that the militia movement took root in rural America, it was more often a creature of rural growth than rural decline. Though several of the individuals who inspired the movement in its early days lived in rural communities isolated from metropolitan America, the movement itself was largely a creature of the suburbs. In these communities the threat of state violence represented by paramilitary policing, the growing reach of the Christian Patriot public sphere, the resurrection of the libertarian memory of the Revolution, and the political and cultural friction generated by suburbanization all came together to produce the militia movement.

AN EXPLORATION OF MILITIA IDEOLOGY: THE
WHIG DIAGNOSIS OF POST–COLD WAR AMERICA

In *Armed and Dangerous,* the first of many reports on the militia movement issued by civil rights organizations, the Anti-Defamation League described the movement's preoccupation with gun control. But it also noted that militia figures had expressed a much broader range of political and constitutional concerns: "Although thwarting gun control is the chief aim of the militias, they seek to turn the clock back on federal involvement in a host of other issues as well." The report then asked an astute question: was the movement's threat to use violence limited to the issue of gun control, or did it extend to "the 'turning around' of the U.S. itself from what the militants see as the 'treasonous' directions of the federal government's present policies"? What, the ADL asked, do "the 'militias' intend to do with their guns"? Though astute, for the ADL the question was rhetorical: it implied that the militia's challenge to the state's monopoly on violence could not be limited to a single issue. Any challenge to the state that transgressed "the time honored means provided by the constitution," the ADL suggested, would necessarily spin out of control and incite a wave of "lawless" violence.[1]

The question of what the militias intended to do with their guns went to the heart of the movement's challenge to the twentieth-century political order. The answer to that question is, like the movement itself, multifaceted and complex. Part of the complexity stems from the fact that different militias, and sometimes even different members of a particular militia, gravitated toward two distinct explanations of the rise in state violence. Constitutionalists within the movement accepted an explanatory framework with roots in eighteenth-century Whig ideology. As constitutionalists looked back over the twentieth century, they perceived that corruption, usurpation, and state coercion, a process that had undermined republics throughout history, lay behind the growing power and violence of the federal government. Adherents of this diagnosis believed that the threat they faced was political and constitutional in nature and that militia organization offered a model of political activism and armed deterrence most likely to yield a solution. More millennial voices within the movement, however, perceived the rise in state violence as the onset of tribulations marking the end of time. They warned of an impending invasion by the forces of the New World Order, a shadowy group of alien conspirators with a despotic and genocidal program. This diagnosis pointed to different solutions, ranging from survivalist withdrawal from society to proactive violence against the forces of the conspiracy.

Constitutionalists within the movement saw armed organization as a legitimate response to a rise in state violence. They attributed that violence to the paramilitarization of law enforcement, to authoritarian attitudes in the halls of government, and to the expansion of the powers of the federal government. As a solution, they proposed the devolution of power back to states and local communities. They argued that devolution would facilitate a second goal, the restoration of civil society at the local level. Constitutionalists insisted that these goals could only be accomplished by political means, and that armed conflict would undermine them.

But the constitutional militia members also argued that the state's unchecked monopoly on violence had produced more violence, in the form of paramilitary raids, rather than less. They sought to create an armed deterrent in order to reverse that trend. Insurgent violence, or at least the deterrent capacity to engage in it, was thus an essential part of the militia's program. Spokespersons for the movement took pains to identify a series of "redlines," government activities that would trigger a violent response. Constitutionalists also sought, less coherently, to lay out norms of legitimate insurgent violence that would avoid the brutality that they perceived in the paramilitary warriors of the BATF and the white supremacist Right. Among constitutionalists, the challenge to the state's monopoly on violence transcended the issue of gun control, but it did not encompass the entirety of the movement's political program.

Millenarians within the movement were less concerned with long-term programs of political and constitutional reform. Some wished to withdraw from civil society rather than devote themselves to strengthening it. Others emphasized survivalist preparation. Millenarians contemplated different forms of violence as well: at least three groups associated with the millenarian wing of the militia movement planned proactive assaults on public facilities likely to cause hundreds of civilian casualties. Constitutionalists within the movement brought all three conspiracies to the attention of law enforcement.

Between 1995 and 1998, the movement gradually separated into distinct constitutionalist and millenarian wings. Members of the two wings disagreed over their diagnosis of events, over the role of the militia as a public organization, and over the norms of legitimate insurgent violence. Nevertheless, militias from the two wings continued to communicate and in some cases cooperate. They shared a preoccupation with the threat of state violence and the belief that a state monopoly on violence was incompatible with a free society.

"It Is Standard Policy and It Is Growing": Militia Perceptions of State Violence

Many members of the militia movement observed that Ruby Ridge and Waco changed the way they looked at the world. As Russell Smith of the Dallas County TCM put it, "Waco was the second shot heard round the world. It woke us up to a very corrupted beast."[2] The catalyst of the movement was not so much the events themselves as the broader examination of state violence that they triggered. Militia members perceived in Ruby Ridge and Waco a callous disregard for the value of human life and liberty. As they gazed more broadly upon activities of law enforcement at all levels, they saw a corrupt preoccupation with victimless crime, a growing authoritarianism within police paramilitary culture, a tolerance for individual brutality, and a wholesale assault on individual privacy. They concluded that Ruby Ridge and Waco were not isolated incidents, but rather evidence of a systemic threat to their liberty, property, and lives. What emerged from militia deliberations on the topic of state violence was thus a broad indictment of the repressive apparatus of the state.

Greg Friedholm, a member of the Howard County regiment of the ICVM, noted that he "would never have joined a militia before Waco." Oral Deckard attributed his motivation to join the movement to Ruby Ridge and Waco: "I guess I got into the militia when I saw our police forces attacking the citizens and murdering innocent people." In his survey of Usenet posts, Stan Weeber observed that three-quarters of the militia members who described the concerns that brought them into the movement agreed with Friedholm and Deckard: they identified Ruby Ridge or Waco as the precipitant cause.[3]

Many of those joining the movement perceived in the events of Ruby Ridge and Waco not tragedy but policy, grounded in a malicious disregard for human life. Carl Worden, a spokesman for the Southern Oregon Militia, explained Ruby Ridge and Waco as follows: "Both cases were triggered by one common event: a federal agent or agents had been killed by those the FBI later slaughtered. Perhaps the FBI wanted to send a clear message that such behavior, even in self-defense, would not be tolerated." Oral Deckard agreed, asserting that the assault on the Waco compound "definitely was murder, and that it was not only an isolated account, but it is standard policy and it is growing."[4]

Ruby Ridge and Waco caused those in the movement to look for other examples of state violence. They soon found them: militia publications were filled with articles on paramilitary raids gone bad, many of which empathized with the victims. In 1996, *E Pluribus Unum*, a newsletter closely associated with the Ohio Unorganized Militia, published brief summaries of fifteen botched raids by the BATF, the Drug Enforcement Agency, and local law enforcement agencies between 1988 and 1996, three of which resulted in civilian deaths. *Taking Aim*, the newsletter of the Militia of Montana, ran a similar story that emphasized abuses by social services agencies. *Necessary Force,* the newsletter of the Missouri 51st Militia, ran several detailed stories on a 1995 raid on the Kuriatnyk household in Longview, Missouri. While these articles often presented a one-sided version of events, they reinforced militia members' perception that they or their neighbors could easily fall victim to the paramilitary violence of the state.[5]

That perception was widely held among those who joined the movement. As John Hakes put it, "Doesn't something like Waco scare you? You know that could happen right here in Brown County. We have small religious groups like that." The *E Pluribus Unum* story ran under the headline, "Just who are the terrorists?" and concluded with a statement by one of the victims: "If they could do this to us, they could do it to anybody." The newsletter of the Gadsden Minutemen ran a commentary on the Lekan siege in 1995 that concluded with the following observation: "Mr. Lekan's only crime was being a gun owner, a patriot, a political activist, and being an outspoken critic of the government. Wake up people, this is a clear description of ourselves." Of the militia members posting to Usenet studied by Stan Weeber, two-thirds expressed a fear of the federal government and specifically its capacity for violence.[6]

As they contemplated this capacity, many of them for the first time, members of the movement came to the conclusion that the federalization and militarization of law enforcement had fostered a paramilitary culture of violence. Harold Sheil, editor of *Necessary Force,* asked in 1995, "Does anyone remember when peace officers became law enforcement officers? It just sort of sneaked up on us." Sheil noted that in the course of expanding its policing powers, the federal government had sidestepped the Posse Comitatus Act's prohibition on the use of standing military forces for the purpose of law enforcement: "Since the military force cannot be used against the civilian populace then law enforcement simply becomes military. This bodes evil." Sheil explained the danger: "A SWAT Team is an assault team. An assault team's only job is to make dynamic entry and to kill, kill, kill. Rules of engagement are preset instructions on who, what, and when to kill."[7]

Others in the movement saw the same danger. The North Carolina

Militia Corps warned that "the government has established well armed, trained, and equipped militarized federal agencies that are in reality an extension of the government's army, and have acted as such against the people." When questioned by the Senate in May 1995, Bob Fletcher of the Militia of Montana took pains to emphasize the dangers of the paramilitarization of law enforcement: "Any time that any nation of the world starts to utilize local police with their federal enforcement and starts to federally arm police at the local level . . . that nation is probably moving into a dictatorship."[8]

Militia members also grew incensed by the increasingly aggressive behavior exhibited by law enforcement. Too many officers of the various federal police agencies, Harold Sheil complained, wanted to "wear a ninja suit and hobnailed boots. They dream of 'Rambo.'" Sheil's wife Kay, who would serve as executive officer of the Missouri 51st Militia after his death, wrote a detailed description of a police raid on the home of Laura and Michael Kuriatnyk in McDonald County, Missouri. She placed particular emphasis on the fact that the officers involved in the raid had leveled their guns on the couple's six-year-old daughter in an effort to control her. Oral Deckard also expressed anger over police brutality: "We get reports all the time, a steady stream of people being brutalized beyond reason, and they are mostly black. They're brutalized in a fashion that can only reasonably be called a lynching. They're done by city police officers, county sheriff's departments, BATF, FBI, basically anybody in uniform." Deckard argued that police brutality and the code of silence that fostered it played a significant role in the emergence of the movement: "Guys like me wouldn't have to form desperate little organizations, hoping against hope that we can do something to revive legitimacy in government, and an end to tyranny, if the people who have sworn an oath to do that would get off their dead ass." Deckard pointed specifically to the beating of Rodney King, while James M., a Cleveland militiaman, offered the rape of Abner Louima as an example of the abuses that he believed had become common.[9]

Militia members saw in the centralization and paramilitarization of law enforcement a threat not just to their lives and persons, but to their privacy as well. Kay Sheil complained that the loosening of standards for the issuing of search warrants had led to untold abuses: "Thousands of innocent people in our country have suffered the loss of reputation, property, money, and some have even died because of these laws." *E Pluribus Unum* warned of emerging surveillance technologies that would strip away privacy rights. In its very first issue, *Taking Aim* warned of a broad government program of warrantless surveillance involving taps on central nodes in the telephone routing system, and the use of supercomputers to run keyword searches on millions of captured phone conversations. The technologies identified in the article were more recently implicated in a scandal over warrantless surveillance authorized by President George W. Bush.[10]

Members of the movement believed that the war on drugs was a significant factor in the increase in violence and abuse. Many argued that waging war on a victimless crime was a fruitless and ultimately destructive enterprise. James M. noted that he had come to view the war on drugs "as being not worth its price in loss of liberty and the suffering that it has caused particularly in the inner city." Joe Pilchak described the drug war as unlawful and unwise: "I don't believe in drug use. I don't believe in anything that's mind altering or that would basically go out and injure the body, but that's the individual's free choice. We never had a drug problem in this country until we made drugs illegal." Jeff Randall, cofounder of the Gadsden Militia, complained that the violent enforcement of laws regulating victimless crimes was abusive by definition, asking rhetorically, "Should I have my door kicked in and possibly be killed for harming no one?"[11]

Most in the movement expected that a war on guns would soon take its place beside the war on drugs. But some painted a starker picture of what was to come. Mike Vanderboegh suggested that the 1994 crime bill, aggressive and arbitrary tax enforcement, property seizures under environmental laws, antiterror legislation, and government efforts to intimidate dissenters had combined to create a vast new class of citizens who would henceforth be targeted by law enforcement. It was only a matter of time, Vanderboegh argued, before the news media began to tacitly endorse the violent enforcement of these laws, much as they had endorsed the war on drugs. "What will we do when we begin to read such stories,"

Vanderboegh asked, "what will we do when the name in the story is someone we know, someone from work or the gun club? What will we do when, or if, it's OUR name on the warrant?"[12]

Sometimes members conveyed the menace they perceived in the growth and centralization of government power by describing government as a physical presence in their lives. John Hakes suggested a threatening physical proximity when complaining of government growth: "We have government in our face now, and that's another thing: I want to be left alone by my government, you know, I just want them to go away and leave me alone. . . . We're being overrun by our own government." Norm Olson described Waco as the result of "the federal government coming into all areas of our lives." In her book *Women and Guns*, Deborah Homsher recounted a similar conversation with Sherry, a member of the Chemung County Militia in central New York. Sherry said that her colleagues in the militia were "people who feel that the government is pushing so hard that they don't want to be pushed any more. So they're saying: 'look, this is the line; this is the constitution; live by it. We intend to.'" This sense of physical intrusion is also reflected in militia fears that their government was intent on disarming them. As they imagined the process of disarmament, it most often involved door-to-door gun confiscation.[13]

Kay Sheil expressed the conclusion that many militia members came to at the end of their examination of the state's capacity for violence: "Here and now, in America in 1996, our government routinely violates people's rights. It's on a smaller scale than Nazi Germany, for now, but the trend is accelerating. The highest law in the land, the U.S. Constitution, has been brushed aside. What else holds them back? What makes you think this trend won't get totally out of control?" For Sheil, the paramount question was "Where does it stop?"[14] But for others, a different question assumed greater importance: how and why did it begin?

Competing Explanations of the Threat:
Whig and Millenarian Diagnoses of State Violence

In 1994, pondering Waco, the assault weapons ban, and proposed follow-on gun legislation, Mike Vanderboegh found inspiration in Gordon

Wood's discussion of the "Whig science of politics" in *Creation of the American Republic*. In particular, Vanderboegh cited John Dickinson's admonition that the crucial question was "not what evil *has actually attended* particular measures—but, what evil, in the nature of things, *is likely to attend* them." After quoting Wood at length, Vanderboegh offered the following commentary: "How much like our ancestors are we that we aim to deflect tyranny before it arrives? Truly, we do not yet have gun confiscation, nor a national ID card (although we have a web of databases that amount to as much), nor (with some revealing exceptions) has the government jackboot been felt upon our necks. Yet our ancestors did not wait before responding. . . . Were they guilty then, as some accuse us today, of exaggerated fears and paranoia because they saw the threat and avoided it?"[15]

Few militia members were as well read in American history as Vanderboegh, but his observation captures the manner in which eighteenth-century libertarian texts evocative of Whig ideology and the libertarian memory of the Revolution shaped militia members' perception of the threat posed by state violence. As constitutionalists within the militia movement looked at the problems facing the United States in the 1990s, they perceived that the nation had fallen victim to a classic Whig crisis of corruption, centralization, and constitutional decay. Jim Wade, commander of the Fifth Brigade, Indiana Citizens Volunteer Militia, described the problems facing the country as "manifestations of a government's tendency to empower itself. A tendency that has historically proven to lead to genuine tyranny if left unchecked." Michael McKinzey, cofounder of the Missouri 51st Militia, saw Waco as a symptom of this process: "The amassing [of] a great deal of power at the federal level is exactly what's happened. . . . These guys, the founding fathers, they read the philosophers, they knew human nature, and they knew what the problem was going to be and, exactly what they feared is exactly what has come to be, and that's incredible to me." J. J. Johnson, a leading constitutional militiaman in Ohio, suggested in 1995 that the militia movement was based upon the premise that "the delegates to the constitutional convention didn't trust any form of government, including the one they had just created. They knew that it was only a matter of time before the government would grow and attempt to usurp the rights of the people. History had proven this fact."[16]

Mike Vanderboegh's encounter with the "Whig science of politics" also suggested to him that it was time to look for patterns and trends in threatening events such as Waco. As he and other militia members contemplated their situation, the patterns that they saw alarmed them. As Vanderboegh later put it, "it didn't take much of a leap of logic to see that an administration which would carry out a Waco while simultaneously pushing the envelope of gun control put us all on notice that anybody could be next year's Davidians." Bob Clark, a member of the Michigan Militia, saw a similar progression: "First the feds put that Reverend Moon character in jail for tax evasion, I thought that was a great idea. Then they went after that guy from India with all those limousines in Oregon, which was OK with me too. But I started getting worried when I learned what happened to Randy Weaver. When the FBI killed all those people in Waco, I asked myself who they were going to come after next, the Baptists?" Tom Plummer, one of the founders of the Ohio Unorganized Militia Advisory and Assistance Command, described a similar growing unease as he watched the advent of no-knock searches, the passage of the Brady bill, and then the Waco siege.[17]

The search for patterns also led members of the movement to ponder the broader history of state violence in America and abroad. Some came to recognize that the inhabitants of America's inner cities had suffered from state violence for decades. Thus, J. J. Johnson denounced "the militarization of our law enforcement, those 'peace officers' who can be found clad in their black ninja suits while they storm inner city neighborhoods indiscriminately shooting and beating residents while fighting their 'war on drugs.'" Another Ohio militiaman noted that "if something like Waco happened once, it can happen again. And Waco wasn't the first Waco. There was the incident in Philadelphia at the MOVE headquarters almost ten years before that."[18]

Other militia members offered the holocaust as the end result of the abuse of the state's monopoly on violence. In a column in *E Pluribus Unum* James Barber compared a proposed bill authorizing the creation of a twenty-five-hundred-man federal paramilitary police force to the creation of Nazi Germany's Order Police. Barber drew extensively upon Christopher Browning's *Ordinary Men* in discussing the Order Police's role in the Holocaust. At the end of his column, Barber reminded readers that in *Federalist No. 46*, James Madison had ridiculed the Whig fears expressed by Anti-Federalists that the federal government would "accumulate a military force for the projects of ambition." Barber responded to Madison's charge that such fears represented the "misguided exaggerations of a counterfeit zeal" by asking simply, "Misguided exaggerations, or sober apprehensions?"[19]

If the Whig diagnosis of the nation's ills caused militiamen to look for patterns across time and space and to empathize with victims of different backgrounds, it also suggested that the problem they faced was with their own government and that it was political in nature, stemming from the spread of authoritarian ideology among government officials. In J. J. Johnson's 1998 novel, *Cracking the Liberty Bell*, an FBI official gives voice to the authoritarianism that Johnson believed had led to the atrocities at Waco: "In order to preserve, protect, and defend the Constitution, the government must maintain its authority over the people. If the people will not submit to the power of the government, then their constitution and their rights mean nothing. The authority and integrity of government must be maintained at all costs."[20] Mike Vanderboegh attributed similarly authoritarian attitudes to the Clinton administration:

> The Clinton administration especially was famous for playing hardball all the time, whether it was necessary or not. And everybody knew that. The people knew it, the law enforcement guys. . . . everybody was complaining that this administration was getting out of control. That was the overarching message of everything—from the gun stuff to Waco to the Traders Gun Shop raid, you know, this was an administration that was kicking in doors and didn't give a hoot in hell about the Constitution.[21]

The centralization of government power was a second focus of militia criticism. Militia members argued that the federal exercise of expanded powers over policing, economic production, and the general welfare tended to undermine local autonomy and civil society and to stimulate political violence as more and more individuals came under the scrutiny of militarized federal law enforcement agencies. More importantly, they saw this accumulation of power as an example of the historical process of centralization described in Whig ideology, a process that the founders had warned would undermine the republic.

Members of the movement examined the accumulation of federal power through the lens of constitutional fundamentalism, a mode of interpretation that insisted on a strict adherence to the plain meaning of the text of the Constitution of 1787. Jon Roland's *Texas Militia Papers* was the movement's most extensive exposition of that constitutional fundamentalism. Roland argued that the federal government had vastly exceeded the powers delegated to it in Article I, Section 8 of the Constitution. He pointed to the jurisprudential revolution that occurred during the New Deal as the moment in which the federal government had abandoned its fidelity to the Constitution. He regarded that revolution as illegitimate because it was based on judicial construction rather than constitutional amendment. As a consequence, he regarded the vast powers accumulated under the general welfare and interstate commerce clauses since the New Deal as simply usurped. Further, he pointed to the growth of bureaucratic regulation, the evolution of a distinct body of administrative law, and the accumulation of authority enacted by executive order, and asserted that none had any foundation in the text of the Constitution. For Roland, the scale of usurpation had by the 1990s created a crisis of legitimacy: "What we have then is two bodies of jurisprudence: one based on the Constitution, the other not based on it, and, indeed, in fundamental conflict with it."[22]

Roland's analysis was widely shared in the movement. The Web site of the Michigan Militia, for example, reminded visitors that "the federal government was intended to perform 18 powers (See Article I, Section 8 of the federal constitution) and all other powers were to be left to the states and the people." In Kay Sheil's view, the Constitution provided for a "central government with certain enumerated powers with all other power given to the states or the people."[23] Under this strict constructionist interpretation, the New Deal revolution represented the corrupt usurpation of power that the founders had warned against.

Militia members feared that this expansion of federal power had ini-

tiated a self-perpetuating cycle: because the growth of government undermined civil society, it created an ever greater need for further government intervention. Mike Vanderboegh noted that the growing reliance
on government tended to diminish popular understandings of civic obligation: "The idea of government as protector is a corrosive one that eats
at everything. It eats at those people who are normally citizens who
should act out. I mean, human behavior is a matter of doing what you're
used to doing. . . . The problem is that the burdens of citizenship have
not been passed on, in large measure, so that when a disaster comes
people say, 'Well, I pay the government to do that.'"[24] Charlie Morrison
argued that the New Deal Revolution had set this dynamic in motion:

> The Constitution is the law of the land. . . . Well, that law of the land has been
> twisted, and when they twisted it, society has changed. . . . Back when it
> meant something, people would help each other. Now if something ever
> goes wrong they just dial 911. You don't ever see someone go to their next-
> door neighbor and help pull the tree off the roof or anything anymore.
> People don't care about each other.[25]

Another militia newsletter described the end of this process: "governments have always sought to enlarge their powers, to assume an even
greater dominion over society, both political and civil. To control and direct the lives of those it purports to serve. In its most advanced stage,
government virtually annihilates civil society, creating a mass of atom-
ized individuals."[26] As this process progressed, militia members predicted, every individual would experience an increasing exposure to the
coercion and violence of the state.

Eighteenth-century Whig ideology thus gave constitutionalists within
the militia movement an intellectual framework with which to diagnose
the causes of the state violence they saw around them. But this Whig diagnosis sat in tension with a second, more millennial explanation propagated by John Trochman, Bob Fletcher, and Mark Koernke. According to
this much more apocalyptic perception of events, Ruby Ridge and Waco
were dress rehearsals for an impending invasion by the forces of the New
World Order. Instead of defending the nation against this invasion,

Trochman, Fletcher, and Koernke charged, the U.S. government was in league with the plot and pushing gun control legislation in an effort to strip the American people of the capacity to defend themselves.

Conspiracy theories centered on efforts by an international cabal to subvert the American government with the aid of domestic traitors have been a feature of American conservatism since the 1790s. Such theories informed William Dudley Pelley's millennial vision in 1936, and were a staple of Birch Society literature in the 1960s and 1970s. Pat Robertson gave such theories a new life in his 1991 volume, *The New World Order*.[27] Trochman, Fletcher, and Koernke repackaged these themes for a post-Waco audience in a series of oral presentations that were videotaped and distributed nationally. Koernke's presentation *America in Peril* dates from late 1993. The Militia of Montana produced Fletcher's presentation *Invasion and Betrayal* and Trochman's presentation *Enemies Foreign and Domestic* in early 1995.[28]

As presented by millennial voices within the militia movement, New World Order conspiracy theory revolved around four themes: the identification of the threat as foreign in origin; the ascription of genocidal intent; the claim that the unseen enemy was diabolically evil and thus possibly of unearthly origin; and the perception of a set timetable in which the conspiracy must achieve its goals. Jack McLamb's 1992 book *Operation Vampire Killer 2000*, which had a significant influence on millenarians within the movement, warned of a plan "for an oligarchy of the world's richest families to place ½ the masses of the earth in servitude under their complete control, administered from behind the false front of the United Nations. To facilitate management capabilities, the plan calls for the elimination of the other 2.5 billion people through war, disease, abortion, and famine by the year 2000."[29]

Other militia proponents of a millennial diagnosis identified a more specific set of conspirators. Joe and Clara Pilchak, members of the Michigan Militia, described the conspirators as follows:

> JP: They call it the Committee of 300, the Rothschilds, the Rockefellers, some of the royalty in Europe. Go back and find out people that belong in this country, the Council on Foreign Relations—

CP: Trilateralists.

JP: Trilateralists. Go back and find out who belongs to, which it still does exist, the Illuminati, the Bildebergers. Just take this list. Those are the people that would be behind that.[30]

In warning of a cabal involving the Rothschilds, the CFR, and the Rockefellers, millenarians fell back on themes that had been a staple of conspiratorial anti-Semitism throughout the twentieth century. Furthermore, toward the end of the 1990s Mark Koernke began to emphasize the Jewishness of the alleged conspirators behind the New World Order, referring to them as the "Kosher Mafia" and the "oiu boys."[31] Nevertheless, such overt anti-Semitism was rare in militia discourse, even among millenarians. Trochman and Fletcher made no mention of Jewish conspirators in their videos, nor did Koernke in *America in Peril*. Thus, some militia members may have accepted New World Order conspiracy theories without a full awareness of their anti-Semitic roots.[32]

Some of the spokesmen offering this millennial diagnosis did, however, explicitly invoke race. In the first minutes of his video *America in Peril*, Koernke warned that "the Crips and the Bloods are now being trained, equipped, and uniformed by, with federal funding" for the purpose of executing house-to-house gun confiscation. Koernke suggested that the government would motivate these African American street gangs by granting them tacit permission to loot and rape in the course of their operations. An "intel report" published in *Taking Aim* in June 1994 touched on the same themes: "Be aware that the Bloods, Crips, and Guardian Angels have finished their basic training and are now practicing deployment via Helicopter. They wear either a bandana, arm band, or tag showing their colors. An ATF agent told me that congress as of approx. 6-6-94, is secretly considering a measure for Americans to have to turn in all of their assault rifles regardless of when they were purchased."[33]

New World Order conspiracy theory offered an apocalyptic diagnosis of state violence that carried enormous emotional power. The best illustration of that emotional power is the opening of Bob Fletcher's video *Invasion and Betrayal*, in which the credits play against a backdrop of a burning farmstead. A black helicopter hovers in the foreground, shooting its machine gun at an unseen target. The first hour of Fletcher's presentation is dominated by references to the militarization of law enforcement, disarmament under the guise of gun control, government invasions of privacy through wiretapping and a traceable national ID, and emergency legislation authorizing martial law and large-scale detentions. He thus covers topics and materials that evoke a fear of state power similar to that found in the Whig diagnosis. But Fletcher's narrative is distinct: he offers no constitutional or historical analysis. Instead, he displays pictures of Soviet-origin military equipment on U.S. soil and juxtaposes them with pictures documenting the destruction of surplus U.S. equipment at the end of the Cold War. Fletcher uses these images to assert that an invasion is imminent, and that when it comes, Soviet and UN troops will mate with their "preplaced" equipment, defeat a disarmed populace, and establish a military dictatorship over the United States.

The second hour of the tape emphasizes the genocidal intent of that dictatorship. Fletcher argues that the conspirators have mastered control of the weather and the earth's tectonic plates. He suggests that recent famines and earthquakes are part of a plan to reduce the earth's population by several billion people. He concludes that all of the disparate pieces of information add up to one concerted pattern, a plot to create one-world socialism under the auspices of the New World Order by the year 2000.

The ending credits serve as a bookend, mirroring the opening and giving shape to what has come between. They play over footage of UN helicopters and armored personnel carriers juxtaposed with footage of the use of helicopters and APCs at Waco. A final shot of a National Guard helicopter buzzing the Branch Davidian compound calls to mind the opening sequence of a helicopter assault on a burning farm, conveying the message that Waco was a rehearsal for what is to come.[34] Whereas constitutionalists embraced a Whig diagnosis that warned that Waco could happen to anyone, Fletcher's millennial diagnosis carried a more apocalyptic message: Waco *will* happen to *everyone.*

This apocalyptic vision of impending invasion further distinguishes the constitutionalist and millennial wings of the militia movement. Constitutionalists were certainly willing to discuss the New World Order, especially when asked, but in general they tended to view it as a set of economic trends, policies, and ideas playing out within a global political process. As Mike Vanderboegh put it, "Obviously there are well-placed people who believe in globalism and believe in moving the United States more into the world government kind of ideal, you know? In terms of ideas and things like that, you have only to read *Foreign Affairs* and other things to see people advocating that." Tom Plummer offered a similar analysis: "I think it's kind of the result of societal and historical and financial and geopolitical forces. There are a lot of people that think global socialism is a good thing. There are a lot of people that believe—unfortunately the majority of the U.S. Senate believes at least in part that we shouldn't have borders to trade. That it's great to be one big world economy."[35]

Though they accepted the reality of the New World Order as an international political movement for a more globalist political and economic system, constitutionalists tended to respond with disdain when encountering milliennial warnings of imminent invasion. One Ohio militiaman took pains to distance himself from the millennial worldview: "The hype is that it's all these evil people in black helicopters getting ready to secretly take over the United States and enslave everybody in huge prison camps. I think the reality is not quite as fantastic as that." Michael McKinzey also expressed frustration with militia groups that never got past "black helicopter mentality."[36]

Here again, familiarity with a Whig understanding of history seems to have inoculated constitutionalists against warnings of a diabolical conspiracy. Oral Deckard described the New World Order as a manifestation of the same historical process that had prompted the founders to break free of England:

> Yeah, there is an attempt to produce a single worldwide government, and it's very well documented. It's not a surprise to any person actually thinking, because if you understand how a flame works, you understand how power works, and if everybody today who were wanting to produce a one-world

government were to magically just drop dead, given a couple of years, there'd be the same problem back. So it's not the situation of some individuals who are evil beyond human nature. It is an ongoing problem that we'll always have to guard against. Thomas Jefferson said, "The price of liberty is eternal vigilance."[37]

For Deckard and other constitutionalists, the New World Order represented simply the newest manifestation of the age-old problem of centralization and the growth of arbitrary power. For these militiamen and women, the obsession with black helicopters paled before the Whig science of politics.

Restoring the Constitutional Order: The Militia, the Revitalization of Civil Society, and a New Balance of Political Violence

Members of the militia movement saw government expansion and state violence as interrelated problems. Constitutionalists offered two solutions, one political and one martial. They believed the militia would play a central role in both. They conceived of the militia as part of a larger vision for the restoration of civil society. They saw their voluntary service in militias of association as a model of the political and civic involvement that could reverse the corrosion of civil society and reduce the involvement of the state in their lives and communities. They also sought to discourage further expansions of government power by suggesting that future legislation in certain areas, particularly gun control, might meet armed resistance. Finally, they believed that the institution of the militia would balance the state's potential for political violence and deter the violent enforcement of the laws. Militia members thus understood their purpose as civic, political, and martial. They argued, furthermore, that their vision of the devolution of power, the revitalization of civil society, and the restoration of a balance of political violence marked a return to the social and political vision of the founding generation.

The first point in the militia movement's political program was the devolution of power from the federal government back to states and local communities. The Web site of the Michigan Militia complained that every year the government accumulated more power, and announced that the MMC's purpose was to "restore the Federal and state governments to their historical, limited, and constitutional function." Norm Olson described his desire to "dissipate and decentralize government as quick as I could. I would abide by the Tenth Amendment to our constitution that gives powers back to the states and I would get it down to the county and the township, down to the people making decisions. What's happening now is that you're seeing centralized, consolidated power going up, up, up. We're trying to empower the people to make decisions for themselves." Carolyn Hart, editor of *Necessary Force,* agreed with Olson that the militia's purpose was to bring the government back into compliance with the Tenth Amendment.[38]

The transfer of power back to local communities would, militia members believed, begin a larger process of rebuilding civil society. Some in the movement envisioned a process in which civil society would naturally reemerge in the absence of state authority. J. J. Johnson described this natural reawakening in *Cracking the Liberty Bell.* In the novel, Johnson imagined the breakdown of government authority in Columbus, Ohio. As two dazed FBI agents drive through the streets of Columbus, they witness a reawakening of civic obligation rather than a descent into anarchy. Civilians step forward to direct traffic and collect the city's garbage. Drug dealers turn away casual users so as to supply customers with medical needs. Citizens peacefully carry their firearms to work, and join together to do what little policing this new society requires.[39]

Not all militia members held Johnson's utopian vision of civic reawakening. Most recognized that the process would take leadership, investment, and some degree of cultural evolution. They saw militia organization as a first step in the process. Charlie Morrison described the purpose of the Central Ohio Unorganized Militia as the promotion of civic engagement in the larger community. The militia, he noted, had provided security for a community festival, and offered CPR and suturing clinics to the general public. Jon Roland also saw the rebuilding of civil society as one of the militia's first tasks: "In this age in which too many people don't know their own next door neighbors, it is time to break down the barriers of anonymity and rebuild the community spirit on which our society depends. Able bodied citizens should be expected to perform regular civic duties in much the same way that they perform jury duty. The constitutional framework for doing that is the militia."[40]

The most detailed vision of a civic reawakening came from Samuel Sherwood, whose proposed "Shire Constitution" envisioned the rebirth of a vigorous civil society in local communities. His constitutional plan for these communities was grounded on the expectation of overwhelming public participation in community affairs. For example, his constitution provided that any tax must be approved by at least 60 percent of registered voters, in an election in which at least 80 percent of registered voters turned out to vote. It also provided that no penalty other than denial of services be assessed for the nonpayment of taxes, thus making payment essentially voluntary. It empowered the shire government to regulate the workplace and the environment for the health and safety of the community and to provide for the education of the public. Nevertheless, it envisioned that a significant degree of voluntary self restraint and civic contribution would be necessary to make the community's education, social welfare, and labor systems function.[41]

Sherwood's plan for the shire rested on the belief that civil society will reemerge only in a polity in which citizens are free to choose whether or not to meet their civic obligations and in which the government refrains from stepping into the void. The freedom to choose thus fosters the responsible choice and also depends upon it. One of Sherwood's observations on the issue of environmental protection nicely summed up this dynamic: "Freedom is not irresponsibility, it is the opposite. If we are to be free, we must be responsible for our own health and welfare. You cannot be free as a people or as a nation if you strip cut all the trees in your nation and have none left."[42]

There were some in the militia movement who rejected this political program of civic reawakening. Among members of the millennial wing of the movement, the theory of sovereign citizenship offered a vision of individual secession from civil society. Under this theory, fully sovereign individuals who had dissolved their bonds to the United States owed no obedience to the laws and no obligations of citizenship. Such individuals held themselves, for example, exempt from state and federal regulations and taxes. John Trochman declared himself a sovereign citizen in 1992, and Mark Koernke began to sign his name in a style often adopted by sovereign citizens in 1999. Joe and Clara Pilchak were closely considering undergoing the process of withdrawing from their bonds with the state and federal governments in 1998, but were worried about the economic implications of such a move. Part of the process of severing their bonds to the state involved returning the government-issued deed to their farm and taking out a "land patent" instead. As Joe noted, "A land patent is a real nice document. The problem is, try to refinance your house. The bank won't touch it." They also worried that some who engaged in this process seemed to be interested in freeloading on their fellow sovereigns, and they wondered whether a community of sovereign citizens in southeast Michigan could sustain itself through barter.[43] Despite sovereign citizenship's allure among more millenarian militia folk in Montana and southeast Michigan, this hyperindividualist rejection of civic obligation appealed only to a small minority within the movement.

Most of those in the movement recognized that the devolution of political power back to states and local communities and the rebuilding of civil society was a long-term political project. They saw the organization of militias as part of this larger reawakening of civic obligation. The connection between armed organization and political and social reformation led some observers to believe that the militias intended to impose their political program by force of arms. Many in the movement took pains to explain that this was not the case. As one New York militia member put it, forming a militia "doesn't mean we're going to pick up our guns and shoot people if they vote in laws we don't like." Oral Deckard expressed a similar conviction that "you can have illegitimate government by people legitimately elected but exercising undelegated powers, which is really what we've got right now real bad, and you can't legitimately go out and start shooting these bastards, because you, as the public, don't have sense enough to throw them out of office at the next election."[44]

Rather, the movement recognized that the achievement of its political objectives would come through engagement in the political process. Thus, Jon Roland argued that constitutionalists "must work to repeal unconstitutional legislation, based on their unconstitutionality and not just on our policy preferences, and to reduce funding for unconstitutional federal activities if we cannot completely eliminate them. We must be prepared to support some constitutional amendments to delegate powers to government for which a consensus has developed." Roland noted that electric energy, communications, air transportation, and the environment were all areas requiring federal regulation not provided for in the Constitution.[45]

Though militia members believed that devolution and civic reawakening could only be accomplished through a long campaign of education and political action, in their view, the threat posed by growing state violence and the militarization of law enforcement required a more immediate and forceful response. Militia men and women concluded that they needed to directly challenge the state's monopoly on violence in order to reverse these trends. They based that challenge on the fundamentally Lockean proposition that government authority and the political violence on which it rested was legitimate only so long as it served the ends for which that government had been created. In essence, they argued that the legitimacy of political violence stemmed from these ends rather than from the authority of those wielding it. "A key point of the idea of legitimacy," argued Jon Roland, "is that legitimacy attaches to actions, not to persons, writings, institutions, or offices."[46]

The militia movement grounded this normative assertion in an appeal to the libertarian memory of the Revolution. Samuel Sherwood cited the creation of the Fairfax County, Virginia, Militia Association by George Washington and George Mason as the precedent for his own United States Militia Association. Washington and Mason, he noted, had acted without government sanction, and had offered as justification only their belief that they were "Threatened with the Destruction of our Civil-rights & Liberty." Michael Johnson pointed to the Declaration of Independence when discussing the founders' intention "to ensure that despotic and tyrannical governments would not come to have power over them or their descendants. Indeed, as voiced in the Declaration, they felt that an absolute duty existed to rebel against a tyrannical and oppressive government." The October 1998 issue of the *Ohio Minuteman,* OUMAAC's newsletter, reprinted an excerpt from a column by Alan Keyes that made precisely the same point: "the principle on which our polity is based, as stated in the Declaration, recognizes that any government, at any level, can become oppressive of our rights. And we must be prepared to defend ourselves against its abuses."[47]

For members of the movement, the Second Amendment was the most important vessel of this memory. Militia men and women argued that the militia clauses and the Second Amendment gave their movement explicit constitutional sanction. Dan White, a member of the Missouri 51st Militia, argued in an essay on the right to keep and bear arms that "the primary purpose intended by those who created the Second Amendment was to guarantee the right of the people to possess firearms, and to use those firearms as a final recourse should their liberties be violated by external or internal military forces." Tom Plummer cited *Federalist No. 46* as evidence that the Framers conceived of an insurrectionary purpose for the militia: "The writings of our Founding Fathers, following the Constitutional convention but preceding the ratification of the Constitution, make clear that the militia has another purpose: to deter the national government from becoming tyrannical and oppressing the people."[48]

Appealing to the insurrectionary interpretation of the Second Amendment, militia members argued that the framers had never intended the state to hold a monopoly on political violence. Rather, the militias insisted, they had intended to create a balance of political violence that would give the people, embodied in the militia, the capacity to resist, and if necessary, overthrow, an abusive government.

This interpretation of the purpose of the militia and the right to keep and bear arms had deep historical roots, but the militia movement also adapted the libertarian memory of the Revolution to meet its own ends. In the eighteenth century, the universal militia was the institutional creature of the state government, regulated by law and under the command authority of the governor and his subordinate officers. In drawing on historical memory to create a popular deterrent to state violence, the

militia movement recrafted the memory of the Founding period to support the assertion that the Framers had intended the militia to remain
independent of any organized government.

There was, as discussed in the first chapter, historical precedent for
the creation of fully independent militias of association in response to
tyranny. Samuel Sherwood's discussion of the Fairfax Militia Association
indicates that he was aware of the precedent set in 1774, when local communities in New England, Pennsylvania, and Virginia organized extralegal militias. But the early organizers of the militia movement more often grounded their argument for militia independence in appeals to
logic and natural law, and they occasionally relied on bogus quotations.
Thus, in "Reviving the Ready Militia," Jon Roland argued that militias
had traditionally been led by local officials and independent of government control except when called into service: "Just as militias are essentially local, so also are they essentially independent of established authorities, since the militia may have to challenge or bypass those
authorities if they abuse their authority or fail to perform their lawful
duties." In "Is the Citizen Militia Lawful?" Norm Olson argued that
"whereas the National Guard is solely the creation of statutory law, the
militia derives its existence from the inherent inalienable rights of man
which existed before the Constitution." For his part, John Trochman's
Militia of Montana *Information and Networking Manual* offered three
quotations from the Federalist in support of the assertion that the
Framers intended the militia to be independent of both state and federal
governments. Of the three quotes, two were spurious, and the third was
edited to remove an explicit reference to state control.[49]

The assertion that militias were independent of established authority
raised the issue of how militia violence might be controlled and how the
social costs of such violence might be contained. Given that many militias were purely private associations, the movement had even less claim
to public sanction than had the militias of association in 1774, which
were at least broadly representative of their local communities. Some in
the movement recognized the tenuous nature of their claim to act on behalf of the public. Bill Utterback urged members of the movement to be
cautious about acting in the name of the people: "many patriots are con-

fused about what is required to act under the authority of the people. They think, 'I and my five friends are people, therefore we can do what we want under the authority of we the people.' Wrong!" Oral Deckard recognized that the social costs of militia violence would be high and insisted that the movement should act only when it had broad public backing: "If you don't have enough of the general population with you to win an election, number one, you're going to lose, and, number two, you don't have the consent of the governed."[50]

Members also attempted to bolster the movement's legitimacy by demonstrating that the objectives for which they would resort to violence were consistent with the public good. In public declarations and in private conversations with federal law enforcement agencies, militia members articulated a set of redlines that identified the exercises of government power they sought to place out of bounds. Different individuals within the movement drew the lines in slightly different places, but in general there was agreement on a core set of concerns. First, the movement issued explicit warnings to the government that any repeat of Waco would result in widespread violence. This message was conveyed with particular intensity during the siege of the Freeman compound in Montana in 1996 and the standoff with militants from the Republic of Texas in 1997.

Most in the movement had little sympathy for the Freemen or the Republic of Texas, but they were determined to prevent another exercise of "Waco rules." Mike Vanderboegh offered the Republic of Texas as an example of the problem: "Everybody understood these guys were loons; nobody liked them. You know, they were chasing little fairies of history dust. . . . Our problem was we want to let the Feds know that it's not okay to provide a Waco solution to this problem. At the same time we want to let the Republic of Texas know, 'We're not going to come to your defense. We're not encouraging you boys.' "[51]

During the Freeman siege, over a dozen spokesmen for the militia movement signed a statement declaring that "should any citizen be injured, or suffer loss of life, now or in the future, by unlawful authority, and/or without due process . . . we will then no longer restrain our brethren from the use of whatever force is necessary to eliminate the threat of unlawful federal enforcement authority." This public message was reinforced in a series of private discussions around the country. Norm Olson traveled to Montana to monitor the siege, and later reported warning officials that "if they treat this Montana thing like they treated Waco, that I was right there. And I told them, 'You will all die, you will all die.'"[52]

The FBI received similarly blunt warnings in Alabama, Missouri, and New Mexico. Jim McKinzey later recounted one of these conversations:

> During the Freeman incident, the FBI here in Kansas City would call me every week, if not every other week, just to give me an update. They'd call, say, "This has come down and this is something we might do. What would be the militia's reaction?" And, I would be up front and honest with him. One of the responses, I don't really remember what the scenario was, but I said, "If you try that, we're going to shoot at you. But if those Freemen come out of their house with guns ablazing, take 'em out. You have a right to protect yourself like everybody else, but if you charge that house with guns ablazing, you better watch your back, plain and simple."[53]

According to Mike Vanderboegh, several members of the Tri-States Militia Network took pains to explain that retaliation for another atrocity might be national in scope: "This was an aspect of the situation that they had never considered. They were worried about us going *there*, wherever there was. We had to make them understand that a provocation in one place would have consequences in others."[54]

Beyond this prohibition, militia leaders warned of a violent response to any declaration of martial law or the suspension of habeas corpus, the use of foreign troops against U.S. citizens, and any campaign of mass detention or internment of American citizens. Few militia members anticipated that such wholesale suspensions of constitutional government were imminent, but they were unwilling to wholly discount the possibility. Tom Plummer explained, "I certainly don't believe that the government is getting ready to round up anybody and ship them off to concentration camps. . . . The point is that sometimes governments go bad, and if a government goes bad the citizens have two options: number one is to allow themselves to be victimized, or, number two, to fight back."[55]

Militia members also declared that they would resist no-knock searches, and that they would retaliate for any injury to members of the movement and their families resulting from "dynamic entry" tactics. For example, J. J. Johnson testified before the Senate Subcommittee on Terrorism that he would submit to a search or arrest, so long as the state provided a legal warrant and refrained from kicking in his door at three in the morning. Joe Pilchak, taking inspiration in Johnson's stance, warned, "When you kick in my front door, I'll drop you."[56]

The last redline concerned the attempt to enact further gun control legislation. Michael Johnson captured the movement's stance on this issue when he declared, "In order to protect against tyranny, arms are a necessity. Therefore, I will not yield my arms to any man for any reason." Charles Morrison Sr. of OUMAAC similarly announced in a 1996 email that he would not "be complying with laws in the future which will regulate what I do with the weapons I have in my possession." Militia members from around the country, including Bill Utterback and J. J. Johnson, publicly backed this stance. A survey of Ohio militia members circulated by OUMAAC in 1998 indicated unanimous agreement with the proposition that "it would be appropriate for the people of the United States to resist, with whatever level of force is necessary, any attempt to disarm them by whatever party under whatever pretext." The Wayne County Brigade of the Michigan Militia made a similar declaration in 1995, as did the Missouri 51st in 1997.[57]

As militia members articulated them, most of these redlines revolved around scenarios that began with state violence. All ceded the initiative, and thus, in their view, the responsibility for the outbreak of violence, to the state. As they saw it, none of these prohibitions interfered with the "normal" operations of law enforcement, at least as they had been conducted prior to the proliferation of no-knock searches and paramilitary raids during the war on drugs. In essence, the militias sought to reverse the trend toward paramilitarization by deterring state violence and enforcing constitutional due process.

The militias' stance against gun control, however, transcended this concern with government abuses. Here the militias sought to check an anticipated exercise of popular sovereignty, translated into policy by the act of a democratically elected legislature. To head off any further gun control legislation, the movement resurrected the tradition of popular nullification dating back to the era of the American Revolution: they declared collectively, within the public sphere, that they would not obey proposed legislation that infringed their constitutional rights, in this case the right to keep and bear arms. They understood that their interpretation of the asserted right was contested by their lawful democratic government, but they insisted that they would defend their interpretation, even by armed force if necessary.

Looking for Lexington Green: The Norms of Violence in the Militia Imagination

Many in the movement were appalled by the acts of Timothy McVeigh, and felt the need to reassure themselves and the public that militia violence would not trigger a descent into terrorism and anarchy. That task required the public discussion of "rules of engagement" that distinguished between legitimate and illegitimate acts of violence. Yet those engaged in this discussion faced significant legal constraints: any discussion of violence that carried even the suggestion of advocacy might lead to prosecution under the law of conspiracy. Under these constraints members of the movement struggled to craft rules to govern the movement's actual use of violence.

The memory of the American Revolution played a role in one facet of this conversation. For many militiamen, especially in the constitutional wing of the movement, the memory of Lexington and Concord was a normative model that stipulated that insurgent violence was legitimate only when it was reactive. Mike Vanderboegh specifically cited this model in the organizational guidelines for the Sons of Liberty clubs that marked his first foray into militia organization: "Remember your principles. Don't lose sight of our objective. The opposition will do its best to provoke some precipitate action on our part to discredit us and our cause. Follow the orders of Captain Parker at Lexington: Stand your ground. Don't fire unless fired upon, but if they mean to have a war, let it begin here." Norm Olson also articulated this normative model when he described what it would take for the militia to strike out: "it will take a Lexington, or another Waco to bring us out for we are enduring, patient, and resilient. We, like our Forefathers before us will suffer many wrongs and we will find that many of them are sufferable."[58]

This essentially reactive stance embedded in the militias' understanding of legitimate violence made the movement much less dangerous than it might otherwise have been. Olson himself courted confrontation with government at various levels. For much of the late 1990s he appeared to be a man in search of Lexington Green. He traveled to Montana during the Freeman siege in 1996, and he placed his own militia brigade on standby during confrontations with several local governments in Michigan. But in the years that Olson's militia was active, the state never served up a Major Pitcairn with whom Olson could bring his vision of legitimate revolution to fruition, and Olson never departed from the script by lashing out proactively.[59]

After the Oklahoma City bombing, some militia members acknowledged that their discussions of violence, even reactive violence, may have played a role.[60] They sought to initiate a broader discussion of the norms of legitimate insurgent violence. Again, these discussions lacked the openness and coherence that characterized their articulation of redlines, because any public articulation of legitimate tactics or targets courted prosecution under the law of conspiracy. As a consequence, militia members approached the topic via a series of negative commandments and through the use of fiction to shield themselves from prosecution.

As militia members contemplated Timothy McVeigh, they recognized the tendency of violence to corrupt those who engaged in it. As Mike Vanderboegh remembered these discussions, "We understood that if you set out to fight evil it's important not to become evil yourself. And what does that cut out? It cuts out collateral damage. That means no collateral damage. It means no innocents killed. That means not even innocents of the families of people who are carrying out regime decisions." Gordon MacCrae of the Regiment of Dragoons, one of the few militias in New England, cited the Geneva Convention in support of the same principle: "Under the Geneva Accords, civilians may not be deliberately attacked." To reinforce this message, the Tri-States Militia distributed a training manual on the laws of land warfare in October 1995.[61]

Discussions of acceptable, as opposed to unacceptable, tactics and targets were particularly constrained. In 1996, Doug Fiedor, a Kentucky constitutionalist closely allied with the militia movement, suggested that the time might have come for "a Boston Tea Party or two. And, so long as people are not personally harmed, this is quite acceptable in the scheme of things." Michael McKinzey also described restrained acts against property when discussing potential militia violence: "If we wanted to disrupt society, we're not going to throw a pipe-bomb at something. We're going to turn the gas off, electric off. We're going to put viruses in your computers. We're the people who built this society and we maintain it. We certainly know how to turn it off."[62]

To flesh out these suggestions, militia members turned to fiction. In 1997, Mike Vanderboegh imagined what such a "tea party" might look like. His short story "Once upon a Tea Party" opens with a terrorist attack on Detroit that is quickly blamed on the militia movement. Three months later Congress passes the "Assault Weapon Confiscation Act." In response, militia groups begin staging "4473 parties" to destroy the records of purchases held by local gun stores. After one such party, the local community turns out under arms to repel federal agents who have come to confiscate the records of a local gun store. Confronted by a crowd of customers in the gun store, the agents retreat to their car:

> Without realizing it, they had stepped out of Charlie's door into the middle of two lines of armed men, facing each other and the ATF agents. Some were in uniform. Some in work clothes. Beyond the men on the opposite side of the street stood Sheriff Tolliver, his deputies and the town mayor, as well as representatives of the local press. . . . The two lines of men (and some women, the agents noted) formed a corridor from the door of Charlie's to their car. . . . Every one held a semiautomatic military-style rifle—the same kind banned by the new Act the ATF men had come to enforce.[63]

In this passage Vanderboegh describes the popular nullification of the new law, conducted at the local level and ritually performed within the public sphere. The performance is entirely reminiscent of those by the Massachusetts militiamen who closed the courts in Worcester in 1774 and the Democratic-Republicans who released the prisoners in Bethlehem, Pennsylvania, during Fries' Rebellion. The ritual is nonviolent, but only because the local militia successfully faces the agents down.

Vanderboegh recognized that a determined attempt to confiscate guns would not be deterred by nonviolent demonstrations. His story presents the escalation of popular resistance to the enforcement of the law in a series of headlines describing the violent repulse of a BATF raid by local law enforcement, the sabotage of federal records warehouses and computer databases, a militia raid on a federal prison to rescue captured militiamen, and finally a mutiny by the National Guardsmen ordered to enforce the new law.[64]

At one point the story suggests that assassination is one of the tools at the disposal of the state and hints that it might be employed by the militia movement as well. According to Vanderboegh, the propriety of assassination was widely debated within the movement. The Tri-States Militia condemned assassination in the November 1995 issue of its newsletter, *Liberty Alert*, arguing that "assassination is a loser's tool, employed by those who have lost confidence in their own principles and their ability to convince others of the righteousness of their cause. . . . Assassination and terrorism are the tools of politically bankrupt movements who must coerce those whom they cannot convince."[65]

J. J. Johnson, on the other hand, justified the recourse to assassination in *Cracking the Liberty Bell*. The novel centers on a BATF raid on a small independent church suspected of ties to the militia movement. The raid, conducted during services, goes awry in a manner reminiscent of Waco: federal agents retreat after killing several congregants and suffering casualties of their own. Federal authorities then lay siege to the church. The militias of the Midwest are mobilized to come to the besieged church's defense. They slip supplies through the government's perimeter and sabotage local military facilities being used to stage a follow-on assault on the church, killing dozens of federal agents in the process.

The government responds by declaring martial law in the entire state of Ohio and suspending habeas corpus. A militiaman then assassinates a

federal judge who has sustained this suspension of constitutional liberties and also bombs a bar where many of the city's federal law enforcement agents are known to congregate. Finally, one of the novel's heroines
assassinates the federal officials who have given an order to napalm the
church as a last-ditch attempt to bring the standoff to a close on the government's terms.

Johnson's vision of righteous violence is broader and more disturb-
ing than Vanderboegh's. Johnson portrays assassination as a justified response to the suspension of the Constitution and to murder if those
committing the acts have the capacity to place themselves beyond accountability. He suggests that the capacity of the government to manipulate public opinion makes it unlikely that those who act in egregious
defiance of legal and constitutional norms will ever be brought before a
jury. Many in the militia movement see the refusal of the Department of
Justice to prosecute Lon Horiuchi and those who gave him his orders as
proof of this assertion. Indeed, Johnson gives the character that per-
forms the final assassination the name Vicki, a clear allusion to Vicki
Weaver.[66]

While most constitutional militia members, including Johnson, insisted that insurgent violence must only come in response to state violence, some members of the millennial wing gravitated toward more
proactive fantasies. In 1997, Battle Creek, Michigan, resident Ken Carter
started a militia group called the North American Militia. In announcing
his new militia, Carter explained his millenarian motivation: "we believe
that the United Nations is the law makers of Satan, we believe that IFOR
is the military force of Satan, we believe that the New World Order is the
stage for the Coming of Satan, and the end of life as we know it."[67]

Michael Barkun, a leading scholar of far right millenarian thought,
has noted that millenarian groups sometimes take on a deterministic
role to bring on the apocalypse, "to act, as it were, to make the inevitable
yet more certain." Carter seems to have followed this path. According to
a BATF undercover agent, Carter planned proactive attacks on a local
military base, the Battle Creek federal building, a TV station, and a high-
way interchange, as well as the assassinations of prominent federal
officials. He apparently hoped "to attack, create chaos and hold on for

three or four days, at which time the entire country would rise up against the government." He tentatively scheduled the attack for June 7, 1997, but called the plan off three days later when he found few allies willing to support him.[68]

Two other millennial minded militiamen traveled this road in the late 1990s. In 1996 Oklahoma militiaman Willie Ray Lampley was convicted of planning a bombing campaign targeting gay bars, abortion clinics, and the offices of the ADL and SPLC. In 1997, Kansas militiamen Bradley Glover and Michael Dorsett made preparations for an assault on Fort Hood, Texas, which they believed was the site of a UN invasion force composed of Communist Chinese troops. They were arrested the day before the planned attack.[69]

Each of these conspiracies could have ended in tragedy, and each has been cited as evidence of the militia movement's potential to lash out at any moment. But these three incidents also share several other characteristics. First, the defendants were significantly influenced by the ideologies of the white supremacist Right. Carter was a former Aryan Nations member, and Lampley was a Christian Identity adherent. These affiliations may have exposed them to white supremacist texts, including *The Turner Diaries*, that celebrated proactive violence. In each case, the participants had been cast out of the constitutional wing of the militia movement. Leaders of the Michigan Militia expelled Carter, and the Tri-States Militia severed ties with Lampley and Glover. Finally, in all three cases, members of the constitutional wing of the movement played a role in alerting authorities to the conspiracy. The leadership of the Michigan Militia warned authorities about Carter's violent tendencies. Tri-States Militia founder John Parsons alerted the authorities to Lampley's bombing plot and testified against Lampley at his trial. Other members of the Tri-States Militia Network alerted the authorities when Glover threatened to retaliate against Parsons for his testimony and later complained when prosecutors failed to charge him with witness tampering.[70]

The impulse toward proactive violence was present within the millennial wing of the movement. It did not, however, characterize the movement as a whole. Most militia members recognized that proactive violence would undermine the twin goals of rebuilding civil society and establishing a credible deterrent against state violence. Moreover, few in the movement looked upon violence as a desirable outcome.

Violence lay at the core of militia identity, but there was very little celebration of violence when militiamen imagined performing the martial functions of citizenship. The significant presence of combat veterans within the movement lent a sober tone to most militia discussions of violence. *Necessary Force*, the newsletter of the Missouri 51st, reprinted an essay called "Rambo Wasn't There" in 1995. The author, who identified himself as "Danang, 1968," wrote of "lying on my face in a rice paddy, bullets tearing at my clothes, my pectoral muscles trying to dig me in deeper, thinking I was going to vomit and defecate at the same time." Editor Harold Sheil, signing as "Pyongyang, 1951," closed the story with his own remembrance of the smell of blood.[71] The newsletter of the Gadsden Minutemen published "An Open Letter on Warfare and America," which contained a similar reminiscence by Vietnam veteran Vernon Wilkins. The letter is a monologue written largely in the second person. Addressing himself, Wilkins describes training young militiamen in the techniques of guerilla warfare out of anger at his government for its atrocities at Waco and its curbs on civil liberties. He then narrates a dream in which he relives his experiences in Vietnam:

> Did you tell them about the stench of death? Human charred, decaying death? Like no other smell you will ever experience and will never forget? Did you tell them about the 18-year-old boy who entered the Imperial City of Hue in the house to house combat? Did you tell them how afraid he was? Did you tell them about the twisted people on the street, or the fires and the thick black smoke, so thick at times it was impossible to tell night from day? Did you tell them it looked the way one would envision hell?

Wilkins's flashback then turns darker, as he relives his participation in the killing of innocents:

> Did you tell them about the L-t's order to clear everything and everyone out of that building? Did you tell them that people were speaking loud and frightened? The platoon sergeant told them to put there hands up and di-di

mau, didn't he? But they did not comply, did they? They must have been the VC that the L-t was talking about. After all, an old man and woman and three kids were often used by the VC. The L-t said that small arms fire was coming from those two flats, right? Did you tell them that was why you smoked them all? 'Cause you found the weapons, right? WRONG!

This encounter with the terrible reality behind Gibson's new war fantasy leads the author to viscerally repudiate the warrior dream, both in the past and the present. He repents having peddled a vision of glorious insurgency without confronting his young followers with the hideous reality:

> Then, only then it hits you. If you do win, what do you win? Thousands of predatory little bandit kings, fighting not for the Constitution or the Bill of Rights, but for its own private gain. Yes, and you thought about it too! Power, Field Marshall, power. Thousands of young men loyal to you and you alone![72]

Like many in the movement, Wilkins concluded that violence represented only the horrific consequence of political failure: "The way of reformation is not the rifle, but self expression of an awakened populace— the *pen;* the *BALLOT BOX.*" Mike McKinzey, another Vietnam veteran, noted that "the main stream media has portrayed the militia movement as a bunch of white angry men that think they are going to shoot their way to solving our country's problems. We know different. The rifle is not the answer, never has been, never will be. . . . when all the gun smoke has cleared and the bodies have been buried, the problems would still have to be solved politically, specifically by voting in people who would do the right things."[73]

In rejecting the glorification of violence for its own sake that lay at the core of the new war fantasy, militiamen forged a masculine identity in which adherents of the warrior dream served as a powerful negative referent. The hostility between constitutional militiamen and the white supremacist Right stemmed largely from the militia movement's disgust at the genocidal fantasies in white supremacist discourse. An exchange between Norm Olson and Martin Lindstedt offered an example of this antagonism. Lindstedt, a Christian Identity adherent and follower of Louis Beam, published the *Modern Militiaman*, a newsletter designed to persuade those in the militia movement to make common cause with the white supremacist "resistance movement." On October 13, 1997, Lindstedt sent an email to *Outpost of Freedom*, a prominent militia discussion list, that contained the following sentiment:

> Thus we must finish off the remains of the civilization that our forefathers built for their and our benefit, so that the predators and parasites and their human herd animals must die. Only then can we rebuild a civilization free of the worm that infested that particular apple. Under such a doctrine, the preemptive extermination of entire populations of murderers, slavers, and their collaborators is justified. . . . Let me remind people that morality and Christianity are the hallmarks of the superior minority. For is it not Christianity's central tennant that the life of one superlative moral man is worth far more than that of the billions of lesser lives lived less righteously?

Two days later, Olson replied:

> Ah, Excuse me, Martin . . . As a minister of the Gospel, I'd like to take issue with this statement. . . . To think that we are deserving of grace and are placed in some kind of position to look down on others among the "billions of lesser lives" would seem to make fertile the ground of imperialism where those who are not of our Christian persuasion are not deserving of justice or mercy. As an aside, allow me to note that such a view is repugnant to Christians who see themselves as sinners saved by grace rather as those deserving of God's grace and mercy because of their race or creed or culture.[74]

The following year Mike Vanderboegh also denounced Lindstedt's incessant calls for a genocidal civil war: "Fires in the night, screams in the dark, bloated bodies of children on the road—there is no reluctance here. No sense of horror at what is about to be unleashed upon the innocents of his own nation. No 'Don't fire unless fired upon' of the founders. Impatience to strike. Impatience to kill."[75]

Revulsion at the warrior dream on display at Waco was a powerful stimulant to militia organization. When Harold Sheil ridiculed paramilitary police officers for wanting to "play Rambo," he spoke from an identity for which Rambo was a negative referent. For constitutionalists within the militia movement, the figure of the Aryan warrior served the same function. Many in the movement felt revulsion at the acts of Timothy McVeigh. In pondering their own insurgent response to state violence, militiamen hoped, perhaps naively, that their violence would be different.

One Movement or Two? The Separation of the Constitutionalist and Millennial Wings of the Militia Movement

By early 1995, two distinct belief systems could be discerned within the emerging militia movement. One set of militias dedicated themselves to open and public operation, celebrated the principle of the equality of all citizens, and announced that membership was open regardless of race or religion. For the most part these groups embraced a Whig analysis that explained state violence as the product of creeping authoritarianism among the officers of government, and described political organization, civic involvement, and armed deterrence as the best solutions. Proponents of this belief system organized the U.S. Militia Association, the Texas Constitutional Militia, the Indiana Citizens Volunteer Militia, the Michigan Militia, and the Missouri 51st Militia.

A second set of militias embraced the organizational vision of John Trochman and Mark Koernke. Generally speaking, such militias organized covertly, and some embraced or at least tolerated membership by white supremacists and sovereign citizens. These militias tended to be much more millennial and apocalyptic in their interpretation of events, and their members took warnings of black helicopters and foreign troops as literal signs of the impending onset of open hostilities with their own government and the forces of the New World Order. Among the militias embracing this worldview were the Militia of Montana, some elements of the Ohio Unorganized Militia, and some of the brigades of the MMC, particularly in the southeastern portion of Michigan where Mark Koernke's influence was strongest.

This distinction between the constitutionalist and millenarian orientation captures an important dynamic in the emergence of the militia movement prior to the Oklahoma City bombing on April 19, 1995. Still, it should not be overstressed. Not all covert militias had a millenarian orientation.[76] Constitutionalist militias sometimes cooperated with millenarian groups, and some groups had members of both orientations. Two of the movement's earliest organizers, Samuel Sherwood and Norm Olson, had a foot in each camp. Both had insisted on open, public organization and racial inclusion, but both were significantly motivated by biblical prophecy and were inclined to view the future in apocalyptic terms. Though neither accepted the theories peddled by Trochman and Koernke, each warned of tribulations to come. Olson viewed the New World Order as the "culmination of history," the fulfillment of end-times prophecy. An early version of the Michigan Militia manual spoke of "the time of approaching chaos and unrest . . . when the cities begin burning."[77] Samuel Sherwood, alarmed by what he perceived as federal responsibility for the Oklahoma City bombing, warned of approaching unrest in the spring of 1995, and urged members to stock food and consider relocating to the rural West.[78]

Nevertheless, the public scrutiny that arrived after the Oklahoma City bombing heightened the disagreements between constitutionalists and millenarians. As a result, the period between May 1995 and the end of 1997 witnessed the gradual separation of the two wings of the militia movement. Two of the earliest casualties of the divergence were Olson and Sherwood. Norm Olson's place in the national leadership of the movement became untenable after the Oklahoma City bombing. Though he had actually spent considerable energy as commander of the Michigan Militia in debunking the invasion rumors propagated by Mark Koernke, Olson publicly articulated a particularly far-fetched conspiracy theory that blamed the bombing on the government of Japan. He was forced to resign as commander of the Michigan Militia at the end of April 1995, and thereafter retained command only of the Emmet County militia from which he had built the state organization.[79]

Samuel Sherwood's fall from grace had less to do with his beliefs than with his misrepresentation in the press. In March 1995, the *Boise Weekly* reported that Sherwood was urging his followers to prepare themselves for violence against local officials: "Go up and look Idaho legislators in the face," he was quoted as saying, "because some day you may be forced to blow it off." The quote was later picked up by the Associated Press, and was used by the national press and by civil rights organizations to portray Sherwood and the movement as a whole as unstable and longing for violence. The available evidence suggests that Sherwood was badly misquoted. Mark Tanner, writing an article on the militia movement for *Reason Magazine,* also attended the meeting and later reported that "Sherwood made an impassioned plea for using political action rather than violence in correcting the wrongs that the members of the United States Militia Association see in government. He suggested that if his listeners wanted to grab a gun to shoot their legislators, they should first go look them in the face and recognize that legislators are also American citizens who are fathers, mothers, husbands, and wives. The audience not only understood that he was arguing against violence, they applauded his remarks." Despite this and other evidence that the quote was spurious, Sherwood never fully reestablished his credibility, and he disbanded the USMA in the fall of 1996.[80]

The process of separation grew more overt in late 1995 with the creation of the Tri-States Militia Network. The Tri-States Militia, so-called because of its dedication to God, family, and country, was the creation of John Parsons and was based in South Dakota. In 1995 Parsons began reaching out to militias across the country in an attempt to create a national organization. Leaders from around the country attended command seminars in Gregory, South Dakota, in August 1995, in Denton, Texas, in October, and in Albuquerque in January 1996. Tri-States also organized a national communications center and appointed a seven-member national board.[81]

These gatherings of militias with a variety of worldviews quickly led to questions about what the organization stood for. The presence of Willey Ray Lampley at the Denton meeting forced the issue. Many on the Tri-States board were uncomfortable with Lampley's presence, and Mike Vanderboegh, newly appointed to the board, agreed to publicly confront Lampley. In a speech entitled "J'accuse," a conscious allusion to Émile

Zola's condemnation of the French government during the Dreyfus Affair, Vanderboegh suggested that the time had come to distance the movement from the racists, anti-Semites, and "loose cannons" in their midst. Lampley left the Tri-States meeting immediately after the speech.[82]

Thereafter, Tri-States board members attempted to rally constitutional militias into a coherent national movement. The communications center used its contacts with militias around the country to debunk the various rumors peddled by figures in the millenarian wing, an activity that the FBI decided to fund as a public service. Board members began to conceive of Tri-States as the "Better Homes and Gardens Good Housekeeping Seal of Approval," an organization that would assist in militia formation and training, provide a clearinghouse for rumors, and monitor and harass white supremacists and other "patriots" prone to violence. According to Vanderboegh, "We were constitutionalist militia and what we were trying to do was help out other people who wanted to form constitutional militias and to better network for the general good."[83]

The Tri-States Militia Network collapsed in April 1996 when trial testimony in the Lampley case revealed that John Parsons had accepted money from the FBI to support the Tri-States communication center.[84] Nevertheless, efforts to coordinate the activities of the constitutional wing of the movement continued. One such effort to craft a platform resulted in the "Alabama Declaration," one of the most widely disseminated statements of militia antiracism. Mike Vanderboegh, the declaration's author, proposed the following sentiments as the central ideological tenets of the constitutional militia movement:

> That while the constitutional militia movement defends the Nazis' right to hold whatever opinions they wish about other races and religions, we wish to make it plain that we do not hold such opinions, nor do we condone discrimination and violent acts against others because of their faith or color of their skin . . .
>
> That the ranks of the constitutional militias are filled with men and women of all races, creeds, colors and religions . . .

That we condemn racism and bigotry as antithetical to our belief that all are "created equal" as Thomas Jefferson wrote, and are entitled to equal protection under the law.[85]

Vanderboegh circulated his statement through the Tri-States Militia Network, and it was signed by representatives of constitutional militias around the country.[86]

The separation between constitutionalists and millenarians also manifested itself in Ohio in 1996. After the collapse of the command structure of the original Ohio Unorganized Militia, J. J. Johnson and Tom Plummer rallied militias of a more constitutionalist orientation under a new umbrella organization, the Ohio Unorganized Militia Advisory and Assistance Command. The result was a large measure of separation between OUMAAC and the sovereign citizen / common-law groups that had belonged to the original OUM.[87]

Finally, in the winter of 1997–98, the Michigan Militia split into two factions. After Norm Olson's resignation in 1995, the organization suffered from a lack of strong leadership. Many constitutionalists had dropped their membership, alienated first by rumors of Timothy McVeigh's association with the MMC, and then by Olson's conspiratorial explanations of the Oklahoma City bombing. Day-to-day leadership of the MMC fell to Tom Wayne, appointed executive officer by titular commander Lynn Van Huizen. Wayne had never associated with a county brigade of the MMC before his appointment. He sought to bolster the legitimacy of his position by building up the organization's membership. Some common-law activists and a few Christian Identity adherents took advantage of the leadership vacuum to set themselves up as new MMC brigades and to infiltrate existing brigades. Alarmed at the penetration of their organization, Wayne and Van Huizen attempted in 1997 to regain control by revising the MMC manual to vest policymaking authority in the organization's nine divisional commanders. Brigades in the three divisions covering the southeastern portion of the state rejected the new manual and repudiated the state leadership. In February 1998 this breakaway faction appointed Bruce Soloway, a Christian Identity adherent and associate of Posse Comitatus leader James

Wickstrom, as interim commander. In March this faction elected Joe Pilchak as their state commander. Pilchak and many members of this faction were close associates of Mark Koernke. Wayne and Van Huizen continued to lead the constitutionalist faction of the MMC in the western part of the state, but in Michigan the millennial wing proved the stronger of the two.[88]

Overall, the movement suffered a significant loss of membership in the aftermath of the Oklahoma City bombing. Some militias disbanded in the weeks after the bombing, and others reported that as many as half of their members dropped out. By 1998, however, membership had stabilized and was growing. Statewide militia organizations like the ICVM and OUMAAC began to rebuild county units and publish new Web sites and newsletters. Multistate coordination efforts in the aftermath of the Tri-States Militia's collapse continued under the auspices of two new organizations, the Council of American Militias, whose national advisory board was populated largely by former members of the Tri-States board, and the Southeastern States Alliance.[89]

From 1998 onward, as the country's focus turned toward the new millennium, militia groups around the country gained new members interested in survivalist preparation. Once again, the constitutionalists and the millenarians perceived the millennium and the associated Y2K phenomenon quite differently. For example, Joe and Clara Pilchak predicted that the New World Order would emerge out of the chaos stemming from Y2K breakdowns, which they expected would "bring this country to its knees." John Trochman predicted a complete breakdown of the nation's electrical, communications, and food distribution systems for a period of several weeks. He predicted that most local communities would band together to ride out the crisis, but he believed that the Clinton administration would use the crisis to declare a national emergency, seize control of all private businesses, confiscate all privately owned guns, and marshal survivors into forced labor pools.[90]

Constitutionalists, on the other hand, tended to doubt that the end was nigh. Most were sufficiently technologically savvy to understand that the predictions of chaos were overblown. Most had already achieved a basic level of disaster preparation and looked forward to helping their neighbors through whatever disruptions lay ahead. As Jim McKinzey put it in early 1999, "If you have a militia type of mind, you will be on your way to getting ready for what, if any, trouble this might bring about. I'm looking at it the same way as I would at a bad ice storm hitting. I've been ready for that for a long time."[91]

Nevertheless, constitutionalists were concerned by the government's own speculations that martial law might be necessary to contain public panic in response to any Y2K breakdowns. In the fall of 1998, a number of government officials speculated publicly that martial law was a possibility should Y2K disrupt basic services. These statements showed little understanding of the constitutional implications of a federal declaration of martial law, nor did they explain why such a declaration would be necessary or desirable in response to power outages, local rioting, or food shortages.[92]

Many in the militia movement took note of these statements and coupled them with a series of urban warfare exercises that had been conducted in American cities since 1996. The Web page of Tom Wayne's faction of the Michigan Militia charged that these exercises were a preparation for martial law. OUMAAC cited a planned National Guard exercise designed to test the Guard's ability to muster its entire force without telecommunications.[93] Even those who did not expect Y2K to have a significant impact on the nation's infrastructure were alarmed by the government's preparations. Oral Deckard for example, recognized that Y2K would probably cause very little disruption, but he feared that the government would provoke a conflict:

> We've got the FEMA [Federal Emergency Management Agency] already telling all local law enforcement, be prepared for us to come help you on December 31. We've got them issuing bayonets to every police department in the country. . . . What's the city police department going to do with bayonets? . . . From my perspective as a programmer, I see there to be no legitimate need, but I've also got them telling each other, in plain words, they're going to patrol our streets with the military under martial law, guaranteed. Now, what am I to think from that?[94]

Y2K came and went without disruption. The January 2000 edition of *Taking Aim* was filled with recrimination, as well as suggestions that the problems predicted for Y2K would manifest themselves over the next several months. The issue led with a letter from Ken Raggio acknowledging that "every alarmist on earth, including myself, looks like a complete idiot." The pages of *Necessary Force*, on the other hand, were filled with usual articles on gun control, American history, veteran's reminiscences, and a sermon on the meaning of the Jewish high holy days by the Missouri 51st Militia's chaplain.[95] In the year 2000, the millenarian wing of the movement suffered a serious blow to its credibility. The constitutionalist wing, on the other hand, exhibited a significant measure of stability as it entered the new millennium.

EPILOGUE: THE DEFENSE OF
LIBERTY IN THE AGE OF TERROR

The election of George W. Bush in 2000 set the U.S. government on a markedly different course than that it had pursued in the 1990s. For the militia movement, the most important outcome of the election of 2000 was the appointment of John Ashcroft as attorney general. On May 17, 2001, Ashcroft responded to an inquiry from NRA executive director James Baker with a letter that outlined his views on the meaning of the Second Amendment. In that letter, Ashcroft endorsed in their entirety the individual rights and insurrectionary interpretations of the Second Amendment crafted by gun rights activists and legal scholars over the previous quarter century. He indicated that these interpretations of the amendment would guide federal policy on gun control. While Ashcroft's letter was hardly the last word in the contentious debate over the meaning of the Second Amendment, the gun rights movement saw the letter as strong evidence that the war on guns initiated in the 1990s had come to an early end.[1]

With the uneventful passing of the millennium and the waning of the threat of state violence directed at gun owners, militia activity showed a significant decline. Norm Olson disbanded the Northern Michigan Regional Militia on April 29, 2001, seven years after its founding. He noted that few members were still active, which he attributed to the change in political winds represented by the election of President Bush: "Across the nation, there is a satisfaction among patriots with the way things are going." Other militias, however, continued to meet periodically. The Missouri 51st Militia continued its activities into the summer of 2001, as did other constitutionalist militias. Commander Rick Hawkins observed in May 2001 that "the fact that 'Our Man' sits in the White House does not mean that our rights are no longer in danger. It does mean that as long as nothing blows up, or no one in camo takes out a Mickey D's with an UZI, we're probably OK for a while."[2]

Some in the constitutional wing of the movement intended to preserve their groups as permanent institutions dedicated to political discussion and civic engagement. That goal was undermined by the attacks of September 11, 2001. The patriotic revival in the aftermath of the attacks marked a full force return to the countersubversive patriotism of the Cold War era. As self-professed conservatives, militia members were ill suited to resist this cultural trend. Jim McKinzey, the cofounder of the Missouri 51st Militia who described the wrenching impact of Waco on his understanding of patriotism, found 9/11 equally wrenching. He later said that it was time to "look at what happened on Sept. 11 and understand that there are other enemies out there than Uncle Sam."[3] In the months after the attack most of the remaining Web sites associated with the constitutional wing of the movement went dark.

Yet the movement's warnings about the growth of government surveillance, the rise of state violence, and the potential for illegal detentions in a time of crisis have become all the more relevant in the age of terrorism. Passed in the immediate aftermath of the September 11 attacks, the USA PATRIOT Act gave the federal government surveillance powers that far outstripped those requested by the Clinton administration after the Oklahoma City bombing. Though the ostensible purpose of these new powers was to prevent further terrorist attacks on American soil, the new Department of Homeland Security controlled by a Republican administration has used these powers to suppress dissent and has suggested that a variety of left wing political groups, including some dedicated to nonviolent protest, are part of the terrorist threat facing the nation.[4]

This new politics of antiterrorism has also lent itself to significantly more violent methods of policing dissent. Since protestors succeeded in disrupting the World Trade Organization meeting in Seattle in 1999, police departments have resorted to much more aggressive tactics against peaceful nonviolent disobedience. In the last ten years, the use of pepper spray against nonviolent protestors has become standard operating procedure around the country. In April 2003, rubber bullets were fired at nonviolent demonstrators protesting the Iraq war at the Port of Oakland. Since then, police have fired rubber bullets at peaceful demonstrators during a 2003 protest against free trade in Miami, a 2007 immigration rally in Los Angeles, and a 2007 protest against the Iraq war in Tacoma.[5] Such tactics may, like the use of Tasers and pepper spray, become a routine part of policing.

These new forms of surveillance and policing fall fully upon aliens and citizens alike. Other powers asserted by the Bush administration apply only to foreign nationals. In practice, however, some aspects of these new powers have fallen upon American citizens as well. For example, the Bush administration has created one or more secret surveillance programs, often referred to as the Terrorist Surveillance Program, that involve the collection and analysis of telephone and electronic communications without warrants. It is clear from the little that we have learned about the Terrorist Surveillance Program that the government has intercepted the communications of at least some American citizens without the use of warrants. The administration is at present seeking legal immunity for those telecommunications companies that cooperated with the program in what may well have been a criminal conspiracy to evade the requirements of the Foreign Intelligence Surveillance Act.[6]

The United States has also asserted new powers to detain suspects without trial. At the end of 2001 the Bush administration announced that suspected terrorists captured during military operations against Al Qaeda would be imprisoned indefinitely at a camp in Guantánamo Bay, Cuba. In the ensuing years the camp has expanded and become the central node in a network of secret camps located around the world. The identities of prisoners in these camps have been withheld from the Red Cross; the prisoners have been denied prisoner-of-war status; many have suffered abusive interrogations. Initially the administration claimed that such detention would be applied only to foreign nationals captured under arms against the United States. However, in April 2003 Attorney General John Ashcroft issued a legal opinion stating that illegal immigrants may be held indefinitely without bond. Furthermore, a provision of the Military Commissions Act of 2006 effectively suspended the writ of habeas corpus for all aliens, both legal and illegal, detained by the United States under the provisions of the act. Finally, President Bush has asserted the authority to designate Americans citizens as "enemy combatants" and to hold them in military custody indefinitely.[7]

These detention policies together have created a legal netherworld in which detainees are entitled to neither the privileges of the U.S. Constitution nor the protections afforded to prisoners under the Geneva Conventions. In this netherworld another form of state violence has reared its ugly head: torture. The first reports that the United States was employing torture against captured members of Al Qaeda surfaced in early 2002. In the last five years it has become clear that the U.S. military and the Central Intelligence Agency have employed torture against hundreds of captives and that some of these detainees have died under torture. The U.S. government has also used the practice of extraordinary rendition to deliver additional terror suspects in its custody to foreign governments known to practice torture. Among the techniques employed by agents of the U.S. government are the prolonged use of stress positions; sleep deprivation; hypothermia; and waterboarding, in which a human being is subjected to gradual, controlled drowning.[8]

A few individual militiamen have spoken out against the abuses committed by the United States during the war on terror, but the movement itself has not revived.[9] Nevertheless, in the movement's critique of state violence and in the Whig diagnosis to which the movement gave voice, there lie observations that bear on our present situation: that state violence is not necessarily more legitimate than insurgent violence; that the trend toward government centralization and toward the violent enforcement of the laws will not reverse of its own accord; and that a government granted arbitrary power over the lives of aliens will soon seek to use that power over the lives of its citizens. When considering the erosion of civil liberty in the years since September 11, 2001, the words of Edward Livingston in 1798 seem all too pertinent. Speaking on the Alien Bill then before the House of Representatives, Livingston warned, "Let no man vainly imagine that the evil is to stop here, that a few unprotected aliens only are to be affected by this inquisitorial power; the same arguments that enforce these provisions against aliens apply with equal strength to enacting them in the case of citizens."[10]

Most Americans have rejected the militia movement's recourse to armed organization as a solution to the growth of state violence and the decline of civil liberty. But that rejection does not absolve us of the obligation to ask this question: What is the duty of free men and women in such an age?

APPENDIX

The following table lists those counties that I am confident hosted active militia groups between 1994 and 2000. It is limited to those states for which I have a sufficient familiarity with the movement to make this judgment. It is possible that the table underrepresents the number of counties that experienced militia activity during the 1990s. The table is based on a variety of sources. Particularly important are two lists of militia contacts, the "Minuteman Press Militia Directory," published in October 1997, http://www.afn.org/~mpress/militia.html (accessed October 19, 1998), and "Texas Constitutional Militia: Militia Contacts by County," compiled by Jon Roland and published on the Constitution Society Web site, http://www.constitution.org/mil/tx/mil_ustx.htm (accessed March 13, 2008). I supplemented the information from these documents with information drawn from interviews, militia publications, and news accounts where those accounts incorporated field research sufficient to establish the presence of a militia unit in a particular county. Given that units in metropolitan areas were more likely to come to the attention of the press, the table may undercount rural militias. The statistics for population density and population growth rate are drawn from the 2000 census, http://quickfacts.census.gov/qfd/ (accessed September 1, 2006). The Rural-Urban Continuum codes are drawn from the United States

Department of Agriculture Economic Research Service, http://www.ers
.usda.gov/Data/RuralUrbanContinuumCodes/ (accessed March 13, 2008).

The RUC (Rural-Urban Continuum) codes are defined as follows:

1. Counties in metropolitan areas of 1 million population or more (For
   1993, the Department of Agriculture distinguished between central metropolitan counties, designated 0 and fringe counties, designated 1)
2. Counties in metropolitan areas of 250,000 to 1 million population
3. Counties in metropolitan areas of fewer than 250,000 population
4. Urban population of 20,000 or more, adjacent to a metropolitan area
5. Urban population of 20,000 or more, not adjacent to a metropolitan area
6. Urban population of 2,500 to 19,999, adjacent to a metropolitan area
7. Urban population of 2,500 to 19,999, not adjacent to a metropolitan area
8. Completely rural or less than 2,500 urban population, adjacent to a metropolitan area
9. Completely rural or less than 2,500 urban population, not adjacent to a
   metropolitan area

STATE	COUNTY	DENSITY (PERSONS/ SQ. MILE)	POPULATION GROWTH RATE (%) 1990–2000	MILITIA	1993 RUC CODE	2003 RUC CODE
1. California	Orange	3,606	18.1	Constitutional Militia of S. California	0	1
2. California	San Bernadino	85	20.5	Unknown	0	1
3. California	San Diego	670	12.6	San Diego Militia	0	1
4. Florida	Pinellas	3,292	8.2	77th Regiment Militia	0	1
5. Illinois	Cook	5,686	5.3	Northern Illinois Minutemen	0	1
6. Illinois	DuPage	223	8.6	Northern Illinois Minutemen	0	1
7. Illinois	Kane	777	27.3	Northern Illinois Minutemen	0	1
8. Illinois	Lake	1,440	24.8	Northern Illinois Minutemen	0	1
9. Illinois	McHenry	431	41.9	Northern Illinois Minutemen	0	1
10. Illinois	Will	600	40.6	Northern Illinois Minutemen	0	1
11. Indiana	Lake	975	1.9	Indiana Citizens Volunteer Militia	0	1
12. Indiana	Marion	2,172	7.9	Indiana Citizens Volunteer Militia	0	1
13. Michigan	Macomb	1,641	9.9	Michigan Militia Division 9	0	1
14. Michigan	Oakland	1,368	10.2	Michigan Militia Division 9	0	1
15. Michigan	St. Clair	227	12.8	Michigan Militia Division 9	0	1
16. Michigan	Washtenhaw	455	14.1	Michigan Militia Division 9	0	2
17. Michigan	Wayne	3,356	−2.4	Michigan Militia Division 9	0	1
18. Missouri	Clay	464	19.9	Missouri 51st Militia	0	1
19. Missouri	Jackson	1,083	3.4	Missouri 51st Militia	0	1
20. Missouri	St. Louis	2,001	2.3	1st Missouri Volunteers	0	1
21. New Hampshire	Hillsborough	435	13.4	Regiment of Dragoons	0	2
22. New Jersey	Burlington	526	7.2	New Jersey Militia	0	1
23. New Jersey	Monmouth	1,304	11.3	New Jersey Militia	0	1
24. Ohio	Cuyahoga	3,040	−1.3	Ohio Unorganized Militia	0	1
25. Ohio	Franklin	1,980	11.2	Ohio Unorganized Militia	0	1
26. Ohio	Lake	997	5.6	Ohio Unorganized Militia	0	1
27. Pennsylvania	Bucks	984	10.4	PA Militia 9th Regiment Co. F	0	1
28. Pennsylvania	Chester	573	15.2	Unnamed	0	1
29. Pennsylvania	Delaware	2,990	0.6	United States Militia Association	0	1
30. Pennsylvania	Montgomery	1,553	10.6	United States Militia Association	0	1
31. Texas	Bexar	1,117	17.5	Texas Constitutional Militia	0	1
32. Texas	Dallas	2,523	19.8	Texas Constitutional Militia	0	1
33. Texas	Denton	487	58.2	Texas Constitutional Militia	0	1
34. Texas	Fort Bend	405	57.2	Texas Constitutional Militia	0	1
35. Texas	Galveston	628	15.1	Texas Constitutional Militia	0	1
36. Texas	Harris	1,967	20.7	Texas Constitutional Militia	0	1
37. Texas	Tarrant	1,675	23.6	Texas Constitutional Militia	0	1
38. Utah	Weber	342	24.1	United States Militia Association	0	2
39. California	El Dorado	91	24.1	Unorganized Militia of El Dorado	1	1
40. California	Placer	177	43.8	Placer County Militia	1	1
41. Indiana	Hancock	181	21.7	Indiana Citizens Volunteer Militia	1	1
42. Indiana	Morgan	164	19.3	Indiana Citizens Volunteer Militia	1	1
43. Indiana	Porter	351	13.9	Indiana Citizens Volunteer Militia	1	1
44. Michigan	Lapeer	134	17.6	Michigan Militia Division 6	1	1
45. Michigan	Lenawee	132	8.1	Michigan Militia Division 8	1	4
46. Michigan	Livingston	276	35.7	Michigan Militia Division 9	1	1

(continued on next page)

STATE	COUNTY	DENSITY (PERSONS/ SQ. MILE)	POPULATION GROWTH RATE (%) 1990–2000	MILITIA	1993 RUC CODE	2003 RUC CODE
47. Michigan	Monroe	265	9.2	Michigan Militia Division 9	1	3
48. Missouri	Jefferson	302	15.6	1st Missouri Volunteers	1	1
49. Ohio	Ashtabula	146	2.9	Ohio Unorganized Militia	1	4
50. Ohio	Delaware	249	65.3	Ohio Unorganized Militia	1	1
51. Ohio	Fairfield	243	18.6	Ohio Unorganized Militia	1	1
52. Ohio	Geauga	225	12.1	Ohio Unorganized Militia	1	1
53. Ohio	Madison	86	8.5	Ohio Unorganized Militia	1	1
54. Ohio	Medina	358	23.5	Ohio Unorganized Militia	1	1
55. Ohio	Warren	396	39.0	Ohio Unorganized Militia	1	1
56. Texas	Brazoria	174	26.1	Texas Constitutional Militia	1	1
57. Texas	Comal	139	50.5	Texas Constitutional Militia	1	1
58. Texas	Guadalupe	125	37.2	Texas Constitutional Militia	1	1
59. Texas	Kaufman	91	36.6	Texas Constitutional Militia	1	1
60. Texas	Liberty	61	33.1	Texas Constitutional Militia	1	1
61. Texas	Montgomery	281	61.2	Texas Constitutional Militia	1	1
62. Washington	Clark	89	21.1	United States Militia Association	1	1
63. Alabama	Blount	79	30.0	1st Alabama Cavalry	2	1
64. Alabama	Elmore	106	33.9	Alabama Constitutional Militia	2	2
65. Alabama	Jefferson	595	1.6	1st Alabama Cavalry	2	1
66. Alabama	Mobile	324	5.6	Unknown	2	2
67. Alabama	Shelby	180	44.2	1st Alabama Cavalry	2	1
68. Alabama	St. Clair	102	30.0	1st Alabama Cavalry	2	1
69. California	Kern	81	21.4	Kern County Liberty Corps	2	2
70. California	San Joaquin	403	17.3	San Joaquin County Militia	2	2
71. Florida	Escambia	445	12.2	Escambia County Militia	2	2
72. Florida	Martin	228	25.6	Florida State Militia	2	2
73. Florida	Palm Beach	573	31.0	Florida State Militia	2	1
74. Florida	Santa Rosa	116	43.7	Santa Rosa County Militia	2	2
75. Florida	St. Lucie	337	28.3	Florida State Militia	2	2
76. Idaho	Ada	285	46.2	United States Militia Association	2	2
77. Idaho	Canyon	223	45.9	United States Militia Association	2	2
78. Michigan	Allegan	126	16.7	Michigan Militia Division 7	2	4
79. Michigan	Bay	248	−1.4	Michigan Militia Division 6	2	3
80. Michigan	Calhoun	195	1.5	Michigan Militia Division 8	2	3
81. Michigan	Clinton	113	11.8	Michigan Militia Division 6	2	2
82. Michigan	Eaton	180	11.6	Michigan Militia Division 8	2	2
83. Michigan	Genessee	681	1.3	Michigan Militia Division 6	2	2
84. Michigan	Ingham	500	−0.9	Michigan Militia Division 8	2	2
85. Michigan	Kalamazoo	425	6.8	Michigan Militia Division 7	2	2
86. Michigan	Kent	670	14.7	Michigan Militia Division 5	2	2
87. Michigan	Midland	159	9.5	Michigan Militia Division 6	2	4
88. Michigan	Muskegon	334	7.1	Michigan Militia Division 5	2	3
89. Michigan	Ottawa	421	26.9	Michigan Militia Division 5	2	3
90. Michigan	Saginaw	260	−0.9	Michigan Militia Division 6	2	3
91. Michigan	Van Buren	125	8.9	Michigan Militia Division 7	2	2
92. Missouri	Greene	356	15.6	Missouri 24th Militia	2	2

STATE	COUNTY	DENSITY (PERSONS/ SQ. MILE)	POPULATION GROWTH RATE (%) 1990–2000	MILITIA	1993 RUC CODE	2003 RUC CODE
Nevada	Clark	174	85.6	United States Militia Association	2	1
New Jersey	Mercer	1,552	7.7	New Jersey Militia	2	2
New Mexico	Bernalillo	477	15.8	New Mexico Militia	2	2
New Mexico	Sandoval	24	42.0	New Mexico Militia	2	2
New York	Orange	418	11.0	Militia of Orange County	2	2
Ohio	Montgomery	1,210	−2.6	Ohio Unorganized Militia	2	2
Ohio	Portage	309	6.6	Ohio Unorganized Militia	2	2
Ohio	Stark	656	2.9	Ohio Unorganized Militia	2	2
Ohio	Summit	1,315	5.4	Ohio Unorganized Militia	2	2
Oregon	Marion	241	24.7	Northwest Oregon Regional Militia	2	2
Oregon	Polk	84	25.9	Northwest Oregon Regional Militia	2	2
Pennsylvania	Dauphin	479	5.9	United States Militia Association	2	2
South Carolina	Aiken	133	17.8	South Carolina Civilian Militia	2	2
South Carolina	Anderson	231	14.2	South Carolina Civilian Militia	2	3
South Carolina	Greenville	481	18.6	South Carolina Civilian Militia	2	2
South Carolina	Lexington	309	28.9	South Carolina Civilian Militia	2	2
South Carolina	Pickens	223	18.0	South Carolina Civilian Militia	2	2
South Carolina	Richland	424	12.0	South Carolina Civilian Militia	2	2
South Carolina	Spartanburg	313	11.9	South Carolina Civilian Militia	2	2
Texas	Bell	225	24.5	Texas Constitutional Militia	2	2
Texas	Caldwell	59	22.0	Texas Constitutional Militia	2	1
Texas	Hays	144	48.7	Texas Constitutional Militia	2	1
Texas	Hidalgo	362	48.5	Texas Constitutional Militia	2	2
Texas	Travis	821	40.9	Texas Constitutional Militia	2	1
Texas	Williamson	223	79.1	Texas Constitutional Militia	2	1
Alabama	Calhoun	184	−3.3	Unknown	3	3
Alabama	Etowah	193	3.6	Gadsden Minutemen	3	3
Alabama	Lawrence	50	10.4	Alabama Constitutional Militia	3	3
Alabama	Tuscaloosa	125	9.6	1st Alabama Cavalry	3	3
California	Butte	124	11.6	Butte County Militia	3	3
Florida	Alachua	249	20.0	North Florida Citizens Regional Militia	3	3
Florida	Marion	164	32.9	Marion County Citizens Militia	3	2
Indiana	Clay	74	7.5	Indiana Citizens Volunteer Militia	3	3
Indiana	Delaware	302	−0.07	Indiana Citizens Volunteer Militia	3	3
Indiana	Howard	170	9.7	Indiana Citizens Volunteer Militia	3	3
Indiana	St. Joseph	581	7.5	Indiana Citizens Volunteer Militia	3	2
Indiana	Tippecanoe	170	9.7	Indiana Citizens Volunteer Militia	3	3
Michigan	Jackson	224	5.8	Michigan Militia Division 8	3	3
New Mexico	Santa Fe	68	30.7	New Mexico Militia	3	3
New Mexico	Valencia	62	46.2	New Mexico Militia	3	2
New York	Chemung	223	−4.3	Chemung County Citizens Militia	3	3
Oregon	Jackson	65	23.8	Southern Oregon Militia	3	3
South Dakota	Rapid City	32	8.9	Tri-States Militia	3	3
Texas	Bowie	101	9.4	Texas Constitutional Militia	3	3
Texas	Victoria	95	13.1	Texas Constitutional Militia	3	3
Texas	Wichita	210	7.6	Texas Constitutional Militia	3	3

(*continued on next page*)

STATE	COUNTY	DENSITY (PERSONS/ SQ. MILE)	POPULATION GROWTH RATE (%) 1990–2000	MILITIA	1993 RUC CODE	200 RU COL
139. Washington	Whatcom	79	30.5	Washington State Militia	3	3
140. Alabama	Talladega	109	8.4	Unknown	4	4
141. California	Mendacino	25	7.4	Fort Bragg Unorganized Militia	4	4
142. Florida	Indian River	224	25.2	Florida State Militia	4	3
143. Indiana	Laporte	184	2.8	Indiana Citizens Volunteer Militia	4	3
144. Michigan	Isabella	110	16.0	Michigan Militia Division 5	4	5
145. Michigan	Shiawassee	133	2.7	Michigan Militia Division 6	4	4
146. Nevada	Carson City	366	29.7	United States Militia Association	4	3
147. Ohio	Hancock	134	8.8	Ohio Unorganized Militia	4	4
148. Ohio	Muskingum	127	3.1	Southeast Ohio Defense Forces	4	4
149. Oregon	Josephine	46	20.9	Southern Oregon Militia	4	4
150. Texas	Navarro	45	13.0	Texas Constitutional Militia	4	4
151. Washington	Cowlitz	82	13.2	United States Militia Association	4	3
152. Idaho	Bannock	68	14.2	United States Militia Association	5	3
153. Idaho	Bonneville	44	14.3	United States Militia Association	5	3
154. Idaho	Twin Falls	33	20.0	United States Militia Association	5	5
155. Illinois	Williamson	149	6.2	Southern Illinois Patriots League	5	5
156. Montana	Flathead	15	25.8	Militia of Montana	5	5
157. New Mexico	Lea	13	−0.5	New Mexico Militia/ United States Militia Association	5	5
158. New Mexico	McKinley	14	23.3	New Mexico Militia	5	4
159. New Mexico	San Juan	21	24.2	New Mexico Militia	5	3
160. Oregon	Deschutes	38	53.9	Central Oregon Militia	5	3
161. Alabama	Bibb	33	25.5	1st Alabama Cavalry	6	1
162. Alabama	Cullman	105	14.6	1st Alabama Cavalry	6	6
163. California	Tehama	19	12.9	Tehama County Militia	6	4
164. California	Tuolumne	24	12.5	Tuolumne County Militia	6	4
165. Florida	Okeechobee	46	21.2	Florida State Militia	6	4
166. Indiana	Greene	61	9.1	Indiana Citizens Volunteer Militia	6	3
167. Indiana	Henry	124	5.9	Indiana Citizens Volunteer Militia	6	4
168. Indiana	Marshall	102	7.0	Indiana Citizens Volunteer Militia	6	6
169. Indiana	Owen	57	26.1	Indiana Citizens Volunteer Militia	6	3
170. Indiana	Starke	76	3.6	Indiana Citizens Volunteer Militia	6	6
171. Michigan	Barry	102	13.4	Michigan Militia Division 7	6	2
172. Michigan	Branch	90	10.3	Michigan Militia Division 8	6	6
173. Michigan	Cass	104	3.3	Michigan Militia Division 7	6	2
174. Michigan	Gladwin	51	18.8	Michigan Militia Division 6	6	6
175. Michigan	Gratiot	74	8.5	Michigan Militia Division 6	6	6
176. Michigan	Hillsdale	78	7.1	Michigan Militia Division 8	6	6
177. Michigan	Ionia	107	7.9	Michigan Militia Division 5	6	6
178. Michigan	Montcalm	87	15.5	Michigan Militia Division 5	6	6
179. Michigan	Newaygo	57	25.3	Michigan Militia Division 5	6	2
180. Michigan	Tuscola	72	5.0	Michigan Militia Division 6	6	6
181. Ohio	Champaign	91	8.0	Ohio Unorganized Militia	6	6
182. Ohio	Darke	90	−0.06	Ohio Unorganized Militia	6	6
183. Ohio	Highland	74	14.4	Ohio Unorganized Militia	6	6

STATE	COUNTY	DENSITY (PERSONS/ SQ. MILE)	POPULATION GROWTH RATE (%) 1990–2000	MILITIA	1993 RUC CODE	2003 RUC CODE
184. Pennsylvania	Greene	71	2.8	Unnamed	6	6
185. Pennsylvania	Warren	50	−2.6	Keystone Militia	6	6
186. Texas	Anderson	52	15.8	Texas Constitutional Militia	6	5
187. Texas	Atacosa	31	26.5	Texas Constitutional Militia	6	1
188. Texas	Cherokee	44	13.7	Texas Constitutional Militia	6	6
189. Texas	Dewitt	22	6.2	Texas Constitutional Militia	6	6
190. Texas	Grimes	30	25.0	Texas Constitutional Militia	6	6
191. Texas	Kendall	36	62.7	Texas Constitutional Militia	6	1
192. Texas	LaVaca	20	2.8	Texas Constitutional Militia	6	6
193. Utah	Box Elder	8	17.2	United States Militia Association	6	4
194. Idaho	Bingham	20	11.0	United States Militia Association	7	6
195. Idaho	Madison	58	6.4	United States Militia Association	7	6
196. Illinois	Warren	35	−2.3	Western Illinois Militia	7	7
197. Michigan	Alger	11	9.9	Michigan Militia Division 2	7	9
198. Michigan	Alpena	55	2.3	Michigan Militia Division 4	7	7
199. Michigan	Cheboygan	37	23.6	Michigan Militia Division 3	7	7
200. Michigan	Clare	55	25.2	Michigan Militia Division 5	7	7
201. Michigan	Delta	33	2.0	Michigan Militia Division 2	7	5
202. Michigan	Emmet	67	25.5	Michigan Militia Division 3	7	7
203. Michigan	Grand Traverse	167	20.8	Michigan Militia Division 3	7	5
204. Michigan	Houghton	36	1.6	Michigan Militia Division 1	7	5
205. Michigan	Huron	43	3.2	Michigan Militia Division 6	7	7
206. Michigan	Iosco	50	−9.5	Michigan Militia Division 4	7	7
207. Michigan	Manistee	45	15.3	Michigan Militia Division 3	7	7
208. Michigan	Mason	57	10.7	Michigan Militia Division 5	7	7
209. Michigan	Menominee	24	1.6	Michigan Militia Division 1	7	7
210. Michigan	Ogemaw	38	15.9	Michigan Militia Division 4	7	9
211. Michigan	Otsego	45	29.8	Michigan Militia Division 4	7	7
212. Michigan	Roscommon	49	28.8	Michigan Militia Division 4	7	7
213. Michigan	Wexford	54	15.6	Michigan Militia Division 3	7	7
214. Montana	Lincoln	5	7.8	Militia of Montana	7	7
215. Montana	Ravilli	15	44.2	Militia of Montana/North American Volunteer Militia	7	6
216. Oregon	Baker	6	9.3	Eastern Oregon Militia	7	7
217. Oregon	Crook	6	35.9	Central Oregon Militia	7	6
218. Oregon	Jefferson	11	39.0	Central Oregon Militia	7	6
219. Oregon	Union	12	3.9	Eastern Oregon Militia	7	7
220. Pennsylvania	Potter	17	8.2	Bucktail Militia	7	9
221. Texas	Freestone	20	13.0	Texas Constitutional Militia	7	7
222. Texas	Kerr	40	20.2	Texas Constitutional Militia	7	4
223. Texas	Nueces	375	7.7	Texas Constitutional Militia	7	2
224. Texas	Uvalde	17	11.1	Texas Constitutional Militia	7	7
225. Texas	Young	20	−0.1	Texas Constitutional Militia	7	6
226. Indiana	Brown	48	6.2	Indiana Citizens Volunteer Militia	8	1
227. Michigan	Arenac	47	15.9	Michigan Militia Division 6	8	8
228. Michigan	Oceana	50	19.7	Michigan Militia Division 5	8	8

(continued on next page)

STATE	COUNTY	DENSITY (PERSONS/ SQ. MILE)	POPULATION GROWTH RATE (%) 1990–2000	MILITIA	1993 RUC CODE	2003 RUC CODE
229. Michigan	Sanilac	46	11.6	Michigan Militia Division 6	8	6
230. New Mexico	Torrance	5	64.4	New Mexico Militia	8	2
231. Texas	Bandera	22	67.1	Texas Constitutional Militia	8	1
232. Texas	Blanco	12	41.0	Texas Constitutional Militia	8	8
233. Idaho	Teton	13	74.4	United States Militia Association	9	9
234. Michigan	Alcona	17	15.5	Michigan Militia Division 4	9	9
235. Michigan	Antrim	49	27.1	Michigan Militia Division 3	9	9
236. Michigan	Benzie	50	31.1	Michigan Militia Division 3	9	9
237. Michigan	Crawford	26	15.4	Michigan Militia Division 4	9	7
238. Michigan	Kalkaska	30	22.8	Michigan Militia Division 3	9	7
239. Michigan	Lake	20	32.0	Michigan Militia Division 5	9	8
240. Michigan	Leelanau	61	27.8	Michigan Militia Division 3	9	9
241. Michigan	Missaukee	26	19.2	Michigan Militia Division 3	9	9
242. Michigan	Montmorency	20	15.4	Michigan Militia Division 4	9	9
243. Michigan	Oscoda	17	20.1	Michigan Militia Division 4	9	9
244. Montana	Sanders	4	18.0	Militia of Montana	9	8
245. South Dakota	Gregory	5	−10.6	Tri-States Militia	9	9
246. Texas	Real	4	26.3	Texas Constitutional Militia	9	9

NOTES

The URLs given in these notes were valid at the time that this research was conducted. However, some of these Web pages may no longer be available.

Introduction

1. Norm Olson, founder of the Michigan Militia, interview by the author, Alanson, MI, November 3, 1998, 7; and Olson, "Is the Citizen Militia Lawful?" http://mmc.cns.net/text/lawfulmilitia.txt (accessed November 1, 1996).

2. Bill Utterback, cofounder, Texas Constitutional Militia, interview by the author, San Antonio, TX, January 6, 2006, 5–6; Charles Morrison Jr., and Tom Plummer, members of the Central Ohio Unorganized Militia, interview by the author, Columbus, OH, October 25, 1998, 4; and Norm Olson, interview, 9. An examination of the texts demonstrates that Olson's manual is the foundation of the manuals of the Texas Constitutional Militia, the Missouri 51st Militia, the Pennsylvania Citizens Militia, and the California Militia. See Norm Olson, "Establishing a Militia in Michigan" (Revision 1, June 28, 1994), Michigan Militia Multi-Information Archive (hereafter MMC Archive); "Formation of a Texas Constitutional Militia," in Kenneth S. Stern, *Militias, a Growing Danger: An American Jewish Committee Background Report* (New York: American Jewish Committee, 1995), app. 28; "Missouri 51st Militia By-Laws," http://www.tfs .net/~sbarnett/bylaws.htm (accessed August 4, 1997); *Pennsylvania Citizens Militia Manual*, version 1.1, March 6, 1995, http://www.users.fast.net/~klh/pa.pa

triot/manual.html (accessed November 1, 1996); and Stephen L. King, *California Militia Manual*, posted to misc.activism.militia (accessed January 24, 1996).

3. John Trochman, *Enemies Foreign and Domestic* (1995), provided courtesy of John Trochman; Militia of Montana, *Information and Networking Manual*, provided courtesy of Donald Cohen, director, Detroit Regional Office of the Anti-Defamation League, 7; *Charter of the Unorganized Militia of the Ohio Republic*, Ohio Unorganized Militia information booklet, provided courtesy of Tom Plummer; and Jonathan Karl, *The Right to Bear Arms: The Rise of America's New Militias* (New York: Harper, 1995), 67–74.

4. The Michigan Militia's claim of a membership approaching ten thousand in early 1995 is plausible in light of news coverage of county militia meetings drawing between one hundred and two hundred attendees each. The Indiana Citizens Volunteer Militia may have enrolled five thousand members in the same period. If these claims are accurate, then a national total in the range of one hundred thousand is a distinct possibility.

5. On the white supremacist roots of the movement, see Southern Poverty Law Center, *False Patriots: The Threat of Antigovernment Extremists* (Montgomery: SPLC, 1997); Anti-Defamation League, *Armed and Dangerous: Militias Take Aim at the Federal Government* (New York: ADL, 1994); Morris Dees with James Corcoran, *Gathering Storm: America's Militia Threat* (New York: HarperCollins, 1996); and Kenneth S. Stern, *A Force upon the Plain: The American Militia Movement and the Politics of Hate* (New York: Simon and Schuster, 1996). On militias as a millenarian phenomenon, see Richard Abanes, *American Militias: Rebellion, Racism, and Religion* (Downers Grove, IL: InterVarsity Press, 1996); Michael Barkun, "Religion, Militias, and Oklahoma City: The Mind of Conspiratorialists," *Terrorism and Political Violence* 8 (1996): 50–64; and Martin Durham, "Preparing for Armageddon: Citizen Militias, the Patriot Movement, and the Oklahoma City Bombing," *Terrorism and Political Violence* 8 (1996): 65–79. For comparisons to earlier populist vigilantes see Catherine McNichol Stock, *Rural Radicals: Righteous Rage in the American Grain* (Ithaca: Cornell University Press, 1996); and Joel Dyer, *Harvest of Rage: Why Oklahoma City Is Only the Beginning* (Boulder, CO: Westview Press, 1998).

6. For the narrative of 1995, see Southern Poverty Law Center, *False Patriots;* Anti-Defamation League, *Armed and Dangerous;* Abanes, *American Militias;* Dees, *Gathering Storm;* Thomas Halpern and Brian Levin, *The Limits of Dissent: The Constitutional Status of Armed Civilian Militias* (Northampton, MA: Alethia Press, 1996); and Stern, *Force upon the Plain.*

7. Steven M. Chermak, *Searching for a Demon: The Media Construction of*

the Militia Movement (Boston: Northeastern Press, 2002). Chermak finds that militia "experts" provided commentary in over 65 percent of all news stories on the militia movement.

8. Leo P. Ribuffo, *The Old Christian Right: The Protestant Far Right from the Great Depression to the Cold War* (Philadelphia: Temple University Press, 1983), esp. chap. 5.

9. The narrative of 1995 was part of a larger lobbying campaign conducted by the Anti-Defamation League, the Southern Poverty Law Center, and other civil rights organizations. Their objective was to convince state governments to enact and enforce legislation that would prohibit paramilitary training. The model antiparamilitary training statutes published by these civil rights organizations were broad enough to criminalize membership in a militia group. In this sense, the legal suppression of the movement was the avowed purpose of these organizations. On this lobbying campaign, see Stern, *Force upon the Plain*, 234. For the texts of the SPLC and ADL model antiparamilitary training statutes, see Halpern and Levin, *Limits of Dissent*, 113–20.

10. David H. Bennett, *The Party of Fear: From Nativist Movements to the New Right in American History* (New York: Vintage, 1995); Stock, *Rural Radicals;* Barbara Perry, "'Button-Down Terror': The Metamorphosis of the Hate Movement," *Sociological Focus* 33 (2000): 113–31; and Manuel Castells, *The Power of Identity,* vol. 2, *The Information Age* (Malden, MA: Blackwell, 2004), 87–100.

11. John Keith Akins, "God, Guns, and Guts: Religion and Violence in Florida Militias," Ph.D. diss., University of Florida, 1998, 73.

12. Sean P. O'Brien and Donald P. Haider-Markel, "Fueling the Fire: Social and Political Correlates of Citizen Militia Activity," *Social Science Quarterly* 79 (1998): 456–65; Joshua D. Freilich, *American Militias: State-Level Variations in Militia Activities* (New York: LFB Scholarly Publishing, 2003); and Nella Van Dyck and Sarah A. Soule, "Structural Social Change and the Mobilizing Effect of Threat: Explaining Levels of Patriot and Militia Organizing in the United States," *Social Problems* 49 (2002): 497–520.

13. Michael Kimmel and Abby L. Ferber, "'White Men Are This Nation': Right Wing Militias and the Restoration of Rural American Masculinity," *Rural Sociology* 65 (2000): 582–604. The authors acknowledge the contributions of Chip Berlet, senior analyst at Political Research Associates. Berlet, for his part, has gently admonished Ferber for conflating the militia movement and the white supremacist Right. For Berlet's corrective and Kimmel and Ferber's somewhat inadequate response, see Abby L. Ferber, ed., *Home Grown Hate: Gender and Organized Racism* (New York: Routledge, 2003), xi, 14, and 28–39. Chip Berlet and

Mark Pitcavage, two of the closest observers of the movement in the civil rights community, have attempted to steer academics clear of the errors embedded in the narrative of 1995. See Berlet, "Militias in the Frame," *Contemporary Sociology* 33 (2004): 514–21; and Mark Pitcavage, "Camouflage and Conspiracy: The Militia Movement from Ruby Ridge to Y2K," *American Behavioral Scientist* 44 (2001): 957–81. Pitcavage was the creator of www.militia-watchdog.org, an early Web site tracking the militia movement, and is currently director of fact-finding for the ADL.

14. Lane Crothers, "The Cultural Foundations of the Modern Militia Movement," *New Political Science* 24 (2002): 221–34; Crothers, *Rage on the Right: The American Militia Movement from Ruby Ridge to Homeland Security* (Lanham, MD: Rowman and Littlefield, 2003), chap. 3; Michael Barkun, "Religion, Militias, and Oklahoma City"; and Durham, "Preparing for Armageddon."

15. Chermak, *Searching for a Demon;* David C. Williams, *The Mythic Meanings of the Second Amendment: Taming Political Violence in a Constitutional Republic* (New Haven: Yale University Press, 2003); and D. J. Mulloy, *American Extremism: History, Politics, and the Militia Movement* (New York: Routledge, 2004).

16. Jürgen Habermas, *The Structural Transformation of the Public Sphere: An Inquiry into a Category of Bourgeois Society,* trans. Thomas Burger with the assistance of Frederick Lawrence (Cambridge: MIT Press, 1991); and Dena Goodman, "Public Sphere and Private Life: Toward a Synthesis of Current Historiographical Approaches to the Old Regime," *History and Theory* 31 (1992): 1–20. Civil rights groups such as the ADL and SPLC have for half a century policed radio, television, mainstream press, and corporate publishing houses, seeking to systematically exclude far right content and speakers on the basis of their fundamental "irrationality." For discussions of the role of civil rights groups in policing the public sphere, see Glen Jeansonne, *Gerald L. K. Smith, Minister of Hate* (New Haven: Yale University Press, 1988), 206–8; Frederick J. Simonelli, *American Fuehrer: George Lincoln Rockwell and the American Nazi Party* (Urbana: University of Illinois Press, 1999), 52–71; and Jeffrey Kaplan, "Right-Wing Violence in North America," in Tore Bjørgo, ed., *Terror from the Extreme Right* (London: Frank Cass, 1995), 76–77 and 94 n. 74.

17. For discussions of the communications nodes of this public sphere, see Neil A. Hamilton, *Militias in America: A Reference Handbook* (Santa Barbara: ABC-CLIO, 1996), 213–20; and Chip Berlet, "Who Is Mediating the Storm? Right-Wing Alternative Information Networks," in Linda Kintz and Julia Lesage, eds., *Media, Culture, and the Religious Right* (Minneapolis: University of Minnesota Press, 1998), 249–73.

18. This assessment of the dynamics of discussion within the Christian Patriot public sphere is based on my observation of discussions on three email discussion lists, misc.activism.militia, Patriots Information Mailing List, and Fratrum.

19. For example, Ken O'Toole of Montana Human Rights Network famously likened the ideological ferment on the far right to a funnel "scooping up" reasonably normal human beings and "popping out" a McVeigh. O'Toole is quoted in Stern, *Force upon the Plain*, 107. See also Carolyn Gallaher, *On the Fault Line: Race, Class, and the American Patriot Movement* (Lanham, MD: Rowman and Littlefield, 1993), 92; Pitcavage, "Camouflage and Conspiracy," 961–62; and Akins, "God, Guns, and Guts," 144–46. One exception to this observation is Chip Berlet, whose analysis in "Who Is Mediating the Storm" is largely neutral.

20. For example, two Illinois teenagers created the "Illinois Constitutional Militia" Web site to attract an audience for their own particular tastes in rock music. See "Illinois Constitutional Militia FAQ," http://www.geocities.com/CapitolHill/Lobby/4266/FAQ.html (accessed July 31, 1997). Missouri white supremacist Martin Lindstedt styled himself a member and spokesperson of the 7th Missouri Militia. I have never seen evidence that there were any other members of the group. See the 7th Missouri Militia Web site, http://www.mo-net.com/~mlindste/7momilit.html (accessed March 13, 2008).

21. For examinations of the paramilitary arm of the white supremacist movement see *Hate, Violence, and White Supremacy: A Decade Review, 1980–1990* (Montgomery: Klanwatch Project of the Southern Poverty Law Center, 1989); James Ridgeway, *Blood in the Face: The Ku Klux Klan, Aryan Nations, Nazi Skinheads, and the Rise of a New White Culture*, 2nd ed. (New York: Thunder's Mouth Press, 1995); James Coates, *Armed and Dangerous: The Rise of the Survivalist Right* (New York: Noonday Press, 1987); and Akins, "God, Guns, and Guts."

22. The material from Political Research Associates was provided courtesy of Chip Berlet. The material from the ADL was provided courtesy of Donald Cohen, director of the Detroit Regional Office. Material from the SPLC was provided courtesy of Mark Potok. The Michigan Militia Multi-Information Archive consists of binders with thousands of documents stored in the home of Rick Haynes, commander, Eighth Division, MMC. This material was provided courtesy of Joe Pilchak and Rick Haynes. In addition, Jim and Michael McKinzey, Joe and Clara Pilchak, Tom Plummer, Samuel Sherwood, Mike Vanderboegh, Jim Wade, and Robert Wright were extremely generous in sharing militia material with me. As time passes, the recovery of militia texts grows more challenging. Many militia Web sites went dark between 2000 and 2002 after their host groups

disbanded. Although the Usenet discussion lists misc.activism.militia and talk.politics.guns are archived at http://groups-beta.google.com, many other discussion lists through which the movement communicated were never archived. It is to be hoped that researchers will undertake the task of archiving the materials that they have gathered in the process of researching the movement.

23. It is not clear how significant a limitation this is. Civil rights activists and white supremacists have both dismissed the public portion of the movement as the less threatening tip of a much more dangerous iceberg, but both communities had ample reason to exaggerate the existence of a radical underground. Members of the constitutional wing of the movement have consistently argued that the bulk of the movement was above ground, and that most of those who avoided publicity shared the principles of those who courted it.

24. The interviews with militiamen were conducted under the auspices of the Rutgers University Institutional Review Board for the Protection of Human Subjects and the University of Hartford Human Subjects Committee. Most interview subjects have given permission for the tapes and transcripts of the interviews to be preserved in an archive to be established at the John Hay Library of Brown University. For an excellent overview of the controversy over the practice of deceiving human subjects, see Charlotte Allen, "Spies Like Us: When Sociologists Deceive Their Subjects," *Lingua Franca* 7 (November 1997): 31–39.

25. For analyses of the militia movement that emphasize class, see Stock, *Rural Radicals;* Dyer, *Harvest of Rage;* and Gallaher, *On the Fault Line.* Like Stock, Dyer exhibits little familiarity with the militia movement: most of his journalistic contacts appear to have been in the common-law court movement or the most radical fringes of the militia movement like the Freemen and the Republic of Texas. But his assertion that militia activity was the product of working-class economic distress has nevertheless significantly influenced the perception of the movement's class composition. Gallagher's analysis is much stronger, but her exposure to the militia movement was also limited.

26. Eduardo Bonilla-Silva, *White Supremacy and Racism in the Post–Civil Rights Era* (Boulder, CO: Lynne Rienner, 2001); Bonilla-Silva, *Racism without Racists: Color-Blind Racism and the Persistence of Racial Inequality in the United States* (Lanham, MD: Rowman and Littlefield, 2003); and Bonilla-Silva, " 'New Racism,' Color-Blind Racism, and the Future of Whiteness in America," in Ashley Doane and Eduardo Bonilla-Silva, eds., *White Out: The Continuing Significance of Racism* (New York: Routledge, 2003), 271–84.

27. On the evolution of American ideals of manliness, see E. Anthony Rotundo, *American Manhood: Transformations in Masculinity from the Revolution*

to the Modern Era (New York: Basic Books, 1993); and Michael Kimmel, *Manhood in America: A Cultural History* (New York: Free Press, 1996).

28. James William Gibson, *Warrior Dreams: Violence and Manhood in Post-Vietnam America* (New York: Hill and Wang, 1994). For the application of his work to the militia movement, see Dees, *Gathering Storm;* Freilich, *American Militias;* and Kimmel and Ferber, "White Men Are This Nation."

29. Gibson, *Warrior Dreams,* 9–14, 26–32.

30. Chermak, *Searching for a Demon,* 145–46.

31. R. W. Connell, *Masculinities: Knowledge, Power, and Social Change* (Berkeley and Los Angeles: University of California Press, 1995), 77–79.

32. See Maurice Halbwachs, *On Collective Memory* (Chicago: University of Chicago Press, 1992). On the use of the concept of collective memory by American historians, see the special March 1989 issue of *Journal of American History* devoted to the topic, and especially the editor's introduction, David Thelen, "Memory and American History," *Journal of American History* 75 (1989): 1117–29.

33. John Bodnar, *Remaking America: Public Memory, Commemoration, and Patriotism in the Twentieth Century* (Princeton: Princeton University Press, 1992).

34. For the impact of Dodd's conspiracy on the elections of 1864, see G. R. Tredway, *Democratic Opposition to the Lincoln Administration in Indiana* (Indianapolis: Indiana Historical Bureau, 1973); and Frank L. Klement, *Dark Lanterns: Secret Political Societies, Conspiracies, and Treason Trials in the Civil War* (Baton Rouge: Louisiana State University Press, 1984).

35. Bodnar, *Remaking America,* 13–19.

The Precedent of 1774

1. Suffolk County (Massachusetts) Resolutions, September 6, 1774, reprinted in Peter Force, ed., *American Archives,* 9 vols. (Washington, DC: M. St. Clair and Peter Force, 1837–53) (hereafter Force), 4th ser., 1:776–79.

2. David Ammerman, *In Common Cause: American Response to the Coercive Acts of 1774* (New York: Norton, 1974), 5–10.

3. Richard Bland, *The Colonel Dismounted,* in Bernard Bailyn, ed., *Pamphlets of the American Revolution,* vol. 1 (Cambridge: Harvard University Press, 1965), 320. For a general overview of this strain of Whig thought, see Bernard Bailyn, *The Ideological Origins of the American Revolution* (Cambridge: Harvard University Press, 1967), 94–143 and 160–212.

4. Middlesex County (Virginia) Resolutions, July 15, 1774, Force, 1:551–52; Resolutions of the Inhabitants of Sussex County, Delaware, July 23, 1774, Force, 1:665–67.

5. Sussex County (New Jersey) Resolutions, July 16, 1774, Force, 1:594; Huntington (Suffolk County, New York) Resolutions, June 21, 1774, Force, 1:453. The first volume of Force's *American Archives* is filled with such resolutions. See, for example, Queen Anne (Maryland) Resolutions, May 13, 1774, Force, 1:366; Prince William (Virginia) Resolutions, June 6, 1774, Force, 1:388; Lancaster (Pennsylvania) Resolutions, June 15, 1774, Force, 1:415–16; Morris County (New Jersey) Resolutions, June 27, 1774, Force, 1:452–53; and New Kent County (Virginia) Resolutions, July 12, 1774, Force, 1:536–37.

6. For an overview of this more libertarian strain of Whig ideology, see John Philip Reid, *The Concept of Liberty in the Age of the American Revolution* (Chicago: University of Chicago Press, 1988) and *Constitutional History of the American Revolution: The Authority of Rights* (Madison: University of Wisconsin Press, 1986).

7. Jonathan Mayhew, *A Discourse Concerning Unlimited Submission*, Bailyn, *Pamphlets*, 233.

8. Ibid., 237–38.

9. Ibid., 236.

10. Thomson Mason, *The British American, IX*, Williamsburg, July 28, 1774, Force, 1:648–54; and Thomas Jefferson, *A Summary View of the Rights of British America* (Philadelphia: John Dunlap, 1774). See also Frederick County (Virginia) Resolutions, June 8, 1774, Force, 1:392–93; Woodstock (Virginia) Resolutions, June 16, 1774, Force, 1:417–18; and Resolutions of the Pennsylvania Convention, July 15, 1774, Force, 1:555–57. Both Mason and Jefferson placed considerable emphasis on Parliament's lack of jurisdiction over the colonies. Nevertheless, both came closest to advocating outright resistance while contemplating the assault on liberty embodied by the Coercive Acts.

11. Suffolk County (Massachusetts) Resolutions, September 6, 1774, Force, 1:778; Middlesex County (Massachusetts) Resolutions, August 31, 1774, Force, 1:750–52; and Resolutions of the Convention of Bristol County, September 29, 1774, in William Lincoln, ed., *The Journals of Each Provincial Congress of Massachusetts* (Boston: Dutton and Wentworth, 1838), 626–27.

12. Suffolk County (Massachusetts) Resolutions, September 6, 1774, Force, 1:778; Cumberland County (Massachusetts) Resolves, Force, 1:798–99; and Resolutions of the Convention of Essex County, September 7, 1774, Lincoln, *Journals*, 616.

13. Proceedings of the Massachusetts Provincial Congress, October 26, 1774, Force, 1:843. In the spring of 1776, after a year of warfare, this theme of state violence would loom larger in the local resolutions urging Congress to declare in-

dependence. See Pauline Maier, *American Scripture: Making the Declaration of Independence* (New York: Vintage, 1998), 79–82.

14. Suffolk County (Massachusetts) Resolutions, September 6, 1774, Force, 1:776–79; Middlesex County (Massachusetts) Resolutions, August 31, 1774, Force, 1:750–52; Worcester County (Massachusetts) Resolutions, Force, 1:795–98; Cumberland County (Massachusetts) Resolves, Force, 1:798–99; Resolutions of the Convention of Essex County, September 7, 1774, Lincoln, *Journals*, 615–18; Resolutions of the Convention of Hampshire County, September 23, 1774, Lincoln, *Journals*, 618–21; Resolutions of the Convention of Plymouth County, September 27, 1774, Lincoln, *Journals*, 621–25; and Resolutions of the Convention of Bristol County, September 29, 1774, Lincoln, *Journals*, 626–27.

15. Boston, September 5, 1774, Force, 1:762–64; and Douglass Adair and John A. Shutz, eds., *Peter Oliver's Origin & Progress of the American Revolution: A Tory View* (San Marino, CA: Huntington Library, 1963), 153.

16. Boston, September 1, 1774, Force, 1:747–49.

17. Cumberland County (Massachusetts) Resolves, Force, 1:798–99; and "At a Meeting of the Delegates of the Towns in the Counties of New London and Windham," September 8, 1774, *Early American Imprints*, ser. 1, no. 42660.

18. Proceedings of the New Jersey Provincial Congress, June 3, 1775, Force, 2:691; and Fairfax County (Virginia) Association, January 17, 1775, Force, 1:1145. See also Bucks County (Pennsylvania) Committee, May 8, 1775, Force, 2:542; Meeting of the Inhabitants of Westmoreland, Pennsylvania, Force, 2:615–16. Mason's articles of association are misdated in Force. The correct date is February 6, 1775. See Robert Rutland, ed., *The Papers of George Mason, 1725–1792*, 3 vols. (Chapel Hill: University of North Carolina Press, 1970), 1:212–17.

19. Proceedings of the Continental Congress, October 14, 1774, Force, 1:910–11.

20. For the best recent analysis of the Declaration, especially the section on colonial grievances, see Maier, *American Scripture*, chap. 3.

21. "An Act for Regulating of the Militia," 1693, Massachusetts Session Laws, *Records of the States of the United States of America* (Washington, DC, 1949). For a comparative study of militia obligations, see Robert H. Churchill, "Gun Regulation, the Police Power, and the Right to Keep Arms in Early America: The Legal Context of the Second Amendment," *Law and History Review* 25 (Spring 2007): 139–75.

22. Benjamin Hoadley, *The Works of Benjamin Hoadley* (London: W. Bower and J. Nichols, 1773), 2:36–53; Francis Hutcheson, *A System of Moral Philosophy* (New York: Augustus M. Kelley, 1968), 1:266–82 and 342–47; Algernon Sydney,

Discourses Concerning Government, ed. Thomas G. West (Indianapolis: Liberty Classics, 1990), 217–29 and 519–24; John Trenchard and Thomas Gordon, *Cato's Letters,* ed. Ronald Hamowy (Indianapolis: Liberty Classics, 1995), nos. 55 and 59, 1:367–76 and 405–13; and John Locke, *Second Treatise of Government,* ed. C. B. McPherson (Indianapolis: Hackett, 1980), 100–124. On this point I disagree with Pauline Maier and David C. Williams. See Maier, *From Resistance to Revolution: Colonial Radicals and the Development of American Opposition to Britain, 1765–1776* (New York: Norton, 1991), 27–42; and Williams, *The Mythic Meanings of the Second Amendment: Taming Political Violence in a Constitutional Republic* (New Haven: Yale University Press, 2003), 21–39.

23. For Massachusetts, see Suffolk County (Massachusetts) Resolutions, September 6, 1774, Force, 1:776–79, Worcester County (Massachusetts) Resolutions, September 21, 1774, Force, 1:795–97; Cumberland County (Massachusetts) Resolves, Force, 1:798–99; Resolutions of the Convention of Hampshire County, September 23, 1774, Lincoln, *Journals,* 621; Resolutions of the Convention of Plymouth County, September 27, 1774, Lincoln, *Journals,* 624; and Resolutions of the Convention of Bristol County, September 29, 1774, Lincoln, *Journals,* 626–27. For military activity in other provinces, see the resolutions of a meeting of delegates of the towns of Windham and New London counties, Connecticut, September 8, 1774, *Early American Imprints,* ser. 1, no. 42660; and Governor Thomas Gage to the Earl of Dartmouth, Boston, September 20, 1774, Force, 1:795. For the actions of the provincial governments to authorize and organize military preparations, see the Proceedings of the Massachusetts Provincial Congress, October 26, 1774, Force, 1:843–45; "Extract of a letter from a gentleman in Connecticut to his friend in Newport, Rhode Island," January 11, 1775, Force, 1:1134–35; and "Extract of a letter to a gentleman in New York," December 14, 1774, Force, 1:1041. Though the Continental Congress had suggested on October 3, 1774 that the militia of the colonies "be put on a proper footing," that body had no authority to order such preparations. The Congress did not even go so far as to "recommend" this measure. See Proceedings of the Continental Congress, October 3, 1774, Force, 1:907.

24. "From a Gentleman in Boston, to Mr. Rivington, in New York," Boston, December 20, 1774, Force, 1:1053–55; Andrew McCleary to the New Hampshire Provincial Congress, April 23, 1775, Force, 1:1775. The Provincial Congress authorized the raising of an army of two thousand on May 20, but its control over the militia was still not formalized until June. See the Proceedings of the New Hampshire Provincial Congress, May 20, 1775, Force, 2:652; and General Fulsome to the New Hampshire Committee of Safety, June 23, 1775, Force, 2:1070.

25. This generalization does not apply to Connecticut, where Whig governor Jonathan Trumbull maintained his government and his authority over the militia throughout the crisis.

26. Proceedings of the Maryland Convention, December 8–12, 1774, Force, 1:1031–33; and Proceedings of the South Carolina Provincial Congress, January 17, 1775, Force, 1:1118.

27. "Fairfax County Militia Association," September 21, 1774, Mason, *Papers*, 1:210–21; James Madison to William Bradford, November 26, 1774, in William T. Hutchinson and William M. E. Rachal, eds., *Papers of James Madison*, 17 vols. (Chicago: University of Chicago Press, 1962–91), 1:129; "Extract of a letter from the Earl of Dunmore to the Earl of Dartmouth," Williamsburg, December 24, 1774, Force, 1:1061–63; and Proceedings of the Virginia Convention, March 23, 1775, Force, 2:167–68.

28. Proceedings of the New Jersey Provincial Congress, June 3, 1775, Force, 2:691–94; Meeting of the Inhabitants of Morris County, New Jersey, May 2, 1775, Force, 2:457; Town Meeting, Upper Freehold (Monmouth County), New Jersey, May 4, 1775, Force, 2:504–5.

29. The tumult in New York is described in the Proceedings of the Council of New York, May 1, 1775, Force, 2:459–60; and a "Letter from a Gentleman now at New York to the Committee of Correspondence in Portsmouth, New Hampshire," April 30, 1775, Force, 2:448–49. See also the Proceedings of the New York Committee, May 15, 1775, Force, 2:604–5.

30. Association of New York, April 29, 1775, Force, 2:471; Proceedings of the New York Provincial Congress, May 29, 1775, Force, 2:1260–61; and Proceedings of the New York Provincial Congress, May 30, 1775, in Berthold Fernow, ed., *Documents Relating to the Colonial History of the State of New York*, 15 vols. (Albany: Weed Parsons, 1887), 15:5. The returned lists of associators and nonassociators are printed in Force, 3:581–616. Some versions of the articles of association lacked any reference to taking up arms. For articles that make such reference, see the returns from Islip and Easthampton, Suffolk County, Force, 3:612–13; the return from New Paltz, May 24, 1775, Force, 3:583; the return from Newburgh, July 14, 1775, Force, 3:596; the return from Rhinebeck, Dutchess County, July 5, 1775, Force, 3:608; and the return from Brookhaven, Suffolk County, July 1, 1775, Force, 3:615–16. See also the Proceedings of the New York Provincial Congress, August 22, 1775, Force, 3:542–46; and the Resolutions of the Newburgh (New York) Committee, May 15, 1775, Force, 2:606–7.

31. New Castle County (Delaware) Committee, December 21, 1774, Force, 1:1022; and York County (Pennsylvania) Committee, February 14, 1775, Force, 1:1235.

32. "Philadelphia, April 26, 1775," Force, 2:399–400. On Berks County, see the "Extract from a letter from Reading," *New York Journal*, May 11, 1775. On Bucks County, see Bucks County (Pennsylvania) Committee, May 8, 1775, Force, 2:542. On Chester, see Chester County (Pennsylvania) Committee, May 15, 1775, Force, 2:588–89. On Northampton, see the Resolutions of the Committee of Correspondence, May 22, *Pennsylvania Evening Post*, June 10, 1775. On Lancaster, see Richard Alan Ryerson, *The Revolution Is Now Begun: The Radical Committees of Philadelphia, 1765–1776* (Philadelphia: University of Pennsylvania Press, 1978), 118. On Bedford, see To the Philadelphia Committee, May 9, 1775, Force, 2:542. On Cumberland, see "Extract from a letter from Carlisle," May 6, 1775, Force, 2:516. On Westmoreland, see Meeting of the Inhabitants of Westmoreland, Pennsylvania, Force, 2:615–16. On Kent, see Kent County Upon Delaware, May 25, 1775, Force, 2:704. Pennsylvania was the only colony that had never established a statutory militia because of the pacifist objections of the Quaker proprietors of the colony.

33. On the Assembly's authorization of the militia, see Ryerson, *Revolution Is Now Begun*, 121–22. For the militia's role in overthrowing the colonial government of Pennsylvania, see Ryerson, 207–46; "Philadelphia, June 10, 1776," Force, 6:784–87; and the Protest of the Philadelphia Committee of Privates, Force, 6:935–36.

34. Michael Lienesch, "Reinterpreting Rebellion: The Influence of Shays's Rebellion on American Political Thought," in Robert A. Gross, ed., *In Debt to Shays: The Bicentennial of an Agrarian Rebellion* (Charlottesville: University Press of Virginia, 1993), 169–70.

35. For a discussion of the framing of the militia clauses, see Jack Rakove, "The Second Amendment: The Highest Stage of Originalism," *Chicago-Kent Law Review* 76 (2000): 126–32.

36. Centinel, no. 1, October 5, 1787, in Bernard Bailyn, ed., *The Debate on the Constitution: Federalist and Antifederalist Speeches, Articles, and Letters during the Struggle over Ratification*, 2 vols. (New York: Library of America, 1993), 1:57; "A Democratic Federalist," October 17, 1787, in Bailyn, 1:70–71; and Brutus, nos. 8 and 9, in Merrill Jensen, ed., *Documentary History of the Ratification of the Constitution*, 18 vols. to date (Madison: State Historical Society of Wisconsin, 1976–), 15:335–38 and 393–98 (hereafter, *DHRC*).

37. Federal Farmer, no. 3, October 10, 1787, in Bailyn, *Debate on the Constitution*, 1:269–70.

38. *Dissent of the Minority of the Pennsylvania Convention*, Bailyn, *Debate on the Constitution*, 1:536.

39. Ibid., 533.

40. My discussion of the different strains of Anti-Federalism follows the typology outlined by Saul Cornell in *The Other Founders: Anti-Federalism and the Dissenting Tradition in America, 1788–1828* (Chapel Hill: University of North Carolina Press, 1999); and Cornell, "Commonplace or Anachronism: The Standard Model, the Second Amendment, and the Problem of History in Contemporary Constitutional Theory," *Constitutional Commentary* 16 (1999): 221–45.

41. Cornell, "Commonplace or Anachronism," 231–37.

42. Federal Farmer no. 18, in Herbert J. Storing, ed., *The Complete Anti-Federalist*, 7 vols. (Chicago: University of Chicago Press, 1981), 2:341–42.

43. Speech of George Mason before the Virginia Ratifying Convention, June 13, 1788, in Jonathan Elliot, ed., *The Debates in the Several State Conventions on the Adoption of the Federal Constitution*, 5 vols. (Salem, NH: Ayer Company reprint edition, 1987), 3:378–81.

44. Luther Martin, *Genuine Information*, no. 7 (January 18, 1788) and no. 10 (February 1, 1788), *DHRC*, 15:410–14 and 16:8–11.

45. On the importance of these Anti-Federalist texts and their reception, see Cornell, *Other Founders*, 25 and the editor's headnote to Martin, *Genuine Information*, no. 1, *DHRC*, 15:146–50.

46. "Impartial," *Independent Gazetteer*, October 16, 1787.

47. Noah Webster, "A Citizen of America," October 17, 1787, Bailyn, *Debate on the Constitution*, 1:155.

48. The "Letter from New York" purported to be a response to an Anti-Federalist "Letter from Massachusetts," which was itself probably a Federalist airing of Anti-Federalist arguments circulating privately, possibly including those that would be published several weeks later by the Federal Farmer. See "Letter from Massachusetts" and "Letter from New York," *Connecticut Journal*, October 17, 24, and 31, 1787, *DHRC*, 3:389–90.

49. For another Federalist essay from October 1787 that describes the universal militia as placing a "powerful check" on "schemes of conquest or oppression," see Tench Coxe, "An American Citizen No. 4," *DHRC*, 13:435–36. On Madison's role in disseminating the essay, see Madison's letter to Coxe, October 26, 1787, *DHRC*, 13:437.

50. Alexander Hamilton, *Federalist No. 28*, in Isaac Kramnick, ed., *The Federalist Papers* (New York: Penguin, 1987), 204–7.

51. Hamilton, *Federalist No. 29*, 208–12.

52. James Madison, *Federalist No. 46*, 301.

53. Ibid., 297–302.

54. "The Republican: To the People," January 7, 1788, *DHRC*, 3:529–31; and Tench Coxe, *A Pennsylvanian*, no. 3, *Pennsylvania Gazette*, February 20, 1788 (spelling and italics in original). See also Alexander White, "To the Citizens of Virginia," February 22 and 29, 1788, *DHRC*, 8:404 and 438–44.

55. "Proposed Amendments Agreed Upon by the Anti-Federal Committee of Richmond and Dispatched to New York," Mason, *Papers*, 3:1070–71.

56. For scholarship interpreting the amendment as a statement of concurrent powers, see Carl T. Bogus, "The Hidden History of the Second Amendment," *University of California at Davis Law Review* 31 (1997): 309–408; and Don Higginbotham, "The Federalized Militia Debate: A Neglected Aspect of Second Amendment Scholarship," *William and Mary Quarterly*, 3rd ser., 55 (1998): 39–58. On an individual right, see Joyce Lee Malcolm, *To Keep and Bear Arms: The Origins of an Anglo-American Right* (Cambridge: Harvard University Press, 1994); Robert J. Cottrol, *Gun Control and the Constitution: Sources and Explorations on the Second Amendment* (New York: Garland, 1994); Stephen Halbrook, *That Every Man Be Armed* (Albuquerque: University of New Mexico Press, 1984); Don B. Kates, "Handgun Prohibition and the Original Meaning of the Second Amendment," *Michigan Law Review* 82 (1983): 204–73; and the special Second Amendment issue of the *Tennessee Law Review* 62 (Spring 1995). On the preservation of a universal militia, see Williams, *Mythic Meanings*. For the assertion that the amendment was drafted as a statement of principle without enforceable meaning, see Garry Wills, "To Keep and Bear Arms," *New York Review of Books* 42 (1995): 62–73; and Rakove, "Second Amendment." Most recently, Saul Cornell has argued that the amendment protected the right to keep and bear arms of those individuals that the federal government designated as having the obligation to enroll and serve in the militia. Cornell's interpretation thus ill fits the positions outlined in the text, but takes something from first, second, and fourth. See Saul Cornell, *A Well Regulated Militia: The Founding Fathers and the Origins of Gun Control in America* (New York: Oxford University Press, 2006).

57. Speech of George Mason before the Virginia Ratifying Convention, June 13, 1788, in Elliot, *Debates*, 3:378–81.

58. Speeches of James Madison and Patrick Henry, June 13, 1788, Elliot, *Debates*, 3:381–84 and 384–88; and Speech of George Mason, June 14, 1788, Elliot, *Debates*, 3:425–26.

59. Neil H. Cogan, *The Complete Bill of Rights: The Drafts, Debates, Sources, and Origins* (New York: Oxford University Press, 1997), 181–83.

60. "Proposed Amendments Offered to the Ratifying Convention by Patrick Henry," Mason, *Papers*, 3:1117.

61. *Dissent of the Minority of the Pennsylvania Convention,* Bailyn, *Debate on the Constitution,* 1:533; Jeremy Belknap to Ebenezer Hazard, February 10, 1788, *Collections of the Massachusetts Historical Society,* 3:17–18; and Amendments Proposed by the New Hampshire Convention, Elliot, *Debates,* 1:325–27.

62. "Amendments to the Constitution, June 8, 1789," in *Papers of James Madison,* 12:196–210.

63. A Pennsylvanian (Tench Coxe), "Remarks on the First Part of the Amendments to the Federal Constitution," *Philadelphia Federal Gazette,* June 18, 1789.

64. For evidence that contemporaries did read an individual right to keep arms into the amendment, see Churchill, "Gun Regulation," 168–75.

65. This suggestion is made by Rakove in "Second Amendment," 121.

66. Linda Grant De Pauw, ed., *Documentary History of the First Federal Congress of the United States of America,* 14 vols. (Baltimore: Johns Hopkins University Press, 1972–97), 4:8.

67. De Pauw, *Documentary History,* 4:44.

68. Speeches of Thomas Fitzsimons and James Jackson, December 16, 1790, in De Pauw, *Documentary History,* 14:73–74.

69. Speech of Roger Sherman, December 17, 1790, De Pauw, *Documentary History,* 14:92–93.

70. "An Act more effectually to provide for the National Defense, by establishing an Uniform Militia throughout the United States," 1792, in *Laws of the United States of America,* 3 vols. (Philadelphia: Richard Folwell, 1796), 2:92–98.

71. See Rakove, "Second Amendment," 159.

72. Here I concur with David C. Williams. See Williams, *Mythic Meanings,* 1–14.

The Revolution as Living Memory

1. Deposition of David Penrose, MSC-536, William Rawle Family Papers, vol. 2, "Insurrections in Northampton County, Pennsylvania, 1798–1800," Historical Society of Pennsylvania, Philadelphia (hereafter Rawle Papers), 39; and testimony of Cephas Childs, in Thomas Carpenter, *The Two Trials of John Fries* (Philadelphia: William Woodward, 1800), 76–77.

2. On 1798, see Lance Banning, *The Jeffersonian Persuasion: Evolution of a Party Ideology* (Ithaca: Cornell University Press, 1978); Richard Buel Jr., *Securing the Revolution: Ideology in American Politics, 1789–1815* (Ithaca: Cornell University Press, 1972); Stanley Elkins and Eric McKitrick, *The Age of Federalism* (New York: Oxford University Press, 1993); Dumas Malone, *Jefferson and the Ordeal of Liberty* (Boston: Little, Brown, 1962); James Morton Smith, "The Grass Roots

Origins of the Kentucky Resolutions," *William and Mary Quarterly* 27 (1970), 221–45; Richard R. Beeman, *The Old Dominion and the New Nation, 1788–1801* (Lexington: University Press of Kentucky, 1972); Adrienne Koch and Henry Ammon, "The Virginia and Kentucky Resolutions: An Episode in Jefferson's and Madison's Defense of Civil Liberties," *William and Mary Quarterly* 5 (1948): 145–76; and James Rodgers Sharp, *American Politics in the Early Republic: The New Nation in Crisis* (New Haven: Yale University Press, 1993).

3. See for example William Watts Hart Davis, *The Fries Rebellion, 1798–99* (New York: Arno Press, 1969); Jane Shaffer Elsmere, "The Trials of John Fries," *Pennsylvania Magazine of History and Biography* 103 (1979): 432–45; Dwight F. Henderson, "Treason, Sedition, and Fries' Rebellion," *American Journal of Legal History* 14 (1970): 308–18; Peter Levine, "Fries Rebellion: Social Violence and the Politics of the New Nation," *Pennsylvania History* 40 (1973): 240–58; and Russel B. Nye, *A Baker's Dozen: Thirteen Unusual Americans* (East Lansing: Michigan State University Press, 1956). Accounts that focus on the particular ethnic variables involved in the rebellion include Kenneth Keller, "Rural Politics and the Collapse of Pennsylvania Federalism," *Transactions of the American Philosophical Society* 72, no. 6 (1982); Paul D. Newman, "The Fries Rebellion of 1799: Pennsylvania Germans, the Federalist Party, and American Political Culture," Ph.D. diss., University of Kentucky, 1996; and A. G. Roeber, "Citizens or Subjects? German Lutherans and the Federal Constitution in Pennsylvania, 1789–1800," *Amerikastudien/American Studies* 34 (1989): 49–68.

4. Elkins and McKitrick, *The Age of Federalism*, 571–75.

5. For an assessment of the balance of power in the Atlantic World, see Simon P. Newman, "The World Turned Upside Down: Revolutionary Politics, Fries' and Gabriel's Rebellions, and the Fears of the Federalists," *Pennsylvania History* 67 (2000): 15.

6. Sharp, *American Politics*, 167 and 180–81.

7. Virginia, General Assembly, House of Delegates, *The Virginia Report of 1799–1800* (New York: Da Capo Press, 1970), 18–21.

8. See Joanne B. Freeman, *Affairs of Honor: National Politics in the New Republic* (New Haven: Yale University Press, 2001); and Freeman, "Explaining the Unexplainable: The Cultural Context of the Sedition Act," in Meg Jacobs, William J. Novak, and Julian E. Zelizer, eds., *The Democratic Experiment: New Directions in American Political History* (Princeton: Princeton University Press, 2003), 20–49.

9. The Officers of the Militia of Sussex County, Delaware to John Adams, and Adams's Reply, *Porcupine's Gazette*, June 25, 1798. Such exchanges between the

president and groups of admiring Federalists were a staple of Federalist political discourse during the Alien and Sedition Act crisis. See also "To the Patriotic Ladies of Lancaster, Pennsylvania, by Capt. Thomas Boude of the Lancaster Troop of Horse," *Porcupine's Gazette*, July 10, 1798.

10. "Americanus" to P. Johnson of Prince Edward County of Virginia, *Porcupine's Gazette*, December 13, 1798; and "Congress," *Porcupine's Gazette*, December 4, 1798.

11. Charge to the Grand Jury delivered by Justice Iredell, April 11, 1799, in Carpenter, *Two Trials*, 1 and 4; and the Address of the Freeholders of Prince Edward County and Timothy Pickering's reply of September 29, 1798, *Philadelphia Aurora and General Advertiser* (hereafter *Aurora*), November 6, 1798. See also Debate on the Franklin County Petition, *Chambersburg Farmers' Register*, March 6, 1799.

12. *Porcupine's Gazette*, September 13, 1798; *Aurora*, May 9 and August 3, 1798; and *Vermont Gazette*, September 8, 1798. On the ideological conflict between Republican Friends of Liberty and Federalist Friends of Order, see Thomas P. Slaughter, *The Whiskey Rebellion: Frontier Epilogue to the American Revolution* (New York: Oxford University Press, 1986).

13. Buel, *Securing the Revolution*, 180. Cobbett is quoted in James Morton Smith, *Freedom's Fetters: The Alien and Sedition Laws and American Civil Liberties* (Ithaca: Cornell University Press, 1956), 101. On the diffusion of the Illuminati conspiracy theory, see Buel, 166–83. For other examples, see Address of the Pennsylvania House of Representatives to President John Adams, *Porcupine's Gazette*, December 21, 1798; Harrison Gray Otis, Speech on the Alien Bill, *Porcupine's Gazette*, July 14, 1798; and Robert Goodloe Harper's speech on the Alien Bill, quoted in Smith, *Freedom's Fetters*, 106. For an analysis that compares Federalist countersubversive ideology to Cold War preoccupations with national security, see Newman, "Fries Rebellion of 1799," chap. 4.

14. Knox's letter to Adams, quoted in Elkins and McKitrick, *The Age of Federalism*, 645–46; Speech of George K. Taylor, December 14, 1798, Virginia House of Delegates, *Virginia Report of 1799–1800*, 37; and the Speech of General Henry Lee, December 20, 1798, *Virginia Report of 1799–1800*, 105.

15. "The Catastrophe, #9," *Aurora*, May 17, 1798.

16. On arguments against internal taxation in the Revolutionary and early national periods, see Bernard Bailyn, *The Ideological Origins of the American Revolution* (Cambridge: Harvard University Press, 1967); Banning, *The Jeffersonian Persuasion*; and Slaughter, *The Whiskey Rebellion*.

17. *New London Bee*, July 18, 1798; and "Queries from an Essex Dutchman,"

reprinted from the *Newark Sentinel of Freedom* in *Aurora*, November 9, 1798. See also *Aurora*, February 9, 1798.

18. Resolutions of the Freeholders of Dinwiddie County, Virginia, *Aurora*, December 6, 1798; and "From the *Vermont Gazette*," *Aurora*, July 31, 1798. For similar statements see also *Boston Independent Chronicle*, January 17, 1799; and Resolutions of the Citizens of Louisa County, Virginia, *Boston Independent Chronicle*, November 5, 1798. For discussions of the army as a source of patronage power, see Address of the General Assembly to the People of the Commonwealth of Virginia, *Boston Independent Chronicle*, February 7, 1799; and *New London Bee*, April 24, 1799.

19. Speech of Edward Livingston's to the House of Representatives, delivered July 2, 1798, as quoted in the *Washington (PA) Herald of Liberty*, August 6, 1998.

20. Resolutions of the Citizens of Mifflin County, Pennsylvania Living North of Tussey's Mountain, *Aurora*, January 23, 1799; "The Catastrophe #9," *Aurora*, May 17, 1798; and Petition and Remonstrance of the Citizens and Inhabitants of Washington County, Pennsylvania, *Aurora*, December 11, 1798. See also Resolutions of the Freeholders of Dinwiddie County, Virginia, *Aurora*, December 6, 1798; and Memorial of the Freeholders and Other Inhabitants of Caroline County, Virginia, *Aurora*, November 27, 1798.

21. Resolutions of the Citizens of the Second Battalion District of Amelia County, Virginia, *Newark Sentinel of Freedom*, October 2, 1798; Resolutions of the Citizens of Orange County, New York, *Boston Independent Chronicle*, December 10, 1798; "A Well Armed Militia," reprinted from the *Chronicle* in the *Aurora*, May 11, 1799; and Address of the People of Orange County, Virginia, *Virginia Argus*, December 1, 1798. See also Resolutions of the Citizens of Goochland County, Virginia, *Aurora*, September 3, 1798; and "Mr. Cooper's Address," reprinted in *Aurora*, July 12, 1799.

22. "Address of the General Assembly to the People of the Commonwealth of Virginia," *Boston Independent Chronicle*, February 7, 1799.

23. *Newark Sentinel of Freedom*, December 18, 1798; and "Mr. Cooper's Address," *Aurora*, July 12, 1799. Major statements reflecting moderate constitutional opposition include the Resolutions of the Citizens of Clark County, Kentucky, *Aurora*, September 2, 1798; Resolutions of the Inhabitants of Woodford County, Kentucky, *Boston Independent Chronicle*, October 4, 1798; Resolutions of the Citizens of Mason and the adjoining Counties, Kentucky, *Boston Independent Chronicle*, October 22, 1798; Resolutions of a Town Meeting of Dracutt, Massachusetts, *Boston Independent Chronicle*, March 14, 1799; Resolutions of the Inhabitants of Woodbridge Township, New Jersey, *New York Journal and Patriotic*

Register, February 16, 1799; Address and Remonstrance of the Inhabitants of Essex County, New Jersey, *Newark Sentinel of Freedom,* January 29, 1799; Memorial of the Inhabitants of Queens County, New York, *Porcupine's Gazette,* February 9, 1799; Address and Petition of the Inhabitants of Fayette County, Pennsylvania, *Washington (PA) Herald of Liberty,* February 25, 1799; Petition and Remonstrance of the Inhabitants of Franklin County, Pennsylvania, *Chambersburg Farmers' Register,* January 9, 1799; Petition of the Inhabitants of Lancaster County, Pennsylvania, *Aurora,* March 6, 1799; Petition of the Inhabitants of Northampton County, Pennsylvania, *Aurora,* February 12, 1799; Petition and Remonstrance of the Citizens and Inhabitants of Washington County, Pennsylvania, *Aurora,* December 11, 1798; Petition of the Inhabitants of York County, Pennsylvania, *Aurora,* January 22, 1799; Remonstrance of the Citizens of Albemarle County, Virginia, *Washington (PA) Herald of Liberty,* November 19, 1799; Resolutions of the Citizens of the Second Battalion District of Amelia County, Virginia, *Newark Sentinel of Freedom,* October 2, 1799; Resolutions of the Freeholders of Dinwiddie County, Virginia, *Aurora,* December 6, 1798; Resolutions of the Citizens of Goochland County, Virginia, *Aurora,* September 3, 1799; Resolutions of the Citizens of Louisa County, Virginia, *Boston Independent Chronicle,* November 5, 1799; Address of the People of Orange County, Virginia, *Virginia Argus,* October 12, 1798; and Address of the Freeholders of Prince Edward County, Virginia, *Aurora,* November 6, 1798.

24. "A letter from a Gentleman in Virginia to his Friend in Kentucky," *Aurora,* November 3, 1798. See also "A Real Democrat," *Washington (PA) Herald of Liberty,* August 20, 1798.

25. *Washington (PA) Herald of Liberty,* November 19, 1798; and *Chambersburg Farmers' Register,* January 23, 1799.

26. Alexander Hamilton, *Federalist No. 78,* in Isaac Kramnick, ed., *The Federalist Papers* (New York: Penguin, 1987), 438. For a discussion of nullification as a theme of popular constitutionalism, see Larry D. Kramer, *The People Themselves: Popular Constitutionalism and Judicial Review* (New York: Oxford University Press, 2004).

27. Memorial of the People of Essex County, Virginia, *Aurora,* December 7, 1798; editorial from the *Albany Register* reprinted in the Boston *Independent Chronicle,* February 25, 1798; and Address of the Citizens of Richmond, Virginia to John Clopton, Esq., *Aurora,* August 20, 1798. See also Resolutions of the Citizens of Buckingham County, Virginia, *Virginia Argus,* November 10, 1798.

28. Resolutions of the Citizens of Orange County, New York, *Boston Independent Chronicle,* December 10, 1798; and the Speech of Edward Livingston to the

House of Representatives, July 2, 1798, as quoted in the *Washington (PA) Herald of Liberty*, August 16, 1798.

29. Statements of radical Republican opposition include the Resolutions of the Citizens of Bourbon County, Kentucky, *Boston Independent Chronicle*, October 25, 1798 (according to the *Kentucky Gazette*, September 5, 1798, these resolutions were adopted verbatim by the inhabitants of Franklin and Mercer counties, Kentucky); Resolutions of the Citizens of Fayette and the Adjacent Counties, Kentucky, *Boston Independent Chronicle*, October 4, 1798; Resolutions of the Seventh Regiment and Citizens of Madison County, Kentucky, *Aurora*, January 4, 1799; Resolutions of the Citizens of Orange County, New York, *Boston Independent Chronicle*, December 10, 1798; Resolutions of the Citizens of Mifflin County, Pennsylvania Living North of Tussey's Mountain, *Aurora*, January 23, 1798; Resolutions of a Company of the Militia of Amelia County, Virginia, *Alexandria Times*, September 12, 1798; Resolutions of the Citizens of Buckingham County, Virginia, *Virginia Argus*, November 10, 1798; Memorial of the Freeholders and other Inhabitants of Caroline County, Virginia, *Aurora*, November 27, 1798; Memorial of the People of Essex County, Virginia, *Aurora*, December 7, 1798; Resolutions of the People of Hanover County, Virginia, *Boston Independent Chronicle*, November 12, 1798; Resolutions of the Inhabitants of Powhatten County, Virginia, *Boston Independent Chronicle*, October 29, 1798; Resolutions of the Inhabitants of Spotsylvania County, Virginia, *Aurora*, November 20, 1798; and the Address of the Citizens of Richmond, Virginia to John Clopton, Esq., *Aurora*, August 20, 1798.

30. Address of the Citizens of Richmond, Virginia to John Clopton, Esq., *Aurora*, August 20, 1798. Clopton seemed caught off guard by this sentiment and avowed that he had "full confidence that the requisite energy and vigilance of the people of this Country over their rights will not be exerted in any other manner than that prescribed by the constitution." See also "From the *Albany Register*," *Aurora*, November 27, 1798.

31. Resolutions of the Inhabitants of Powhatten County, Virginia, *Boston Independent Chronicle*, October 29, 1798.

32. Resolutions of the Citizens of Fayette and the Adjacent Counties, Kentucky, Boston *Independent Chronicle*, October 4, 1798.

33. The first section of the Sedition Act had made it a crime to "unlawfully combine or conspire together with intent to impede or oppose any measure or measures of the government of the United States." It was not clear in the summer of 1798 whether the Fayette County resolutions might constitute such an "unlawful combination."

34. Memorial of the People of Essex County, Virginia, *Aurora*, December 7, 1798; and Resolutions of the Citizens of Bourbon County, Kentucky, *Boston Independent Chronicle*, October 25, 1798. See also Resolutions of the People of Hanover County, Virginia, *Boston Independent Chronicle*, November 12, 1798.

35. Resolutions of the Citizens of Bourbon County, Kentucky, *Boston Independent Chronicle*, October 25, 1798. The Hanover and Essex resolutions also contained language disclaiming any intent to overthrow the Constitution.

36. *Aurora*, July 6, 1798.

37. Resolutions of a Company of the Militia of Amelia County, Virginia, *Alexandria Times*, September 12, 1798; and Resolutions of the Seventh Regiment and Citizens of Madison County, *Aurora*, January 4, 1799.

38. Resolutions of the Citizens of Bourbon County, Kentucky, *Boston Independent Chronicle*, October 25, 1798; and Resolutions of the Citizens of Fayette and the Adjacent Counties, Kentucky, *Boston Independent Chronicle*, October 4, 1798. In November 1798, a letter published in the *Kentucky Gazette* cited the Second Amendment of the Constitution in support of this resolution. See "To the Freemen of Kentucky," *Kentucky Gazette*, September 19, 1798.

39. *Aurora*, July 6, 1798; and *Washington (PA) Herald of Liberty*, August 13, 1798. On the role of Independence Day festivity in national political culture in the 1790s, see Simon P. Newman, *Parades and the Politics of the Street: Festive Culture in the Early American Republic* (Philadelphia: University of Pennsylvania Press, 1997), chap. 3.

40. *Washington (PA) Herald of Liberty*, August 13, 1798.

41. *New York Journal and Patriotic Register*, August 25, 1798; and *Aurora*, July 30, 1798. See also *Boston Independent Chronicle*, August 6, 1798; and *New York Journal and Patriotic Register*, June 16, 1798.

42. *New York Journal and Patriotic Register*, August 1, 1798; and *Newark Sentinel of Freedom*, March 12, 1799. For similar ritual celebrations, see *Newark Sentinel of Freedom*, July 17, 1798, November 13, 1799, and June 19, 1800; *New York Journal and Patriotic Register*, July 18 and August 1, 1798; *New London Bee*, September 5, 1798; and *Aurora*, May 13 and July 6, 1799.

43. *Newark Sentinel of Freedom*, July 17, 1798.

44. The Virginia Resolutions of 1798, Virginia House of Delegates, *Virginia Report of 1799–1800*, 22; and *The Report of 1800*, in *Virginia Report of 1799–1800*, 231–32.

45. Jefferson's fair copy of the Kentucky Resolutions of 1798, *Papers of James Madison*, 17:179.

46. Ibid., 17:177 and 181.

47. Smith, "Grass Roots Origins," 328–40.

48. This narrative is based on the testimony contained in Carpenter, *Two Trials*, which published a transcript of the trials of the insurgents, and in the depositions used by federal prosecutors to bring the insurgents to trial, collected in the Rawle Papers. See also Davis, *Fries Rebellion*; and Paul D. Newman, *Fries's Rebellion: The Enduring Struggle for the American Revolution* (Philadelphia: University of Pennsylvania Press, 2004).

49. On the tension between Pennsylvania Whigs and the state's large pacifist community, see Douglas M. Arnold, *A Republican Revolution: Ideology and Politics in Pennsylvania, 1776–1790* (New York: Garland, 1989).

50. On Republican success in garnering support among the Kirchenlute, see Harry Marlin Tinkcom, *The Republicans and Federalists in Pennsylvania, 1790–1801: A Study in National Stimulus and Local Response* (Harrisburg: Pennsylvania Historical and Museum Commission, 1950).

51. This discussion is based on more detailed descriptions of ethnocultural conflict in the affected counties found in the work of Paul D. Newman and Kenneth Keller. See especially Newman, "Fries Rebellion of 1799"; and Keller, "Rural Politics."

52. Deposition of Philip Schlough, Rawle Papers, 79, and Deposition of Duvalt Albrecht, Rawle Papers, 64. See also the Deposition of Andrew Sleichter, Rawle Papers, 41; and Deposition of John Wetzell Jr., Rawle Papers, 8.

53. "Letter to a Legislator in Montgomery County from a Gentleman in Reading," *Aurora*, July 27, 1798; and the Deposition of Philip Kremer, Rawle Papers, 13. See also Indictment of Henry Engle, Henry Barnet, and Nicholas Fox, Northampton County, Court of Oyer and Terminer, October, 1790, MSC 2049, Tench Coxe Papers, Historical Society of Pennsylvania, Philadelphia. I am indebted to Owen S. Ireland for pointing out the long-standing complaints about tax collection in Pennsylvania. For an analysis of Fries' Rebellion that emphasizes the economic burden of the direct tax, see Terry Bouton, "'No Wonder the Times Were Troublesome': The Origins of Fries' Rebellion," *Pennsylvania History* 67 (2000): 21–42.

54. Deposition of John Butz, Rawle Papers, 9; Deposition of John Fogel Jr., Rawle Papers, 10; and Deposition of Samuel Mifler, Rawle Papers, 6. On Anti-Federalist objections to vesting the power of internal taxation in the federal government, see Thomas P. Slaughter, "The Tax Man Cometh: Ideological Opposition to Internal Taxes, 1760–1790," *William and Mary Quarterly*, 3rd ser., 41 (1984), 566–91. In 1798 the Pennsylvania German community renewed these complaints: petitions from York and Lancaster counties requested that Congress

repeal the house tax and allow the states to raise the funds necessary as they saw fit. See Petition of the Inhabitants of York County, Pennsylvania, *Aurora*, January 22, 1799; and Petition of the Inhabitants of Lancaster County, Pennsylvania, *Aurora*, March 6, 1799.

55. Deposition of David Penrose, Rawle Papers, 3. See also Deposition of James Williamson, Assessor for Plainfield, Rawle Papers, 78; Deposition of Philip Arndt, Rawle Papers, 1; Trial Testimony of Marshal William Nichols, Carpenter, *Two Trials*, 38; and Deposition of Frederick Seiberling, Rawle Papers, 6.

56. Deposition of Henry Hunsicher, Rawle Papers, 72; Deposition of Henry Ohl, Rawle Papers, 91; Deposition of Jacob Arndt Jr., Rawle Papers, 75, and *Gazette of the United States*, March 28, 1799. See also Deposition of John Jarrett, Rawle Papers, 62; and Deposition of Peter Ripple, Rawle Papers, 80.

57. For conspiracy theories of a particular ethnic cast, see Deposition of Michael Bobst, Rawle Papers, 58; Deposition of George Miller, Rawle Papers, 4; Deposition of James Williamson, Rawle Papers, 78; Deposition of Jacob Huber, Rawle Papers, 88; and Testimony of Jacob Oswald, Carpenter, *Two Trials*, 186.

58. Deposition of James Williamson, Rawle Papers, 78; and Testimony of Cephas Childs, Carpenter, *Two Trials*, 76–77.

59. See *Readinger Adler*, July 24 and 31, and August 7, 1798. For a brief analysis of the *Adler's* editorial comment, see Newman, "Fries Rebellion of 1799," 162–63.

60. It may be that Fogel and Ohl were merely attempting to displace the blame for their own acts of resistance. It seems unlikely that Republican congressmen would court prosecution under the Sedition Act in this manner, particularly given that McClenachen, in particular, would have been speaking to strangers. See the Deposition of Henry Ohl, Rawle Papers, 91; Deposition of Henry Hunsicher, Rawle Papers, 72; Deposition of John Fogel Jr., Rawle Papers, 69; and Deposition of Jacob Gorr, Rawle Papers, 125.

61. Deposition of John Serfas, Rawle Papers, 11; Testimony of Jacob Oswald, Carpenter, *Two Trials*, 186; Deposition of James Williamson, Rawle Papers, 78; and Testimony of Jacob Eyerly, Carpenter, *Two Trials*, 49–50.

62. Smith, *Freedom's Fetters*, chaps. 11, 12, and 17.

63. It is probably significant that the enforcement of the direct tax was delayed in Kentucky. As a consequence, the insurgents of Northampton County faced the choice of resistance or submission before the radical Republicans of Kentucky. For evidence that the execution of the Direct Tax of 1798 had not yet begun in Kentucky, see *Kentucky Gazette*, March 7, 1799.

64. For constitutional arguments see the Examination of John Fries, Rawle Papers, 43, and the Deposition of John Serfas, Rawle Papers, 11. For substantive

discussions of the law, see the Deposition of John Fogel Jr., Rawle Papers, 69; the Deposition of Christian Heckwelder, Rawle Papers, 68; and the Deposition of John Snyder, Rawle Papers, 125. For statements arguing the legitimacy of resistance in defense of liberty, see the Deposition of John Klein Sr., Rawle Papers, 48; the testimony of Cephas Childs, Carpenter, *Two Trials*, 76–77; and "Extract from a letter from Northampton," *Gazette of the United States*, March 28, 1799. On this point I disagree with Paul D. Newman, who argues that the insurgents' desire to defend the Constitution and the Bill of Rights was an expression of emerging German-American nationalism. See Newman, "Fries Rebellion of 1799," 189.

65. Testimony of Jacob Eyerly, Carpenter, *Two Trials*, 49–50; and Petition of the Inhabitants of Northampton County, Pennsylvania, *Aurora*, February 12, 1799. Most of the insurgents probably signed the petition, but it did not dissuade them in the least from using force to nullify the house tax.

66. Deposition of Daniel Weidner, Rawle Papers, 39; Deposition of Israel Roberts, Rawle Papers, 104; and Deposition of John Moritz, Rawle Papers, 56.

67. Deposition of John Moritz, Rawle Papers, 56; Deposition of James Williamson, Rawle Papers, 78, and his trial testimony in Carpenter, *Two Trials*, 187.

68. Deposition of Peter Zeiner, Rawle Papers, 82; Deposition of George Lintz, Rawle Papers, 7; and Deposition of Christian Heckwelder, Rawle Papers, 68. See also Deposition of John Rodrock, Rawle Papers, 26.

69. On the formation of associations, see the Deposition of Michael Bobst, Rawle Papers, 4; Deposition of Philip Stetler, Rawle Papers, 6; Deposition of Samuel Mifler, Rawle Papers, 6; Deposition of John Heninger, Rawle Papers, 85; Deposition of Henry Strauss, Rawle Papers, 15; Deposition of Duvalt Albrecht, Rawle Papers, 64; and the Deposition of George Mitchell, Rawle Papers, 102. I am indebted to Paul D. Newman for pointing out the distinction between these associations and the various petitions circulating the region. On militia companies, see the Deposition of James Chapman, Rawle Papers, 27; Deposition of John Fogel Jr., Rawle Papers, 10; Deposition of Isaac Hartzell, Rawle Papers, 32; Deposition of Frederick King, Rawle Papers, 89; Deposition of Michael Bobst, Rawle Papers, 58; Deposition of Alexander Benjamin, Rawle Papers, 36; and Deposition of George Ringer, Rawle Papers, 5.

70. Deposition of James Williamson, Rawle Papers, 78; and Examination of Valentine Brobst, Rawle Papers, 84.

71. Deposition of Michael Bobst, Rawle Papers, 58; Testimony of Jacob Eyerly, Carpenter, *Two Trials*, 50; and Testimony of William Nichols, Carpenter, *Two Trials*, 40.

72. Deposition of Jacob Sterner, Rawle Papers, 9.

73. Testimony of William Nichols, Carpenter, *Two Trials*, 38.

74. On this negotiation between Nichols and Fries, see the Deposition of Philip Schlough, Carpenter, *Two Trials*, 79; and the Testimony of William Nichols, Philip Schlough, and Joseph Horsfield, Carpenter, *Two Trials*, 37–44.

75. Depositions of Adam Wetzell, Rawle Papers, 64, and the Testimony of John Jamison and Israel Roberts, Carpenter, *Two Trials*, 111–13. On a planned trip to Virginia to meet with Washington, see the Deposition of Michael Bobst, Rawle Papers, 58; and the Deposition of Jacob Gorr, Rawle Papers, 125.

76. For evidence of continuing resistance after the march on Bethlehem, see the Deposition of Frederick King, Rawle Papers, 89; the Deposition of David Okley, Rawle Papers, 53; the Deposition of Michael Bobst, Rawle Papers, 58; the Deposition of Philip Steller, Rawle Papers, 61; the Memorandum of Christian Heckwelder, Rawle Papers, 37; and the Testimony of Richard Peters, Carpenter, *Two Trials*, 85.

77. *Gazette of the United States*, March 11, 1799.

78. *Gazette of the United States*, April 26, 1799.

79. *Porcupine's Gazette*, March 30, 1798.

80. For an account of these incidents, see the *Aurora*, May 13, 16, and 24, 1799.

81. The depositions taken immediately after the rescue document the very confused situation in Bethlehem on March 7, and indicate that the insurgents arrived in three or four distinct groups. See especially the Deposition of John Mulhallon, Rawle Papers, 28; Deposition of Joseph Horsfield, Rawle Papers, 18; Deposition of Isaac Hartzell, Rawle Papers, 32; and the Deposition of Jacob Eyerly and Stephen Balliett, *American State Papers*, Class 10 (Miscellaneous), Vol. 1, 187. For the description of the insurgents as a unified force, see the Testimony of William Henry, Carpenter, *Two Trials*, 25; and the Testimony of William Nichols, Carpenter, *Two Trials*, 39. On cockades, contrast the Deposition of John Moritz, Rawle Papers, 107, with Jacob Eyerly's testimony that every man in Anthony Stahler's infantry company wore "French" cockades, Rawle Papers, 46. See also Newman, *Parades and Politics*, 161. For John Fries's comment on France, compare the notes of the testimony of Israel Roberts in the trial of Henry Shiffert et al. on charges of conspiracy, Rawle Papers, 105–9, with the testimony of James Chapman in Fries's first trial, Carpenter, *Two Trials*, 70. For Rawle's summation of these points, see, Carpenter, *Two Trials*, 152–56.

82. Carpenter, *Two Trials*, 169.

83. Thomas Jefferson to Edmund Pendleton, February 14, 1799, in Paul Leicester Ford, ed., *The Writings of Thomas Jefferson* (New York: G. P. Putnam's Sons, 1896), 7:356.

84. For Dallas's argument, see Carpenter, *Two Trials*, 97. On the unconstitutionality of both sections of the Sedition Act, see the Speech of William Daniel to the Virginia House of Delegates, December 19, 1798, Virginia House of Delegates, *Virginia Report of 1799–1800*, 93. On the trials of lesser insurgents, see Henderson, "Treason, Sedition," and the Minute Books for 1796–99 and 1799–1800, Records of the United States District Court for Eastern Pennsylvania, Record Group (RG) 21, Microfilm Publication M987, National Archives and Record Administration, Philadelphia. On the acceleration of sedition prosecutions in 1799, see Smith, *Freedom's Fetters*, part 3.

85. The last liberty pole to which I can find reference was erected near Slaughterdam, New York, on February 23, 1799. The petitioning campaign ended in February as well. For Republican repudiations of the insurgents, see *Aurora*, March 12 and 22, 1799; *Newark Sentinel of Freedom*, May 7, 1799; "From N.Y. Argus," *Newark Sentinel of Freedom*, July 9, 1799; and *Aurora*, May 17, 1799.

86. *Aurora*, July 9, 1799; and *Newark Sentinel of Freedom*, July 9, 1799, and June 17, 1800.

87. *Aurora*, April 18, 1799, and July 30, 1799. On depredations committed by members of the standing army, see *Aurora*, August 3, 1799, and April 29, 1800; *Kentucky Gazette*, March 28, 1799; and the *New London Bee*, June 19, July 10, and August 14, 1799, and April 2, 1800.

88. *Aurora*, March 25, April 5, and July 15, 1799. For other Republican papers that accepted Duane's narrative, see the *New London Bee*, January 8, 1800; and the *Newark Sentinel of Freedom*, September 23, 1800.

89. *Aurora*, September 2, 26, and 30, and October 8, 1799.

90. Virginia House of Delegates, *Virginia Report of 1799–1800*, 191 and 231–32.

91. The Kentucky Resolutions of 1799 as reprinted in the *Washington (PA) Herald of Liberty*, January 20, 1800.

92. My description of the episode is based on Sharp, *American Politics*, 250–75. See also James E. Lewis Jr., "'What Is to Become of Our Government': The Revolutionary Potential of the Election of 1800," in James Horn, Jan Ellen Lewis, and Peter S. Onuf, eds., *The Revolution of 1800: Democracy, Race, and the New Republic* (Charlottesville: University of Virginia Press, 2002), 3–29.

93. Sharp, *American Politics*, 268–71. For Jefferson's warning, see Thomas Jefferson to James Monroe, February 15, 1801, in *Writings of Thomas Jefferson*, 7:490–91.

94. Jefferson's fair copy of the Kentucky Resolutions of 1798, *Papers of James Madison*, 17:180.

Part I Conclusion

1. Speech of Robert Y. Hayne, January 25, 1830, in Herman Belz, ed., *The Webster-Hayne Debate on the Nature of the Union: Selected Documents* (Indianapolis: Liberty Fund, 2000), 35–80.

2. Speech of Daniel Webster, January 26–27, 1830, Belz, *Webster-Hayne Debate*, 139–44.

3. Ibid., 125.

4. Speech of Robert Y. Hayne, January 27, 1830, in Belz, *Webster-Hayne Debate* 182.

5. *Richmond Enquirer,* July 11, 1826.

6. *Richmond Enquirer,* July 11, 1826; for a similar toast in Nashville, see Andrew Burstein, *America's Jubilee* (New York: Vintage, 2001), 247.

7. Speech of Ezekiel Bacon, December 4, 1807, *Annals of Congress: The Debates and Proceedings in the Congress of the United States,* 42 vols. (Washington, DC: Gales and Seaton, 1834–56), 17:1042.

8. Joseph Story, *Commentaries on the Constitution of the United States* (Boston: Hilliard, Gray, 1833), 3:746.

9. *Aymette v. State,* 21 Tenn. 154, at 158.

10. Larry D. Kramer, *The People Themselves: Popular Constititonalism and Judicial Review* (New York: Oxford University Press, 2004).

11. Edward Livingston, Speech before the Senate, March 15, 1830, *Congressional Register,* 270.

12. Ibid.

13. Ibid., 268.

14. Jean H. Baker, "The Ceremonies of Politics: Nineteenth-Century Rituals of National Affirmation," in William J. Cooper Jr., Michael F. Holt, and John McCardell, eds., *A Master's Due: Essays in Honor of David Herbert Donald* (Baton Rouge: Louisiana State University Press, 1985), 161–78.

15. John K. Mahon, *History of the Militia and the National Guard* (New York: Macmillan, 1983; and Kimberly K. Smith, *The Dominion of Voice: Riot, Reason, and Romance in Antebellum Politics* (Lawrence: University of Kansas Press, 1999).

16. On the Dorr War, see George M. Dennison, *The Dorr War: Republicanism on Trial, 1831–1861* (Lexington: University Press of Kentucky, 1976).

17. Joseph Story to John Pitman, February 10, 1842, in William W. Story, ed., *Life and Letters of Joseph Story* (Boston: Charles C. Little and James Brown, 1851), 2:416.

18. *Luther v. Borden*, 48 U.S. 1 (1849); On the judicial politics of the decision, see Dennison, *Dorr War*, 141–92.

19. Richard Hildreth, *Despotism in America* (1840, reissued 1854), quoted in Albert J. Von Frank, *The Trials of Anthony Burns: Freedom and Slavery in Emerson's Boston* (Cambridge: Harvard University Press, 1998), 160.

20. Von Frank, *Trials of Anthony Burns*, 62–70, 206–19, and 240.

21. "Legal Resistance to Unrighteous Law," *New York Independent*, June 15, 1854.

The Roots of Modern Patriotism

1. Speech of Clement Vallandigham of Ohio in the House of Representatives, February 23, 1863, *Congressional Globe*, 37th Congress, Third Session, 172–77.

2. For a detailed discussion of these measures, see Frank L. Klement, *The Copperheads in the Middle West* (Chicago: University of Chicago Press, 1960), 40–78; and Kenneth Stamp, *Indiana Politics during the Civil War* (Indianapolis: Indiana Historical Bureau, 1949), 128–57. For a detailed analysis of the suspension of habeas corpus and the extent of military arrests during the war, see Mark E. Neely Jr., *The Fate of Liberty: Abraham Lincoln and Civil Liberties* (New York: Oxford University Press, 1991).

3. Herman Belz, *Abraham Lincoln, Constitutionalism, and Equal Rights in the Civil War Era* (New York: Fordham Press, 1998), 94; and "Union Mass Meeting at Columbus," *Indianapolis Daily Journal*, February 4, 1863. For the best analyses of Lincoln's evolving understanding of the doctrine of necessity, see Belz, and also Neely, *Fate of Liberty*. See also the Resolutions of the "Union Meeting in Tipton," *Indianapolis Daily Journal*, January 29, 1863; "Great Union Meeting," *Indianapolis Daily Journal*, January 27, 1863; and Resolutions of Company G, 70th Indiana Regiment, *Indianapolis Daily Journal*, April 24, 1863.

4. Kenneth Stamp, *Indiana Politics during the Civil War*, 158–85; and Mark E. Neely Jr., *The Union Divided: Party Conflict in the Civil War North* (Cambridge: Harvard University Press, 2005), 57.

5. Philip Shaw Paludan, *"A People's Contest": The Union and Civil War, 1861–1865* (New York: Harper and Row, 1988), 240–43; and *Indiana State Sentinel*, April 14 and May 11, 1863. See also Frank L. Klement, *The Limits of Dissent: Clement L. Vallandigham and the Civil War* (Lexington: University Press of Kentucky, 1970).

6. *Indiana State Sentinel*, June 4, 1863.

7. *Indiana State Sentinel*, May 4 and 18, 1863.

8. George M. Frederickson, *The Inner Civil War: Northern Intellectuals and the Crisis of Union* (New York: Harper and Row, 1965), chap. 9; and Melinda Lawson, "'A Profound National Devotion': The Civil War Union Leagues and the Construction of a New National Patriotism," *Civil War History* 48 (2002): 338–62. On the Constitution of the Union League Club of New York, see Frederickson, 131.

9. Resolutions of the Union Meeting in Johnson County, *Indianapolis Daily Journal*, June 24, 1863; and "Union Mass Meeting," *Indianapolis Daily Journal*, February 26, 1863. See also *Indianapolis Daily Journal*, February 13, April 28, May 6, and June 3, 1863; and *Putnam Republican Banner*, April 23, 1863.

10. Neely, *The Union Divided*, 41–47; and "Resolutions of the 8th and 18th Regiments and 1st Battery," *Indianapolis Daily Journal*, March 10, 1863.

11. *Indiana State Sentinel*, July 28, 1863; and Robert D. Sampson, "'Pretty Damned Warm Times': The 1864 Charleston Riot and 'the Inalienable Right of Revolution,'" *Illinois Historical Journal* 89 (1996): 111. See also John Mansfield to Governor Morton, June 15, 1863, Indiana Legion Manuscripts, Indiana State Archives, Manuscripts Division, Indianapolis (hereafter Indiana Legion Manuscripts).

12. G. R. Tredway, *Democratic Opposition to the Lincoln Administration in Indiana* (Indianapolis: Indiana Historical Bureau, 1973), 27–28.

13. *Indiana State Sentinel*, April 20, 1863; and *Sullivan Democrat*, July 9, 1863.

14. The files of the Indiana Legion Manuscripts are replete with such warnings. In particular, see W. B. Squire to Gov. Morton, June 25, 1861, Sullivan County Correspondence, box 27; L. G. Vanderwalker to Morton, February 3, 1863, Noble County Correspondence, box 19; and G. E. Fuller to Morton, June 14, 1863, Fulton County Correspondence, box 8.

15. For a general overview that debunks the Knights of the Golden Circle conspiracy theories propagated by Republicans, see Frank L. Klement, *Dark Lanterns: Secret Political Societies, Conspiracies, and Treason Trials in the Civil War* (Baton Rouge: Louisiana State University Press, 1984), chap. 1.

16. *Indianapolis Daily Journal*, August 4, 1862, and January 19 and 27, 1863.

17. *Indianapolis Daily Journal*, March 12, 1863.

18. *Indianapolis Daily Journal*, July 30 and November 8, 1864. Republican KGC conspiracy charges have been thoroughly debunked by Frank Klement. Nevertheless, their details serve as a vivid illustration of the contours of Republican paranoia. Though members of the Sons of Liberty were conspiring against the Union in 1864, one must distinguish between the real details of the plot and representation thereof within the Republican imagination.

19. "Proceedings of the Brown County Democracy," *Indiana State Sentinel,* January 9, 1863. See also Resolutions of the Democratic Mass Convention of the 10th and 11th Congressional Districts, *Indiana State Sentinel,* May 4, 1863; and *Bloomfield Southern Indianan,* June 4, 1863.

20. Resolutions of the Democratic Mass Convention of the 10th and 11th Congressional Districts, *Indiana State Sentinel,* May 4, 1864. See also Resolutions of the Martin County Democratic Convention, *Indiana State Sentinel,* June 20, 1864.

21. Daniel W. Voorhees, "The Liberty of the Citizen," February 22, 1863, as printed in the *Indiana State Sentinel,* March 2 and 3, 1863.

22. Ibid. For other invocations of classical Whig themes, see *Indiana State Sentinel,* March 30, May 4, and June 26, 1863. See also Jean H. Baker, *Affairs of Party: The Political Culture of Northern Democrats in the Mid-Nineteenth Century* (Ithaca: Cornell University Press, 1983), 143–76.

23. *Indiana State Sentinel,* July 7, 1863; and *Huntington Gazette,* January 7, 1864. See also *Indiana State Sentinel,* June 9 and July 13, 1863, and January 7, January 19, and June 29, 1864.

24. *Indiana State Sentinel,* January 1 and 5, 1863.

25. *Indiana State Sentinel,* February 10, 1863. See also the Resolutions of the Rush County Democratic Convention, *Indiana State Sentinel,* February 3, 1863.

26. *Indiana State Sentinel,* May 4, June 26, and January 9, 1863.

27. "From Washington," reprinted from the *Chicago Times,* in *Indiana State Sentinel,* August 12, 1863. See also the "Resolutions of Senator Davis," *Indiana State Sentinel,* January 16, 1864; J. J. Bingham's editorials, *Indiana State Sentinel,* August 3 and October 7, 1864; and "Secret Union League Circular," reprinted from the *Albany Atlas and Argus, Indiana State Sentinel,* October 7, 1864.

28. "From Washington," reprinted from the *Chicago Times,* in *Indiana State Sentinel,* March 9, 1863; *Indiana State Sentinel,* January 3, 1863. See also "Resolutions of Senator Davis of Kentucky," *Indiana State Sentinel,* January 16, 1864.

29. *Indiana State Sentinel,* January 3, 1863.

30. *Indiana State Sentinel,* February 14, April 24, and June 18, 1863.

31. *Indiana State Sentinel,* January 3 and February 7, 1863; and *Washington Democrat,* February 19, 1863.

32. *Indiana State Sentinel,* February 3, 1863.

33. *Indiana State Sentinel,* February 7, 1863; *Huntington Democrat,* February 26, 1863; and *Indiana State Sentinel,* March 20, 1863. See also *Fort Wayne Sentinel,* March 7, 1863; *Indiana State Sentinel,* March 7, 1863; and *Huntington Democrat,* March 12, 1863. In his speech at the festival Hendricks commented, "It is a Demo-

cratic sentiment that the laws must be respected and obeyed." He also condemned resistance to the arrest of deserters. It may be that the resolution caught Hendricks by surprise.

34. *New Albany Ledger,* March 23, 1863; and *Bloomfield Southern Indianan,* April 9, 1863.

35. *Indiana State Sentinel,* May 21, 1863.

36. *Indiana State Sentinel,* May 21, 1863. See also *Indiana State Sentinel,* June 9, 11, and 20, 1863; and *Sullivan Democrat,* June 25, 1863; *Paoli American Eagle,* June 18, 1863; and Letter from Hon. D. W. Voorhees, *New Albany Ledger,* July 6, 1863.

37. *Indiana State Sentinel,* June 25, 1863. For similar warnings of the consequences of revolution, see *New Albany Ledger,* March 30, 1863; *Sullivan Democrat,* March 26, 1863; *Bloomfield Southern Indianan,* April 9, 1863; and *Indiana State Sentinel,* May 22, 1863.

38. On bourgeois masculinity, see E. Anthony Rotundo, *American Manhood: Transformations in Masculinity from the Revolution to the Modern Era* (New York: Basic Books, 1993), especially chaps. 1 and 3.

39. *Indiana State Sentinel,* February 9, 1863; *Bloomfield Southern Indianan,* March 8, 1863; and *Indiana State Sentinel,* July 17, 1863. See also *New Albany Ledger,* March 30, 1863; *Fort Wayne Sentinel,* March 26, 1864; and *Indiana State Sentinel,* May 15, August 11, and September 22, 1863.

40. Proceedings of the Democratic conventions of the Ninth, Tenth, and Eleventh congressional districts, *Indiana State Sentinel,* January 12, 16, and 19, 1864.

41. For warnings of "Copperhead" loyalties in the legion, see Col. John Wiley to Laz Noble, June 11, 1863, box 4, Indiana Legion Manuscripts; Greene County Union Central Committee to Governor Morton, June 8, 1863, Seventh District, Indiana, letters received, Records of the Provost Marshal General's Bureau (Civil War), RG 110, National Archives and Records Administration, Washington, DC (hereafter RG 110); and Hiram Sale to Governor Morton, June 27, 1863, Wells County Correspondence, box 32, Indiana Legion Manuscripts. For Democratic suspicions of the legion, see J. J. Bingham's comments in the *Indiana State Sentinel,* August 3, 1864.

42. I have found reliable evidence of such associations in twenty-one of Indiana's ninety-two counties: Vanderburg, Martin, Orange, Washington, Crawford, Harrison, Scott, Sullivan, Greene, Monroe, Clay, Putnam, Parke, Morgan, Johnson, Brown, Rush, Jasper, Randolph, Huntington, and Wells counties. For Democratic resolutions critical of secret societies, see the Paoli *American Eagle,*

March 19, 1863; and the *Indiana State Sentinel,* September 2, September 11, and October 2, 1863 and July 16, 1864. For associations that met furtively, see the Deposition of John Jackson, General Courts Martial File NN2716, Records of the Office of Judge Advocate General (Army), RG 153, National Archives and Records Administration, Washington, DC (hereafter NN2716); Jacob Evans to Henry B. Carrington, April 13, 1864, NN2716; and the testimony of Wesley Tranter in Benn Pitman, *The Trials for Treason at Indianapolis* (Cincinnati: Moore, Wilstach, and Baldwin, 1865), 94. For associations acting in the open, see the *Bloomfield Southern Indianan,* June 4, 1863; and the *Putnam Republican Banner,* November 5, 1863.

43. For the condemnation and absolution that has characterized historical assessments of these associations, see George F. Milton, *Abraham Lincoln and the Fifth Column* (New York: Vanguard Press, 1942); and Tredway, *Democratic Opposition.*

44. Proceedings of trial of Andrew Jackson Perry, *Indianapolis Daily Journal,* February 26 and 28, and March 2, 1863. For resistance in Rush County, see the *Indianapolis Daily Journal,* March 21, 1863; *Indiana State Sentinel,* March 21, 1863; and *Weekly Wabash Express,* March 25, 1863. For Brown County, see the *Indiana State Sentinel,* August 6, 1863.

45. *Sullivan Democrat,* June 11, 1863; *Worthington Gazette,* June 11, 1863; and testimony of Elisha Cowgil, Pitman, *Trials for Treason,* 142.

46. *Indianapolis Daily Journal,* June 11, 1863.

47. *Indianapolis Daily Journal,* June 15, 1863; the *Indiana State Sentinel,* June 15, 1863; and Amanda Chittenden to George F. Chittenden, June 14, 1863, George F. Chittenden Papers, Manuscript Collection L31, Indiana State Library, Indianapolis.

48. *Putnam Republican Banner,* June 18, 1863; and *Indiana State Sentinel,* October 2, 1863.

49. *Sullivan Democrat,* June 25 and July 2, 1863. See also Seventh District Provost Marshal R. W. Thompson to Assistant Provost Marshal General Conrad Baker, June 18, 1863, in United States War Department, *War of the Rebellion: A Compilation of the Official Records of the Union and Confederate Armies* (Washington, DC: Government Printing Office, 1880–1901), ser. 3, 3:392; Thompson to Baker, June 23, 1863, Seventh District, Indiana, letters received, RG 110. For similar intimidation in Illinois, see S. A. Andrews to Captain M. O'Kean, June 26, 1863, Acting Assistant Provost Marshal General, Illinois, letters received from the Eleventh District, RG 110.

50. *Indianapolis Daily Journal,* June 24 and July 4, 1863; *Indiana State Sentinel,*

June 29, 1863; and *White River Gazette,* June 25, 1863. See also G. Patrick to R. W. Thompson, June 22, 1863, Seventh District, Indiana, letters received, RG 110.

51. Robert E. Sterling, "Civil War Draft Resistance in Illinois," *Journal of the Illinois Historical Society* 64 (1971): 244–66; and Kenneth H. Wheeler, "Local Autonomy and Civil War Draft Resistance: Holmes County, Ohio," *Civil War History* 45 (1999): 147–59.

52. The files of the federal district and circuit court proceedings against draft resisters were transferred during the war to the office of the Solicitor of the Treasury. As a consequence, these files, some of which probably contained pretrial depositions, are no longer present in the National Archives. A thorough search for these files in the District and Circuit Court Record Groups (RG 21 and RG 276) at the Great Lakes Branch Archives in Chicago and in the Records of the Solicitor of the Treasury (RG 206) in College Park, MD, proved fruitless.

53. Statement of Franklin Newkirk, December 13, 1864, Seventh District, Indiana, letters received, RG 110; *Mattoon Independent Gazette,* August 26, 1863, quoted in Sterling, "Civil War Draft Resistance," 262; and Jacob Evans to Henry B. Carrington, April 13, 1864, NN2716. See also Deposition of Wesley Tranter, NN2716; Samuel R. Yegarder to Henry B. Carrington, August 24, 1864, Carrington Family Papers, Yale University Archives, New Haven, Connecticut; and *New Albany Ledger,* June 18, 1863.

54. Statement of Franklin Newkirk, December 13, 1864, Seventh District, Indiana, letters received, RG 110; and testimony given in the examination of witnesses before U.S. Commissioner Davis in the case of John A. Burgess, as reported in the *Indiana State Sentinel,* June 26, 1863. See also letter of G. Cassidy printed in the *Putnam Republican Banner,* April 23, 1863; "Excerpts from the letters of Jack Baker," no date, Seventh District, Indiana, letters received, RG 110; and Joseph Jones to Laz Noble, October 4, 1864, Miscellaneous Correspondence, Indiana Adjutant General Manuscripts, Indiana State Archives, Manuscripts Division.

55. On this point, see also Thomas E. Rodgers, "Liberty, Will, and Violence: The Political Ideology of the Democrats of West-Central Indiana during the Civil War," *Indiana Magazine of History* 92 (1996): 133–59.

56. *Indianapolis Daily Journal,* June 20, 1863; Opinion of the United States District Court on a motion for a new trial in the case of *U.S. v. Abram Hufford,* file 327, Mixed Case Files, Records of the United States District Court for the Southern District of Indiana at Indianapolis, RG 21, National Archives and Records Administration, Great Lakes Branch, Chicago; and testimony of John McAvoy in *United States v. George Scott,* as printed in the *Indianapolis Daily Journal,* May 30, 1865.

57. Depositions of William F. Wells, April 11, 1864, and Benjamin Wells, April 12, 1864, Charleston Riot Depositions, Coles County Clerk's Office, Charleston, Illinois; and *Bloomfield Southern Indianan,* June 4, 1863. See also *Bloomfield Southern Indianan,* June 18, 1864; and *Matoon Independent Gazette,* August 5, 1863.

58. Mutual protection societies were active in townships on the border of Greene and Sullivan counties that lay fifteen miles from the nearest rail connections, in Brown, Rush, and Wells counties that had no rail connections at all, and in regions of Orange, Martin, and Crawford counties isolated by hills and dense forest. For a sense of the geographic isolation of many of these communities, see *Maps of Indiana Counties in 1876* (Indianapolis: Indiana Historical Society, 1968). The connection between isolation and resistance can be overstated, as resistance also broke out in areas of Morgan, Johnson, and Boone counties that were closely connected to the Indianapolis market.

59. *Sullivan Democrat,* June 18, 1863. For household subsistence strategies within yeoman society, see Thomas Rodgers, "Northern Political Ideologies in the Civil War Era: West Central Indiana, 1860–1866," Ph.D. diss., Indiana University, 1991; and John Mack Faragher, *Sugar Creek: Life on the Illinois Prairie* (New Haven: Yale University Press, 1986).

60. For resistance by women, see Tredway, *Democratic Opposition,* 16; *New Albany Daily Ledger,* June 8, 1863, and June 18, 1863; and *Indianapolis Daily Journal,* June 29, 1863. Though newspaper editors recorded these incidents, they did so with a tone of amusement. They did not record any statements on the part of the women involved, and none of the women were brought to trial. These women may have been motivated by constitutional concerns or by conscription's disruption of the gendered division of labor. Unfortunately, the available sources conceal their voices.

61. Testimony of William Clayton, Transcript of the Court Martial of Harrison H. Dodd, NN2716; and testimony of Horace Heffren, Pitman, *Trials for Treason,* 126. See also Jacob Evans to Henry B. Carrington, April 13, 1864, NN2716; and Hiram Sale to Oliver P. Morton, June 27, 1863, Wells County Correspondence, box 32, Indiana Legion Manuscripts.

62. Testimony of Elisha Bidwell, taken before John Hume, March 8, 1865, Seventh District, Indiana, letters received, RG 110; and "A Speck of War in Ohio," *New Albany Ledger,* June 22, 1863. See also testimony of William Stephenson in the trial of Mitchell Perry as reported in the *Indianapolis Daily Journal,* March 2, 1863.

63. *Weekly Wabash Express,* April 1, 1863; *Indianapolis Daily Journal,* April 17,

1863; and *Sullivan Democrat,* October 1, 1863. See also *Indianapolis Daily Journal,* June 3, 1863.

64. Testimony of William Harrison, Pitman, *Trials for Treason,* 87; and testimony of W. G. Ewing, Transcript of the Court Martial of Benjamin M. Anderson et al., *House Executive Documents,* 39th Congress, Second Session, no. 50 (hereafter *House Docs.*), 317. Pitman's *Trials for Treason* is an edited transcript of the court martial proceedings against the Indianapolis Sons of Liberty conspirators. The original transcript of the trials, as well as considerable depositional material, may be found in NN2716 and in General Courts Martial File NN3409, Records of the Office of Judge Advocate General (Army), RG 153, National Archives and Records Administration, Washington, DC (hereafter NN3409). An alleged plot to attack Camp Douglas and burn Chicago produced the trial of Benjamin Anderson et al. The proceedings of this second court martial, held in Cincinnati, are recorded in the *House Executive Documents.* I have cited Pitman's transcript where it is a substantively reliable rendering of the manuscript original, as it is more widely available. Where Pitman departs materially from the original, I have cited the latter. Frank Klement is quite correct that the evidence against the Chicago conspirators was thin at best. In extending this thesis to the Indianapolis conspiracy, however, he displays a systematic bias in his treatment of the evidence. For Klement's claim that the Sons of Liberty had no real existence, see Klement, *Dark Lanterns,* especially 108.

65. Testimony of J. J. Bingham, Pitman, *Trials for Treason,* 98–99; Testimony of Samuel Winter, Pitman, *Trials for Treason,* 173–74.

66. Lesson affirmed by initiates of the first degree, "Ritual of the Order of Sons of Liberty," reprinted in Pitman, *Trials for Treason,* 304.

67. Testimony of Stephen G. Burton, Transcript of the Court Martial of William Bowles et al., NN3409; and testimony of Wilson B. Lockridge, NN3409.

68. Letter of H. H. Dodd published in the *Indiana State Sentinel,* March 30, 1863.

69. *Indiana State Sentinel,* September 9 and 14, 1863; and *Indianapolis Daily Journal,* September 15, 1863.

70. Testimony of William Harrison, Pitman, *Trials for Treason,* 80.

71. Tredway, *Democratic Opposition,* 131–32; and the ritual of the Order of Sons of Liberty and the "Proceedings of the Grand Council of the State of Indiana," February 16 and 17, 1864, reprinted in Pitman, *Trials for Treason,* 302–8 and 315–19.

72. Testimony of Clement Vallandigham, *House Docs.,* 516.

73. S. Corning Judd to Abraham Lincoln, March 3, 1865, Nicolay-Hay Papers, Illinois State Historical Library, Springfield.

74. Testimony of James B. Wilson, Pitman, *Trials for Treason*, 143.

75. Felix Stidger to Captain Stephen E. Jones, May 13, 1864, NN2716; Deposition of Wesley Tranter, March 13, 1864, NN2716; Statements of George Washington Goodman and Franklin Newkirk, Seventh District, Indiana, letters received, RG 110; testimony of Joseph Johnson, Pitman, *Trials for Treason*, 172; and Deposition of John Jackson, March 4, 1864, NN2716.

76. Testimony of James B. Wilson, Pitman, *Trials for Treason*, 126–27; testimony of Felix Stidger, Pitman, *Trials for Treason*, 23–24; and testimony of James B. Wilson, *House Docs.*, 567–70. Frank Klement has argued that the plot was a figment of Dodd's imagination. A close reading of the evidence, however, reveals that the conspiracy involved at least a dozen men: Dodd, William A. Bowles, William Harrison, Horace Heffren, James B. Wilson, and John C. Walker from Indiana; Joshua Bullitt, W. R. Thomas, Mr. Williams, and Dr. Kalfus from Kentucky; and James Barrett, Charles Walsh, Robert Holloway, and B. B. Piper from Illinois. See Klement, *Dark Lanterns*, 153–64.

77. Testimony of Felix Stidger, Pitman, *Trials for Treason*, 24; testimony of William Harrison, Pitman, *Trials for Treason*, 90–91; and testimony of J. J. Bingham, Pitman, *Trials for Treason*, 101–2.

78. Testimony of B. F. Ibach, Pitman, *Trials for Treason*, 179; and Testimony of Felix G. Stidger, Pitman, *Trials for Treason*, 21 and 115. See also Deposition of Wesley Tranter, March 13, 1864, NN2716; Jacob Evans to Henry B. Carrington, April 13, 1864, NN2716; Felix Stidger to Stephen E. Jones, Provost Marshal, District of Kentucky, May 31, 1864, NN2716; and Testimony of Felix Stidger, Pitman, *Trials for Treason*, 108–13.

79. Testimony of Felix Stidger, Pitman, *Trials for Treason*, 23; Testimony of James Wilson, Pitman, *Trials for Treason*, 145; Testimony of Amos Green, *House Docs.*, 185–86; Examination of Joseph Kirkpatrick, August 25, 1864, in the file "Notes on the Civil War and Treason Trials," Albert Gallatin Porter Papers, Manuscript Collection L125, Indiana State Library; and testimony of William Harrison, Pitman, *Trials for Treason*, 88.

80. Testimony of James Wilson and Felix Stidger, Transcript of the Court Martial of William Bowles et al., NN3409.

81. Testimony of William Harrison, Pitman, *Trials for Treason*, 90–93.

82. Testimony of J. J. Bingham, Pitman, *Trials for Treason*, 101–2; Testimony of James Wilson, Pitman, *Trials for Treason*, 148; J. S. Hoagland to J. H. McKinley, August 21, 1864, Carrington Family Papers; Samuel R. Yegarder to Carrington, August 24, 1864, Carrington Family Papers; J. A. Cravens to M. W. Wines, August 6, 1864, Charles Worden Papers, Manuscript Collection 1456, Indiana State Li-

brary; Dr. Vogle to Laz Noble, August 3, 1864, NN3409; *Indianapolis Daily Journal*, August 6, 1864; testimony of Felix Stidger, Pitman, *Trials for Treason*, 114; and the Report of the Grand Secretary in the "Proceedings of the Grand Council of the State of Indiana," reprinted in Pitman, *Trials for Treason*, 320.

83. Testimony of J. J. Bingham, Pitman, *Trials for Treason*, 101–3.

84. Klement, *Dark Lanterns*, 164–72.

85. Testimony of Horace Zumro, Transcript of the Court Martial of William A. Bowles et al., NN3409; Statement of George Washington Goodman, Seventh District, Indiana, letters received, RG 110; and William S. Hall to Charles B. Lasalle, August 4, 1864, Charles B. Lasalle Papers, Indiana State Library. Hall was identified as a leader of a mutual protection association operating in Rush County in the testimony of James Mason, Pitman, *Trials for Treason*, 141.

86. *Indianapolis Daily Journal*, October 3 and 11, 1864; Robert E. Sterling, "Civil War Draft Resistance in the Middle West," Ph.D. diss., Northern Illinois University, 1974, 510–20; *Weekly Wabash Express*, August 31, 1864; and *History of Greene and Sullivan Counties* (Chicago: Goodspeed Brothers, 1884), 599. For statistics on the failure to report for the draft of July 1864, see the Final Report made to the Secretary of War, by the Provost Marshal General, *House Executive Documents*, 39th Congress, 1st Session, no. 1, 190 and 198. For the state as a whole, the rate was 16 percent.

87. S. W. Shuseterson to R.W. Thompson, October 26, 1864, Seventh District, Indiana, letters received, RG 110; and Thompson to Lt. Fox, November 28, 1864, Seventh District, Indiana, letters received, RG 110.

88. Unsworn Examinations of Junius Lomax, William Sanders, Lorenzo Knight, Joseph Allen, and Martin Belcher in *Operations of the Indiana Legion and Minutemen* (Indianapolis: W. R. Holloway, 1865), 82–84; *Indianapolis Daily Journal*, October 3, 1864; G. W. Colelasure to W. H. H. Terrell, December 23, 1864, Orange County Correspondence, Indiana Legion Manuscripts; and Deposition of James Brown, December 4, 1865, Clark County Correspondence, Indiana Legion Manuscripts. The *New Albany Ledger*, the district's leading Democratic newspaper, later dismissed the incident as a drunken brawl involving only a few drafted men in Crawford County, but the *Ledger's* account does not mention incidents reported in Orange and Floyd counties that suggest a failed attempt to stage a general rising. For the *New Albany Ledger's* version, see October 3, 5, and 7, 1864.

89. *Indiana State Sentinel*, September 22, 1864.

90. *Sullivan Democrat*, October 13, 1864; *Putnam Republican Banner*, December 31, 1863 and August 25, 1864; and *Indianapolis Daily Journal*, August 24, 1864.

91. Testimony of J. J. Bingham, Pitman, *Trials for Treason*, 103. The Central

Committee's "Address" was printed in the *Indiana State Sentinel*, August 15, 1864.

92. W. H. H. Terrell (Adjutant General of the State of Indiana) to J. T. Wilder, September 6, 1864, J. T. Wilder Manuscripts, Manuscript Collection S2600, Indiana State Library.

93. For the state election returns, see the *Indianapolis Daily Journal*, November 7, 1864. For the federal election returns, see the *Indiana State Sentinel*, November 30, 1864.

94. *Indianapolis Daily Journal*, November 8, 1864; and Klement, *Dark Lanterns*, chap. 7.

95. The best account of the court martial proceedings remains Tredway, *Democratic Opposition*, 224–48. Both Tredway and Frank Klement criticize the conduct of the military commission and cast doubt upon the reliability of Benn Pitman's published record of the trials.

96. William Harrison testified in a subsequent lawsuit that he had informed Milligan of the details of the plot when he saw him in Huntington. This conflicts with his testimony at the court martial of the conspirators in 1864. In any case Milligan refused to take part. See Harrison's testimony in *Milligan v. Hovey*, as reported in the *Indianapolis Daily Journal*, May 25, 1871.

97. Closing Statement of J. R. Coffroth, Pitman, *Trials for Treason*, 248.

98. Closing Statement of Major H. L. Burnett, Pitman, *Trials for Treason*, 260 and 293.

99. For a published record of *ex parte Milligan*, see Samuel Klaus, ed., *The Milligan Case* (New York: De Capo Press, 1970). For a recent analysis of the case, see William H. Rehnquist, *All the Laws but One: Civil Liberties in Wartime* (New York: Knopf, 1998). Milligan proceeded to sue the members of the commission and the officials responsible for his arrest and confinement. He won this suit in the U.S. circuit court in 1871, but an indemnity act prevented him from recovering damages. For an account of Milligan's civil suit, see Tredway, *Democratic Opposition*, 257–62.

100. *Ex parte Milligan*, 71 U.S. 2 (1866), at 126.

101. Neely, *The Fate of Liberty*, 175–84.

Cleansing the Memory of the Revolution

1. On the new patriotic organizations of the Gilded Age, see Cecelia Elizabeth O'Leary, *To Die For: The Paradox of American Patriotism* (Princeton: Princeton University Press, 1999); Stuart McConnell, *Glorious Contentment: The Grand Army of the Republic, 1865–1900* (Chapel Hill: University of North Carolina Press, 1997); and Woden Sorrow Teachout, "Forging Memory: Hereditary

Societies, Patriotism, and the American Past, 1876–1898," Ph.D. diss., Harvard University, 2003.

2. Teachout, "Forging Memory," 168–85.

3. O'Leary, *To Die For*, 50–61; Teachout, "Forging Memory," 293–99.

4. On the National Guard, see Nell Irvin Painter, *Standing at Armageddon: The United States, 1877–1919* (New York: Norton, 1987), 22; Jerry Cooper, *The Rise of the National Guard: The Evolution of an American Militia, 1865–1920* (Lincoln: University of Nebraska Press, 1997), 23–86; and John K. Mahon, *History of the Militia and the National Guard* (New York: Macmillan, 1983), 108–24. See also *Presser v. Illinois*, 116 U.S. 252 (1886).

5. Teachout, "Forging Memory," 328–45.

6. Ibid., 259–67.

7. On the 1902 dedication of the Indiana Soldiers and Sailors Monument, see John Bodnar, *Remaking America: Public Memory, Commemoration, and Patriotism in the Twentieth Century* (Princeton: Princeton University Press, 1992), 81; *Indianapolis News*, May 14–16; and *Indianapolis Sentinel*, May 14–16.

8. *Indianapolis Sentinel*, May 16, 1902. For the speeches at the Democratic state mass meeting on May 20, 1863, see *Indianapolis State Sentinel*, May 21–23, 1863. The Indiana State House was rebuilt between 1863 and 1902, and the east portico of the new state house sits slightly north of where it did in 1863.

9. *Indianapolis Sentinel*, May 15, 1902.

10. For the reconfiguration of patriotism, see O'Leary, *To Die For*, 54–55; Rotundo, *American Manhood: Transformations in Masculinity from the Revolution to the Modern Era* (New York: Basic Books, 1993), 222–46; David W. Blight, *Race and Reunion: The Civil War in American Memory* (Cambridge: Harvard University Press, 2001), 351–66, 381–97; and Matthew Frye Jacobson, *Whiteness of a Different Color: European Immigrants and the Alchemy of Race* (Cambridge: Harvard University Press, 1998), 139–70.

11. On *The Birth of a Nation*, see O'Leary, *To Die For*, 206–8; and Michael Rogin, "'The Sword Became a Flashing Vision': D. W. Griffith's The Birth of a Nation," *Representations* 9 (1985): 150–95.

12. For recent examinations of the first Ku Klux Klan, see Carole Emberton, "The Limits of Incorporation: Violence, Gun Rights, and Gun Regulation in the Reconstruction South," *Stanford Law and Policy Review* 17 (2006): 615–34; and Stephen Kantrowitz, "One Man's Mob Is Another Man's Militia," in Jane Dailey, Glenda Elizabeth Gilmore, and Bryant Simon, eds., *Jumpin' Jim Crow: Southern Politics from Civil War to Civil Rights* (Princeton: Princeton University Press, 2000), 67–87.

13. René Hayden, "Root of Wrath: Political Culture and the Origins of the First Ku Klux Klan in North Carolina, 1830–1875," Ph.D. diss., University of California, San Diego, 2003, 218–19.

14. Ibid., 178–80, 277.

15. Ibid., 249–69.

16. *Indianapolis Star,* May 30 and 31, 1918.

17. *Indianapolis Star,* May 31, 1918.

18. On the wave of postwar violence and the role of returning veterans, see Painter, *Standing at Armageddon,* 344–80; William M. Tuttle, *Race Riot: Chicago in the Red Summer of 1919* (Urbana: University of Illinois Press, 1996); William Pencak, *For God and Country: The American Legion, 1919–1941* (Boston: Northeastern University Press, 1989), 149–62; and James S. Hirsch, *Riot and Remembrance: The Tulsa Race War and Its Legacy* (New York: Houghton Mifflin, 2002).

19. On migration, see Steve Babson, *Working Detroit: The Making of a Union Town* (New York: Adama Books, 1984), 22–28. On ethnic tensions and the rise of the KKK, see Kenneth T. Jackson, *The Ku Klux Klan in the City, 1915–1930* (New York: Oxford University Press, 1967), 127–43.

20. On Michigan in the Depression, see Babson, *Working Detroit,* 51–60; and Frank B. Woodford and Arthur M. Woodford, *All Our Yesterdays: A Brief History of Detroit* (Detroit: Wayne State University Press, 1969), 310–21.

21. George Wolfskill, *The Revolt of the Conservatives: A History of the American Liberty League, 1934–1940* (Boston: Houghton Mifflin, 1962); and National Lawyers Committee of the American Liberty League, *Report on the Constitutionality of the National Labor Relations Act,* September 5, 1935. See also William E. Leuchtenburg, *The Supreme Court Reborn: The Constitutional Revolution in the Age of Roosevelt* (New York: Oxford University Press, 1995); and Barry Cushman, *Rethinking the New Deal Court: The Structure of a Constitutional Revolution* (New York: Oxford University Press, 1998).

22. On the alliance between unions and the Democratic Party and the sit-down strikes of 1936–37, see Babson, *Working Detroit,* 68–86; Henry Kraus, *Heroes of an Unwritten Story: The UAW, 1934–1939* (Urbana: University of Illinois Press, 1993), 236–94; and Sidney Fine, *Sit Down: The General Motors Strike of 1936–37* (Ann Arbor: University of Michigan Press, 1969).

23. Wolfskill, *Revolt of the Conservatives,* 72–73 and 109–22; and Raoul Desvernine, *Americanism at the Crossroads,* January 15, 1936, American Liberty League Pamphlet Series, no. 88.

24. Leo P. Ribuffo, *Right, Center, Left: Essays in American History* (New Brunswick: Rutgers University Press, 1992), 70–105; Geoffrey S. Smith, *To Save a*

Nation: American Counter-Subversives, the New Deal, and the Coming of World War II (New York: Basic Books, 1973), 53–65; Leo P. Ribuffo, The Old Christian Right: The Protestant Far Right from the Great Depression to the Cold War (Philadelphia: Temple University Press, 1983), 25–79; John McIntyre Werly, "The Millenarian Right: William Dudley Pelley and the Silver Legion of America," Ph.D. diss., Syracuse University, 1972; and Pelley's Weekly, April 8, April 15, May 20, and June 10, 1936.

25. On Coughlin and the Union Party Campaign of 1936, see David H. Bennett, Demagogues in the Depression: American Radicals and the Union Party, 1932–1936 (New Brunswick: Rutgers University Press, 1969); Glen Jeansonne, Gerald L. K. Smith, Minister of Hate (New Haven: Yale University Press, 1988), 46–63; Ribuffo, Old Christian Right, 140–49; Smith, To Save a Nation, 11–52; and Donald Warren, Radio Priest: Charles Coughlin, the Father of Hate Radio (New York: Free Press, 1996). For Coughlin's statements during the campaign, see the Detroit News, August 28 and September 25, 1936.

26. On anti-Communist vigilantism, see the Detroit Free Press, June 4, 1936; Detroit News, August 6, 1936; and New York Times, June 28, 1937.

27. On the career of Dr. William Shepard, see Peter Amann, "Vigilante Fascism: The Black Legion as an American Hybrid," Comparative Studies in Society and History 25 (1983): 493–501. For examples of inducements used in recruitment, see the memorandum of August 31, 1935, FBI file 62-779, box 1, file 5, Peter Amann Papers, Archive of Labor and Urban Affairs, Walter Reuther Library, Detroit, Michigan (hereafter Amann Papers); and the statement of Harold Hubbard of Genesee County, May 24, 1936, Michigan State Police file on the Black Legion, no. 5947 (hereafter MSP 5947). For examples of coercion, see the testimony of Clement Teuterbaugh in the preliminary hearing of Donald Swindle, Flint Journal, September 12, 1936; the testimony of Samuel Stiff in Swindle's trial for perjury, Flint Journal, October 6, 1936; and the letter from a Greenfield, Ohio informant, May 25, 1936, FBI file 61-7398, box 1, file 7, Amann Papers. For a detailed description of a legion initiation, see testimony of Arlington Jones, Wilson v. City of Highland Park, 284 Michigan Supreme Court Records and Briefs (hereafter MSCRB) 96, 45–58. On legion floggings, see the reports of May 23 and 25, 1936, on Jackson County floggings, MSP 5947; and the Toledo Blade, May 27, 1936. On the second Klan, see Kathleen Blee, Women of the Klan: Racism and Gender in the 1920s (Berkeley and Los Angeles: University of California Press, 1991); David M. Chalmers, Hooded Americanism: The History of the Ku Klux Klan (New York: Franklin Watts, 1981); Jackson, Ku Klux Klan; Leonard J. Moore, Citizen Klansman: The Ku Klux Klan in Indiana, 1921–1928 (Chapel Hill: University

of North Carolina Press, 1991); and Nancy MacLean, *Behind the Mask of Chivalry: The Making of the Second Ku Klux Klan* (New York: Oxford University Press, 1994).

28. On the purposes and extent of Shepard's Legion, see the *Detroit News*, May 27 and 28, 1936; and *Detroit Times*, May 27, 1936.

29. Amann, "Vigilante Fascism," 502.

30. Testimony of Dayton Dean, *Wilson v. City of Highland Park*, 284 MSCRB 96, 188–89 and 223–25; testimony of Arthur Harris, *Calvert v. Pontiac Police and Fire Trial Board*, 288 MSCRB 401, 86–89; Charles F. Dexter (writing as "Anonymous"), "I Was a Captain of the Black Legion," part 2, *True Detective Mysteries*, February 1937, 129; and *Toledo Times*, October 9, 1936.

31. A notebook confiscated from Arthur Lupp contains a partial list of Michigan regiments and their commanders. A typescript of the book's contents is in the Detroit Police Department file on the murder of Charles Poole. On the legion in Ecorse, see the *New York Times*, June 8, 1936. For the Detroit area estimate, I have figured three city regiments at full strength, the businessman's regiment at five hundred members, and I have accepted the *New York Times* estimate of two thousand in Ecorse. State prosecutor Owen Dudley estimated the Jackson regiment at five hundred men, *Detroit Times*, May 28, 1936. For a range of estimates of legion strength in Oakland County, see the testimony of Sherry Mapey before the Oakland County grand jury, inserted into the record of *Mapey v. Pontiac Police and Fire Trial Board*, 288 MSCRB 396, 172; and the *Report of Black Legion Activities in Oakland County* (Circuit Court for Oakland County, Michigan, August 31, 1936), 6–7. For Genesee County, see the *Flint Journal*, May 23, 1936. On the Monroe County regiments, see Amann, "Vigilante Fascism," 506–7. The commanders of legion units in Saginaw, Battle Creek, and Grand Rapids are identified in the address book confiscated from Arthur Lupp. Their respective ranks give a rough estimate of the size of the units.

32. On Toledo, see the *Toledo Blade*, May 28 and October 21, 1936. On Lima and Allen County, see the memorandum of May 28, 1936, FBI file 61-7398, box 2, file 13, Amann Papers; and *Lima News*, May 25, 1936. On Bucyrus, see Amann, "Vigilante Fascism," 506–7. On Akron, Sandusky, and Wayne County, see the *Detroit Times*, May 28, 1936; *Sandusky Star-Journal*, May 27, 1936; and a letter from a Greenfield, Ohio, informant to the FBI, May 25, 1936, FBI file 61-7398, box 1, file 7, Amann Papers. For Ohio KKK grand dragon James Colescott's estimate of legion strength in eastern Ohio, see *Akron Beacon Journal*, May 27, 1936. On Fort Wayne, see *Fort Wayne News Sentinel*, May 27, 1936; and *Fort Wayne Journal-Gazette*, May 30, 1936. On South Bend, see the *Fort Wayne News Sentinel*, May 28,

1936. On Pennsylvania, West Virginia, and Los Angeles, see *Detroit News,* May 31 and October 14, 1936.

33. For purposes of comparison, most contemporaries estimated the strength of the legion at forty thousand. Peter Amann put the minimum figure at twenty-four thousand, but thought that Indiana and Illinois contingents were probably as strong as those in Michigan and Ohio. He thus argued that sixty to one hundred thousand was a likely range. There is no evidence, however, of a strong legion presence in either Indiana or Illinois. See Amann, "Vigilante Fascism," 506–8.

34. No complete membership records survive from any Black Legion unit bigger than a company, so it is not possible to reconstruct a full typology of legion membership. These conclusions are based on information gleaned from the membership roster of one Detroit company and background information on the defendants in a dozen legion-related trials. See "Confidential report on the Black Legion," June 12, 1936, MSP 5947. Membership lists confiscated from Leonard Lipps indicate a much higher percentage of blue-collar workers. See the typescripts of books marked "Perfection" and "Memorandum," June 2, 1936, Detroit Police file on the murder of Charles Poole. On a separate "businessman's regiment" in Detroit, see Charles F. Dexter, "I Was a Captain of the Black Legion," part 1, *True Detective Mysteries,* January 1937, 28. For a list of public employees who belonged to the legion in Oakland County, see the *Report of Black Legion Activities in Oakland County,* 23–24.

35. *Detroit News,* May 29, 1936; April 27, 1937, memorandum to Judge John Maher outlining a court-appointed psychologist's evaluation of the defendants in *People v. Black, et al.,* box 13, file 38, Amann Papers; *Report of Black Legion Activities in Oakland County,* 3; and the account of Dayton Dean in "Secrets of the Black Legion," *Official Detective Stories,* October 1, 1936, 35.

36. The description of this meeting is based on the testimony of Bert Kilmer, *Wilson v. City of Highland Park,* 284 *MSCRB* 96, 295–310; the *Report of Black Legion Activities in Oakland County,* 8–13; and the copy of the Black Legion's ritual confiscated from Ray Ernst, MSP 5947.

37. "Declaration of Principles of the Black Legion," *Flint Journal,* September 26, 1936.

38. Testimony of Dayton Dean, preliminary hearing of *Virgil Effinger, et al.,* on charges of criminal syndicalism, quoted in the *Detroit Free Press,* October 23, 1936; and Statement of Harold Hubbard, May 24, 1936, MSP 5947.

39. *Report of Black Legion Activities in Oakland County,* 12; and memorandum to Judge John Mayer, April 27, 1937, box 13, file 38, Amann Papers. The memo-

randum to Judge Mayer emphasized the defendants' tenuous claim to bourgeois status as the source of the considerable economic anxiety that permeated legion ideology. My discussion on this point is significantly informed by Nancy MacLean's analysis of the second Ku Klux Klan in *Behind the Mask of Chivalry,* 136–40.

40. *Report of Black Legion Activities in Oakland County,* 9–10; the advertising supplement to the *Rail Splitter* describing the content of Clark's writing, box 11, file 6, Amann Papers; the Affidavit of Dayton Dean, reprinted in the *Detroit Times,* August 21, 1936; and Memorandum to Judge John Mayer, April 27, 1937, box 13, file 38, Amann Papers.

41. Memorandum to Judge John Mayer, April 27, 1937, box 13, file 38, Amann Papers. A copy of the flyer with which the legion hoped to discredit Sugar is in box 7, file 23, Amann Papers.

42. Ritual of the Black Legion, confiscated from Ray Ernst, MSP 5947; interview with Virgil Effinger, *Toledo News-Bee,* March 11, 1938, quoted in report of May 29, 1940, FBI file 61-9662, box 2, file 16, Amann Papers; leaflet seized by Michigan authorities, reprinted in Dexter, "I Was a Captain," part 2, 29; testimony of Arlington Jones, *Wilson v. City of Highland Park,* 284 *MSCRB* 96, 45; statement of Lloyd Modglin, *Detroit News,* June 30, 1936.

43. On discussions of race, sex, and lynching during legion initiations, see the testimony of Bert Kilmer, *Wilson v. City of Highland Park,* 284 *MSCRB* 96, 299; and the account of Dayton Dean in "Secrets of the Black Legion," *Official Detective Stories,* October 1, 1936, 7.

44. Leaflet on the candidacy of Maurice Sugar, box 7, file 23, Amann Papers.

45. *Detroit Times,* July 26, 1936; and the *Detroit Tribune,* August 1, 1936.

46. Statement of a former Klan organizer, taken by Harry Colburn, August 6, 1936, box 13, file 18, Amann Papers; Memorandum to Judge John Mayer, April 27, 1937, box 13, file 38, Amann Papers; "Black Legion General Held in Jackson," *Detroit News,* May 24, 1936; testimony of Sherry Mapey before the Oakland County Grand Jury, June 19, 1936, read into the record of Mapey's dismissal hearing before the Pontiac Police and Fire Trial board, *Sherry Mapey v. Pontiac Police and Fire Trial Board,* 288 *MSCRB* 396, 172; Amann, "Vigilante Fascism," 500–501.

47. Testimony of Dayton Dean, *Wilson v. City of Highland Park,* 284 *MSCRB* 96, 222–26; testimony of Bert Kilmer, 284 *MSCRB* 96, 306–30; and *Report of Black Legion Activities in Oakland County,* 10.

48. On the murder of Charles Poole, see Heinrick Pickert, "Black Legion Secrets Never Told Before," part 1, *True Detective Mysteries,* October 1936; testimony of Detective John Harvill and Dayton Dean in the preliminary hearing of

People v. Davis, et al., reprinted in the *Detroit News,* June 2 and 3, 1936; Dean's testimony in the trial, *Detroit Times,* September 18, 1936; and the statements of Hershell Gill, Marcia Rushing, Ruby Lane, Michael Layton, and Dayton Dean, and the "Notes on Witness Interviews," Detroit Police file on the murder of Charles Poole.

49. On the shooting of James Armour, see the *Detroit Times,* July 26, 1936; and the *Detroit Tribune,* August 1, 1936.

50. On the murder of Silas Coleman, see the *Detroit News,* July 21, 1936; *Detroit Times,* November 27, 1936; and the transcript of the testimony of Dayton Dean in the preliminary hearing of the Coleman case, Detroit Police file on the murder of Silas Coleman.

51. *Toledo News-Bee,* May 30, 1936.

52. Testimony of Carl Moore in the trial of Donald Swindle, *Flint Journal,* October 6, 1936; and interview with Wilbur Robinson, *Detroit Times,* May 29, 1936. See also interview with Roy Hepner, *Detroit News,* June 17, 1936.

53. The Far Right in the 1930s was divided between native groups such as the legion and the Silver Shirts, and groups such as the Order of Sons of Italy and the German American Bund, which were expressions of expatriate nationalism and, as such, beyond the hegemony of Americanism. Expatriate fascists demonstrated a much stronger tendency to paramilitary organization and subversive conspiracy, as illustrated by the Italian-American members of the Khaki Shirts who marched on Washington and the activities of German- and Irish-American members of the Christian Front in New York. For a recent evaluation of fascist movements during the Depression, see Philip Jenkins, *Hoods and Shirts: The Extreme Right in Pennsylvania, 1925–1950* (Chapel Hill: University of North Carolina Press, 1997).

54. Letter of Charles Harris, December 21, 1935, United States Department of Justice file 202600-2866, box 5, file 6, Amann Papers; report of May 26–27 describing an interview with an anonymous informer in Genesee County, MSP 5947; and testimony of Dayton Dean in the preliminary hearing of *People v. Effinger, et al.,* on a charge of criminal syndicalism, *Detroit News,* October 22, 1936.

55. Dayton Dean, "Secrets of the Black Legion," *Official Detective Stories,* October 1936; affidavit of Dayton Dean, reprinted in the *Detroit Times,* August 21, 1936; interview with George Scheid described in FBI report of May 24, 1936, FBI file 61–7398, box 2, file 12, Amann Papers; and Scheid's conversation with his son, as related in an interview between George Scheid Jr. and Peter Amann in 1979, quoted in Amann, "Vigilante Fascism," 510. See also the testimony of Charles F.

Dexter in the preliminary hearing of *People v. Effinger, et al, Detroit News,* October 23, 1936.

56. For example, William Dudley Pelley predicted a "Judeo-Bolshevik" coup would take place in the summer of 1936. He also scheduled a patriotic counterstrike, led by his Silver Shirt Legion, for September 16. When the "cabal" refrained from launching its summer coup, Pelley told his followers to stand down. Bound by the countersubversive tenets of one hundred percent Americanism, Pelley could not bring himself to attempt a proactive fascist revolution. The Liberty League and Coughlin also briefly flirted with revolutionary language, but never seriously advocated antistate violence. See *Pelley's Weekly,* April 15, May 20, and June 10, 1936; and American Liberty League pamphlets by James A. Reed, *The Constitution—the Fortress of Liberty,* February 11, 1936, no. 105, George W. Maxey, *What the Constitution Means to the Citizen,* March 1936, no. 106; Raoul E. Desvernine, *The Principles of Constitutional Democracy and the New Deal,* July 11, 1935, no. 52, and James M. Beck, *What Is the Constitution between Friends?* March 27, 1935, no. 22; Wolfskill, *Revolt of the Conservatives,* 72–73 and 109; and the *Detroit News,* August 28 and September 25, 1936.

57. Typescript marked "History," MSP 5947.

58. Interrogation of Andrew Martin by the Michigan State Police, discussed in the report of August 31, 1936, FBI file 62-799, box 1, file 5, Amann Papers; testimony of Andrew Martin in *Effinger v. Lima News, Toledo Blade,* May 24, 1940; and "Declaration of Principles of the Black Legion," *Flint Journal,* September 26, 1936.

59. Interview with Virgil Effinger, report of April 14, 1936, FBI file 61-7398, box 2, file 13, Amann Papers; and Arthur Lupp, Lecture on Gun Control, Detroit Police file on the murder of Charles Poole.

60. After the exposure of the Black Legion in May 1936, Effinger's thought seems to have turned explicitly fascist and more violently anti-Semitic. See *Pelley's Weekly,* July 8, 1936; and statement of a former Klan organizer, taken by Harry Colburn, August 6, 1936, box 13, file 18, Amann Papers.

61. *Detroit News,* May 22, June 11, and July 21, 1936; *Flint Journal,* May 30, 1936; and *Detroit Times,* July 26 and August 21, 1936.

62. *Detroit News,* May 24, 1936; Governor Fitzgerald's foreword to Michigan attorney general David H. Crowley's account, "Black Legion Secrets Never Told Before," part 3, *True Detective Mysteries,* December 1936; and Governor Earle's address, *Detroit News,* June 7, 1936.

63. Fitzgerald, foreword to "Black Legion Secrets," part 3; "Liberals Urge

F.D.R. to Back U.S. Probe of Legion," clipping from *Washington News*, FBI file 61–7398-A; and *Washington Times*, May 29, 1936.

64. "Black Legion," *Indianapolis News*, May 29, 1936; Governor Fitzgerald's letter to Attorney General Crowley, *Flint Journal*, May 30, 1936; and *New York Post*, May 28, 1936.

65. *Daily Worker*, June 11, 1936; *New York Times*, June 7 and 12, 1936; *Detroit News*, June 11, 1936; and Governor Earle's address, *Detroit News*, June 7, 1936.

66. "Stamp It Out," *Detroit Free Press*, May 25, 1936; *Detroit News*, May 24, 1936; "More Work for G-Men," clipping from *Asbury Park Evening Press*, FBI file 61–7398-A; *Washington News*, May 27, 1936; *Hartford Times*, June 16, 1936; and *Washington Times*, June 1, 1936.

67. Ribuffo, *Old Christian Right*, 178–83; and Smith, *To Save a Nation*, 66–69.

68. Ribuffo, *Old Christian Right*, 179–93.

69. Ibid., 184–87.

70. Ibid., 77–79, and 184–224.

71. Ibid.

72. Pauline Maier, *American Scripture: Making the Declaration of Independence* (New York: Vintage, 1998), 209–12.

Part II Conclusion

1. Alan F. Westin, "The John Birch Society: 'Radical Right' and 'Extreme Left' in the Political Context of Post World War II," in Daniel Bell, ed., *The Radical Right: The New American Right Expanded and Updated* (Garden City, NY: Anchor Books, 1964), 242. For astute analyses of the literature of liberal pluralism, see Leo P. Ribuffo, *The Old Christian Right: The Protestant Far Right from the Great Depression to the Cold War* (Philadelphia: Temple University Press, 1983), 237–57; and D. J. Mulloy, *American Extremism: History, Politics, and the Militia Movement* (New York: Routledge, 2004), 17–33. In addition to Bell, *The Radical Right*, important liberal pluralist works include Theodore Adorno, Else Frenkel-Brunswik, Daniel Levinson, and Nevitt Sanford, *The Authoritarian Personality* (New York: Harper and Row, 1950); Richard Hofstadter, *The Paranoid Style in American Politics and Other Essays* (New York: Alfred A. Knopf, 1965); and Seymour Martin Lipset and Earl Raab, *The Politics of Unreason: Right-Wing Extremism in America, 1790–1970* (New York: Harper and Row, 1970).

2. Hofstadter, "The Pseudo-Conservative Revolt," in Bell, *The Radical Right*, 77.

3. Westin, "John Birch Society," 267–68.

4. Ibid.

5. For the role of the AJC and ADL in liberal pluralist scholarship, see Ribuffo, *Old Christian Right*, 237–38; and the copyright page of the first edition of Lipset and Raab, *Politics of Unreason*. On "dynamic silence," see Glen Jeansonne, *Gerald L. K. Smith, Minister of Hate* (New Haven: Yale University Press, 1988), 206–8; and Frederick J. Simonelli, *American Fuehrer: George Lincoln Rockwell and the American Nazi Party* (Urbana: University of Illinois Press), 52–71.

6. On the ADL's activisties to counter right-wing "extremism," see Jeffrey Kaplan, "Right-Wing Violence in North America," in Tore Bjørgo, ed., *Terror from the Extreme Right* (London: Frank Cass, 1995), 76–77 and 94 n. 74; Simonelli, *American Fuehrer*, 65; and "History of ADL," http://www.adl.org/ADL History/ intro.asp (accessed April 12, 2005).

7. On Williams, see Timothy B. Tyson, *Radio Free Dixie: Robert F. Williams and the Roots of Black Power* (Chapel Hill: University of North Carolina Press, 1999), esp. 78–87 and 198.

8. The evolution of Identity theology was an enormously complicated process that is painstakingly analyzed in Michael Barkun, *Religion and the Racist Right: The Origins of the Christian Identity Movement* (Chapel Hill: University of North Carolina Press, 1994).

9. On Gale, see Barkun, *Religion and the Racist Right*, 207–8 and 217–23; and Daniel Levitas, *The Terrorist Next Door: The Militia Movement and the Radical Right* (New York: Thomas Dunne, 2002), 108–10 and 284–89. On the Posse Comitatus movement more broadly, see James A. Aho, *The Politics of Righteousness: Idaho Christian Patriotism* (Seattle: University of Washington Press, 1990), 44–47; Ridgeway, *Blood in the Face: The Ku Klux Klan, Aryan Nations, Nazi Skinheads, and the Rise of a New White Culture*, 2nd ed. (New York: Thunder's Mouth Press, 1995), 127–59; and James Corcoran, *Bitter Harvest: Gordon Kahl and the Posse Comitatus* (New York: Viking, 1990).

10. Barkun, *Religion and the Racist Right*, 207–8; and Levitas, *Terrorist Next Door*, 284–89.

11. Barkun, *Religion and the Racist Right*, 217–23; and Levitas, *Terrorist Next Door*, 183–91.

12. On Kahl, see Corcoran, *Bitter Harvest*; and Levitas, *Terrorist Next Door*, 192–200 and 217–20.

13. Andrew McDonald (William L. Pierce), *The Turner Diaries* (New York: Barricade Books, 1996). On Pierce, see Levitas, *Terrorist Next Door*, 291–92.

14. McDonald, *Turner Diaries*, 172–74.

15. On the Order, see Barkun, *Religion and the Racist Right*, 228–33; and James

Coates, *Armed and Dangerous: The Rise of the Survivalist Right* (New York: Noonday Press, 1987), 41–76. On the death of Robert Matthews, see Levitas, *Terrorist Next Door,* 106.

16. For the 1980s exposés of the white supremacist Right, see *Hate, Violence, and White Supremacy: A Decade Review, 1980–1990* (Montgomery: Klanwatch Project of the Southern Poverty Law Center, 1989); *Extremism on the Right,* rev. ed. (New York: Anti-Defamation League, 1988); *The "Identity Churches": A Theology of Hate* (New York: Anti-Defamation League, 1983); *Aryan Nations: Far Right Underground* (Atlanta: Center for Democratic Renewal, 1986); Ridgeway, *Blood in the Face;* and Coates, *Armed and Dangerous.*

The Origins of the Militia Movement

1. The best measure of this sense of loss is the groundswell of support for the independent presidential candidacy of H. Ross Perot.

2. For an overview of this research, see Peter B. Kraska and Victor E. Kappeler, "Militarizing American Police: The Rise and Normalization of Paramilitary Units," *Social Problems* 44 (1997): 1–18; Kraska and Louis J. Cubellis, "Militarizing Mayberry and Beyond: Making Sense of American Paramilitary Policing," *Justice Quarterly* 14 (1997): 607–29; and Kraska and Derek J. Paulsen, "Grounded Research into U.S. Paramilitary Policing: Forging the Iron Fist inside the Velvet Glove," *Policing and Society* 7 (1997): 253–70.

3. On military training of PPUs, see Kraska and Paulsen, "Grounded Research," 262–63. On the role of the military in training the Waco assault team, see David B. Kopel and Paul H. Blackman, *No More Wacos: What's Wrong with Federal Law Enforcement and How to Fix It* (Amherst: Prometheus Books, 1997), 85–90. For a description of the "bottoms up" roundup in Shreveport, Louisiana, as well as an attempt to debunk the various rumors about the operation swirling around the Christian Patriot public sphere, see William F. Jasper, "About Those Black Helicopters," *New American,* October 31, 1994.

4. "Attention! This Is Only a Drill," *Cleveland Plain Dealer,* June 22, 1995; "Military May Attack Book-Cadillac," *Detroit Free Press,* July 23, 1994; and Kopel and Blackman, *No More Wacos,* 339–40.

5. On the Brady Gun Control Act and the Assault Weapons Ban, see D. J. Mulloy, *American Extremism: History, Politics and the Militia Movement* (London: Routledge, 2004), 12. See also S.1878, "A Bill to Amend Title 18, United States Code, to Promote the Safe Use of Guns and to Reduce Gun Violence," February 28, 1994.

6. The best account of the Weavers and the events at Ruby Ridge is Jess Wal-

ter, *Every Knee Shall Bow: The Truth and Tragedy of Ruby Ridge and the Randy Weaver Family* (New York: Regan Books, 1995).

7. Ibid., 74–115.

8. Some of the details of this initial shootout on Ruby Ridge will never be known. Most observers, including Morris Dees and the authors of the U.S. Senate report on Ruby Ridge, agree that the most plausible scenario begins with a federal agent shooting Striker. See Walter, *Every Knee Shall Bow*, 160–71; and Morris Dees with James Corcoran, *Gathering Storm: America's Militia Threat* (New York: HarperCollins, 1996), 17.

9. Walter, *Every Knee Shall Bow*, 177–203. Horiuchi later testified that he believed that Weaver and Harris represented a threat to a government helicopter flying overhead.

10. Dick J. Reavis, *The Ashes of Waco: An Investigation* (Syracuse: Syracuse University Press, 1995), 31–35 and 120–55.

11. Ibid.

12. Ibid., 221–36, 258–77.

13. The events at Waco and Ruby Ridge played a fundamental role in prompting individuals involved in the gun rights movement to associate in militias. See, for example, Oral Deckard, former member of the Indiana Citizens Volunteer Militia, interview by the author, Terre Haute, IN, October 29, 1998; Charles Morrison, Jr., and Tom Plummer, members of the Central Ohio Unorganized Militia, interview by the author, Columbus, OH, october 25, 1998; and James and Michael McKinzey, founders of the Missouri 51st Militia, interview by the author, Grain Valley, MO, October 30, 1998.

14. For examples of the accounts of paramilitary police abuses circulated by gun rights activists, see Joe Waldron, "Armed and Considered Dangerous: Bureau of Alcohol, Tobacco, and Firearms in the 1990s," July 24, 1995, http://www .ccrkba.org/pub/rkba/articles/general/polabuse.txt (accessed March 13, 2008); and Tom Washington, Open Letter to President Bush, May 10, 1995, *USA Today*, May 15, 1995. Waldron wrote on behalf of the Second Amendment Foundation, and Washington was president of the NRA. Gun rights organizations' accounts of these incidents were one-sided. For a more balanced account of some of these incidents, see "Rifle Association Claims ATF Abuses Civil Rights," *Albany Times Union*, May 21, 1995.

15. For a full account of the Lekan siege, see the *Cleveland Plain Dealer*, April 3 and 4, 1995, and January 5, 1996.

16. *Cleveland Plain Dealer*, April 3 and 4, 1995, and January 5, 1996.

17. James and Michael McKinzey, interview, 6.

18. Radley Balko, *Overkill: The Rise of Paramilitary Police Raids in America* (Washington, DC: Cato Institute, 2006); and Balko, "Botched Paramilitary Police Raids: An Epidemic of Isolated Incidents," http://www.cato.org/raidmap/ (accessed March 13, 2008).

19. Chip Berlet, "Who Is Mediating the Storm? Right-Wing Alternative Information Networks," in Linda Kintz and Julia Lesage, eds., *Media, Culture, and the Religous Right* (Minneapolis: University of Minnesota Press, 1998), 259–60.

20. On the history of APFN, see Jonathan Karl, *Right to Bear Arms: The Rise of America's New Militias* (New York: Harper, 1995), 33; and the American Patriots Friends Network, http://www.apfn.org/apfn.htm (accessed September 1, 2006).

21. Berlet, "Who Is Mediating the Storm?" 255–56. Messages forwarding Thompson's call to arms to the Usenet groups alt.conspiracy and alt.society .civil-liberties suggest that it originated on AEN News, and was then picked up by a larger group of Fidonet nodes called Searchnet. Searchnet coordinator Glenda Stocks and several other individuals then posted the call to several Usenet groups. See Searchnet Zec, "Militia alert," posted to alt.society.civil-liber ties, April 20, 1994. All Usenet messages cited in this work were retrieved using the Google Groups News Archive, http://groups.google.com.

22. For an early Usenet discussion of militia formation, see Frank Ney, "Northern Virginia Free Militia," posted to alt.politics.guns, March 25, 1992. For Roland's and Olson's announcements, see insist, "Militia Day in San Antonio," posted to talk.politics.guns, April 12, 1994; and Glenda Stocks, "Rev. norm," posted to alt.conspiracy, May 1, 1994. The Patriots Information Mailing List was started by Bill Utterback, cofounder of the Texas Constitutional Militia. On patriots@kaiwan.com, see Neil A. Hamilton, *Militias in America: A Reference Handbook,* (Santa Barbara: ABC-CLIO, 1996), 216.

23. The NRA's Institute for Legislative Action organized a weekly email and fax alert system at the beginning of 1993. For a partial archive, see their Web site, http://www.nraila.org/CurrentLegislation/ActionAlerts/Archive (accessed September 1, 2008). For a partial archive of GOA alerts, see their Web site, http://www.gunowners.org/altbatb (accessed March 13, 2008). For a reference to MOM's email alert system see "Addressing the Allegations," *Taking Aim,* April 1995.

24. The best collection of links to Christian Patriot and militia Web sites was assembled by Mark Pitcavage, now director of research for the Anti-Defamation

League, on his Militia Watchdog Web site, www.militia-watchdog.org. The official Michigan Militia Web site prior to the 1998 schism was http://mmc .cns.net.

25. See http://www.constitution.org.

26. On E Pluribus Unum, see Charles Morrison, Jr., and Tom Plummer, interview, 3–4. On the Indiana Patriots, see Jim Wade and John Hakes, members, Indiana Volunteer Citizens Militia, interview by the author, Nashville, IN, July 18, 1999, 9–10. On the Western Missouri Shooters Alliance, see James and Michael McKinzey, interview, 8.

27. For a description of a 1995 expo in Florida, see Leonard Zeskind, "Armed and Dangerous," *Rolling Stone*, November 2, 1995.

28. Dees, *Gathering Storm*, 49–67; and Kenneth S. Stern, *A Force upon the Plain: The American Militia Movement and the Politics of Hate* (New York: Simon and Schuster, 1996), 35–37.

29. For an example of scholarship that broadly accepts the civil rights charge, see Michael Kimmel and Abby L. Ferber, "'White Men Are This Nation': Right Wing Militias and the Restoration of Rural American Masculinity," *Rural Sociology* 65 (2000): 582–604. For an example of equivocation, see Mulloy, *American Extremism*, 8.

30. Bonilla-Silva, *White Supremacy and Racism in the Post–Civil Rights Era* (Boulder, CO: Lynne Rienner, 2001), 22. See also Bonilla-Silva, *Racism without Racists: Color-Blind Racism and the Persistence of Racial Inequality in the United States* (Lanham, MD: Rowman and Littlefield, 2003); and Bonilla-Silva, "'New Racism,' Color-Blind Racism, and the Future of Whiteness in America," in Ashley Doane and Eduardo Bonilla-Silva, eds., *White Out: The Continuing Significance of Racism* (New York: Routledge, 2003), 271–84.

31. Bonilla-Silva, *White Supremacy and Racism*, 141–42; and Bonilla-Silva, *Racism without Racists*, chap. 2.

32. Charles Morrison, Jr., and Tom Plummer, interview, 35.

33. Samuel Sherwood, founder, United States Militia Association, interview by the author, Brentwood, TN, September 10, 2005, 30.

34. Bonilla-Silva, *White Supremacy and Racism*, 142.

35. Militia of Montana, *Information and Networking Manual*, provided courtesy of Donald Cohen, director, Detroit Regional Office of the Anti-Defamation League, 23–24.

36. *Gadsden Minuteman Newsletter*, July 1995, provided courtesy of Southern Poverty Law Center, 8; James and Michael McKinzey, interview, 36–37; and Joe and Clara Pilchak, members, Michigan Militia, interview by the author, St. Clair County, MI, November 3, 1998, 43.

37. "The Regiment of Dragoons," http://www.fxbbs.com/family/dragoon3 (accessed July 31, 1997); and Wayne County Brigade of the Michigan Militia, "In Defense of Liberty," provided courtesy of Donald Cohen.

38. Chuck Wittig, "Wittig Speaks in Dallas," *Necessary Force*, September–October 1995, provided courtesy of Michael McKinzey; and Jim Wade and John Hakes, interview, 16–17.

39. James M., member, Ohio Unorganized Militia, interview by the author, Cuyahoga County, OH, October 25, 1998, 13; Bill Utterback, cofounder, Texas Constitutional Militia, interview by the author, San Antonio, TX, January 6, 2006; Jim Wade and John Hakes, interview, 34; Norm Olson, founder of the Michigan Militia, interview by the author, Alanson, MI, November 3, 1998, 26; and Charles Morrison, Jr., and Tom Plummer, interview, 23.

40. "The Alabama Declaration," September 11, 1996, http://www2.holli.com/~deckard/aldeclar.htm (accessed November 1, 1996); and Oral Deckard, interview, 26.

41. Joseph T. Adams, "Re: Militia Studies," posted to misc.activism.militia, October 13, 1996; and Norm Olson, interview, 50.

42. "Good Ol' Boys II," *Necessary Force*, September–October 1996; Wittig, "Wittig Speaks in Dallas"; Mike Vanderboegh, "re: Worst Nightmare Exposed," email to Bill Utterback, May 7, 1996, provided courtesy of Mike Vanderboegh; and Mike Vanderboegh, commander, First Alabama Cavalry Regiment, interview by the author, Pinson, AL, September 11, 2005, 37–39.

43. Mike Vanderboegh, "J'Accuse," a speech delivered to the Second Annual National Militia Commanders Seminar sponsored by the Tri-States Militia Network, Mountain View, TX, October 14, 1995, provided courtesy of Mike Vanderboegh; and J. J. Johnson, *Cracking the Liberty Bell*, 1998, http://www.jj-johnson.com (accessed October 8, 1999), 2-z.

44. Kimmel and Ferber, "White Men Are This Nation," 584–86; James William Gibson, *Warrior Dreams: Violence and Manhood in Post-Vietnam America* (New York: Hill and Wang, 1994), 9–14 and 26–32; and Gibson, "The Blast That Finished Off Militia Culture," *Los Angeles Times*, May 13, 2001.

45. R. W. Connell, *Masculinities: Knowledge, Power, and Social Change* (Berkeley and Los Angeles: University of California Press, 1995), 67–86; and R. W. Connell, "Men and the Women's Movement," *Social Policy* 23 (Summer 1993): 72–79.

46. Chuck Wittig, "Who Are We," *Necessary Force*, November 1998, http://www.tfs.net/~sbarnett/PG9_DEC_98.htm, (accessed October 8, 1999); and Mike Vanderboegh, interview, Pinson, AL, 58. For the surveys, see Charlotte Meador, "Fantasy Theme Chaining in Cyberspace: A Rhetorical Vision of the

U.S. Militia Movement on the Internet," M.A. thesis, University of Houston, 1996; and "OUMAAC September 1998 Survey of the Ohio Unorganized Militia," *OUMAAC Ohio Minuteman*, November 1998, provided courtesy of Tom Plummer.

47. Mike Vanderboegh, "Skirmishing on the Edge of Battle," an address to the Birmingham, Alabama, Libertarians, October 11, 1999, provided courtesy of Mike Vanderboegh; Charles Morrison, Jr., and Tom Plummer, interview, 51; and Mike Vanderboegh, interview, Pinson, AL, 59. See also Norm Olson, interview, 27; and Oral Deckard, interview, 20.

48. Vanderboegh, "Skirmishing on the Edge of Battle."

49. J. J. Johnson, quoted in Timothy M. Seul, "Militia Minds: Inside America's Contemporary Militia Movement," Ph.D. diss., Purdue University, 1997, 110.

50. Norm Olson, "Establishing a Militia in Michigan" (Revision 1, June 28, 1994), MMC Archive; James and Michael McKinzey, interview, 36–37; Discovery Channel, "An Armed Militia," July 12, 1999, videocassette, provided courtesy of Michael McKinzey; and Mike Vanderboegh, interview, Pinson, AL, 23.

51. Jim Wade and John Hakes, interview, 17–18; and Charles Morrison, Jr., and Tom Plummer, interview, 50. See also Joe and Clara Pilchak, interview, 45.

52. Mike Vanderboegh, interview, Pinson, AL, 57; and Charles Morrison, Jr., and Tom Plummer, interview, 50–51.

53. Oral Deckard, interview, 20–21. For an interesting intramarital debate on this subject, see Joe and Clara Pilchak, interview, 45–46.

54. "Militia Maneuvers," *Necessary Force*, September–October 1995; and Norm Olson, interview, 55–56.

55. Daniel Levitas, *The Terrorist Next Door: The Militia Movement and the Radical Right* (New York: Thomas Dunne, 2002), 286–88; Louis Beam, "Leaderless Resistance," *Modern Militiaman*, no. 3, October 1996, http://www.monet.com/~mlindste/mmmisu3.html#noconstitution (accessed July 31, 1997); and Stern, *Force upon the Plain*, 36.

56. For a survey of law review literature on the Second Amendment, see Robert J. Spitzer, "Lost and Found: Researching the Second Amendment," *Chicago-Kent Law Review* 76 (2000): 349–401.

57. David I. Caplan, "Restoring the Balance: The Second Amendment Revisited," *Fordham Urban Law Journal* 5 (1976), 51.

58. For the first wave of activist scholarship advancing the insurrectionary interpretation of the Second Amendment, see especially Stephen Halbrook, "To Keep and Bear Their Private Arms: The Adoption of the Second Amendment, 1787–1791," *Northern Kentucky Law Review* 10 (1982): 13–39; Halbrook, *That Every*

Man Be Armed: The Evolution of a Constitutional Right (Albuquerque: University of New Mexico Press, 1984); David T. Hardy, "Armed Citizens, Citizen Armies: Towards a Jurisprudence of the Second Amendment," *Harvard Journal of Law and Public Policy* 9 (1986): 559–638; and Hardy, *Origins and Development of the Second Amendment: A Sourcebook* (Chino Valley, AZ: Blacksmith Corporation, 1986). For the second wave of academic scholarship, see Sanford Levinson, "The Embarrassing Second Amendment," *Yale Law Journal* 99 (1989): 637–59; Akhil Reed Amar, "The Bill of Rights as a Constitution," *Yale Law Journal* 100 (1991): 1131–1210; and David C. Williams, "Civic Republicanism and the Citizen Militia: The Terrifying Second Amendment," *Yale Law Journal* 101 (1991): 551–615. Several academic scholars have worked in close cooperation with gun rights activists. See, for example, Glenn H. Reynolds, "A Critical Guide to the Second Amendment," *Tennessee Law Review* 65 (1995): 461–512; and Randy Barnett and Don B. Kates Jr., "Under Fire: The New Consensus on the Second Amendment," *Emory Law Journal* 45 (1996): 1140–1259. For an example of the incorporation of this research into popular gun rights literature, see Halbrook, "'The Arms of All the People Should Be Taken Away,'" *American Rifleman*, March 1989.

59. David E. Young, *Origins of the Second Amendment: A Documentary History of the Bill of Rights, 1787–1792* (Ontonagon, MI: Golden Oak Books, 1991).

60. For Usenet postings, see Ray Terry, "Armed and Dangerous," posted to rec.bicycles, August 8, 1990; Bryan, "2nd & 14th Amends. (preface)," posted to alt.conspiracy, November 9, 1989; Ed Ipser, "Want Gun Control? Enforce the Second Amendment!" posted to misc.legal, March 11, 1990; Christopher J. Crobaugh, "The Embarrassing 2nd," posted to talk.politics.guns, January 28, 1992; and Clayton Cramer, "The Second Amendment (part 3)," posted to ca.pol itics, April 30, 1991.

61. Clayton Cramer, "The Second Amendment (part 4)," posted to ca.politics, April 30, 1991. The Google archive of Usenet posts is not complete, and hence the statistics offered here are only approximations. Nevertheless, they do reflect the historical development of Usenet discussions of the Second Amendment. This statistical analysis was performed on the archive as it existed in September 2006.

62. Mike Vanderboegh, writing as Thomas Paine, "The Renewal of the American Republic: The Past Is Our Present and Our Future," provided courtesy of Mike Vanderboegh. Vanderboegh's discussion of the Revolutionary period was based on Gordon S. Wood's discussion of the "Whig science of politics," in *Creation of the American Republic, 1776–1787* (Chapel Hill: University of North Carolina Press, 1969), 4–6.

63. Jon Roland, "Reviving the Ready Militia," http://www.constitution

.org/mil/rev_read.htm (accessed March 13, 2008); M. Samuel Sherwood, *The Little Republics* (Blackfoot, ID: Founders Press Publications, 1992); Sherwood, *The Guarantee of the Second Amendment* (Blackfoot, ID: Founders Press Publications, 1992); Militia of Montana, *Information and Networking Manual*; Michael Johnson, "Modern Militias," http://www.coolmedia.net/cbg.modern .html (accessed October 7, 1999); and Mike Vanderboegh, writing as Samuel Adams II, "Random Thoughts on the Second American Revolution: Advice to the Sons of Liberty," provided courtesy of Mike Vanderboegh.

64. Sherwood, *The Little Republics*, 9–12, 111–200.

65. Sherwood, *Guarantee of the Second Amendment*, preface, 35–46, and 121–40; and Sherwood, *Establishing Independent Militia in the United States* (Blackfoot, ID: Founders Press Publications, 1994).

66. Samuel Sherwood, interview, 13. The organizational progress of the USMA can also be followed in the pages of the organization's newsletter, *Aide de Camp*. See *Aide de Camp*, January–June 1995, provided courtesy of Samuel Sherwood.

67. On Trochman's background, see Karl, *Right to Bear Arms*, 53–58. Civil rights organizations have persistently asserted that Trochman is a Christian Identity adherent, but have never offered conclusive evidence. Trochman declined to be interviewed for this book. For the changes in language, compare Sherwood, *Guarantee of the Second Amendment*, 121–25 to Militia of Montana, *Information and Networking Manual*, 9–16.

68. Militia of Montana, *Information and Networking Manual*, 17–22. For Trochman's comparison of MOM to a neighborhood watch, see "John Trochman's Speech & Appearance before the Senate Subcommittee on Anti-Terrorism, June 15, 1995," *Taking Aim*, June 1995.

69. Militia of Montana, *Information and Networking Manual*, 23–24.

70. MOM's catalog is on their Web site, http://www.militiaofmontana.com/catolog.htm (accessed March 13, 2008). On the Yale debate, see "Good Things Happening," *Taking Aim*, October 1995. For MOM's organizing activities, see Montana Human Rights Network, *A Season of Discontent: Militias, Constitutionalists, and the Far Right in Montana* (Helena: Montana Human Rights Network, 1994), reprinted in D. J. Mulloy, ed., *Homegrown Revolutionaries: An American Militia Reader* (Norwich, UK: Arthur Miller Centre for American Studies, 1999), 133–40. Though MOM held public meetings across eastern Montana, there is little evidence that the organization took root beyond Flathead, Lincoln, Ravilli, and Sanders counties.

71. *Charter of the Unorganized Militia of the Ohio Republic*, Ohio Unorganized Militia information booklet, 1 and 7.

72. For a reasonably cogent discussion of sovereign citizenship, see the ADL's analysis of the "Sovereign Citizenship Movement," http://www.adl.org/learn/ext _us/SCM.asp?xpicked=4&item=20 (accessed March 13, 2008).

73. Compare *Charter of the Unorganized Militia of the Ohio Republic*, 1–7, with Sherwood, "The Militia Constitution," Article II, *Guarantee of the Second Amendment*, 123.

74. Karl, *Right to Bear Arms*, 41–43.

75. Roland, "Reviving the Ready Militia." For a directory of County Commanders of the TCM that documents the organization's geographical presence as of early 1995, see the Constitution Society Web site, http://www.constitu tion.org/mil/tx/mil_ustx.htm (accessed March 13, 2008).

76. Norm Olson, interview, 6–8; Olson, "Establishing a Militia in Michigan"; and *Northern Michigan Regional Militia Manual 1-1* (rev. 1, May 19, 1994), provided courtesy of Mike Vanderboegh. "Establishing a Militia in Michigan" appears to be an early version of the MMC manual that circulated within the state. The *NMRM Manual 1-1* had a wider circulation and was sent to militia activists around the country. On the spread of the organization across Michigan, see Norm Olson, interview, 10.

77. On Johnson's break with the white supremacists in the early OUM, see Charles Morrison, Jr., and Tom Plummer, interview, 9–15; and James M., interview, 9 and 13. Johnson's disgust at the white supremacist leanings of some members of the early OUM is reflected in his novel *Cracking the Liberty Bell*. For his embrace of the constitutionalist impulse, see J. J. Johnson, "Ohio Minutemanual," February 1995, 1–5, provided courtesy of Chip Berlet, senior analyst, Political Research Associates. On the creation of OUMAAC and its presence in over fifty counties, see Charles Morrison, Jr., and Tom Plummer, interview, 18–21. OUMAAC's newsletter, *Ohio Minuteman*, and their Web site listed contacts in eighteen counties. See the incomplete directory of county contacts, http://www.oumaac.com (accessed October 7, 1999).

78. For evidence of Olson's outreach, see Norm Olson, interview, 9; Charles Morrison, Jr., and Tom Plummer, interview, 7–8; Johnny Johnson, "Texas Militia—Statement," posted to misc.survivalism, February 12, 1995; Stephen L. King, *California Militia Manual* posted to misc. activism.militia (accessed January 24, 1996); *Pennsylvania Citizens Militia Manual* version 1.1, March 6, 1995, http://www.users.fast.net/~klh/pa.patriot/manual.html (accessed November 1, 1996); "Missouri 51st Militia By-Laws." For Roland, see James M., interview, 18–19; J. J. Johnson, "Ohio Minutemanual"; and *Gadsden Minutemen Newsletter*, January 13, 1995.

79. On Koernke's message, see Karl, *Right to Bear Arms*, 67–74; and Koernke, *America in Peril* (1993). For his influence in Michigan, Ohio, and Pennsylvania, see Norm Olson, interview, 9–12 and 32–34; Charles Morrison, Jr., and Tom Plummer, interview, 26–29; and "Local Militias Defend Role," *Pittsburgh Post Gazette*, April 30, 1995.

80. On the ICVM, see Jim Wade and John Hakes, interview, 9–10 and 19–21; and "ICVM Instruction for Militia" (December 5, 1998 revision), provided courtesy of Jim Wade. On the SCCM, see "Armed against Authority: The Militia Movement in South Carolina," http://www.mindspring.com/~kubla/sccm.html (accessed March 13, 2008); *Rock Hill (SC) Herald*, March 31, 1996; *Charleston (SC) Post and Courier*, April 21, 1996; and *Atlanta Journal Constitution*, May 2, 1995. On the Oregon Militia, see the coverage of the *Portland Oregonian*, April 27 and 28, May 13 and June 6, 1995; May 9 and 10, 1996; and April 28, 1997. On New Mexico, see *Albuquerque Journal*, May 10 and 14, 1995.

81. On the Northern Illinois Minutemen, see the *Chicago Sun-Times*, May 7, 1995. On the Florida State Militia, see the *Palm Beach Post*, April 25 and 30, 1995.

82. On the militia movement in Alabama, see Mike Vanderboegh, interview, Pinson, AL, 28–29. On the movement in California, see *Sacramento News and Review*, August 25, 1994; *Sacramento Bee*, January 29, 1995; and *San Francisco Chronicle*, March 12, 1995.

83. See, for example, Joel Dyer, *Harvest of Rage: Why Oklahoma City Is Only the Beginning* (Boulder, CO: Westview Press, 1998); Catherine McNichol Stock, *Rural Radicals: Righteous Rage in the American Grain* (Ithaca: Cornell University Press, 1996); and Carolyn Gallaher, *On the Fault Line: Race, Class, and the American Patriot Movement* (Lanham, MD: Rowman and Littlefield, 1993).

84. See table of militia counties in appendix A.

85. Table of militia counties.

86. Table of militia counties.

87. "A Wave of Distrust in the West," *Los Angeles Times*, February 3, 1995.

88. Table of militia counties. For a sensitive discussion of the dynamic of suburbanization in the rural Midwest, see Sonya Salamon, *Newcomers to Old Towns: Suburbanization of the Heartland* (Chicago: University of Chicago Press, 1993).

An Exploration of Militia Ideology

1. Anti-Defamation League, *Armed and Dangerous: Militias Take Aim at the Federal Government* (New York: ADL, 1994).

2. Smith quoted in "American Movement," *USA Today*, January 30, 1995.

3. Friedholm quoted in Timothy M. Seul, "Militia Minds: Inside America's

Contemporary Militia Movement," Ph.D. diss., Purdue University, 1997, 97; Oral Deckard, former member of the Indiana Citizens Volunteer Militia, interview by the author, Terre Haute, IN, October 29, 1998, 2; and Stan Weeber and Daniel G. Rodeheaver, *Militias in the New Millennium: A Test of Smelser's Theory of Collective Behavior* (Lanham, MD: University Press of America, 2004), 49–50.

4. Carl Worden, Southern Oregon Militia, "The Truth about the American Militia Movement," reprinted in *Necessary Force*, January 1998; and Oral Deckard, interview, 2.

5. "Just Who Are the Terrorists?" *E Pluribus Unum*, April–May 1996; "Why Americans Join the Militia/Patriot Movement," *Taking Aim*, March 1996; and "Missouri Ninjas," *Necessary Force*, November–December 1995. See also, for example, "BATF Thugs Strike the Lamplughs," article from *The Gun Owner* reprinted in *E Pluribus Unum*, January 1995; and "More BATF Horror," *Necessary Force*, July–September 1995.

6. Jim Wade and John Hakes, members, Indiana Volunteer Citizens Militia, interview by the author, Nashville, IN, July 18, 1994, 41; "Just Who Are the Terrorists?" *E Pluribus Unum*, April–May, 1996; *Gadsden Minutemen Newsletter*, April 1995; and Weeber, *Militias in the New Millennium*, 42–43.

7. "Firing from the Foxhole," *Necessary Force*, September–October 1995.

8. "North Carolina Militia Corps Declarations and Resolves," http://members.aol.com/nc3rddiv/index.html (accessed October 19, 1998); and Bob Fletcher, testimony before the Senate Subcommittee on Terrorism, Technology, and Government Information, June 15, 1995, reprinted in D. J. Mulloy, *Homegrown Revolutionaries: An American Militia Reader* (Norwich, UK: Arthur Miller Centre for American Studies, 1999), 191.

9. "Firing from the Foxhole," *Necessary Force*, September–October 1995; "Missouri Ninjas," *Necessary Force*, November–December 1995; Oral Deckard, interview, 32–34; and James M., interview, 45–46.

10. "The Fourth Amendment," *Necessary Force*, July 1999; Simon Davies, director, Privacy International, "The Future, Big Brother, & You," reprinted in *E Pluribus Unum*, April–May 1996; and "Be Careful What You Say: They Are Listening," *Taking Aim*, March 1994. See also "The British Are Listening," *Necessary Force*, January 1999; and "Today in America," *Gadsden Minutemen Newsletter*, April 1995. On the Terrorist Surveillance Program, see "Bush Lets U.S. Spy on Callers without Courts," *New York Times*, December 16, 2005.

11. James M., member, Ohio Unorganized Militia, interview by the author, Cuyahoga County, OH, October 25, 1998, 2; Joe and Clara Pilchak, members,

Michigan Militia, interview by the author, St. Clair County, MI, November 3, 1998, 9; and "Law Enforcement?" *Gadsden Minutemen Newsletter*, April 1995.

12. Mike Vanderboegh, writing under the pseudonym Samuel Adams II, "Random Thoughts on the Second American Revolution," 1994, provided courtesy of Mike Vanderboegh.

13. Jim Wade and John Hakes, interview, 16; Norm Olson quoted in "American Movement," *USA Today*, January 30, 1995; and Sherry, a member of the Chemung County, NY, Militia, quoted in Deborah Homsher, *Women and Guns: Politics and the Culture of Firearms in America* (Armonk, NY: M. E. Sharpe, 2001), 150. One of the most widely read fictional account of door-to-door gun confiscation was Raymond K. Paden's short story "Sundown at Coffin Rock," which was reprinted in *E Pluribus Unum*, January 1995. The story may also be found in Mike Vanderboegh's *Why We Will Fight*, no. 8, May 21, 1998, http://xld.com/public/wwwf/wwwf008.htm (accessed October 8, 1999). It is also mentioned in *Necessary Force*, August 1997.

14. "Eggs and Issues," *Necessary Force*, September–October 1996.

15. Mike Vanderboegh, "The Renewal of the American Republic," 1994, provided courtesy of Mike Vanderboegh. On the "Whig science of politics," see Gordon S. Wood, *Creation of the American Republic, 1776–1787* (Chapel Hill: University of North Carolina Press, 1969), chap. 1.

16. Jim Wade, *Stan Solomon Show*, July 19, 1999, transcript provided by Jim Wade; James and Michael McKinzey, founders of the Missouri 51st Militia, interview by the author, Grain Valley, MO, October 30, 1998, 10–11; J. J. Johnson, "Ohio Minutemanual," February 1995, 1, provided courtesy of Chip Berlet, senior analyst, Political Research Associates. For additional evidence of the influence of eighteenth-century Whiggery, see Charles Morrison, Jr., and Tom Plummer, members of the Central Ohio Unorganized Militia, interview by the author, Columbus, OH, October 25, 1998, 34; and "Frequently Asked Questions of the Michigan Militia," http://mmc.cns.net (accessed November 1, 1996).

17. Mike Vanderboegh, email interview by the author, September 5, 2005, 7; Bob Clark, member of the Michigan Militia, quoted in D. J. Mulloy, *American Extremism: History, Politics, and the Militia Movement* (London: Routledge, 2004), 16; and Charles Morrison, Jr., and Tom Plummer, interview, 3–4.

18. J. J. Johnson, "A Heartfelt Invitation to Black Americans," reprinted in *Necessary Force*, January–February 1996; and James M., interview, 6–7.

19. James Barber, "Views on the News," reprinted in *E Pluribus Unum*, February 1996.

20. J. J. Johnson, *Cracking the Liberty Bell*, 1998, http://www.jj-johnson.com (accessed October 8, 1999), 8-f.

21. Mike Vanderboegh, commander, First Alabama Cavalry Regiment, interview by the author, Pinson, AL, September 11, 2005.

22. Jon Roland, "Summary of Constitutional Rights, Powers, and Duties"; "Declaration of Constitutional Principles"; "The Modern Constitutionalist Movement"; "The Patriot's Dilemma"; and "Law and Antilaw," http://www.constitution.org/mil/tmp.htm (accessed March 13, 2008).

23. Michigan Militia, "Thanks for Checking Us Out," http://mmc.ncs.net/thanks (accessed November 1, 1996); and Kay Sheil, quoted in Mulloy, *American Extremism,* 102.

24. Mike Vanderboegh, interview, Pinson, AL, 24.

25. Charles Morrison, Jr., and Tom Plummer, interview, 24–25.

26. "Strengthening the Bonds of Civil Society," *Minuteman Magazine,* Winter 1997.

27. For an excellent overview of far right conspiracism, see Michael Barkun, *A Culture of Conspiracy: Apocalyptic Visions in Contemporary America* (Berkeley and Los Angeles: University of California Press, 1993).

28. Mark Koernke, *America in Peril* (1993), provided courtesy of Chip Berlet; Bob Fletcher, *Invasion and Betrayal* (1995), provided courtesy of John Trochman; and John Trochman, *Enemies Foreign and Domestic* (1995), provided courtesy of John Trochman.

29. Jack McLamb, *Operation Vampire Killer 2000* (Phoenix: American Citizens and Lawmen Association, 1992), 3, 12, and 16.

30. Joe and Clara Pilchak, interview, 26–27.

31. Mark Koernke, *The Intelligence Report,* April 7, 1999, wysiwyg://402/http://intelreport.freeservers.com (accessed October 8, 1999).

32. Martin Durham comes to the same conclusion in *The Christian Right, the Far Right, and the Boundaries of American Conservatism* (New York: Manchester University Press, 2001), 136.

33. Koernke, *America in Peril;* and "Intelligence Reports," no. 22, *Taking Aim,* June 1994.

34. Fletcher, *Invasion and Betrayal.*

35. Mike Vanderboegh, interview, Pinson, AL, 50; and Charles Morrison, Jr., and Tom Plummer, interview, 28.

36. James M., interview, 3–4; and James and Michael McKinzey, interview, 9.

37. Oral Deckard, interview, 30–31.

38. Michigan Militia, "Thanks for Checking Us Out"; Norm Olson, quoted in Mulloy, *American Extremism,* 108; "Militia Patriotism," *Necessary Force,* March–April 1996.

39. Johnson, *Cracking the Liberty Bell,* 4-m.

40. Charles Morrison, Jr., and Tom Plummer, interview, 24–25; and Jon Roland, "Constitutionalists Organize," http://www.constitution.org/mil/tmp .htm (accessed March 13, 2008).

41. M. Samuel Sherwood, *The Little Republics* (Blackfoot, ID: Founders Press Publications, 1992), 111–49.

42. Ibid., 161.

43. Kenneth S. Stern, *Force upon the Plain: The American Militia Movement and the Politics of Hate* (New York: Simon and Schuster), 69; Mark Koernke, *The Intelligence Report,* April 7, 1999; Joe and Clara Pilchak, interview, 48–51.

44. Sherry, quoted in Homsher, *Women and Guns,* 150–51; Oral Deckard, interview, 20.

45. Jon Roland, "The Patriot's Dilemma" and "Summary of Constitutional Rights, Powers, and Duties."

46. Jon Roland, "Legitimacy and the Militia," posted to misc.activism.militia, May 2, 1997.

47. Samuel Sherwood, *The Guarantee of the Second Amendment* (Blackfoot, ID: Founders Press Publications, 1992), 31–33; Johnson, "Modern Militias"; and Alan Keyes, "Defense of Second Amendment Essential to Defense of Liberty," reprinted in *OUMAAC Ohio Minuteman,* October 1998.

48. Dan White, "The Last Resource," *Necessary Force,* July–August 1996; and Tom Plummer, "Basic Facts on the Militia," provided courtesy of Tom Plummer.

49. Jon Roland, "Reviving the Ready Militia," http://www.constitution.org/ mil/rev_read.htm (accessed March 13, 2008); Norm Olson, "Is the Citizen Militia Lawful?" http://mmc.cns.net/text/lawfulmilitia.txt, 1 (accessed November 1, 1996); and Militia of Montana, *Information and Networking Manual,* 8.

50. Bill Utterback to Mike Vanderboegh, May 24, 1998, *Why We Will Fight,* no. 10, http://xld.com/public/wwwf/wwwf010.htm (accessed October 8, 1999); and Oral Deckard, interview, 22.

51. Mike Vanderboegh, interview, Pinson, AL, 45.

52. "Knob Creek Declaration," http://users.monet.com/mlindste/mm misu1.html (accessed October 19, 1998); and Norm Olson, founder of the Michigan Militia, interview by the author, Alanson, MI, November 3, 1998, 35–36.

53. James and Michael McKinzey, interview, 16.

54. Mike Vanderboegh, email interview.

55. Samuel Sherwood, founder, United States Militia Association, interview by the author, Brentwood, TN, September 10, 2005, 28–29; Jim Wade and John Hakes, interview, 42; Charles Morrison, Jr., and Tom Plummer, interview, 45–46;

and Tri-States Militia Network, "Declaration of Grievance," reprinted in *Rapid City Journal,* September 17, 1995.

56. J. J. Johnson, testimony before the Senate Subcommittee on Terrorism, Technology, and Government Information, June 15, 1995, reprinted in Mulloy, *Homegrown Revolutionaries,* 196; and Joe and Clara Pilchak, interview, 33–34.

57. Charles Ray Morrison, "Drawing the Line" and "Drawing the Line: Supporter's Responses," http://home.megalinx.net/~eplurib/epu (accessed July 31, 1997); "OUMAAC September 1998 Survey of the Ohio Unorganized Militia," *OUMAAC Ohio Minuteman,* November 1998, provided courtesy of Tom Plummer; Wayne County Brigade of the Michigan Militia, "In Defense of Liberty," provided courtesy of the ADL; and "The 'Line in the Sand' Has Been Drawn," *Necessary Force,* Winter 1996–97.

58. Mike Vanderboegh, "Organizational Guidelines for Sons of Liberty Clubs," provided courtesy of Mike Vanderboegh; Norm Olson, "What Has the Militia Ever Done for Me?" reprinted in *Modern Militiaman,* no. 5, April 19, 1997, http://www.geocities.com/CapitolHill/Lobby/1076/mmmisu5.html (accessed October 19, 1998).

59. "N.Y. Man Asks Militia Groups to Aid in Fight to Save Home," *Chicago Sun-Times,* July 30, 1995; "Militias Differ in Standoff," *St. Louis Post Dispatch,* April 1996; "Family's Y2K Prep Judged Illegal," posted to misc.activism.militia, August 13, 1999; "Waiting for Apocalypse, Militia Falls on Hard Times," *Washington Post,* September 9, 1999; and "Militia Founder Disbands Faction," *South Bend Tribune,* May 1, 2001.

60. Oral Deckard, interview, 13–14; Mike Vanderboegh, interview, Pinson, AL, 47–48; Norm Olson, interview, 44–45; and Samuel Sherwood, interview, 46–47.

61. Mike Vanderboegh, interview, Pinson, AL, 46–47; C. F. R. MacCrae, "Live Free or Die: The Cultivation, Care, and Feeding of Homegrown Militias," http://fxbbs.com/Family/chapt.3.html (accessed August 4, 1997); and Tri-States Militia Training Command, "Militias and the Law of Land Warfare," provided courtesy of Mike Vanderboegh.

62. Doug Fiedor, "An Open Letter to Mike Kemp," August 9, 1996, http://www2.hooli.com/~deckard/kempltr.htm (accessed November 1, 1996); and James and Michael McKinzey, interview, 53.

63. Mike Vanderboegh, "Once Upon a Tea Party," posted to eplurib@ infinet.com, December 21, 1997.

64. Ibid.

65. Ibid.; Mike Vanderboegh, interview, Pinson, AL, 46; and "Assassination, a

Loser's Tool," *The Liberty Alert: A Publication of the Tri-States Militia*, November 1995, provided courtesy of Robert Wright, commander, First Brigade, New Mexico Militia. See also Joseph T. Adams, "re: Militias Coming or Going?" posted to misc.activism.militia, September 28, 1997.

66. Johnson, *Cracking the Liberty Bell*, 6-d and 8-p.

67. Kenneth J. Carter, "To all Christian Brothers and Sisters," posted to misc.activism.militia, March 9, 1997.

68. "Undercover Agents Describe Plan to Create Chaos, National Uprising," *Battle Creek Enquirer*, March 20, 1998.

69. "Sheriff Links Bomb Talk to Lampley," *Tulsa World*, April 4, 1996; and "Undercover Police Were at Militia Meeting," *Austin American Statesman*, October 17, 1998.

70. "Undercover Agents Describe Plan"; "Dangerous Militiamen Stay in Jail, *Oakland Press*, March 20, 1998; "Terror from the Right," Southern Poverty Law Center, *Intelligence Report*, Summer 2001; "Militia Coordinator on Federal Payroll," *Tulsa World*, April 7, 1996; Anti-Defamation League, "Extremism in America: Christian Identity," http://www.adl.org/learn/Ext_US/Christian_Identity .asp?LEARN_Cat=Extremism&LEARN_SubCat=Extremism_in_America& xpicked=4&item=Christian_ID (accessed March 13, 2008); and Mike Vanderboegh, "Worst Nightmare Exposed," email to Bill Utterback, May 7, 1996, provided courtesy of Mike Vanderboegh.

71. "Rambo Wasn't There," *E Pluribus Unum*, November 1995, reprinted with commentary by editor Harold Sheil, *Necessary Force*, November–December 1995.

72. Vernon Wilkins, "An Open Letter on Warfare in America," *Gadsden Minutemen Newsletter*, July 1995.

73. Ibid.; and Michael McKinzey, "Spray and Pray," *Necessary Force*, November–December 1995.

74. Martin Lindstedt, "Business at Roby Ridge," October 13, 1997; and Norm Olson to OutPostofFreedom@illusions.com (Olson's response), October 15, 1997, reprinted in Lindtstedt's *Modern Militiaman's Internet Gazette*, http://www2.mo-net.com/~mlindste/mmgaz9.html (accessed October 19, 1998).

75. Mike Vanderboegh, *Why We Will Fight*, no. 9, http://xld.com/public/ wwwf/wwwf009.htm (accessed October 8, 1999).

76. For example, the Sons of Liberty, a network of covert militias operating in Ohio, Alabama, and other states, had a largely constitutionalist orientation. See Mike Vanderboegh, interview, Pinson, AL, 11–15.

77. Norm Olson, interview, 31–32; and Olson, "Establishing a Militia in Michigan."

78. "The Coming Breakdown of Law and Order," *Aide de Camp*, May 1995.

79. Norm Olson, interview, 27–35; on Olson's attempt to debunk conspiracy theories, see Ken Adams, "Resolution of Conflict in Southern Region," fax to all MMC brigades, February 8, 1995, MMC Archive. On Olson's resignation, see the *Memphis Commercial Appeal*, April 30, 1995.

80. For the different versions of Sherwood's statement, see "Travel Agency," *Washington Post*, March 15, 1995; Mark Tanner, "Extreme Prejudice: How the Media Misrepresents the Militia Movement," *Reason Magazine*, July 1995; and Samuel Sherwood, interview, 25–27. Taken in conjunction with the confirmation by Tanner, who is an independent witness, and his contemporaneous writings, Sherwood's account of this incident is credible. All of Sherwood's writings urged his followers to cooperate with local officials and to seek charters for their militias from local governments. He was in early 1995 cultivating ties with state officials in Idaho, and Idaho lieutenant governor Butch Otter spoke at the meeting in question. Had Sherwood made such a threat, he would have been contradicting everything he had written for the previous three years and jeopardizing his entire political program. On the disbanding of the USMA, see "McVeigh Fallout: Utah Militias Rare," *Deseret News*, June 10, 2001; and "Militia Activist from Fargher Lake Still Conservative," *The Columbian*, March 4, 2000.

81. On the Tri-States Militia, see *Liberty Alert*, August, November, and December 1995; *Albuquerque Tribune*, January 13, 1996; and Mike Vanderboegh, interview, Pinson, AL, 33.

82. Mike Vanderboegh, interview, Pinson, AL, 31–33; and Vanderboegh, "J'Accuse."

83. "Militia Coordinator on Federal Payroll," *Tulsa World*, April 7, 1996; and Mike Vanderboegh, interview, Pinson, AL, 35–36.

84. Mike Vanderboegh, "The King's Shilling," posted to misc.activism.militia, April 15, 1996.

85. Mike Vanderboegh, "The Alabama Declaration," September 13, 1996, http://www2.holli.com/~deckard/aldeclar.htm (accessed November 1, 1996).

86. Ibid.

87. Charles Morrison, Jr., and Tom Plummer, interview, 18–23 and 52–53.

88. Norm Olson, interview, 26–34; "Meet the Commander," http://www.militia.gen.MI.us (accessed July 31, 1997); Thomas R. Wayne, "To All Brigades," November 9, 1995, MMC Archive; "An Open Letter to John Trochman from Tom Wayne," http://www.geocities.com/~cowboy140/ (accessed October 19, 1998);

Michigan Militia Corps, Wolverines, *Manual 1-1 Revised,* http://www.geoci ties.com/~cowboy140/1–1.htm (accessed October 19, 1998); Minutes of a State Meeting at Bruce Soloway's on March 15, 1998, MMC Archive; "Feast of Passover Gathering!!," flyer advertising Brice Soloway as the contact for a Christian Identity service celebrated by James Wickstrom in Fremont, MI, April 11, 1998, provided courtesy of the ADL; and Joe and Clara Pilchak, interview, 34–41.

89. On the post–Oklahoma City drop in membership, see "Bombing's Repercussions Rattle Militias," *Washington Post,* May 6, 1995; Jim Wade and John Hakes, interview, 23–26; and Thomas R. Wayne, "To All Brigades," November 9, 1995, MMC Archive. For evidence of stabilization, see Jim Wade and John Hakes, interview, 23; and "OUMAAC September 1998 Survey of the Ohio Unorganized Militia," *OUMAAC Ohio Minuteman,* November 1998. On the Council of American Militias, see Mike Vanderboegh, "In Defense of Mark T Pitsavage," posted to misc.activism.militia, May 13, 1996. On the Southeastern States Alliance, see "The Articles of Alliance of the Southeastern States Militia Alliance," http://www.geoc ities.com/CapitolHill/9852/saa.htm (accessed October 19, 1998).

90. Joe and Clara Pilchak, interview, 59; and "Y2K Scenario," *Taking Aim,* February 1999.

91. "H.Q. Bunker," *Necessary Force,* January 1999.

92. For the impact of official discussions of Y2K scenarios on the militia community, see Doug Fiedor, "Computers May Cause a Decline of Liberty," *Heads Up,* June 14, 1998, http://www.militia.gen.MI.us (accessed June 14, 1998); "Panic in the Year Zero," *Michigan Militia Weekly Update,* January 11, 1999, http://www.mili tia.gen.MI.us (accessed October 8, 1999); "The Government's Secret Y2K Plans," *Wolverine News Room,* May 6, 1999, wysiwyg://375/www. geocities.com/Penta gon/Quarters/3385/news19.html (accessed October 8, 1999).

93. "United States Marine Corps Urban Advanced Warfighting Experiment," wysiwyg://373/http://www.geocities.com/~cowboy140/uwawe.html (accessed October 8, 1999); and *OUMAAC Ohio Minuteman,* February and March 1999, http://www.oumaac.com/minuteman (accessed October 7, 1999).

94. Oral Deckard, interview, 44–45.

95. "Y2K or D2K," and "Stand Down," *Taking Aim,* Janurary 2000; and *Necessary Force,* January 2000.

Epilogue

1. John Ashcroft, Attorney General of the United States, to James Jay Baker, Executive Director, National Rifle Association, May 17, 2001, http://www.vpc .org/ studies/ashapa.htm (accessed March 13, 2008).

2. Norm Olson, quoted in "Citing Declining Membership, a Leader Disbands His Militia," *New York Times*, April 30, 2001; and Rick Hawins, "No Time to Rest," *Necessary Force*, May 2001.

3. McKinzey quoted in "The Militia Movement May Have Lost Its Steam," *St. Petersburg Times*, June 23, 2002.

4. "F.B.I. Watched Activist Groups, New Files Show," *New York Times*, December 20, 2005.

5. "Oakland Nears Final Payouts for Protesters Hurt by Police," *New York Times*, March 20, 2006; and "Protestors, Police Clash during Miami Free Trade Demonstrations," Associated Press, November 20, 2003. For footage of the police use of nonlethal ammunition at Tacoma and Los Angeles, see Tacoma Police Riot Rubber Bullets Fired—Camera #1, http://www.youtube.com/watch?v=q1_lmvhkv3c (accessed March 13, 2008); and Rubber Bullets Fired at L.A. Protesters, http://www.youtube.com/watch?v=2GeiozyD3Tc (accessed March 13, 2008).

6. "Bush Lets U.S. Spy on Callers without Courts," *New York Times*, December 16, 2005.

7. "Guantanamo Bound: Taliban, al Qaeda Prisoners Going to U.S. Military Base in Cuba," *San Francisco Chronicle*, December 28, 2001; "Secret World of US Jails," *The Observer*, June 13, 2004; "Ashcroft Rules on Immigrants' Detention," *New York Times*, April 24, 2003; Military Commissions Act of 2006, http://thomas.loc.gov/cgi-bin/bdquery/z?d109:S.3930: (accessed March 13, 2008); Congressional Research Service, "Detention of American Citizens as Enemy Combatants," March 15, 2004, http://www.fas.org/irp/crs/RL31724.pdf (accessed September 5, 2008).

8. "Outsourcing Torture: The Secret History of America's 'Extraordinary Rendition' Program," *New Yorker*, February 14, 2005; "Secret U.S. Endorsement of Severe Interrogations," *New Yorker*, October 4, 2007; "Pentagon Will Not Try 17 G.I.'s Implicated in Prisoners' Deaths," *New York Times*, March 26, 2005; and Marty Lederman, "Lowering the Bar: Well, At Least We're Not as Barbaric as the Spanish Inquisition," February 14, 2008, http://balkin.blogspot.com/2008/02/lowering-bar-well-at-least-were-not-as.html (accessed March 13, 2008).

9. For militiamen condemning the targeting of civilians in the war on terror, see Carl Worden, "Knowest Not Thine Enemy?" *Command Briefs*, July 2003, http://indianamilitia.homestead.com/knowestnot.html (accessed March 13, 2008); and Joseph T. Adams, "Re: Patriotism," posted to misc.activism.militia, July 7, 2004.

10. "Mr. Livingston's Speech on the Alien Bill," *Washington (PA) Herald of Liberty*, August 6, 1798.

INDEX